Eyles Irwin

A Series of Adventures in the Course of a Voyage up the Red-Sea

On the Coasts of Arabia and Egypt

Eyles Irwin

A Series of Adventures in the Course of a Voyage up the Red-Sea
On the Coasts of Arabia and Egypt

ISBN/EAN: 9783337144494

Printed in Europe, USA, Canada, Australia, Japan

Cover: Foto ©Andreas Hilbeck / pixelio.de

More available books at **www.hansebooks.com**

A

SERIES OF ADVENTURES

IN THE COURSE OF

A VOYAGE UP THE RED-SEA,

ON THE COASTS OF ARABIA AND EGYPT;

AND OF

A ROUTE through the Desarts of THEBAIS,

HITHERTO UNKNOWN TO THE EUROPEAN TRAVELLER,

IN THE YEAR M.DCC.LXXVII.

IN LETTERS TO A LADY.

BY EYLES IRWIN, ESQ.
IN THE SERVICE OF THE HON^{BLE}. THE EAST-INDIA COMPANY.

ILLUSTRATED WITH MAPS AND CUTS.

INFANDUM, REGINA, JUBES RENOVARE DOLOREM.
VIRGIL.

LONDON:
PRINTED FOR J. DODSLEY, PALL-MALL.

M.DCC.LXXX.

TO THE HONOURABLE

THE EAST-INDIA COMPANY,

THIS WORK,

CONTAINING

THE PARTICULARS OF A JOURNEY

UNDERTAKEN ON THEIR SERVICE,

IS, WITH GREAT DEFERENCE, INSCRIBED,

BY THEIR MOST FAITHFUL

AND MUCH OBLIGED SERVANT,

THE AUTHOR.

London, 1ft
February 1780.

ADVERTISEMENT.

ON the publication of a work of this nature, something may be expected by way of prelude. If the plaudit of the public is not to be purchased, their indulgence may possibly be secured. But neither of these motives has influenced the author to trespass upon their time. He would deprecate their pardon, not for having given birth to this production, but for having introduced it immaturely to the observation of the public. What little polish would the close application of two years throw upon a body of this magnitude! And yet, amid a variety of other avocations, two years only has the author been allowed to transcribe, correct, and finish it. He says, allowed, as necessity prescribes the term, and his duty calls him to a distant part of the globe, to perform other engagements, to pay other debts, than what the desire of pleasing prompts, or the love of fame exacts from him.

Under this conviction, therefore, he waits silently the probe of criticism. But the candid critic, like the skilful surgeon, is sparing of the knife, and, but in desperate cases, is inclined to proceed to extremities. Into such hands it may be the lot of the author to fall. Where the eye takes more delight in beauty than in deformity, where the disposition is more apt to praise than to censure, no doubts could deter an author from appearing at the bar of criticism. In a description of countries little travelled, and of men little known, there may possibly be mistakes that have arisen from misinformation, or even misconception of things. In a detail of adventures committed often to paper in moments of peril and distress, there may, indeed, be a repetition of sentiment, and sometimes a contradiction of opinions before advanced, which the greatest attention, during a two years revisal, has not been able to correct. But if impartiality has uniformly directed his pencil, and his pictures are not even so highly coloured as nature would have permitted; if he has rather consulted the public amusement, than the gratification of his own vanity, this early publication, with all its imperfections, will not want an advocate among the *literati*.

And here he was about to congratulate himself on having gained so essential a point. To the private approbation of Mr. Reed of Staples-Inn, was the author confirmed in the hope of success, and to his open recommendation of this work to some who knew the value of Mr. Reed's judgment, the reader, probably,

bably, owes that it is now submitted to his view. To the friendship of Mr. Braithwaite of the Post-Office, he may place this, and other material helps he has experienced in the course of publication. But he should ask these gentlemen's forgiveness, for involving them in a question, where their names are used less to their advantage than to that of the author.

It behoves him to say a word or two on the head of the Plates. His knowledge of drawing is so confined, that more than a sketch of the places through which he passed, exceeded the author's art. The antiquities of Egypt have given employment to the pencils of a Norden and a Pococke, and were not to be expected from the title of these travels. But drawings of particular scenes, in which he was engaged, and representations of the singular customs of the country, would have brought them forward to the reader's eye. He must ever lament the deficiency of his work in this respect: but he is happy at the same time to observe, that there is a remedy at hand, for those who delight in novel pictures. The reputation of Mr. Dalton, his Majesty's antiquarian, was established by the work which he produced in 1752, consisting of plates of various antiquities in Greece and Egypt. The connoisseurs, therefore, are not likely to be disappointed in the Supplement to that work, which Mr. Dalton

Dalton is about to publish. The designs which relate to Egypt, obtained as they must have been with great difficulty, and executed as they are with great spirit, will prove such an elucidation to his labors, that the author must beg Mr. Dalton's pardon, if he presumes to recommend those designs to the reader, which are so peculiarly adapted to this work, that nothing but its unworthiness should divide them from each other.

He has but one thing more to add, which concerns the companions of his travels. To the two gentlemen who accompanied him to Europe, he trusts an apology is needless, as they will readily acquit him of a design to pay any but a proper tribute to their characters. By the other person, whom the hand of mischance separated from their company, he would wish to be understood. The circumstances which produced that separation should have been buried in oblivion, had not a regard for his own honor obliged the author to place the intentions of his companions and himself in their true light. The narrative of that affair—as it appears in this work—was signed by Major Henry Alexander, Mr. Anthony Hammond, and the author, and transmitted to India at the time. The paper may have miscarried, but the parties are alive to testify the fact. All that delicacy and humanity could suggest,

gest, has been observed on the occasion. The name of the unhappy person is suppressed, and self-vindication alone could have induced him to revive a subject, which more nearly affected the author and his companions, than all their subsequent misfortunes!

To conclude. Were books, any more than men, to be judged only by their good intentions—were no regard to be paid to the figure which they make in the world—this work would have a better chance to maintain its ground. But as there are other points to be considered; as truth can only be rendered efficacious in an amiable dress, and as the justest descriptions must be disgraced by inelegant language, the author cannot divest himself of certain sensations, which must disturb the firmest mind, on the eve of committing its thoughts to the discussion of the public.

CONTENTS.

LETTER I. Page 1.

*A*DDRESS—*The author pursues his voyage from Madras to Suez—Tedious passage across the Indian ocean.—Makes the island of Socotra, Cape Guardafoy, the Arabian shore—Enters the Red-sea by the straits of Babelmandel—Hard Gale—Arrival in Mocha road—Occurrences at that city—Embarks again—Contrary winds—The vessel driven by currents on the Arabian coast—In imminent danger of being wrecked among the shoals and breakers—Obliged to put into the port of Yambo for a pilot—The author, &c. seduced ashore, and made prisoners by the vizier of that place—Incidents during their confinement—The craft and villainy of the Arabs apparent in their attempts to possess themselves of the vessel—Stratagem for that purpose—Its success—The vessel brought into the harbor, and the author, &c. return aboard under a guard, until an answer is received from the Xerif of Mecca, touching their destiny—A description of the town and environs of Yambo—Interviews with the vizier—Instances of his duplicity and pride—Various disappointments in the hope of a speedy answer—The shawbunder of Judda at length arrives, charged with powers from the Xerif, to dispose of the vessel and crew—Negociations on that head—The vessel is carried to Judda, under charge of an Arabian pilot, and the author and his fellow-travellers are allowed to proceed—Presents to the vizier on this occasion—Egregiously imposed upon by this minister in the hire of a vessel—They embark on an open boat for Suez.*

CONTENTS.

Journal of the boat Imposition—Detained by contrary winds at the mouth of the harbor—Alarm at the sudden disappearance of one of the author's fellow-travellers and the interpreter—They are sent back to the boat by the vizier—The boat sails to the northward, and puts into a bay on the coast—Encounters two barks bound to the southward—Unhappy symptoms of a disordered mind appear in the gentleman who absconded—He awakens the apprehensions of the Arabs, who insist on his quitting the boat, and returning on one of the barks to Judda—The absolute necessity of complying with this requisition—The distress of the author and his companions on this melancholy occasion—The boat sails again—Difficulties of this extraordinary navigation—Touches at several islands on the Arabian coast—Tedious passage to the gulf of Akaba—Strange instance of the notion of the dominion of evil spirits—Makes the shore adjacent to Mount Sinai—Cape Mahomet—Enters the gulf of Suez—The boat is run over to the Egyptian shore in the night, and instead of Suez, by the treachery of the Arabs, is carried to Cosire, a port of Upper Egypt, near four degrees to the southward of Suez—The vexation of the author and his companions—Conclusion.

LETTER II. Page 119.

ADDRESS—The author, &c. land at Cosire—Their reception and accommodation there—Occurrences at that place—The demands of the government for its protection of our travellers—Unaccountable behavior of the Arab shaik—They set out with the caravan for Ghinnah on the Nile, under the care of the shaik's son—Part with the caravan—Alarm—Inconveniency of this mode of travelling—Intense heat of the sun—They replenish their skins at some springs—Pursue their way, and experience extreme distress from thirst, heat, and fatigue—Relieved by their arrival at the Nile—Surprized at being carried to Banute instead of Ghiunah—Remonstrate with the young shaik, who consents to take them to that city—

Set

Set out accordingly, and in six hours are safely housed at Ghinnah—The villainy of their host and his family—Are visited by the vizier of the place—Attempts to chouse them out of their money and effects—Find themselves close prisoners—Their baggage searched and repeatedly pillaged by the host and his associates—Visit from the hakeem of the city, by the order of his master, the Shaik Ul Arab—Enquiry into their wrongs—Tumult in the house on that account—Uncommon instance of courage and fidelity in an Arab domestic—The hakeem removes our travellers to his own habitation—He is supplanted in his office by an Abyssinian, who, at the express commands of the shaik, takes them under his protection—The meanness and rapacity of this slave—Advice comes to Ghinnah of a robbery and murder committed on their late inhuman host, in a dispute with the young shaik of Cosire about his ill-gotten booty—Reflections on this tragical event—The arrival of the Shaik Ul Arab—His interview with our travellers—His person and character described—His politeness and humanity—Exemplary instances of his impartiality and justice—Unhappy state of the country of Egypt—Rebellion on the Nile—The passage to Cairo by the river shut up—Doubts how to proceed—Our travellers resolve to pursue their route through the deserts of Thebais—Are confirmed in this intention by the good shaik, who provides them with a conductor, and essentially interests himself in their safety—They take leave of their generous benefactor, and enter the deserts with a body of sixteen—The rugged and mountainous face of the country—Unexpectedly fall in with a party of camels, which proves to be a band of robbers, journeying from the Red-sea towards Cairo—A treaty concluded with the captain of the robbers—An Arab feast—The two parties proceed in company—Difficulties of the road—Continual ranges of mountains every where present themselves to the traveller—Sudden transitions from heat to cold in the course of the journey—Replenish their water-skins twice in the desart—Provisions begin to fail with the author and his companions.
—Readily

—*Readily relieved by the robbers—Their forbearance and strict observance of their word—Halt in the neighborhood of the Nile to procure water—Alarm—Strike into the desart, and pass over rocks of granite or Thebaic marble—Obtain a sight of the Nile, and come upon the encampment of the robbers—The author, &c. part with these singular people—Remarks on their hospitality and good faith—Rejoin the Nile—Travel on its banks—Pass the villages of Vel Hadie and Ifcour, and discern the pyramids to the westward of the river—Halt at Tinnah, and engage a boat to convey them the remaining short distance—Joyfully embark for the capital—Happy arrival there, and friendly reception by the* Company's *agent.*

Occurrences at Grand Cairo—Cursory observations on the city and its antiquities—Concise narrative of the late revolution in Egypt—Our travellers return letters and presents to the worthy Shaik Ul Arab by the camels, and embark for Alexandria—Delightful voyage down the Nile—Review of the towns and country on its banks—Arrive at Rosetto—Beauty of its situation—The road to Alexandria infested with robbers—Reimbark in a boat bound to that port—Critical situation at the bogage, or mouth of the Nile—The boat strikes the sands, but luckily escapes, and enters the Mediterranean—Dreary appearance of the coast of Egypt—They safely reach Alexandria, after a passage of sixteen hours—Some account of that city, and the elegant remains in its neighborhood—Droll anecdote of some English captains—Affecting story of the death of the late French Consul of Alexandria—Occurrences at that city—The author and his companions embark on a French ship for Marseilles—Conclusion—Postscript.

APPENDIX. Page 394.

*A*N *Ode to the Desart, and another to the Nile, referred to this place from the body of the Work.*

ERRATA.

Page 17. Line 2. *for* cabin *read* cabbin.
—— do. —— 8. *for* shipwrecked *read* wrecked.
—— 123. —— 10. *for* visitors *read* visitors.
—— 178. —— 12. *for* eat *read* eaten.
—— 238. —— 19. *for* human *read* humane.
—— 267. —— 21. *for* were *read* was.
—— 356. —— 10. *for* Neiburh *read* Niebuhr.

Lately Published for J. DODSLEY,

By the Author of this Work,

Saint Thomas's Mount, a Poem, 2s. 6d.

Bedukah, a Poem, 2s. 6d.

Eastern Eclogues, a Poem, 2s. 6d.

A

SERIES OF ADVENTURES, &c.

IN THE YEAR M.DCC.LXXVII.

IN LETTERS TO A LADY.

LETTER I.

MADAM,

WERE ability subservient to inclination, were the efforts of the heart to be seconded by the efforts of the imagination, I should with less scruple begin upon the task which you have allotted me. But the seas which I have passed, and the sands which I have wandered over, appear now to have been fraught with less danger than the adventure I am about to engage in. Once launched into the literary world, what has not a poor author to fear from the blasts of ridicule, and the rocks of envy! But as the want of an ostentatious display has secured my footsteps from the assault of the wild Arab, so may I hope, that the modesty of my pretensions may prove my passport through the waste of criticism. Happy at all events, in the prospect of your influence, to protect the strain that is guided by truth, and owes its existence to the commands of friendship.

The occurrences of our voyage from Madras to Mocha, are like the generality of sea-affairs, too trivial to become interesting, and too unvaried to afford amusement. Since the fables of the ancients have been banished our creed, a modern voyager finds it difficult to diversify or embellish his journal. Neptune ceases to assert his empire over the waves, and Amphitrité no longer skims the surface of the deep, seated in a coral chariot drawn by Mermaids, and surrounded by a choir of musical Nereids. A storm therefore loses the majesty which a Divinity would give it; and our calms are really dull, for want of the company of such a beautiful Goddess. I question whether the voyage of Æneas, if deprived of these fictitious ornaments, would not become equally insipid with those published by recent discoverers, whose heroes visited people more strange, and seas more remote than Æneas, and encountered gulphs far more dangerous than Scylla or Charybdis!

There was nothing remarkable in our passage to Mocha, but the length of it. We were above eight weeks in effecting a passage, which frequently requires but three. The lateness of the season made us apprehensive of delays, but not the continual ones we met with. At several periods we thought of nothing less than of getting to Suez by water. My fellow-travellers and myself were, however, resolved to prosecute our journey by land, should the snow Adventure reach any port in the Red-Sea. But the sight of land presented us with better prospects.

We had been two-and-forty days in crossing the wide ocean which divides India from Africa, when on the 31st of March we saw indistinctly the island of Socotra, which lies about 35 leagues from the main. On the 2d of April we made Cape Guardafoy, which is a prodigious mountainous and craggy shore. From hence we stood over to the coast of Arabia, and

by

by an easterly current, were driven so far towards the ocean, that it was the 6th before we past Cape Aden. Here the remains of a Portuguese fort are still visible, which is an humiliating monument of their former superiority in these parts. On the 9th we ran through the straits of Babelmandel, with a fine gale, which, joined to a strong current, set us through in a quarter of an hour. There is a very ugly sea in these straits, and they being the usual entrance into the Red-Sea, I have annexed a plate of them, which was drawn upon the spot. Vessels may pass to the westward of the island, but this is attended with danger. The gale encreased to such a degree, that we were fain to run under the land at noon, in a bay about half-way between the straits and Mocha. Here we rode out a very violent storm, and thought ourselves lucky in being so well sheltered from the fury of it. The wind abated a little at day-break on the 10th, when we weighed and stood for Mocha. Though still boisterous, the wind was fortunately fair, and we were not many hours in running the distance. At twelve o'clock we dropped our anchor in Mocha road, but were obliged to wait until the weather moderated, before we ventured to debark. The month of April was advanced, but we went ashore at Mocha the same evening, in full confidence of being agreeably accommodated to Suez, on board the Adventure. We looked only upon the brighter side of the perspective; as the difficulties and dangers annexed to a journey of 11 or 1200 miles by land, along a barren and barbarous coast, could afford us no very pleasing reflections.

Mocha, the ancient capital of Arabia Felix, is situated upon a sandy soil, about 12 leagues from the straits of Babelmandel, and in the latitude of 13° 15′ north. This city is of great antiquity, and displays a very handsome appearance towards the sea. But its beauty will not bear a close inspection.

Like the deformities which are so frequently discovered beneath a fair exterior, the inside of its buildings is by no means answerable to the expectations which they raise. To survey the desart on which it stands, a stranger must be surprized at the plenty which reigns in the markets. There is not a tree within ken, that produces any fruit, but the date, or herbage of any kind, to support the cattle which are daily exposed for sale. But to the simplicity of the Arabian manners this circumstance is to be attributed. Where the natives are content with the coarsest food that a country produces, it is no wonder that the more delicate viands are readily procured, by the few Europeans who visit their shores. And indeed, when we are informed that the sheep which are sold here, are all brought from the opposite coast of Abyssinia, and the simplest vegetable, at no less a distance than fifteen miles from Mocha, conjecture would lose itself in accounting for such plenty, were a clue not given to unravel the mystery.

Mocha is under the authority of a governor, as the Imaun, who unites the offices of high-priest and king of Arabia Felix, always resides at Sennaa, a city about ten days journey from hence, delightfully situated in a valley, with which this mountainous country abounds. The Turks have lost the influence which they formerly possessed in this kingdom. They seem content, at present, to receive their proportion of the duties of the other provinces of Arabia, without pretending to exert the arbitrary sway, which marks their government in the districts that are more imediately within the reach of their arms. There is one privilege that the Imaun claims here, which custom has rendered familiar to the subjects of a despotic state, however oppressive it may appear to the ideas of an European. He has an indisputable property in all horse-flesh. So that if a stranger takes a liking to an horse, it is of no consequence to whom

it

it belongs, provided he be content to pay the price, which the governor may fix on it in the name of his master. But the owner is seldom exposed to the mortification of being obliged to part with his property: the value of the beast, however beautiful it may be, seldom proving in the least adequate to the price which is demanded for it.

In their horses the chief pleasure and pride of the Arabs consist. Pampered to an excess that renders them fitter for shew than use, they stand in the stable, or are picketted at the doors of their masters, from one sabbath-day to another. But on this festival, they are adorned with a load of rich and unwieldy furniture, with which they parade the streets from morning to night: and they now receive the only exercise which they are permitted to take. The governor's stud, which consists of a number of choice horses, are particularly drawn up in the square before his house. They are opposed to each other in squadrons, and at the word of command, the riders set off at full gallop, and as they pass each other, dart the pike or spear with great dexterity.

We paid a customary visit to the governor on our landing, and found him to be a grave and elderly man, meager in his body, and slovenly in his apparel. But with this unpromising appearance, he has the character of being a very good and intelligent man; and much more inquisitive after the manners and discoveries of European nations, than the generality of his countrymen. This peculiarity in his disposition plainly evinces itself in the furniture of his audience chamber, which is ornamented with a broken figured clock, a French thermometer, and an English quadrant. He received us very politely, and is a professed friend of the English nation, whose genius and spirit he affects to admire. This piece of intelligence we obtained from our resident here, who at the same time communicated to us

an

an anecdote of his life, which is not unworthy of mention. It not only carries with it an evidence of the intriguing temper of the Arabs, but sets off to advantage the character of a man, to whom the English are materially obliged.

In the reign of the father of the present king of Sennaa, this man was the vizier and favorite. So universally was his administration approved of, and so necessary did the old king think him to the welfare of the state, that he recommended him on his death-bed to the protection of his son, in the most earnest terms. The prince was deeply impressed with a charge delivered to him at so solemn a moment, and promised his father, to make the knowledge and advice of the vizier the sole guides of his future life. And to this promise he very faithfully adhered, for some years after his accession to the throne.

In the course of this time, the young monarch had formed inconsiderate attachments for courtiers of his own age and disposition. Though this did not immediately interfere with the minister's influence in matters of government, it nevertheless suggested, to a discerning mind, the approaches of neglect and disgrace. To prevent the execution, therefore, of what he considered as inevitable, should he continue in his present office, he very wisely formed the resolution of retiring from court. A resolution inspired by the soundest philosophy, wavered not until an opportunity offered to put it into practice.

One day when he was alone with the king, he took the liberty to speak of the length of his services, and of the decline of his life. He touched modestly upon his known affection, and zeal for the honor of his sovereign; and bespoke his majesty's indulgence for the petition which he was about to prefer. He concluded with an humble desire, that he might be permitted to resign his trust to one, whose faculties and health were

were more vigorous, and able to transact the important affairs, in which he had been so long employed. The better to cover his design, he affected an inclination to visit Mocha, where he purposed to remain until his name was forgotten, and that time should weaken the malice of a faction, which is the inseparable attendant of the best administration. It was not without reluctance, that the king complied with this unexpected request. He had a particular value and respect for the minister, and was not prepared to forego his services, although the latter had been artful enough to recommend for his successor, one of the chief favorites of his master. The struggle, however, was of no long continuance. The king's pride was touched at the idea of being at a loss for a servant, and he hastened to invest the very favourite who had been pointed out to him, with the dignity of the abdicated minister.

But little did the minister dream of the consequences of this resignation. Little did he foresee, that his successor would lay hold of the wish which he had expressed to visit Mocha, to load him again with the cares of government; where his influence would be considerably lessened, though his dignity would appear greater than before. No sooner had the new vizier possessed himself of his office, than he was determined to remove for ever, so virtuous an observer of his administration. Poison or the sword, was too dangerous an implement, against such a character. He had recourse to a remedy which wholly answered his intentions; and, by blinding the eyes of his sovereign, and advancing the opinion of his principles among the vulgar, must be held as a masterpiece of courtly artifice.

With the greatest appearance of warmth, therefore, he represented to the king the outcry which would be raised against him, should he suffer an old servant of his father's, and the

guardian

guardian of his own youth, to vifit Mocha, without being diftinguifhed by fome public character. He then infinuated the lucky occafion which prefented itfelf, to reward his fervices with the government of that city. It was impoffible to fufpect the treachery of this advice; and it is not wonderful, that the monarch greedily took the bait. He that very day forwarded a commiffion to Mocha, which the old man had the mortification to find, on his arrival here. To him, however, the trick was obvious. He readily dived into the fcheme of his fucceffor, who, judging of others from himfelf, had taken an unneceffary ftep to detach him from the vanity of court-favor. The vexation of the governor is not to be defcribed. But rather than difturb the peace of his mafter with complaints, he has the virtue to encounter the fatigues of bufinefs, though repugnant to his inclinations; and is content to live a voluntary exile from his native place, fecure of the affection of the people, and confcious of the efteem of the king. A king! who ftill continues under the delufion of having preferred a faithful fubject, agreeably to his own choice. What a leffon fhould this be to the fovereigns of more enlightened nations! who may juftly apprehend the intrigues of defigning men, when the refinements of party prevail within the narrow fcope of Arabian politics!

The women in Arabia are kept in much ftricter confinement, than thofe of their religion in India. The females of rank are fhut up in their apartments, and never ftir abroad, except now and then, to accompany their hufbands on an excurfion to the vallies. They are vailed at thefe times from head to foot, and fent off upon horfeback under cover of the night. But this fimple recreation does not fall often to their lot. The civilized Arabs are, of all nations, the leaft inclined to action; and it is to be fuppofed, that women born here, live and die, without ftirring out of the walls of Mocha: fuch is the tax that is laid

on

on birth and greatness, even in the remote country of Arabia. How then can we be surprized at the vexations, which cloud the lives of the followers of a powerful court? if female beauty be doomed to solitude in these rude parts, is not the liberty which is allowed it in more polished countries, too often the source of calamities more grievous than confinement, of persecutions more intolerable than the commands of an imperious master? I doubt not, but there is many a toast that blazes in the circle of St. James's, that sighs for the privilege of obscurity, and would willingly hide the remains of a shattered reputation in an Arabian seraglio!

To those of a lower degree, there is some deviation permitted from the severity of this custom. Though there are no public Hummums for the women to resort to as in Turkey, they are indulged with the freedom of visiting their neighbors, when the dusk of the evening can skreen their persons from observation: for the thick vails in which their faces are buried, utterly preclude the possibility of distinguishing their features. We have met them ourselves in the streets, and have conceived a favorable idea of their faces, from the symmetry of their figures.

Incontinence is held much more criminal among the single than married females. Though adultery is punished with a heavy fine, the seduction of a virgin is attended by a more serious correction. In this they differ from the laws of more enlightened kingdoms, where an injury of this nature, is not only unpunishable by any course of law, but the matter itself is treated in a very light manner. And here the character of the Arabian legislator rises far beyond the boasted policy of European states. To his justice it is owing, that the destruction of innocence is held in such abhorrence; and to his rectitude of thinking, that the mere accomplice of a lewd woman should encounter less rigorous treatment, than the mean betrayer of unexperienced simplicity.

plicity. How juft this obfervation may be, I fubmit with pleafure to the decifion of a lady, who can fo charitably diftinguifh between the follies and vices of her fex; and who can feparate the errors of inexperience from the impulfes of a depraved inclination!

We were furprized at the number of Chriftian renegadoes that refide at Mocha. Not, that the apoftacy of men, who perhaps had no fenfe of religion until they profeffed Mahometanifm, could provoke our wonder; but how their worldly interefts could be advanced by the change. Reduced to a pitiful fubfiftence, and held in deferved contempt by the natives, we fhould have furmifed their defection to be merely the effects of defpair; and that the fugitives from juftice alone, fought their fafety at this price, had not the example of a Greek prieft fomewhat fhaken our opinion. This prieft, by name Ananias, I remember to have heard mentioned in Bengal, as a miracle of piety. And yet in the feventieth year of his age, did he publicly abjure the Chriftian religion, in the courfe of a pilgrimage to Mount Sinai. He was circumcifed, and received into the Mahometan church; and, to crown the whole of this ftrange proceeding, was led about the city for three days, according to cuftom, mounted on an afs, to receive the alms of the faithful, which every convert is entitled to on his admiffion to their myfteries. This happened during our fhort ftay at Mocha; and is one of the greateft inftances of the infirmity of human nature, which has come within the fphere of my obfervation.

The Englifh are the only nation who have a refident here; and this is but a late regulation. The Eaft India Company were accuftomed to fend a fhip here every feafon; but now the coffee is tranfported on country bottoms to Bombay, from whence our Indiamen convey it to Europe. By this plan they are eafed of a confiderable expence; as the appointments of fupercargoes to

this

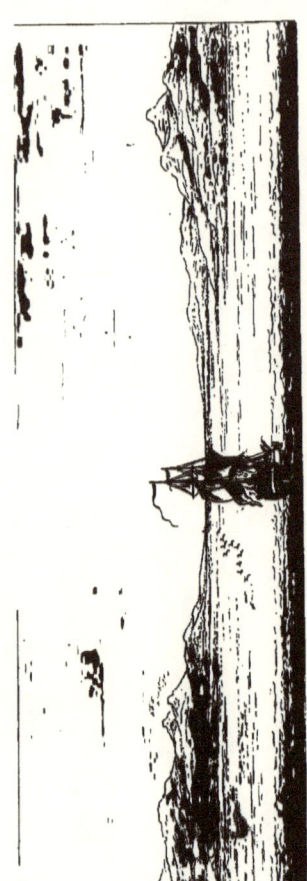

A View of the Straits of Babelmandel in Lat: 12:40: N.

A View of Mocha on the Road of Arabia Felix in Lat: 13:19: N.

this station, and the heavy duties of this port, must have lessened the advantages which result from this trade. No better means could have been devised to ingratiate ourselves with the natives, than the appointment of a resident among them. It is a pleasure to me to add, that nothing could have better ensured the end in view, than the choice of the present gentleman who fills that post. His mild demeanor cannot fail to engage the esteem of the people; as his acknowledged abilities will lead him to improve every occasion, to restore this drooping branch of commerce to its original value. Neither is the presence of Mr. Horseley at Mocha, of less moment to the interests of travellers, who prefer this short cut to Europe, to the old track by the Cape of Good Hope. Hospitality and politeness are acceptable in all places, but doubly so to the way-worn traveller, who the least expects to meet with them in a remote and uncivilized region.

I have annexed a view of the town and suburbs of Mocha, which I took from our vessel on the day of our arrival here. There is a wall runs round the town, but there are no cannon mounted on it, except a few on a battery towards the sea. The northern and southern extremities of the town are flanked by two castles of a circular form, which are likewise ornamented with guns, and were meant as a defence to the place. How much these Arabian engineers were mistaken in their ideas of fortification, will clearly appear from a circumstance, which occurred here about six or seven years ago, and will set their pretensions to power in a proper light.

The captain of a trading vessel from India, was ashore at the English factory, and correcting a slave for some fault or other, the boy ran away, and took refuge in an Arabian house, where he was prevailed upon to become a Mahometan. In this country no Christian is permitted to keep a slave of this persuasion. The boy availed himself of this privilege, and went abroad again, without any fear of his master's resentment. One day, however, as he ventured to pass the factory, he was observed by the captain, whose English blood boiled with indignation at this seeming insult. Unheedful of his situation, he gave way to a sudden impulse of passion, and ordered his servants to seize the boy, and flog him severely within the yard of the factory. This rash action could not escape notice, and was attended by consequences which he little expected. The factory was at that time uninhabited, except by the supercargoes and captains during their short stay here. It was not in the best repair, and but little calculated to make a defence. The mob, which now gathered about it, easily forced the gates; and not finding the object of their research, whom they meant to have sacrificed on the spot, contented themselves with plundering his effects. On the first alarm, the captain wisely retreated to the terrace of the factory; and it was with no little difficulty, that he escaped along the roofs of the houses to the sea-side, where he immediately took a boat for his vessel.

This disturbance was too sudden to have been checked under the best-regulated government; but it might have been remedied: satisfaction might have been made to the sufferer, had the governor been inclined to do him justice. A deaf ear was turned to his remonstrances, and the captain was obliged to carry his complaint to Bombay: here, to the honour of the British name, it was properly attended to. The councils were vigorous; and two sloops of war were directly fitted out for Mocha, to enforce redress. They accordingly appeared before the town, with all the implements for a bombardment; and a message was sent ashore, to advertise the governor of their errand. It is impossible to conceive the terror of the inhabitants at these tidings. They deserted the castles, which they had once considered as impregnable, and were about to quit the city itself; but this the

governor

governor prevented. He thought proper to comply with the demands, which were made in the name of the sufferer, and sent off 4,000 dollars to the commodore of the expedition; happy, to preserve the city from destruction, and to appease the resentment of the English, at so cheap a rate. And even the money to make good this payment, was raised unjustly, though it was to satisfy a just demand. The Banian, or Gentoo merchants who are settled here, and transact all the business of the port, fell within the gripe of government on this occasion. They have assured us more than once, that they were obliged to advance the sum in question, for which they have not yet been satisfied. It is necessary to add, that this occurrence, so disgraceful in its nature, was antecedent to the administration of the present governor; of whose character I have had occasion to speak in the most favorable terms.

To these Banians we were obliged for a part of our amusements at this place. There is a wood of date-trees, which extends from the southern suburbs of Mocha, for some miles towards the inland mountains. There is no mark of cultivation in this neighborhood besides; and in this wood, one of the principal Banians has a country seat. We have no conveyance here, except asses, on which we ride about for our diversion. In one of our excursions we called at this seat, which is above three miles from the town, and on our way home, had an opportunity of observing a curious process in the vegetable world. It has already been taken notice of by naturalists, but is too uncommon to be known to readers of every class. The date-trees were now in blossom; and we remarked the Arabs to be busied about the branches. It is necessary to ingraft all fruit-trees, to obtain good fruit; but the propagation of the date is in another manner, and intimately resembles that of the animal creation. There is a male as well as female date-tree, which are distinguished

from

from each other by the color and shape of the blossoms. The male tree yields no fruit; but the gardener must be careful, every spring, to cull as many blossoms from the male, as will serve his purpose. One of these at least he must inwrap and bind up in a blossom of the female tree; without which she will prove as barren as the male. The singularity of this operation is heightened by its being discovered by a people, who are at present grossly ignorant of every branch of natural philosophy *.

It is to our resident that I am indebted for an ingenious conjecture, relative to the barren coasts of Arabia Felix, with which I shall close my remarks on this celebrated territory. For the space of fifteen or sixteen miles from the beach, the land rises on a gradual ascent towards the foot of the mountains. Here the scene suddenly changes from a sandy waste, to a verdant and fertile soil; from a scarcity of palatable water, to a profusion of chrystal springs and running streams. In this desart barrier there are found quantities of shells, and other productions of the ocean, which seem to have lain there for many ages: this, joined to the shelving appearance of the ground, renders the idea very probable, that this tract of land has been won from the sea, by the secret operations of nature. There is, indeed, no information to be gathered of this event, among a people whose annals carry no perspicuity with them, beyond the days of their prophet. But the perpendicular shores of the opposite coast of Africa, upon which the waters may have proportionably encroached, are an additional evidence in favor of this opinion. No stranger, in traversing this shore, could possibly conceive her right to the

---

* There is little force in this compliment, when it is known that the Egyptians have so far improved on this mode, as to plant only a male date-tree in the middle of many females. The wind scatters the male seed, which impregnates the female tree, without the trouble of the Arabian culture.

title

title of Happy. But place him in her middle regions, beneath her balm-dropping woods, and amidſt her delightful vales, where the fruits of every climate court his taſte, and the breezes of caſſia refreſh his ſenſes, and he will pronounce, that ſhe juſtly retains the flattering appellation with which ſhe was honored by the antients.

On the 16th of April we had completed our wood and water, and taken on board a ſufficient ſtock of proviſion to ſerve us on our paſſage. We chearfully embarked, therefore, on the Adventure, captain Bacon, and with an additional paſſenger from India, ſpread our ſails for the long-wiſhed-for port of Suez. For ſome days we were favored with a fair breeze, and moderate weather: but the wind changed ſuddenly to the northward, and began to blow with great violence againſt us. The moon was now at the full, and we were to look for a continuance of the gale. In narrow ſeas the waters are ſoon agitated; and we experienced ſuch a diſagreeable motion, from the inceſſant working of the veſſel, that ſome of my fellow-paſſengers were again confined to their cabbins. As for my own part, I have had the good fortune to be free from ſickneſs during our tedious voyage, if I except an head-ach of four-days ſtanding, which I conſider, indeed, as a natural infirmity. Our hopes were once more revived, from the winds abating. We were by this time in the latitude of Judda; and though the wind was ſtill contrary, we made a ſhift to creep on daily towards our deſired port. Our greateſt progreſs was from ten to twenty miles in our way. We could not, with propriety, run more than thirty miles upon one tack; and it was our cuſtom to make one ſhore about ſun-ſet, then to tack, and ſtand for the oppoſite ſide, until day-break.

We had beaten up in this manner, to the 24th degree of north latitude, and were within 150 leagues of Suez, when, in the afternoon of the 6th of May, we diſcovered breakers ahead. The vessel's head was to the north-east, and the captain judged himself, from his journal, to be in mid-channel. It may be supposed, therefore, that this circumstance much alarmed us, as nothing but a strong easterly current, could have thrown us among the rocks and shoals, with which this part of the Arabian coast abounds. Nor were our fears without foundation. The weather had been so hazy all day, that we could scarcely see two leagues distance. The vessel had been put about at the alarm before recited, and we were sailing with great security towards the open sea, when the departing sun warned us of the destruction on which we were running. The sky cleared up for a moment as the sun set, and presented to our view, a line of rocks and shoals immediately before us, and on which, in a quarter of an hour, we must have struck, had not Providence, in this unexpected manner, delivered us from the ravenous deep. The most experienced among us were appalled at this sight. We had breakers to the northward and westward of us, and an unknown coast to the east. The wind fortunately favoring the only safe course which was now left us, the vessel wore and stood to the southward; her two boats being sent a mile ahead to lead the way. In this manner we proceeded until midnight, when one of the boats fired a gun, as a signal of distress. Our sails were backed on this alarm; and the boat presently bore down to inform us, that she heard the surf break close to her, and that there was no ground with fifty fathom of line. Our danger now became pressing. We were exposed to impending destruction while the vessel was in motion, and there was no probability of finding anchorage for her on this coast.

In this dilemma the vessel's head was put towards the land. The weather happily continued moderate, and we made a shift to steer clear of the perils that encircled us, though not without frequent alarms. So desperate did our situation appear, so

few

few were the chances of safety, that about two in the morning I retired to my cabin, and secured what little money and valuables I could conveniently carry about me. I loaded my pistols, and took out a packet of consequence from my chest, which I kept by me, in expectation of the vessel's striking on the rocks. In case of such an accident, we were only to trust to our boats for our deliverance. This we had learnt from the captain and officers of the snow Aurora, which was shipwrecked on this part of the coast, not six months preceding our arrival. We met them at Mocha on their return to India; and were advised of the particulars of their disaster, which doubled our apprehensions at the present crisis. The Aurora had been standing, like us, for the Arabian coast, and just before day-break, she struck, without the least warning, on a sunken rock. By the violence of the wind, she was driven so far upon the rock, as to bulge her bows, while at her stern no ground was to be found with ninety fathom of line. It was impossible that the vessel could hold long together in this position; and the captain and crew had scarcely time to take to their boats, when she separated and went down. There was an island in view, to which they made, and which would have preserved them from shipwreck, had the day broke but half an hour sooner. But we were at length relieved from our perplexity. With constant sounding we hit upon a narrow bank in fifty fathom, and joyfully dropped an anchor at four in the morning. There was no ground, however, to be found by the boats that sounded round the vessel. The bottom was rocky; and should the wind freshen, there was little dependance to be placed upon our anchor. Our satisfaction consequently was imperfect and precarious.

The light, which had been so long expected, now dawned, and enabled us at least, to discover the dangers that lurked around us. As the sun rose over the coast, we plainly discerned the

D   mountains

mountains of Arabia; and to the splendor of that glorious luminary, we were once more indebted for a gleam of hope, to revive our drooping spirits. We hastened therefore to take advantage of this intelligence. We weighed our anchor, with as much expedition as the depth of water would admit of, and were rejoiced to get it safe on board again. Our course was still directed towards the land, which was often obscured by the mists which hung over it. About noon we were close enough to distinguish a large town, which, from our charts, we concluded to be Yambo. To this town we attempted to get. After various intricate traverses, as the channel between the sands and rocks occasioned, we arrived at the mouth of the harbour, without which there is no ground, though the boats sounded at the edge of the shoals.

And now did we heartily congratulate ourselves on the conclusion of our troubles. We had heard at Mocha of the hospitality of this port, from the very persons who had owed to the inhabitants, their life and freedom. Captain Adams, and the survivors of the snow Aurora before mentioned, had been released by the governor of Yambo from the hands of the wild Arabs. These banditti had seized them, on their reaching the continent in their boat, stripped them of their cloaths, and brought them here with a view of selling them. Not content with this act of humanity, he had furnished them with camels, and generously supplied them with money and necessaries to carry them to Judda, where they were certain of finding English vessels. Nay, the very commerce that is carried on between the English and the inhabitants of Judda, which, as well as Yambo, is subject to the Xerif of Mecca, dispelled any doubt which might arise concerning the good faith of these people. We knew that there were several English vessels at Judda at the very time. We had landed a considerable sum of money at Mocha, which was a

present

present from the nabob of the Carnatic to the temple of Mecca; and we doubted not of meeting with the most favorable treatment at a place, which is in the neighborhood of Medina. How dim is the perception of mortals! What avails their boasted sagacity! Their funds of lettered knowledge! Their idle dreams of security! What appears the most reconcileable to their judgment, turns out in the experiment, to have been trusted without cause, and embraced without the evidence of conviction!

I have been the more particular in recapitulating the circumstances, on which we built a confidence in these people, as there are not wanting persons, idle and malicious enough, to condemn even the steps, by which their fellow-creatures have entailed misery and destruction upon themselves. The captain would have been censured for bringing his vessel into an uncivilized port, and the credulity of the passengers held up in a ridiculous light, for trusting themselves among a savage tribe, unversed in the tender offices of humanity, and unrestrained by the laws of social life. And to such this recital will be of use. While the generous breast shall plead our cause, and make allowances for the frailty of our natures, those worse than Arab spirits shall be robbed of the enjoyment of their spleen, and of liberty to pass sentence upon us, unheard. Entangled in a chain of sands and rocks, without a correct chart to direct us, or a seaman on board acquainted with the path of safety, there remained no alternative but to enter a port, that seemed to open her friendly arms for our relief. We were certain there were pilots here who could conduct us to Suez; and to escape shipwreck at sea, necessity would have obliged us to hazard slaughter ashore, even had we not been taught to look for the most hospitable reception. It will appear in the course of this narrative, that had we not considered the vessel's safety prior to our own, our lives had probably never been endangered, and we had

escaped

escaped a fund of trouble and disquietude. But to our ignorance of the Arabian policy must our conduct be attributed, and that opposition, which brought us to the brink of destruction.

As the adventures which befel us in this place, were either immediately committed to paper, or as soon as I could regain a communication with the pen, I will beg leave to deviate from the mode which I have hitherto observed, and keep a diary of our future transactions. A tale of distress is not only more interesting when thus divided, but more capable of spirit and accuracy. I ask not the colours of fiction to heighten a picture, which cannot fail to affect, when represented by the simplest touches of nature!

WEDNESDAY, 7th MAY 1777.

On the afternoon of this day we anchored at the entrance of Yambo harbor. We had scarcely taken a view of the town through our glasses, when we perceived a boat rowing towards us, which brought on board an Arab of a venerable and pleasing aspect. His appearance bespoke him of no common rank, and we presently found that he was a Shaik, and one of the members of government. This personage was charged with the compliments of the governor, or as he is here styled, the Vizier of Yambo, and his congratulations on our arrival in a port, where we should want for nothing that was in his power to afford. Refreshments we were in little need of. But our spirits were elated with the proffer of a pilot, which the vizier justly divined to be the motive of our errand.

In a few minutes a second boat reached our vessel, from which ascended an Abyssinian slave, handsomely cloathed and armed after the fashion of the country. He proved to be one of
the

the vizier's guard, and came with an invitation from his master, to favor him with our company on shore. We were much taken with the freedom of these people's behavior; and though they acknowledged to us, that no European vessel had put into their port before, we entertained no distrust of their sincerity, and readily promised to take advantage of the vizier's politeness. There were several of us in the ship who talked the Moor language, and were equally deceived by the old shaik, who was a Patan, and understood it perfectly. He conversed with such ease and gravity of face, that the eye of suspicion might have been lulled asleep, and age itself relaxed of its severity of opinion.

After regaling them with coffee and tea, of which they willingly partook, we dismissed them with advice of our intentions to go on shore in the morning. The preliminaries were adjusted; and we agreed to salute the fort at sun-rise, when these messengers promised to come on board for us.

THURSDAY, 8th May.

I was awakened this morning by the vessel's salute, which was irregularly returned by the fort. As soon as breakfast was over, I went into the long-boat with the captain, two supercargoes, our interpreter, and three passengers, who are bound for England as well as myself. We were accompanied by our servants in a fisher-boat, and about the middle of the harbor, were met by the old shaik, the Abyssinian, and others of the vizier's train, who had been sent to conduct us ashore. As we passed a decayed castle on an angle of the fort, a very laughable incident occurred. A gun was fired from thence to welcome us to Yambo; but such a quantity of rubbish fell down from the shock, and such a dust obscured the place, as immediately interrupted

the

the falute, and induced the garrifon to confult their own fafety, by an omiffion of the compliment intended us. Indeed, fo ruinous an appearance did the walls and buildings of this town exhibit, which had not probably been repaired fince the days of Mahomet, that our contempt of it increafed to a degree, that would have ridiculed the idea of danger. At our landing we were met by fome officers of the vizier's houfhold, and ufhered in great ftate to an apartment by the fea-fide. Here were affembled fundry of the principal inhabitants, who were feated on carpets, agreeably to the oriental cuftom. There were chairs provided for our reception, and we were ferved with coffee and perfumes.

After an hour's delay, at which we were fomewhat furprized, but have fince been able to account for, the vizier fent to acquaint us of his being ready to fee us. We were accordingly attended in the fame manner as before, to a building within the fort, and introduced to this minifter. He received us fitting; it being unufual with the Arabs to rife up, to falute thofe of an inferior rank. We advanced however, towards him, by the direction of our interpreter; on which he put his right hand to his breaft with a flight inclination of his head, and gave it to each of us, as a token of his amity. Of all the Muffulmen whom I have yet feen, the vizier of Yambo is the faireft. Without the mixture of red and white, that diftinguifhes Europeans from Afiatics, his complexion did not yield to any of our company. His eyes black and fparkling; his nofe aquiline, and his countenance expreffive of great fweetnefs and fenfibility. He feemed to be between thirty and forty years of age, and was not the leaft embarraffed by the prefence of ftrangers, whom he only knew by report. We had been furprized at the deportment of the vizier's fervants yefterday. But that was a fcene of little admiration,

admiration, when compared with the audience we now obtained. The impreffion will never be effaced from my mind. The powers of Garrick would, if poffible, fall fhort, to fupport the countenance and addrefs of the vizier during an interview of two hours, in which fuch complicated deceit and villainy were ufed, as throw the crooked politics of Machiavel far behind!

After the firft ceremonies were over, and the coffee and perfumes brought in, the vizier repeated his offers of affiftance. He profeffed a great refpect for the Englifh nation, and a regard for the nabob of Arcot—in whofe fervice the captain had declared himfelf—for his generous attention to the poor of Mecca. He flattered us with the profpect of getting eafily to Suez; and as we were in want of a pilot, he fent for the captain of the port, to examine him in our prefence, touching our future paffage. Nothing could be more plaufible than this behavior. We were profufe in our acknowledgments of the minifter's goodnefs, and little imagined that the man who was fummoned before us, had been tutored for the purpofe, during our ftay at the fhaik's houfe.

In a fhort time this officer appeared, and was queftioned by the vizier himfelf on the certainty and length of our voyage to Suez. The particulars of this converfation were conveyed to us by our interpreter, who ftood between them. It had long been our fear, that the foutherly winds were exhaufted, and that the northerly monfoon was about to fet in; which would inevitably prevent our further progrefs. And it was on thefe points that the pilot infifted. He expreffed his doubts of making the paffage, and his apprehenfions of endangering an Englifh veffel; the confequence of which he could not anfwer. At length he pofitively declined the undertaking, as hazardous and impracticable. Much argument did the vizier ufe to render him compliant. He threw out the lure of the reward, which his fuccefs woud entitle him' to; and even affected to be fhocked at his prefumption and pufillanimity. He fubmitted the matter to ourfelves, and offered, if we pleafed, to fend the pilot in irons on board our veffel. To this violence it may be fuppofed, we univerfally diffented; at the fame time that we declared our fenfe of this mark of the minifter's friendfhip. The head pilot was therefore difmiffed, and another fent for, whom the vizier pretended to judge would be more tractable. But with him we had no better fuccefs. He was equally backward with the former, to take charge of the veffel; and after much futile perfuafion, the minifter turned round to us in feeming trouble, and expreffed his regret at our bad fortune.

The captain now totally abandoned all thoughts of proceeding further; and was content with the promife of a pilot to carry him to Judda; the port to which the fhip was ordered, in cafe of the lofs of her paffage to Suez. The travellers deftined for Europe, now preferred their petition. We requefted a boat, to tranfport us to Suez with our baggage; and informed the vizier of our being feverally charged with packets for the Eaft India Company, both from the nabob of Arcot and the governor of Madras. To this he gave a gracious affent; and the pilot engaged to fit out a boat for us in five days. Nay, the price of his trouble was fixed at 50 dollars, which apparently exceeded his expectations. Our conference had been fpun out to a great length, and as our bufinefs was difpatched, we made a motion to retire. It was our intention to have repaired immediately to the veffel, where dinner was provided: but the vizier acquainted us at our departure, that he had directed refrefhments to be prepared for us at the fhaik's houfe, of which he hoped we would partake. As the day was pretty far advanced, and we travellers were anxious to adjuft the particulars of our voyage with the pilot, we unwittingly fwallowed the bait which was thrown out for us, us, and returned with the old fhaik to his houfe, little dreaming that it would become the theatre of our troubles!

On a candid review of the foregoing fcene, even on the very day it occurred, I cannot charge my memory with a fingle circumftance, by which the fincerity of the vizier was liable to fufpicion. So well was the plot laid, with fuch addrefs did the principal characters conduct themfelves, that never fiction fo happily affumed the air of truth. The flighteft alarm would probably have prevented the confequences which enfued, as none of us imagine the fhaik or his attendants were authorized to oppofe our departure, had we made an effort to regain our boat, inftead of returning to the houfe of our conductor. But we were lulled into a fecurity, that was particularly ftrengthened on the part of us travellers, from an information which the vizier gave us. Two Englifh gentlemen had been recommended to his good offices by the Xerif his mafter; and he had difpatched them with a packet to Suez, but a few days before our arrival. This circumftance encouraged our hopes. We conceived the packet to be the fame, which a captain Dibdin was charged with from the ufurped adminiftration at Madras; and we were emulous of not being outftripped in a race, where we contended without reproach.

We had not been half an hour at the fhaik's houfe, when a meffenger came to fummon our interpreter to the vizier's prefence. This man was an Arab by birth, and had performed a pilgrimage to Mecca; an act of devotion which every true Muffulman undertakes, either in perfon or by proxy, before he dies. From this he had obtained the title of Hadgy. He was a fhrewd fenfible fellow, and proved of infinite fervice to us in the fequel, by letting us into the defigns of his countrymen. He returned after a fhort abfence, with evident marks of furprize in his countenance, which foon communicated itfelf to our

our breasts, by the meſſage he brought. It imported, that the vizier could render us no aſſiſtance, until he received an order from the Xerif of Mecca concerning us; and that it would be adviſeable for the captain to direct the officer on board, to bring the veſſel into the harbor. Such a contradiction in his conduct immediately opened our eyes to the wrong that was intended us; and we began to think of the beſt method, to extricate ourſelves from the ſnare we had fallen into. A retreat to our boat naturally ſuggeſted itſelf: but our deliberations were ſoon interrupted, by one of the company obſerving from a window, that there was a guard upon the houſe. To be certified of this, I walked through an area that led to the gateway, which I found beſet by a troop of ſoldiers. There was now nothing left us, but to put the beſt face on the matter. We ſent the interpreter back to the vizier, with expoſtulations on the duplicity of his behavior. We reminded him of our having come aſhore at his own invitation; and that he could not detain us, without a violation of the law of nations, and of hoſpitality: for a regard to which the Arabs were univerſally celebrated. We demanded, what buſineſs he or his maſter could have with a veſſel, which had not entered their port, and was in want of nothing but a pilot, which it was at their option to afford her. We obſerved the odium that would attend ſuch proceedings towards the property of a prince, to whom the Xerif was ſo much indebted, both in reſpect to the commerce which he carried on with the port of Judda, and the very valuable preſent that our veſſel had brought for the temple of Mecca. Finally, we warned him, not to offer any inſult to the Britiſh flag, which the moſt barbarous nations had been taught to reſpect. The interpreter was likewiſe charged to demand an audience for the captain, that he might argue the matter with the vizier. But this effort was unſucceſsful. The poor fellow came back with a

long

long face, and brought a strict injunction to the captain, to order the vessel into the harbor, and a desire that we would make ourselves easy, until the orders respecting us arrived, which would be in six days at furthest. The captain's suit was declined, on pretence of the vizier's being engaged with company.

We now consulted upon the steps to be taken in this exigency. Our junction with the ship was infallibly cut off. The mariners who had been left to take care of the boat, had by this time, been sent to the place of our confinement. From them we learnt, that our boat was carried to an unknown part, at the moment of their seizure. Our own detention was consequently confirmed, and the escape of the vessel from the hands of these robbers — for such we regarded them — was the point to which we turned our views. Indeed, we considered her as the anchor by which our lives were held. It was impossible to answer for the forbearance or humanity of people, who had broken through the most sacred precept of their religion, in their treatment of us, should they once get the vessel into their possession, by whose means alone the circumstances of our detention could be brought to light. With our concurrence therefore, the captain wrote a positive order to his chief mate, to weigh or slip his anchor, with the first favorable wind, make the best of his way to Judda, and there communicate our story to the captains of the English vessels. And even this scheme appeared to us by no means as safe or feasible. The vessel lay in a narrow channel, with shoals and breakers on each side of her; and the northerly winds prevailed the greatest part of the day, which obstructed her departure. Add to this, that her passage to Judda was dangerous without a pilot; to the chance of procuring which, the officer must have trusted to the coasting boats. But all obstacles sunk under the pressure of necessity. The captain and supercargoes were more particularly interested in the preservation of the vessel and cargo; and among the valuables that the passengers had on board, I chiefly considered a packet, which a noble friend * had entrusted to a fellow-traveller and myself. We were, perhaps, singular in our concern for some moveable or other. But we were unanimous in our desire, that the vessel which contained it, should get beyond the reach of these spoilers.

While our interpreter was dispatched with this letter to the vizier, to give a very opposite explanation of the contents, which their utter ignorance of our language enabled him to do with security, we sate down upon a carpet, to partake of a frugal meal which the old shaik had set before us. It consisted of stewed mutton, garnished with raw onions. Flat cakes of flour were our plates, and our fingers stood us in lieu of knives and forks. Notwithstanding the agitation of our minds, and this unusual method of eating, we made a shift to clear the dish in a few minutes, to the no small admiration of the shaik and his attendants. The natives of Arabia are very temperate in their diet; and though we found that the lower class would drink spirituous liquors to excess, we have reason to believe, that the better sort generally adhere to the precept of the Alcoran, which forbids the use of them. Pure water is their common draught, and with this we were obliged to crown our meal.

Our watches had advised us of its being past five o'clock, when the interpreter returned with an order to the shaik, to send a boat off with the letter. It now occurred to us, that the captain had better proffer himself to execute the vizier's pleasure. His escape would have proved an additional security to the vessel; and though we almost despaired of success, we omitted not our endeavors to carry this point. The captain and the two supercargoes were separately proposed to be the bearer of the orders; but all that we could obtain, in the course of two hours solici-

* The right honorable Lord Pigot.

tation,

tation, was leave for a servant to go off with the letter. It was now near eight o'clock, and we had the further mortification to be kept in suspence an hour longer, before the boat was ready. We felt for the situation of the officers on board, who had expected our return to dinner, and had received no intelligence from us since we had been ashore. We knew not what designs might be concerting against the vessel, which lay within half a mile of the coast; and until the officers aboard were cautioned of the danger, our general fate was undetermined. Night had thrown her sable curtains around us, and treachery and stratagem, which shun the light, might now be busy for our destruction. We were entangled in those toils, with which the dauntless lion struggles in vain. The pale glimmering of a lamp served just to afford us a sight of each other, and the posture of a part of our guard, who had civilly intruded themselves into the room, where gentlemen, servants, and mariners, to the number of twenty, were crouded together. The sea surrounded three sides of our prison, and the other was secured by a strong body, armed with matchlocks, pistols, and sabres. Though it afterwards appeared, that our situation could be more alarming than at this period, I should think such another hour dearly purchased with the wealth of the east. I can truly affirm, that when death seemed unavoidable, when the ministers of vengeance stood ready to perform its mandate, my thoughts were more collected, and my resolution more confirmed. So preferable is the knowledge of the worst which can befall us, to a state of uncertainty!

But our minds were at length relieved by the arrival of the boat, which took our servant from the window of our apartment. A desperate scheme now suggested itself for our escape, but was rejected, on a conviction of its folly. There was a guard in the boat as well as in our room; and we had observed soldiers planted on the walls, as spies upon our motions. To have

regained

regained our swords, the only weapons we had brought ashore, we must have betrayed our design. To make the attempt unarmed, would have been worse than madness. We therefore contented ourselves with adding verbal instructions to the servant, for the officer's positive departure, and prepared to take that repose, which the circumstances we were under, might allow of. But here, we reckoned without our host. Sleep and we were not so near, as we expected. The boat had not long left us, when we observed some of the domestics remove the carpets, which had been spread for our beds. We had not time to indulge our conjectures on this incident, when the old shaik appeared, and with much apparent concern acquainted us, that it was the vizier's order, we should be confined in an upper apartment of the house during the night. The place to which he pointed, was a tower, against which our very natures revolted. The order itself had a black appearance; and though it turned out to be only meant for the better securing our persons, it is no wonder that some among us should attribute it to be a project, for the readier perpetration of their villainous purposes. In short, it was agreed upon to oppose the execution of this order to the utmost; and though actual resistance was equally vain and hopeless, we found the good effects of not tamely submitting to this indignity. The shaik was charged to tell the vizier, that we would not go to the dungeon allotted us, unless compelled by force of arms; and again to warn him of treating us harshly. And this commission was so faithfully executed, that in about an hour, our carpets were returned to us, and we were delivered from further persecution for the present.

Our spirits were much raised by the success of this measure; and we began to entertain hopes that no violence was intended us. Our late distress became the subject of mirth; and we affected to regret, that our story would not be enriched with the
adventure

adventure of the round-tower. We betook ourselves, without repining, to our humble lodging on the ground; and I enjoyed a very comfortable nap until day-break, although my nostrils were plentifully regaled with the fumes of tobacco, from the pipe of one of our guard, who had taken post in the seat of a window above me.

FRIDAY, 9th May.

When I awoke this morning, I found our servant had returned, with an answer from the chief mate; which expressed his concern for our situation, and his intention to get away with the first favorable wind, agreeably to the captain's directions. This was very pleasing intelligence; and we drank the coffee which was now brought us, without complaining of its being unpalatable. The Arabs never adulterate their coffee with sugar or milk. These are quite an European addition; as is the case likewise with respect to tea, which is drank pure in China. I must acknowledge, that I prefer our method of preparing these articles of luxury; but were we to use tea and coffee in such quantities as the natives of those countries, we should neither find them pleasant nor salutary, when mixed with other ingredients. There is scarce an hour passes in the day, that coffee is not served up here; and their coloons, or pipes, are never from their mouths, but when they are at meals or asleep.

Our attention was engaged the whole morning towards our vessel, which we could see very plainly from the windows of our apartment. The wind began to blow from the northward according to custom, and before noon encreased with such violence, as not only to cut off the possibility of her departure, but

even

even to alarm us for her safety; as she rode without the harbor, and lay exposed to all the fury of the sea and weather. We now plotted for the recovery of our boat; the absence of which, with the prime part of her crew, might occasion the loss of the vessel, in case of her parting her cable. For this purpose we dispatched our interpreter to the vizier, who was entrusted to express to him our doubts of the officer's obedience. We remarked that the wind blew into the harbor, and the vessel had made no motion to weigh her anchor and stand in; and we attributed the officer's backwardness to his entertaining a notion, that the orders which he had received, had been extorted from us. As a means, therefore, of satisfying him, we proposed that the vizier would permit our boat and mariners to go on board, with a second order from the captain, and a declaration of our having done nothing by compulsion. At the same time we insinuated, that the sight of our boat and people would overcome any scruples, which the officer might have harbored in his breast.

The whole day was spent in this negotiation, and we began to think it would prove fruitless, when this crafty minister was foiled at his own weapons, and allowed himself to be egregiously duped. An Arab boat with a guard, however, was ordered to accompany ours; and the captain wrote a second letter to the officer, conjuring him to depart by the first opportunity, and to detain the ship's boat, and return our servant on the other. He also directed him to appear enraged at the contents of the letter, and to declare to the Arabs that he would sail at daybreak. We took this opportunity to send on board for a shift or two of linen; a convenience which we had been two days debarred of, and which, in other circumstances, would have been sufficiently distressing in a warm climate. I had several valuables about

about me; but I had not a thought of preserving any thing from pillage, except the picture of a dear sister, which I had worn for many years about my neck. From this bosom-friend did I now resolve to part; and the most sensible pang which I endured in our captivity, was at the moment of my delivering this picture into the hands of the servant, who was going off to the vessel. I was ashamed of my weakness, and retired to a window in order to conceal a tear, which rose in my own despite, from the fountain of affection!

We were entertained by our hospitable shaik with a dinner, similar to that of yesterday; with the addition however of water-melons, which are much larger and finer here than in India. It is but doing him justice to say, that he has behaved to us with the greatest civility and attention; insomuch, that our food is frequently served up with his own hands. We were inquisitive about the vizier's intentions, but could get nothing out of the old man, except exhortations to patience, and hopes of a speedy answer from Mecca. The suspence we live in, is the greatest hardship which we labor under. In other respects, our situation is as comfortable as prisoners could expect. Our very guard are as civil as their manners will admit of; and though their presence is troublesome enough, we have hitherto met with none of those insults, which the petty tyrants of our own country are so apt to exercise over the poor wretches in their custody. Though we have fallen into the hands of an arbitrary government, we have not become the prey of its servile and unfeeling instruments.

About nine o'clock at night we were advertized of the return of the Arab boat, but without our servant or linen; the Arabs having been so intimidated at the officer's affectation of anger, as to leave the vessel with precipitation. This news was communicated

nicated to us by our hoſt, who ſeemed much ſurprized at the preſumption of the officer towards his captain, which he could by no means reconcile to his own ideas of ſubordination to his ſuperiors. Our only concern was the want of the linen, and ſome liquors that we had ſent for. But we conſoled ourſelves with the thoughts of procuring them in the morning by ſome accident or other; and in the mean time compoſed ourſelves to reſt.

SATURDAY, 10th May.

The laſt night was paſſed in the ſame manner as the firſt, except that we were leſs crouded, by the departure of our boat's crew; a circumſtance not immaterial in an hot climate, where our apartment did not meaſure more than ſixteen feet by ten. I roſe before day-break, and going out on a ſmall terrace bounded by the ſea, for the benefit of the morning air, was ſurprized at the ſound of female voices, which ſeemed at no great diſtance. I looked up, and found it to proceed from the windows above me; the lattices of which were now open, and filled with women. Theſe were members of the old ſhaik's family, and I little imagined that we could meet with ſuch treatment in the neighborhood of a ſeraglio. We had acceſs to but one room in this manſion; the upper part of which was conſecrated to beauty, under equal reſtraint with ourſelves. Had we been poſſeſſed of the true ſpirit of chivalry, we ſhould have gloried in our fate, that enabled us to wear the ſame chains which enſlaved the 'fair': and, regardleſs of our own deſtiny, we ſhould only have reſolved how to deliver theſe captive damſels from their enchanted caſtle. But alas! there was no Quixote among us; and we ſhall remain as a ſignal inſtance of the degeneracy of theſe latter times.

I liſtened attentively to theſe females, who were very earneſtly

engaged;

engaged; and though I am a stranger to the Arabic language, I judged from the motions which they made use of, that we were the subjects of their discourse. I even flattered myself; that they were touched with pity at our situation, from the tones of their voices at certain intervals; and, though the romantic notions I entertain of the general tenderness and benevolence of womankind, may have rendered me too sanguine in this particular, I have not the least doubt but they interested themselves in our safety, and would have contributed towards our escape. As the light dawned they found themselves observed, and retired from the windows, but not without many respectful obeisances and looks of commiseration.

About seven o'clock the vessel fired a gun and loosed her foretopsail, the customary signals for sailing: and we received a letter from the officer to this effect. This he had sent by our small boat with two sailors, whom he could well spare to provide for our necessities, which were become pressing. We now got a message from the vizier, demanding the result of the officer's determination. To this we replied, that he still denied the captain's authority over him, and was on the point of sailing for Judda, with the account of our detention. Had this design been fortunately executed, the end which we had in view, would probably have been answered: for seeing his prey escape him, which was the ship, the vizier would, it is to be presumed, have sent us after her in our boat, as lumber too unworthy to be with-held.

By this time the vessel was in motion. The rocks had cut her cable as her crew were weighing her anchor, and she swung bodily towards a reef of breakers, before they could bring her up with another anchor. At this moment we tasted the bitterness of anguish. We plainly saw the vessel driving on destruction, and stood idle spectators of a misfortune beyond our power to avert.

avert. Our captain himſelf, a man of ſkill and experience, gave her up as loſt; and we vented the ebullitions of our rage, in impotent threats, and idle imprecations on the author of our diſtreſs. The horrors of our ſituation ruſhed at once upon our minds. All hopes of relief would periſh with the veſſel, and we be left at the mercy of a race, the profeſſed enemies of our religion. The fears of detection might inſpire them with the worſt deſigns; and though our lives might be remitted us, the more grievous alternative of pining away our days in ſlavery, cut off from a communication with our friends and country, might be our portion. Nor were theſe the weak ſuggeſtions of deſpair. Every thing conſpired to darken the proſpect before us. Our hoſt and guard had caught the alarm, and painted the danger of the veſſel in ſuch ſtrong colors to the vizier, as induced him to permit us to ſend our boat to her aſſiſtance. We gladly availed ourſelves of this circumſtance, though the immediate danger was over before the boat reached the veſſel, which now rode at anchor within a fathom of the rocks. Had the wind encreaſed as uſual, her reſpite would have been but ſhort. But Providence decreed otherwiſe. The weather proved ſo moderate the whole day, as to allow the officer to warp her into her old birth again.

While he was employed in a taſk that calmed the perturbation we were under, we obſerved a ſtrange boat paſs near him, and make towards the town. At the ſame time we heard the report of muſkets, but could not diſtinguiſh, whether it came from the veſſel or the boat. We cannot ſay poſitively, whether it was a ſcheme to entrap us, or that the vizier really ſuppoſed our people had commenced hoſtilities againſt the Arabs; but ſo it was: the boat had ſcarcely reached the ſhore, when the vizier ſent for our interpreter, to complain of the outrage, and to let us know that we had no right to expect good treatment from him

him hereafter. It was in vain, that we appealed to the teftimony of the mafter of the boat, who came to us of his own accord, and depofed, that our people had not fired at him. That they had only brought him to, with a mufket, and offered him money for a pilot, which he had refufed them. A formal demand was now made of our fwords; and we fufpected there was fomething uncommon in agitation, from the whifpers of our guard, and the frequent meffengers that came to and fro. One of our company obferved a body of foldiers marching towards the place, where our veffel lay; and not a ftone's throw from us, we faw them unlading a boat of ammunition, which they had tranfported acrofs an arm of the fea, that runs into the town at high water. Thefe preparations plainly indicated their defigns on the veffel, againft which we had previoufly cautioned the officer to prepare himfelf. The Adventure carried eight 3-pounders, befides fwivels; and we had not the leaft doubt of her repelling the whole of their force. But we were unacquainted with the policy of the Arabs, who truft to craft for the accomplifhment of their wifhes; and only affect refolution, when they can do it with impunity.

The hills now re-echoed with the found of cannon; which we learnt was a fummons to the neighboring tribes to join the holy ftandard, which is fet up in times of danger. And this was a prelude to a fcene; that threatened to end very tragically. We were ruminating on the iffue of this extraordinary adventure, when the Arabian mufketry began to play brifkly on the veffel. As a part of the fort fkreened the action from our view, we retired to the front windows of our apartment, where we could better obferve the veffel's motions. I had Thompfon's feafons in my hand, and had, inadvertently, caft my eyes on the fublime hymn which crowns that delightful work, when a band of ruffians rufhed into the room, and ranged themfelves directly before us. Their appearance was rude, and their countenances

very

very different from the people we had hitherto conversed with. They were of the roving race, and promised to prove worthy of the dark purpose in which they were engaged. The matches of their pieces were lighted, and we tottered on the brink of futurity!—

The villainy of the Arabs was now apparent. They were endeavoring to provoke our mariners to return their fire; and we well knew, that the death of one Muffulman is only to be atoned for, by the lives of ten Christians. This is a precept of their religion. But the officer on board, had reflexion enough to consider his countrymen ashore. He felt for our distress, and was so cool as to bear with their repeated infults for the space of two hours; although the musket-balls flew into the vessel, and he was continually urged by the crew, to pour a broad-side among the troops, some of whom were daring enough to wade into the sea, within pistol-shot of the vessel. Nay, we afterwards learnt our situation had been so critical, that nothing but threats of instant death, could prevent the sailors from taking to their arms; and the officer was obliged to parade the deck with a loaded musket, to intimidate them. But it is not strange, that we should apprehend other measures. We knew not what steps they had taken, to facilitate the seizure of the vessel; or how long the forbearance of our people would last: and we expected an engagement every moment, to commence between her and the shore. At this crisis we held a consultation together, and it was unanimously resolved, to demand a parley with the vizier, touching the delivery of the vessel into his hands. Our interpreter was dispatched to him, with this mortifying concession. The matter was become too serious to be trifled with. We had the evidence of our own eyes, to despair of the possibility of the vessel's escape, without a pilot; nor could we answer for the blood, which might be spilled through a fruitless obstinacy. In

this

this awful interval I endeavored to collect myself so, as to meet death with a becoming resignation. I breathed a prayer for the welfare of my friends, and can truly say, that I should have died in peace with all mankind. But the greatest consolation which I found in this exigency, was derived from the sublime hymn that I before mentioned. I read it over with pleasure, and felt my bosom filled with a prophetic confidence from the energy of the latter part; which is so analogous to the situation we were in, that I cannot resist transcribing it, though it is so well known to persons of taste.

> " Should Fate command me to the farthest verge
> Of the green earth, to distant barbarous climes,
> Rivers unknown to song; where first the sun
> Gilds Indian mountains, or his setting beam
> Flames on th' Atlantic isles; 'tis nought to me:
> Since God is ever present, ever felt,
> In the void waste as in the city full;
> And where He vital breathes there must be joy.
> When ev'n at last the solemn hour shall come,
> And wing my mystic flight to future worlds,
> I cheerful will obey; there, with new powers,
> Will rising wonders sing: I cannot go
> Where universal love not smiles around,
> Sustaining all yon orbs and all their sons;
> From seeming evil still educing good,
> &c."

A full hour and more, did we remain under the alarming circumstances I have described, before we obtained the shadow of a reprieve. The fire of the musketry was still continued against the veffel; and the minifters of death ftood over us, each feeming to have fingled out his prey, in a fixed pofture and a mute referve. At length our interpreter returned from his embaffy to the vizier. He was accompanied by three Arabians of diftinction, who were come to pledge their words for the fafety of ourfelves and veffel. The firft of thefe, was the general of the troops at Yambo; and the other two, were the chiefs of the Arab tribes, who had been fummoned to the vizier's affiftance. A writing was drawn up, and figned by them; to the obfervance of which they fwore by their beards, the moft folemn oath that a Muffulman can take. The captain was now cited to the prefence of the vizier, to obtain a fimilar obligation from him. He ftaid only to drink a cup of coffee; and brought back an handkerchief, which he had received, as a token of the minifter's fincerity. Pledges of this nature among the Orientals, amount to the moft ferious engagements. Whatever doubts we might entertain of their value, this was no feafon to exprefs them; and we readily concurred in the captain's orders to the chief mate, to bring the veffel into the harbor. We ftated the matter to him, and furnifhed him with the affurances which had been given us, for our general fecurity. The captain himfelf, harbored no fufpicions of their intention to plunder us; and I muft own that I was of the fame opinion. There was nothing very improbable in the vizier's ftory, now that we came to a right knowledge of it. This was the firft European veffel that had appeared on this part of the coaft; and he had written to the Xerif, to know whether he fhould treat us as friends or not. It is not impoffible but he confidered us as fpies, who meant to pry into the poverty and weaknefs of the country. Given to deceit himfelf, he might have held our tale of a pilot, as fictitious; and our anchoring at the mouth of the harbor, as

a fhallow

a shallow artifice, through which he could difcern. I would be as charitable in my conclufions, as a chriftian ought to be, but muft leave to the event, an explication of his conduct.

The good effects of our late compliance were foon vifible. The troops were recalled from the beach, and our tremendous guefts withdrawn from our apartment. Hope once more dawned in our bofoms; and the difappointed looks of the ruffians, who retired without having earned the wages of iniquity, left us no room to doubt of their inhuman commiffion.

The day was too far advanced to think of moving the veffel, as the channel into the harbour is very narrow. It was therefore ftipulated, that a pilot fhould go on board at day-break, to fetch her in; and that on her coming to anchor, her great and fmall guns, piftols and cutlaffes, fhould be delivered over to the cuftody of an officer, whom the vizier fhould appoint for that purpofe. This article was infifted upon by him, as the only means to quiet the minds of the inhabitants; who trembled for the fafety of the town, while the cannon were on board; and could not conquer their fears of Europeans, who had arms of any kind in their poffeffion. This fhew of terror was, to be fure, a tacit compliment to the European name; and we were at any rate content to fubfcribe to terms, by which alone we were permitted to return to the veffel. The boundary was paffed; and we had no other refource, than to confide in people who held us in fubjection. We were heartily tired of being cooped up in a prifon, and wifhed to return to the veffel; where we fhould at leaft be rid of obfervance, and live agreeably to our own cuftoms, although faddled with the lofs of liberty. We fpent the evening far more cheerfully than ufual, and found the guard lefs watchful of our motions, fince the conclufion of the treaty. Our hoft was particularly attentive to us; and regaled us, for the firft time, with a fupper. This is a meal almoft unknown in Arabia; and was considered by us in the light of a friendly banquet. We resigned ourselves, at our customary hour, to our carpets; where our imaginations were again disturbed, by a review of the unpleasing scenes of the foregoing day.

SUNDAY, 11th May.

This proved by far the most tedious day that we had passed in our confinement. We expected to have got on board to dinner, but were prevented by that indolent and perverse disposition, which prevails among the Eastern nations. At eight o'clock the pilot weighed the vessel's anchor, and before nine she brought up, within half a mile abreast of the town. We now received a visit from Mr. Walters, the chief officer, and were advertised by him of the particulars which I have before recited, respecting the attack on the vessel. Our thanks were justly due to this gentleman, on whose firmness and discretion our lives had depended; and I embrace with pleasure, this public opportunity to declare our sense of his conduct. The captain gave him an order, for the delivery of the arms to the vizier's officer, who now accompanied him in a boat to receive them. They were landed in great form. The small arms were lodged in the fort, and the cannon were mounted on a battery opposite our vessel. This was meant to intimidate us; though it was easy to perceive, that a single discharge would reduce the wall to ruins. Our swords were returned to us, with a compliment from the vizier; and we were in momentary expectation of permission to depart. But the little philosophy we possessed, was yet to be exercised; and happy was he, who could the best make a virtue of necessity.

Frequent were the visits of our interpreter to the minister in the course of this day: but no audience could he obtain. At noon he was retired to his haram, where it was treason to disturb him.

him. Now, he was engaged at dinner; and now he had company with him. As we faw every thing here through the medium of difcontent, we confidered thefe excufes as mere evafions of his word; and fhould he fail in that part of the treaty, where our living on board the veffel was fpecified, we had little reafon to expect his fulfilling the reft of it. Nay, the worft of their former fears recurred to fome of our party; and though I was by this time pretty well reconciled to the malice of fortune, and did not torment myfelf by anticipating evils, I muft confefs, that appearances were not much in our favor. Our property, freedom, and lives, were in the hands of an imperious tyrant, who had fecured us by treachery, and might only be reftrained by fear, from falfifying his engagements. And to this principle, by which his tribe are generally actuated in political concerns, I trufted for our deliverance. The fails of commerce are ever bufy in this fea, and numbers of fmall veffels had arrived at, and departed from this port, during our fhort ftay. Should the vizier be inclined to keep the tranfaction a fecret, his own reflexion muft fuggeft to him, that it muft needs tranfpire by a fea-conveyance, fhould he have influence enough to bar the communication by land: and, whatever might be the tale he trumped up to deceive his mafter, the fact would at length reach him in its native colors. Such did I conceive to be the point, which was difcuffed during this delay. I imaged to myfelf the minifter, fhut up with his creatures in dark cabal, and flattered myfelf that his intereft would teach him for once, to be honeft. Nor was I difappointed. The captain was fummoned to the prefence of the vizier, and returned with very gracious affurances of protection, and a licence to repair to the veffel. In the whole courfe of my life, I do not recollect to have received more acceptable tidings. We could not have wifhed for a ftronger confirmation of the minifter's fincerity; and for my own part, I felt a certain confidence in the thoughts of being on board, although we were deſtitute of arms, to protect us againſt violence, and there was a guard of ſoldiers to be ſtationed in the veſſel. But ſo preferable is the notion of what we term our home, to that of a foreign place, that even in the midſt of danger and diſtreſs, we derive comfort from the partiality, and find ſomething therein, to flatter and to conſole us.

The ſun was juſt ſinking in the boſom of the deep, when we put off from the ſhore. We had taken a very cordial leave of our hoſpitable ſhaik, and invited him to viſit us frequently on board, when we obſerved the ladies of his family were aſſembled to grace our departure. The old man's houſe was one of the largeſt in the town, and ſurrounded on three ſides by the ſea: and the windows were now crouded with females, who waved to us with their handkerchiefs, unperceived by thoſe below. The generoſity of the fair ſex might have atoned for the inhumanity of the men of Yambo, had we been able to benefit by their good-will. But what arms could they aſſail our perſecutors with, whoſe hearts were proof to the irreſiſtible violence of female tears? and what hope could we derive from their gentle interpoſition in a Mahometan region, where petticoat-intereſt is at the loweſt ebb? Still be the tenets of this abſurd faith confined to deſart climes, and an ignorant race! Let them expand themſelves through the Numidian waſte, and let the unlettered Arab cheriſh them in his mind! Never will they get footing in more enlightened lands; never will they uſurp the poliſhed breaſt, which acknowledges the ſoft empire of womankind, and rejects all attempts to depreciate her worth, as the dictates of malice, folly, and pride!

The evening was ſpent in a more agreeable manner, than we had of late experienced. We enjoyed our own cuſtoms with double ſatisfaction, ſince we had known the want of them; and

our

our minds were relieved from a load of suspence, with which they had been oppressed. We had obtained the vizier's leave to write to our friends at Judda; and we retired to our beds, with the pleasing expectations of being soon redeemed from captivity, by the good offices of our countrymen with the Xerif.

MONDAY, 12th May.

The captain this morning wrote a state of our case to captain Anderson; who he knew was at Judda, with a ship in his charge, belonging to the nabob of Arcot. He entreated him to represent our wrongs to the Xerif of Mecca, and to demand our immediate release, under pain of the resentment of the English. This letter was sent to the vizier by his desire, that he might inclose it in his packet. To guard against the double-dealing of a man so well known to us, we had the precaution to write a duplicate of this letter. This was folded up, and directed after the Arabic fashion, by our interpreter; who secretly delivered it to a passenger in the boat, that waited to carry the vizier's dispatches to Judda.

I have said, that there was a ship at Judda in the service of the nabob of Arcot, and that our captain had thought proper to declare the Adventure to be his property. It is not to be inferred from this, that the nabob is a maritime power, or is aiming to extend the commerce of his subjects by an attention to naval affairs. The fact is quite the reverse. The trade of India wholly exists in the spirit and industry of the English. While their vessels are exploring the islands that border on the Pacific ocean, and return with a freight that renders our settlements the mart of oriental productions, a ship or two is sent yearly to Judda by the nabob of Arcot. These vessels, indeed, carry a cargo, and import in exchange, the products of Arabia. But this

is

is the captain's care. The only benefit which the nabob looks for, is the prayers of two or three hundred pilgrims, who are transported at his expence, to perform their vows at the mosque of Mecca! his ships were so crouded this season with these idle mendicants, that through the nabob's interest with the owners, we had the company of above twenty of them in our vessel. This was an honor we were by no means ambitious of; and from which we readily disengaged ourselves at Mocha, where they were landed to prosecute their journey in the best manner they could.

The abuse of reason in these useless undertakings, is the least evil to be complained of. They are such an encouragement to idleness, and so destructive to the welfare of a country, where thousands of the inhabitants are seduced from their families and habitations by a fanatic call, that we may consider their toleration as one of the ruinous principles of a Mahometan government. We have had an opportunity of observing the effect, which these pilgrimages have upon the manners and dispositions of those engaged in them. A froward spirit and a brutal behavior, mark the herd of these pilgrims. And we have been assured from good authority, that their mutinous deportment rises sometimes to such a pitch, that the captains of the ships are obliged to put them in irons, for the preservation of themselves and crew.

The occurrences aboard the Adventure being as unvaried, as may be imagined in a vessel at anchor, I will omit the recital but of such days, as produced any particular events; which may be useful in curtailing a journal already, I fear, too prolix to escape censure. If we were uneasy at the restraint we were under, we had no reason to complain of sensual entertainment during the term of our detention. We were plentifully supplied with provisions and vegetables, at an easy rate; and Apicius himself,

self, might have taken a voyage to the Red-Sea, to have feasted on the delicious fish with which the harbour of Yambo abounds, without the least derogation to the merits of the lamprey of Baiæ.

MONDAY, 19th May.

Our patience was pretty nearly exhausted by this time. But on the evening of this day, we were permitted to wait on the vizier, after many vain solicitations, to learn how soon we might expect our release: the time appointed by him to obtain answers from Mecca, being expired.

We went ashore about five o'clock, and were received by him in greater state, than at our first audience. The room was full of armed men; and we could not but impute this useless precaution, to the terrors of a bad conscience, which views every thing with a suspicious eye. The evident alteration in the vizier's countenance and behavior, which were now marked with inquietude and reserve, in spite of his efforts to conceal them, convinced us of his having repented the step he had taken. He made several enquiries concerning the power and commerce of the English in the East. Nor was there occasion for our magnifying their influence, to awaken his fears. He seemed very attentive to the description of our ships of force; and could not help expressing his surprize, when our interpreter told him, that there were three men of war at Suez. As he was in an inquisitive mood, we would not miss the opportunity to impress him with sentiments, that might serve to regulate his future conduct. But his pride at length, got the better of his timidity. For in the course of our conversation, when the actions of the Portugueze in this sea, and their settlements on this coast, were brought on the carpet, he informed us, that the Arabian historians took

notice,

notice of them; and added, with an air of triumph, that the Portugueze were expelled Arabia by the great Sultan Selim.

We were civilly difmiffed by the minifter, with hopes of hourly intelligence from Mecca, and an invitation to take a view of the town, if agreeable to us. As there was a full hour to fun-fet, we readily embraced the occafion to fatisfy our curiofity, and to ufe a little exercife, of which we had been fo long deprived. We had an officer to attend us, befides two foldiers who had accompanied us from the veffel. And we found this guard neceffary, to keep off the rabble that purfued us in our walk. The firft arrival of a Cherokee Indian in Europe, could not have begotten half the wonder that our appearance did here. If the commonalty of Europe are not more mannerly, they are at leaft better informed than the rude Arab. Bred up in utter ignorance of other countries, and bigotted to the prejudices of illiberal doctrines, he is at a lofs to account for the production of a Chriftian, whom his religion teaches him to hold in abhorrence and contempt. But if the rough minds of the men are hurried away into thefe abfurdities, I muft once more bear witnefs to the moderation of the Mahometan females, who plainly evinced to us, that their bofoms were made of "penetrable ftuff." As we paffed through the ftreets, the windows and terraces of the houfes were filled with women, who were infpired with' no illaudable curiofity to behold the ftrangers. They neither treated us with fcorn, nor followed us with curfes, like the favage throng below; but by their eagernefs of obfervation, and attempts to engage our attention, betrayed the fecret fymptoms of approbation. Nay, the facred thirft of admiration, fo predominant in the fex, was not quenched in their breafts. We obferved many vails drop, as if by accident, as we paffed beneath their owners faces, which were overfpread with a vifible confufion, and verified the poet's idea of

zed in

and is
diately
e Ara-
1 con-
uation,
eakers,
1 navi-
ne has
), with
which
me to
critical
ty be a
em on

ons of
e date-
of sand.
distant
: beau-
degree.
l, seem
of rude
polity,
nature
: in fa-
to the
other,

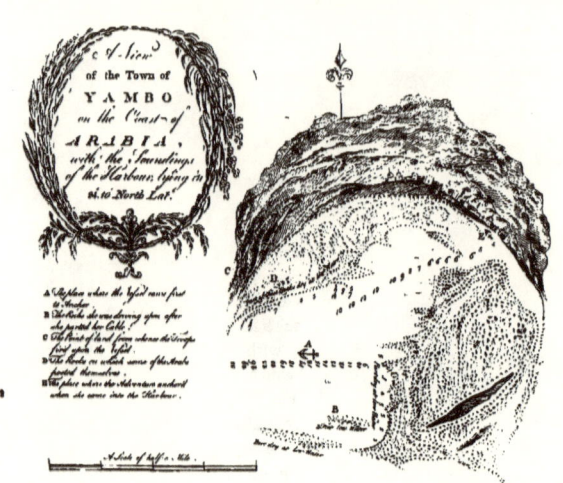

of Mufidora's confolation in her diftrefs, at being furprized in a naked fituation by her lover:

" Ev'n a fenfe
Of felf-approving beauty ftole acrofs
Her bufy thought."

Yambo is fituated in the latitude of 24° 10' north, and is the port, from which the communication is more immediately carried on with Egypt. It is the general refort of all the Arabian veffels that ply on this fea; and has a very fafe and convenient haven for their protection, in bad weather. Its fituation, behind an almoft uninterrupted chain of fhoals and breakers, has hitherto fecluded it from the knowledge of European navigators. But the charm is now broken; and as fortune has thrown it in our way, I have annexed a view of Yambo, with the foundings of the harbor, taken from an actual furvey, which Mr. Walters, chief officer of the Adventure, permitted me to copy from his draught. This will not only explain the critical fituation that our veffel was in during the attack, but may be a guide to future mariners, whofe evil ftars may throw them on this inhofpitable fhore.

The coaft here is infinitely more barren than the environs of Mocha, the foil being too ungrateful to produce even the date-tree or furze-bufh, and is throughout a fhining expanfe of fand. The eye meets with no interruption, until it reaches the diftant mountains, which bound the joylefs profpect. But if the beautiful be wanting here, the fublime exifts in no fmall degree. The mountains in the more remote parts of the world, feem particularly appointed by Providence, to be the refidence of rude and ftraggling nations, unconnected by the laws of civil polity, and unambitious of rambling beyond the limits which nature has prefcribed them. The coaft of Arabia is an evidence in favor of this remark. The interior parts, from one end to the other,

other, exhibit what Shakespear emphatically calls, "Heaven-kissing hills," and the mountains behind the town of Yambo, rival, in height, the American Andees, or the Caucasus of Asia. This restraint, perhaps, has been the cause of as extraordinary a revolution in the face of things, as the world has seen. Mahomet kindled the flame, that under the Caliphs, stirred up the Arabs to break from their dark recesses. Like the fearful eruptions of Etna or Vesuvius, they burst upon the astonished nations, and spread desolation far and near. But the calamity is past, though its effects still remain. This destroying race are retired within their barriers again; there to prey upon each other, until time shall ripen them for another grand event.

FRIDAY, 23d May.

'Four days are now elapsed since our visit to the vizier, and no intelligence is come from Mecca. The year is nearly half-expended, and we have not performed the half of our journey to Europe. Besides, we have the uncomfortable prospect before us, of being obliged to travel in the heats of summer through Egypt. This idea was particularly aggravated by the scorching wind, that blew to-day from the land. It was well for us, that we had been seasoned for this attack, by the land-winds so remarkable on the coast of Coromandel, or else the air would have been intolerable, and our blood been inflamed by the violence of the heat. Fevers would have been no eligible companions to constitutions, that had been exposed to the effects of a long voyage, and in want of a surgeon, to administer relief to them. But it pleased God, that we should maintain our healths in the midst of our distresses, and experience a signal mark of his protection, in the hands of our enemies.

To add to the disagreeableness of our situation, our guard

was

was this day doubled upon the veffel. The fails had been taken down to be mended, on her coming into the harbor; and though the topmafts were ftruck, and her yards lowered down, the vizier excepted at our offering to replace the fails on the yards. He pretended to be apprehenfive of our departure, and fent formally to demand our fails. The captain was juftly nettled at this meffage, which he could not but confider as a wanton infult. He pointed out to the vizier's officer, the impoffibility of the veffel's efcape. For not to mention the unprepared ftate fhe was in, the wind conftantly blew into the harbor, and there was a neceffity for a pilot to carry her out. In truth, we were as much in their hands, as if the veffel had been drawn afhore. The captain, therefore, defired him to inform his mafter, that if he wanted the fails, he muft fend people to fetch them, as he would not voluntarily give them up. This fhew of refolution proved a check on the prefumption of this haughty bafhaw, who withdrew his demand; but at the fame time, contrived to torment us with the company of the additional guard I have mentioned.

The wind did not lofe its rage when the fun went down, but was fo parching the whole night, as to oblige me to quit the deck, where I had taken up my lodging for the fake of coolnefs, ever fince our return to the veffel. But this, to our great joy, is the only land-wind we felt here; which, from its direction and burning heat, probably traverfed the great defart, which extends from the Red-Sea to the coaft of Paleftine, ere it fpent its fury upon us.

SUNDAY, 25th May.

Many camels have come in from the country within thefe two days, but bring no news for us. Thefe creatures are loaded with fruit and vegetables for the town; and with fkins of water, which they fetch from the vallies, for the use of the inhabitants, who can procure no water here, but what the heavens supply them with. It generally rains about once in two years in Arabia Petrea; and then not a drop is lost, which can be caught by the natives who live on the sea-coast. They preserve it very carefully in large reservoirs, and make an article of trade of it, which, however, is sold at a moderate rate. We have drank nothing but rain-water since our arrival, and find it very wholesome and palatable; although some was brought us, which the old shaik declared to be ten years old. Whether he may have exaggerated the age of it or not, it is certain, that they have little or no rain in this country. But the want of it is amply supplied by the heavy dews that fall at night, and make the ground appear as if moistened by a shower. Thus is the vegetable brought to perfection, thus are the trees supplied with never-failing fruit, and the vallies covered with eternal green.

A caravan arrived this forenoon from Medina, which is but two days journey from hence. This was the first I had seen, and though it consisted but of 4 or 500 camels, I must confess myself to have been much struck with the grandeur and novelty of the sight. We discerned it from afar, moving onwards with a quick though solemn pace, and as it passed near the beach, we could distinguish with our glasses the economy of the whole. The major part of the camels were loaded with merchandize, and the rest carried the travellers and the principal camel-drivers. The sun was in his meridian, and not a cloud obscured the heavens, nor a breath disturbed the surface of the deep. The natives were retired to the inmost recesses of their habitations, and not a beast was seen abroad, save the patient camel, that now braved the fiery ray, and marched with steady steps, beneath the united pressure of hunger, thirst, and heat! While the wooden bark ploughs the deep, and wafts from shore to shore the produce of

each

each clime, this living veffel traverfes the pathlefs wafte, fraught with the precious treafures of the Eaft. A caravan of camels exploring the wilds of Arabia, with nothing in view but fand and fky, and conducted by the planets to its defired haven, may well be likened to a fleet of veffels, which are not more ufeful in their way, or wonderful in their ftructure. As the fhip alone can outlive the feas, in which the weaker boat muft perifh, fo is the camel peculiarly adapted to a region, in which no other clafs of beafts could bear fatigue. He too experiences the chance of fublunary things. His mighty ftrength, his dauntlefs heart fink beneath the whirlwind's rage, and like the towering fhip, which winds and waves affail with ceafelefs fury, he yields at length to inevitable fate.

Our expectations were wound up to the higheft pitch this evening, by the return of the boat which carried our packet to Judda. But thefe were foon let down by the information of our interpreter, whom we had fent to the vizier to learn the news. The boat he found had not waited for anfwers; but we had reafon to expect them before now by land. The return of the boat in fo fhort a time, was however a matter of confolation, as it evinced the poffibility of our getting to Suez, though the wind is contrary for the greateft part of the day.

TUESDAY, 27th May.

We obferved two camels travelling with uncommon expedition towards the town, yefterday evening, and flattered ourfelves with the thoughts of their bringing our difpatches. Nor were we deceived. The vizier fent for our interpreter, to acquaint us, of his having juft received orders concerning us, which he would communicate in the morning. This fhort delay was mortifying

-tifying enough, but we had long learnt to have recourfe to patience, as the only remedy in our prefent fituation.

The craft and deceit of thefe people are equally great and inexplicable. To lye for the fake of falfehood, and to overreach in matters of no moment, are paradoxes peculiar to the Arabians. Were the enthufiafts in vice to think, that, like virtue, it is its own reward, the conduct of the vizier would not need a comment. But, why he fhould conceal orders which he muft fubmiffively obey, or trifle with our anxiety when we are at his mercy, is beyond the reach of thought to fathom. We waited this whole morning in expectation of a fummons, according to his voluntary promife. Difappointed in this, we fent our interpreter to befiege his gate in the afternoon, who at dufk, returned with an appointment for an audience the next morning, but with no manner of apology from the minifter, for his extraordinary behavior. We bore the flight with a good grace; and in the height of our charitable fuggeftions, framed excufes for his neglect, and were fanguine enough to believe, that the morrow would put an end to our fufpence. But we knew not the race we had ftumbled upon. Our dealings had been hitherto confined to people, who have fettled principles of action: and, whether fpurred on by intereft or guided by fear, we were fenfible of what we had to expect from the natives of India. But here judgment is at a ftand. No penetration can unravel the mazes of inconfiftency, no reflexion account for the fudden ftarts of barbarous pride!

WEDNESDAY, 28th May.

This day was paffed, like the foregoing, in vain applications and idle repinings. Nay, the infult was aggravated, by the vizier's refufing refusing even to see our interpreter. — He endeavored, it is true, to sweeten the bitter potion, by pleading business as the reason. But we were by this time, too well convinced of his insincerity, to swallow the excuse with our usual facility. Our state was now more deplorable than ever. The arrival of a dispatch from Mecca, had produced nothing in our favor; and we beheld the period which we had assigned to our detention, escape, without disclosing the faintest gleam of hope.

If such were the clouds which obscured our immediate prospect, how were our imaginations fitted to encounter the scene which approached; worked up as they had been by a series of complicated villainy, to apprehend the utmost malice of mankind! We had supped as usual, and some of our company were retired to their cabbins, when a report was made to the officer upon watch, that there was a boat along-side of the vessel. I happened to be on the quarter-deck, and was ruminating on the strangeness of the circumstance at so late an hour, when several armed men approached us without ceremony, and immediately joined their comrades, who commonly mounted guard on the aftermost part of the deck. Their appearance was as much a matter of surprize to our stated guard, as to ourselves. And all we could gather from them, by dint of repeated inquiry, was, that they had orders to remain on board the vessel until day-break.

It is generally allowed, that an air of mystery renders the most trivial incident of consequence, as every object looks larger, that is seen through a mist. At this moment the alarm was given, that there was a guard-boat on each bow; whereas, we had heretofore had the company but of one. Wearied out with a succession of disappointments, and impressed with the most unfavorable ideas of the people we were among, it is no wonder that we gave way to conjectures, by no means to the honor of the vizier's principles. We had too great confidence in the commercial

mercial connections between the English and the Xerif, to suspect that any harm would befall us by his directions. But on the other hand, the minister might be endeavoring to foment the present difference. This was the deepest stroke we had experienced in the desperate game which he had been playing, and was not to be solved by any maxims of policy. His intents were evidently deep and unfriendly; but the hue of them was not clearly to be discerned. Had they been murderous, there was no occasion for the farce which he had been playing. For, what rational creature is so abandoned to humanity, as wantonly to destroy those who have never offended him, or lengthen misery, which it is his interest to shorten? our lives and property had been long at his disposal; and it was not reasonable to imagine, that he would delay the sentence which would secure the prize, had he authority or inclination to execute it. We had been witnesses to so many instances of his folly and caprice, that it was not improbable, but this adventure would terminate without prejudice to us. But it must be confessed, that no little share of resolution is necessary for the support of such argument, where reason is too weak to oppose the evidence of our senses, and reflexion is lost in the tumult of the scene before us. Our minds by degrees resumed their wonted calm, and we retired to rest, with no other safeguard but the eye of a beneficent God, without whose regard there is no protection for the sleeping monarch, surrounded by his guards.

THURSDAY, 29th May.

The dawn of day delivered us from these unwelcome guests, conformably to their report; and the vizier, ashamed, as we suppose, of the transaction, had the grace to pretend an utter ignorance of it. On our remonstrating against the violation of the compact

compact between us, he laid the blame on the general of the troops, who had committed some mistake in issuing orders relative to the vessel. This proof of his being yet sensible of shame, gave us hopes of an amendment in his behavior, and encouraged the captain to press the vizier for another interview for himself only, which he now condescended to grant. Though productive of no real advantage, we derived great consolation from it, as the captain fairly extorted from him the reason of his late reserve. He acknowledged, that his instructions concerning us were come; but that nothing could be done in the affair, until the arrival of the Shawbunder, or captain of the port of Judda, whom the Xerif had ordered to Yambo, to adjust the terms of our departure. We had long suspected, that the vizier's designs were to extort heavy duties from the vessel; and were pleased to hear, that those duties were to be regulated by the port of Judda; which, though unreasonable enough, will certainly come more within the bounds of equity and justice, than the conscience of this Arab might have demanded.

As the name of the Xerif of Mecca so often occurs in this narrative, and as his power and influence ought properly to be ascertained, for the elucidation of the part he bore in our detention, I will endeavor to throw such light upon them, as opportunity and inquiry have afforded me.

The Xerif of Mecca is, in most respects, on the footing of the Pope in the earlier days of Christianity. He is sovereign Pontiff of the Mahometan church, and a temporal as well as spiritual prince. Since the extinction of the Caliphs, whose apparent successor he is, he holds his dominions as fiefs to the Turk; and is more indebted to the zeal of superstition than to the terror of his arms, for the support of his dignity. A prodigious decline indeed, from the importance of those Caliphs, who reigned the masters of the Eastern world, and shook the neighboring kingdoms

kingdoms of the north with dire dismay! But shrunk as he is within the limits of a province, where the Mahometan greatness first originated, the Xerif, in two instances, exceeds the Popes in the fullest plenitude of their power. His honors are hereditary; to possess which, he must prove his descent from the Prophet: and the extent of his influence reaches as far beyond that of the Popes, as the persuasion of Mahomet beyond the Papal tenets. The remotest corners of the East pay homage to his title. The way-worn pilgrim ceaseless toils from Teflis' towers or Mesopotamia's waste, to add his little mite to the treasures of Medina's temple; while Asiatic princes, subahs of Ind, and sultans of the Spicy Isles, which westward bound the Southern ocean, enrich the Prophet's shrine with gems and gold. The large sum of money which our vessel brought for the service of the Mosque, as a peace-offering from the nabob of Arcot, on the decease of his daughter, is a corroborating evidence of the enthusiasm of Mussulmen. It amounted to one lack and an half of rupees, which is near £.20,000 sterling, and was the gift of a prince, whom the world need not be told is so involved in debt, as not to require this drain to exhaust his mortgaged revenues.

The territories of the Xerif lie in the heart of Arabia, and are about three hundred miles long and one hundred broad. Besides the cities of Mecca and Medina, to which the caravans annually bring the produce of distant countries, his revenues are considerably augmented by the commerce, that is carried on with his ports of Yambo and Judda, by the vessels of Africa and India. Whatever sanctity he may pretend to, or indifference to the concerns of this world, like other hypocrites in religion, he prefers his own interest to that of his Maker; and uses his name as an instrument, to advance his own dignity and riches. The caravans, which professedly set out on a pious journey to Mecca, are more encouraged by this Pontiff for the fake of his own glory, than that of the Prophet; as the valuable goods they convey, and the high duties impofed upon the deluded merchants, fufficiently atteft. But what perfuafion is there among the frail race of mankind, which is not open to perverfion, and liable to be difgraced by abfurd rites, and idle ceremonies? the divine purity of the Chriftian religion could not preferve its ftream from being tainted, by the machinations of prieftcraft, and the intemperance of zeal. Nor is there much difference in the folly of the belief, that founds falvation on a pilgrimage to the temple of Mecca, or to the houfe of my lady of Loretto!

The prefent Xerif is a youth under twenty years of age, and, what is remarkable on account of his family, he is as black as a negro. He has been feen by fome of our countrymen, but this is not a common thing, as he feldom ftirs from Mecca, to the neighborhood of which place, and Medina, no approach is allowed to Chriftians. Nay, to fuch a degree has their contempt of us arifen, that neither at Mocha, Judda, nor Yambo, will they fuffer a Chriftian to go out at the gate, which looks towards Mecca. One of his Majefty's frigates was at Judda laft year, to fettle fome articles of trade between the different nations; when the Xerif himfelf made an excurfion to Judda, on purpofe to pay a compliment to the Britifh flag. He went on board the frigate; and, to teftify his fatisfaction at the activity of the failors, and the difcipline of the marines, he left a very princely gratuity to be diftributed among them. On this appearance of good-will in the Xerif towards the Englifh, we rely for redrefs in the injury we have received; though the courfe of juftice may be delayed, by the mifreprefentations of the knave, into whofe clutches we have unfortunately fallen.

SATURDAY,

SATURDAY, 31st May.

This morning we were delighted with the fight of two boats to the fouthward. As they came into the harbor, we learnt from our guard, that the fhawbunder of Judda was in the foremoft. But this funfhine was foon clouded by a meffage from the fhore, which advifed us that the perfon we expected, was in a boat behind. We, who were bound for Europe, thought this a good opportunity to folicit the vizier for our departure to Suez, which he might, on certain conditions, wifh to grant us, before the arrival of another officer to fhare in the profit, which he evidently meant to make of us. With his permiffion, therefore, my three fellow-travellers and myfelf paid him a vifit in the afternoon, when we were received with his wonted politenefs. We preffed him for the immediate provifion of a boat, but he pretended that nothing could be done until the fhawbunder's arrival, except the order for a boat to be ready at a minute's warning. He concluded this affurance with a caution againft the impofitions of his people, and a requeft not to give any prefents, but to fuch as came exprefsly by his order. This was too plain to be mifunderftood; and after our return to the veffel, we judged it expedient to tender this minifter a bribe. We found, from long experience, that he was not to be moved by the force of words, and accordingly prepared a prefent, wherewith to melt his unrelenting breaft. It confifted of a diamond ring, a fine fhaul, and a piece of gold ftuff for a drefs; and was an offering, rather extorted by neceffity, than fuitable to the characters which we affumed. This we fent him by our interpreter, and had the pleafure to learn that it was gracioufly received. We met in return, with a repetition of thofe affurances of his protection, which he had before lavifhed upon us.

I cannot

I cannot help relating here a curious circumstance of the divers of Arabia, whose skill exceeds that of any others which I have read of. The master of a boat, which was just returned from Tor, offered to recover the anchor, which I mentioned to have been lost by our vessel, while she was at the entrance of the harbor. As it lay in sixteen fathom water, the captain gave little credit to the fellow's pretensions, but was willing to try the experiment, as much from a motive of curiosity as any other. The diver was to earn but a third of the fixed reward, should his attempts miscarry. He brought his boat to the vessel to-day, and accompanied our long-boat, with an officer on board, to the mouth of the harbor. And from this officer I had the following particulars.

When they came to the supposed place, the diver went down in sixteen fathoms, with no other preparation than a weight to his feet, and a piece of wood on his nostrils, to prevent his fetching his breath in the water. There was a rope fastened to his arm, by which he gave notice when he wanted to be drawn up. At the signal made, he was run up by his comrades with amazing celerity. He informed the officer that he had seen the anchor at some distance; and taking a rope of sufficient strength to hold it, he dived again to an equal depth, and tied it to the ring of the anchor. Upon weighing it, however, it turned out not to be ours, but a large grapnel belonging to the annual Judda vessel, which sailed from hence some months ago. After this disappointment, to make good what he had asserted of his skill, the fellow went down in two-and-twenty fathoms, though the wind began to freshen, and the sea to be ruffled. He staid between two and three minutes under water, according to the watch of the gentleman present. Nay, after he came into the boat, this amphibious creature did not take the pressure from his nostrils for near a minute longer; and appeared not in the

least

least fatigued or discomposed. He affirmed, that upon occasion, he can dive some fathoms deeper; and in a calm day, can see ten fathoms around him. That he can walk about with great ease at the bottom of the sea, and separate branches of coral from the rocks, with an ax or a saw. As a proof of which, he produced a large branch of coral, which he had taken out of a bay to the northward. I have a piece of this coral in my possession. Anxious as he appeared to be for the recovery of our anchor, we have reason to believe that the poor man had been forbidden by the vizier to get it; as he means to turn it to his own account, after our departure. I am sensible that the divers go to a great depth, in the pearl-fisheries in the Gulph of Persia, where they are assisted by machines of various constructions: but such a marvellous instance as I have related, of natural powers unaided by the efforts of art, should have died in silence for me, had it not fallen, in a manner, under our immediate observation.

The only recreation we enjoy, is sailing about the harbor in one of the ship's boats. And this is rather connived at by our guard, than allowed of by the vizier, whose orders concerning us are very rigid. In the course of these cruizes, we have had opportunities to make ourselves well acquainted with the harbor, and to produce the plate which has been exhibited of it. But all our observations tended nothing towards our own enlargement. There is but one channel into the harbor, and the wind constantly blows into it at this season. It is not, therefore, the loss of our guns, or the presence of a guard, that detains us. Despair would furnish us with arms to rid us of this obstacle, were the door of escape open to our vessel.

MONDAY,

MONDAY, 2d JUNE.

This morning the long-expected boat brought in the shawbunder of Judda. At nine o'clock he came aboard the Adventure, and delivered our captain a letter from the Xerif himself, and another from Captain Anderson. The first letter contained permission for the captain to go where he pleased, on paying the duties of the port of Yambo; an imposition which is levied on all vessels that enter the Xerif's ports, whether they dispose of their cargoes or not. If he preferred going to Judda, no duties were to be paid at Yambo; but in that case, the vessel was to be given as a security, into the charge of the Xerif's servants; and the captain and his officers were to proceed to Judda, on a boat which should be provided for them. The vizier was likewise directed to dispatch the packets, and the gentlemen who had the care of them, in a proper boat to Suez. Such was the substance of the Xerif's orders. They were in some respects, unreasonable enough, and betrayed a greater regard to his own benefit, than a readiness to do us justice. But our situation considered, it will be easily believed, that we were more satisfied than otherwise, at the receipt of these tidings.

The contents of Captain Anderson's letter were not less agreeable. After condoling with us on our misfortune, he tells us, that the Swallow sloop of war, which had been on a voyage to Suez, was just arrived at Judda. That on learning our situation, her commander, Captain Panton, had demanded satisfaction of the government, for the insult that had been offered to the British flag. It was plain from his letter, that the Xerif was unacquainted with this demand, when his instructions relative to us, were forwarded to Yambo. But we doubted not that

our

our wrongs would be redreſſed, by the preſence of a naval officer, of the known ſpirit and humanity of Captain Panton. Captain Bacon and the ſupercargoes of the Adventure, would ſoon have an opportunity of making a perſonal application to him at Judda, on this head. But the gentlemen bound for Europe, thought it expedient to join with me, in a repreſentation of the damages we had incurred, by the treachery of the Xerif's government. This letter we forwarded to Captain Panton by the hands of Captain Bacon; and though no benefit may accrue to us from the reſult, we ſhall be ſatisfied to hear that the inſult is revenged, by the interpoſition of the Britiſh arms.

Our proſpect of getting to England now recurred with tenfold pleaſure; and we were not willing to loſe a moment in taking advantage of the Xerif's permiſſion. The interpreter was immediately diſpatched to the vizier, to remind him of his promiſe. He returned with a Nokidah, or maſter of a boat, whom this crafty miniſter pretended to have ſent us, that we might make our own terms with him. This modeſt fellow had the confidence to aſk us 700 dollars and a dreſs, for the freight of his boat to Suez. I ſay freight, as we were to find proviſions, and even water, ourſelves. When the direct diſtance be conſidered, which ſcarcely exceeds 150 leagues, and the boat itſelf be examined, which is without a deck, and not ſo well found as a Corniſh fiſhing-ſmack, no one will pronounce the demand to be within the bounds of moderation, though preferred by an Arab. But we were in abſolute want of the boat, and were fain to ſee ourſelves cheated, with our eyes open. We found this convenient agent inflexible in his purpoſe, and were glad to ſtrike the bargain at 650 dollars; the major part of which, we ſhrewdly ſuſpected, would go into the vizier's coffers. And this was the return which his gratitude ſuggeſted, for the preſent which we made him! but we were obliged to keep our ſuſpicions

cions and our complaints, equally a secret. It was in the vizier's power to frame a thousand delays in our undertaking, and consequently, our interest to wink at an imposition, by which we secured his protection. On these principles, therefore, we agreed to give more for the hire of a boat, than she was intrinsically worth. And, happy to escape from the snare which beset us, we did not think our liberty dearly purchased, at the price of being handsomely fleeced. When this weighty matter was settled, the Arab retired, to give his employer the agreeable intelligence of his success, while we seriously prepared ourselves to turn a bad bargain to the best account.

SUNDAY, 8th JUNE.

The last week was employed in regulating the affairs of the vessel. There was not the best appearance of harmony between the vizier and the shawbunder; which operated to retard her dispatch. By some blunder of the former, the cargo was ordered ashore; and though this procedure seemed to contradict the Xerif's commands, the captain could not dispute the pleasure of the vizier. By the shawbunder's representation, however, the cargo was forthwith returned to the vessel; but a bale of callicoes was missing. This was undoubtedly embezzled by the vizier and his people, who stoutly denied having received it, though opposed by the testimonies of the supercargoes, and the officers of the Adventure. Two days were spent in fruitless disputes on this subject; and there is no pronouncing to what a length they would have been spun out, had not a seasonable hint which the vizier dropped, finally decided them. He affected to declare, that as his honor was doubted, he must insist upon things resting as they were, until justice had been done to him at Mecca. There needed no more, to convince us of the absurdity of perseverance against such a character. We were ascertained of his being capable of the blackest actions; and the captain wisely resolved to forego his right, and give a receipt for the whole cargo.

These vexatious transactions detained my fellow-travellers and myself at Yambo, as the vessel's departure and ours was to take place together. But every thing being now prepared for the prosecution of our coasting voyage, our debts at this place discharged, and the boat we had agreed for, having been exchanged for another, which the vizier, for reasons best known to himself, pitched upon for us, we this afternoon obtained our audience of leave of this extraordinary personage. We were received with that politeness and affability, which in ministers of state, cover a multitude of imperfections. These are the bright sides of political characters, where an agreeable light is blended with the shades that overcast them. Had our knowledge of this man been confined to externals, we should have quitted Yambo, with the most favorable ideas of his disposition. But the brutality of his conduct could not be softened by the polish of his manners, and the conviction of his treachery flashed through the vail of a smooth tongue and a winning address. We were resolved, nevertheless, to appear satisfied of his sincerity; which, in truth, we now gave him more credit for, than since our acquaintance commenced. He had no longer any probable motive to amuse us; and the Xerif's commands are reputed to be held too sacred, to be sported with by his servants. We took in good part, the wishes he expressed for our safe arrival at Suez; and received the passport which he gave us for the security of our persons, with entire confidence in the virtue of its contents. We took our leave of the vizier, amid a profusion of high-flown compliments, which we had neither the capacity nor inclination to return. The natives of the East are so habituated to this mode of speech, that well-turned compliments fall from their lips with inexpressible readiness. And the Arabian language is so superior in elegance to the rest, that this people, in other respects so remarkable for their simplicity, exceed all other nations in the delicacy of their expression, and the agreeable wildness of their images.

MONDAY, 9th June.

This has been a busy, as well as a joyful day for us. On the eve of recovering our liberty, after a tedious and painful detention, like the birds who escape the cage which with-held them, and flutter abroad without a thought of the consequences, we only rejoiced over the present moment, unheedful of the toils we might fall into, or the dangers that might await us in coasting a wild and unknown shore, and, as the poet finely says, " with no other stay save innocence and Heaven." We could only provide against obvious calamities. We were well furnished with fire-arms and ammunition, to guard against open attacks, and with rice and water, to obviate the calls of hunger and thirst. But the friendship of Captain Bacon set us above answering the mere necessities of nature. He supplied us with many articles, which might have been dispensed with in the voyage which we had undertaken, had we meant to have kept a table suitable to our accommodations in an open boat. But he was willing that we should be as well provided as his ship would afford; and we could not in justice, refuse him the pleasure of crowning his genteel behavior during a four-months voyage, by this more material instance of his attention. It will appear a mystery to people in Europe, who are obliged to pay extravagantly for a passage from one kingdom to another, to learn that the commanders, in general, in the country service in India, think your entertainment sufficiently repaid by the pleasure of your company; and are only studious to render a passage agreeable to you, which can no otherwise redound to their benefit, than what a liberal mind feels on the exertion of an hospitable action. This remark is due to the gentlemen of a service, which has been too much disparaged by the ill conduct of some unworthy members. The character of Captain Bacon, and others that I could mention from experience, will more than atone for the defection of the rest. I should not omit, among the rest of his favors, that he furnished us with a lascar, or mariner, who had some knowledge of the Arabic tongue. It would be painful to conceive the difficulties, to which we might be reduced in the course of our journey, were not this man to be with us, to interpret our wants, and to give the people we dealt with, a more favorable idea of Christians. He is a Mussulman, and is likely to gain some credit with those of his persuasion. And yet we were on the point of setting out, without any interpreter; neither reflecting on possible events, nor providing against human accidents.

We supped for the last time, on board the Adventure; and after taking a parting glass, and a cordial leave of Captain Bacon and the rest of our friends, Major Alexander, Lieutenant * * *, Mr. Hammond, and myself, attended by my European servant, two slave-boys of the major's, one of Lieutenant * * *'s, and Ibrahim our interpreter, stepped into the vessel's pinnace, and were presently conveyed to the boat, which we reached about ten o'clock at night. I would attempt to give the reader some idea of the place we got into, but the description demands an higher coloring than my pencil can give it. If he can imagine, however, the situation of four gentlemen, crouded together in a square of about five feet diameter, with no defence from the noontide suns and midnight dews of the Arabian coast, deprived

of

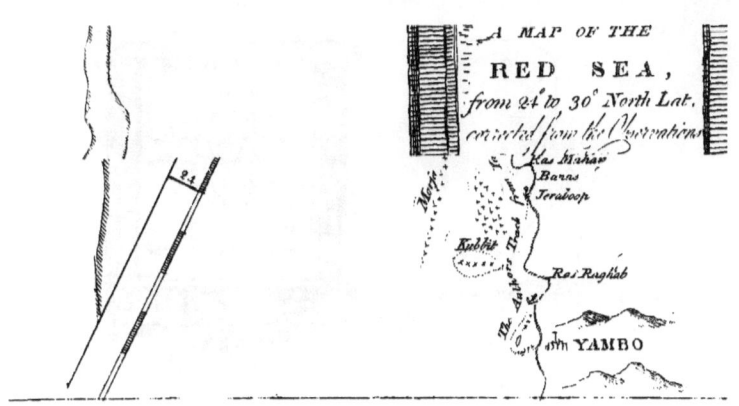

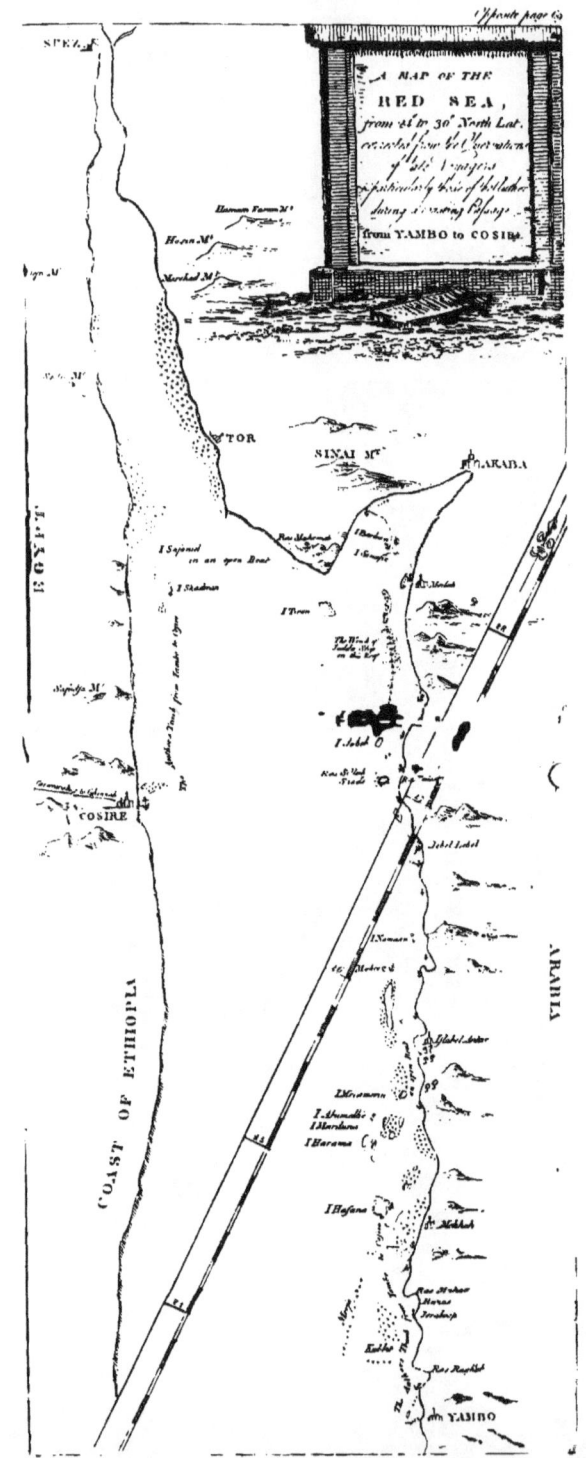

of the smallest exercise of their limbs, and condemned to the constant society of the boat's crew, wholly at the discretion of a perfidious race, and with the prospect of a long and tedious cruize in an unknown sea — he may gather some faint traits of the undertaking we were engaged in. As we sought the danger, there can be no vanity in speaking of it: as something more than an idle temerity, enforced the prosecution of a voyage, the difficulties of which we were sufficiently apprized of.

JOURNAL OF THE BOAT IMPOSITION

FROM YAMBO TOWARDS SUEZ.

TUESDAY, 10th June.

We were disturbed at day-break by the arrival of the nokidah, and pilot who is to navigate the boat, which, from the price we have paid for her, we have named the Imposition. They brought another Arab and three Abyssinian slaves with them, who made up her crew. And these are full sufficient to manage her. Could we consult our ease before our safety, we would willingly dispense with this addition to our numbers, which greatly exceed the size and convenience of our bark. We found no little difficulty, last night, in providing for our repose. Our chests form a square in the center of the boat, and my companions and I, each take up his lodging on his own chest. Our servants disposed themselves in such places, as they could obtain a footing upon; but this increase to our society, will reduce them to the necessity of securing a post for themselves.

We weighed our anchor at 6 A. M. and ſtood to the weſtward, with the wind at N. by W. But we had not got a league out, when the wind hauled round to N. W. This obliged us to run back again, and anchor at the mouth of the harbor.

We had not been here long, when a boat paſſed us, with Captain Bacon and his chief mate on board. They are bound for Judda, and we had but juſt time to hail each other, and renew our wiſhes for our reciprocal welfare. The wind will be fair for their boat, when they get clear of the harbor; and their paſſage promiſes to be a ſpeedy one, in proportion as the wind is unfavorable to us.

The wind was ſtrong all day from the N. W. In the evening we ſaw the Adventure, ſtanding towards us. There were but a few of her ſails ſet; and the Arabian pilots, to whoſe charge ſhe is committed by the Xerif's order, not being able to make any hand of it, brought her to an anchor again in the harbor. This outſet proves the little knowledge of theſe pilots; and it will be well if they carry her ſafely to Judda, conſidering the great difference between working her, and veſſels rigged for coaſting voyages.

I have annexed a chart of the Red-ſea, from Yambo to Suez, that the reader may purſue the track of the boat as he reads the journal.

WEDNESDAY, 11th June.

The nokidah and pilot ſlept upon the poop laſt night. Our arrangement, therefore, is as follows. They have poſſeſſed themſelves of the ſtern; my companions and myſelf occupy the midſpace, and our ſervants and the crew keep in the fore-part of the boat. We have mounted a muſketoon upon the gunnel, and have our fuſees and piſtols loaded. But as we are as yet,

under

under the protection of the fort, we have not began to keep watch during the night.

At 6 A. M. we weighed with the wind at S. W. and stood N. W. and ran about three leagues; but the wind suddenly veering round to the west and W. N. W. the pilot found he could not reach his intended anchoring-place, and, to our great mortification, ran back before the wind, to an opening between the rocks. These rocks are a part of a reef, that extends from Judda to Cape Mahomet, and in which our vessel was unfortunately entangled, when we were driven to the necessity of putting into Yambo. We understand there are particular places upon this coast, which vessels are obliged to reach during the day, or else they must, at times, run back to the birth which they left, for want of anchoring-ground. At one of these stages, our boat brought to, at twelve o'clock, which is the properest term that can be used on the occasion. As the boat approaches the reef, one of the crew jumps from the forecastle, with a hook in each hand, and diving under the reef, fastens the hooks to the rocks, which are rendered porous by the water. The boat rides here in smooth water, with her sides almost touching the rocks. And here a vessel of considerable burden, might ride; as the water is so deep, that we cannot find a bottom with several fathoms of rope.

We took an observation at noon, and found ourselves in the latitude of 24° 10′ north. We have hitherto made little or no progress in our voyage; but are not to despair, because the winds have been contrary for two days. In the afternoon we saw the Adventure, standing to the southward. This denotes that she is clear of the harbor, but she seems to be going under a very easy sail.

THURSDAY,

THURSDAY, 12th June.

The nokidah waded afhore during the night, in order to go to Yambo for a fpar, to replace one which was carried away yefterday. He had not left us long, when a brifk breeze fprung up from the land, with which we might have made a ftretch to the northward, had our mafter been aboard. But this is only on a fuppofition, that thefe people work their boats in the night, which we have, indeed, but too much reafon to doubt. At day-break the wind fhifted to the N. W. fo that when the nokidah returned, he found that it was impoffible for us to ftir. He brought fome intelligence refpecting the Adventure. It feems that the Arabian pilots are fo unfkilful in the management of a veffel of her conftruction, that the fupercargoes and the officer who remain on board, are afraid of being caft away in the paffage to Judda. They have already loft all her own anchors by their ignorance; and it is a great chance, if they fucceed better with the grapnels, which they have taken in, to fupply the lofs. The fituation of this veffel is very peculiar: She was reduced to her prefent diftrefs by the treachery of thefe barbarians; and is in danger of being wrecked by their obftinacy, in not permitting Captain Bacon to take charge of her, when they carry her clear of the rocks. But vengeance, no doubt, awaits the injured. This is not the firft time, that the Englifh flag has redreffed her fubjects, even in this remote fea: and the hour perhaps will come, when the Xerif of Mecca will be forced to do juftice to the fufferers on the fnow Adventure.

About nine o'clock the wind changed to the fouthward; but we could not take advantage of it, on account of the abfence of fome of our company. Lieutenant * * * went afhore at fix o'clock, on pretence of gathering famphire, and took Ibrahim our interpreter with him. We were a little furprized at their ftay; but when the wind became favorable, we difpatched a mariner into the country, to recal them to the boat. But how was our furprize increafed, when the meffenger returned, and informed us, that they were not to be found! Various were our conjectures on this occafion. We at one time, fancied that they had wandered beyond their knowledge, and were gone towards the beach, by tracing which they muft at length find the boat. At another, we apprehended they had been furprized by the wild Arabs, and carried into flavery. The true caufe was the furtheft from our thoughts. But fomething poffeffed our nokidah to believe, that the abfentees were gone to Yambo. Whether he had obferved Lieutenant * * * 's difcontent at his fituation, and fufpected that he was engaged in a bufinefs unfavorable to him, fo it was, the nokidah's penetration exceeded ours, and he determined to feek them at Yambo. It was about noon when he fet out for the town, which is about two leagues from hence; and, that nothing might be wanting on our parts, to recover our friends, we directed two mariners to take different routes in fearch of them, while we hoifted a fignal on our mainmaft, and difcharged our mufketoon repeatedly, in hopes of attracting their notice. At 3 P. M. the wind came about to the N. W. and blew from that point the reft of the day.

Our mariners returned with as little fuccefs, as before. Our opinions now began to waver, and we fufpected that Lieutenant * * * had taken fome extraordinary ftep. Ever fince our imprifonment at Yambo, his conduct had been the reverfe to what we had known it. His prejudice againft the Arabs exceeded all bounds, and his apprehenfions of them feemed to have difordered his intellects. He often expreffed fuch an abhorrence of the voyage we were about to engage in, that we more than once preffed him to forbear accompanying us. We had obferved with concern, that he had betrayed fears for his life ever since he entered the boat; and was always on the watch, while we slept in the security which our situation required. We were too near to Yambo, to expect danger from the country; and all resistance would be vain, were harm intended us by the government. But the night before, he had declared, that our Arabs meant to murder us at supper. Then, that they had deferred it until midnight. These, and many other extravagancies which he committed, we attributed to the effects of distrust, and contented ourselves with laughing at them; although he frequently protested, that he had overheard the Arabs debating on the manner of our deaths.

The day thus passed over our heads, while we labored under a weight of vexation and anxiety. We had missed of as fair a wind as could blow for us; and were uncertain of the fate, which had befallen Lieutenant * * * and Ibrahim. At five o'clock we discovered camels and a guard of soldiers at a distance, which actually turned out to be their escort. Our looks mutually exhibited astonishment and confusion at this meeting. But we pitied the situation of our companion, and forbore to reproach him in the presence of the guard. He seemed much agitated and fatigued, and spoke but little on his arrival. From our interpreter and the guard, we learnt the particulars of his expedition. It appears, that his distrust of our Arabs had so worked upon the mind of Lieutenant * * *, as to induce him to return, in a clandestine manner, to the vizier of Yambo, and communicate his suspicions. On their reaching the shore, he artfully drew Ibrahim towards the town, and, on their getting about a mile, by threats and entreaties, he persuaded the simple fellow to accompany him. On their reaching the town, they were laid hold of by some Arabs; and carried, as they desired, before the vizier. They were received very politely by that minister, and the complaint of Lieutenant * * * was so far attended to, that a guard was ordered to

take

take the boat-people into cuſtody. At this moment the nokidah arrived, and gave evidence of his innocence, by the relation of our behavior on the abſence of the accuſer. The tables were now turned, and Lieutenant * * * was ſent back to us, in the manner before recited. The vizier diſpatched an Hindoo with him, to aſſure us, in the Moor tongue, that we had nothing to fear from the boat-people, whoſe lives ſhould anſwer for our ſafety. We were obliged, in our own defence, to diſown any knowledge of Lieutenant * * *'s intentions; and to thank the vizier for his candid behavior on this occaſion. The guard then departed, with a gratification which we made them for their trouble.

As accuſations and repinings were equally vain, we determined among ourſelves, to be ſilent on this myſterious conduct of Lieutenant * * *. We, however, reprimanded Ibrahim very ſeverely, in his preſence, for the folly which he had been guilty of; and came to a general reſolution, not to go on ſhore on the continent, nor detain the boat for any one, who ventured to do ſo in future. After we went to bed, we obſerved Lieutenant * * * go to the poop, and by means of geſtures, and the few words of Arabic of which he is maſter, hold a kind of diſcourſe with the nokidah and pilot. He came to his ſcrutoire once or twice, and we ſuſpect took out money. What he did with it, or what will be the iſſue of his unhappy turn of mind, we cannot determine. It was late when he laid down, and we have reaſon to believe his reſt is broken and unſound.

FRIDAY, 13th JUNE.

Our boat got under ſail at four o'clock this morning, with a light breeze from the land. Though ſhe is too large to row againſt an head ſea, we found the advantage of having oars on board.

board. The weather was so moderate, we made use of them the greatest part of the morning. At nine A. M. the wind shifted to the S. W. but proved very faint. We felt the rage of the sun to-day pretty severely. While we are under sail, it is not possible for us to put up a canvas awning, with which we are furnished. But to advance quicker in our progress, we must be content to be exposed in this manner. About 3 P. M. the wind came round to the favorite point, the N. W. which obliged us to run into smooth water, and bring to, as before, between the breakers and the shore; from the latter of which we are about a mile distant. The coast here is rather low, but the mountains rise a few miles behind it. The sky was too hazy for us to take an observation at noon; but by our reckoning, we have gained about three leagues to the northward in the last run.

Just as the boat came to anchor, Lieutenant * * *'s infirmity plainly discovered itself. We had been confirmed since yesterday, in our suspicions of his brain being touched. His appetite was gone, his looks were wild and disordered, and his conversation continually bordered upon madness. He told us, when the boat stood out to sea this morning, that the Arabs were carrying us there to murder us; and, when she stood into land, he changed his tone, and pronounced our deaths to be prepared for us here. We little regarded such strange fancies; but were alarmed much at his seizing his sword when we came to anchor, and bidding us to stand upon our defence. The Arabs were now justly frightened at his extravagance, and we had much ado to persuade him to lay by his sword. This circumstance had been overlooked, and we had determined only to keep a strict eye on his conduct; when the arrival of two boats, from the northward, in the cove we are in, opened a strange and unexpected scene.

As they approached us, Lieutenant * * *: betrayed the strongest symptoms

symptoms of uneasiness. He gravely bade us prepare for death; and, unaccountably, made these new-comers privy to our fate. It was in vain that we assured him, they could have no intimation of any ill which was meant us; strangers as they were, and accidental as our meeting had been. Such an unhappy prepossession had he taken against the Arabians in general, that no opinion, no reasoning of ours, could avail. We knew that he had but little knowledge of the Arabic language; but every word that had an affinity to those of wicked purport, was converted, by his distempered imagination, into the very mischief itself; as his infected sight, in like manner, turned sticks into spears, and knives into daggers. The ears of Ibrahim were open as well as his, and his ready apprehension of the language would have advertised us of danger, if any were at hand.

It had been whispered to us, that some money had been given to our nokidah last night; and we were now not a little astonished to find from Lieutenant * * * himself, that the sum was no less than 75 venetians, which he had divided between the nokidah and pilot, to save his life. He lamented, however, that it was in vain; for our deaths were fixed upon, and we should soon follow Captain Bacon and the gentlemen in the Adventure, who, he vehemently affirmed, had been massacred some days before. To divert these strange thoughts as much as possible, a slave-boy of Major Alexander's played on the fiddle, while the Arabs in the other boats, joined us with their kinds of music. We had supped, and were looking at some fish, which were playing about the boat, when Lieutenant * * * suddenly sprang from his seat, with two swords in his hand, and running to the major, gave him one sword to defend himself; and attempted to draw the other, as he said his life was in danger, from a man near the mainmast of the boat, who had a poniard in his hand. The boat was immediately filled with confusion; the crew

crouded

crouded together in the ftern, and called out to the other boat, which pufhed away from us in hafte. The matter was too critical to be trifled with; and the frenzy of our companion had become too confpicuous, to be palliated. He was accordingly feized, and difarmed by us; and, in the ftruggle, the major received a flight wound in the foot, from the other's fword.

We now began to be alarmed for ourfelves. The ftrange boats might judge from appearances, that we had hoftile intentions, and perhaps, attempt to fecure themfelves, in a manner not very agreeable to us. The nokidah of ours came to us, and pofitively declared, that he would not get under fail again, while Lieutenant * * * remained on board. It was to no purpofe that we offered to pledge our lives for the fafety of himfelf and crew; and to keep a conftant watch on our unhappy friend. The man was ftartled at the mad freaks which had been committed; and owned to us, that he thought our lives in equal danger with his own: as in his frantic fits, Lieutenant * * * would not be able to diftinguifh his friends from his imaginary foes. The reader may fuppofe that this infinuation made no impreffion upon us. Our repugnance in parting with our companion in fo melancholy a fituation, awakened all our eloquence, and redoubled our efforts to keep him with us. For fome hours did we argue the matter with our nokidah and pilot, who had now joined him. But they remained deaf to our remonftrances. We found ourfelves reduced to the neceffity of either foregoing our voyage, or complying with thefe fellows' demand, of defiring Lieutenant * * * to return to Yambo upon one of the boats near us. This boat is afterwards to proceed to Judda; where he will find Captain Bacon, and be certain of being accommodated in his veffel.

When we faw there was no alternative, but what had been propofed to us, we were fain to acquiefce, however ftrong our reluctance

reluctance to such a measure. But on a serious review of it, Lieutenant * * *'s interest may have demanded it, as much as our own. The business we are engaged in, is of too great consequence to be forgone; and by his going to Judda, we are ascertained that he is likely to meet with the assistance which his unfortunate case requires, from the surgeon of the Swallow sloop of war. Whereas, by proceeding with us, his malady would daily encrease, by the force of the terrors which he entertains of our Arabs. And some months would perhaps elapse before he could receive the advice of an European surgeon: The opportunity of removing him might never occur again; and the idea of beholding him sunk in the last stage of madness, bound hand and foot, and out of the reach of medicine, presents a picture too distressing to encounter, even in fancy. A letter was therefore written to Captain Bacon, with a summary of the untoward affair. We requested him to supply Lieutenant * * * with the money which he had paid for his share of the boat; for which Captain Bacon was to call on our attornies in India.

Our nokidah now hailed one of the boats, and induced it to draw near us again. He related the cause of the late disturbance, and agreed with the master of it, to land Lieutenant * * * and his slave-boy at Yambo, and afterwards carry him to Judda. He was now asked the amount of the sum, which he had received the last night from Lieutenant * * *. The nokidah and pilot produced 25 venetians, which they declared were all he had given them. It was impossible to discover the truth. Lieutenant * * * might perchance be mistaken, and they be apt to deceive us in such a point. It appears, however, of little moment to our poor friend; who is in a mood to give away all his money to the first man he is distrustful of.

It was now midnight, and Lieutenant * * * seemed desirous
of

of paſſing the night with us; which he once more ſolemnly averred, was the laſt which he or we ſhould ever know. As we were not to part until day-break, we readily aſſented to this deſire. We prevailed on him to lie down on one of our beds, as he was afraid to remain in his own. At his own requeſt, and for the ſatisfaction of our Arabs, Mr. Hammond and myſelf kept watch over him until morning. I do not remember to have ever been engaged in a more diſagreeable office. Our humanity was wounded by the object before us; and our conſciences were touched at a reſolution, which we had been obliged to adopt in our own deſpite. The reader of ſenſibility will feel for our perplexity. Not a wink of ſleep did our charge get during the night. He ſtarted up every moment in his bed, or called out to us to know, what villain ſtood behind him with a drawn ſword! He ſeemed not to apprehend danger from the other boats; or to dream of aſſaſſins, but among our own people.

SATURDAY, 14th JUNE.

At day-break the ſignal was made for ſailing. Lieutenant * * * aroſe, rather more compoſed than uſual, and permitted his baggage to be put into the other boat, without complaining. He had reflection enough at this moment, to ſee the neceſſity of our ſeparation; and aſſured us, that he held himſelf in no more danger in one place than another. It was his firm opinion that our deſtiny was certain, whether in this veſſel or that, at Yambo or at Judda. We paid for his paſſage, and gave the maſter of the boat a verbal meſſage for the vizier, to advertiſe him of our companion's ſituation, and to requeſt his good offices, in getting him conveyed ſafely to Judda. Our letter for Captain Bacon, we committed to the ſlave-boy, together with his maſter's

ſwords

swords and keys. This is a shrewd honest boy, who we make no doubt will be as careful as he can be, of his master, on this short passage. We had the satisfaction to perceive, that Lieutenant * * * left us much more readily, than we could have expected. Though his antipathy to the Arabs is rooted in his present disorder, he distinguishes ours more particularly, in his distrust; and perhaps, the quitting their company, is a temporary relief to his mind. Fortunate did we hold it, that not an angry word was requisite, to hasten his departure; affected as we were at the situation of a person, whom we had some regard for, and averse to embittering the potion which was prepared for him. Our principal consolation arose from the wind being fair for his return. It ensured his reaching Yambo in a few hours; and might throw him even in the way of the Adventure, which we had seen at the mouth of the harbor but two days before. At all events, we depended on the vizier's treating him with the same humanity as before; and complying with the request, which we had made in his behalf.

The boats had not long left us with Lieutenant * * *, when a breeze of wind came off the land. We presently got under sail, and had made a good stretch along shore, when the wind suddenly came ahead, and blew so strong, as to oblige us to tack about, and look for a shelter from its fury. We ran back a good way on this design, and at 11 A. M. entered a large bay encircled by a reef of rocks, to which we fastened our boat, in the manner before described. This bay is called Jeraboop, by the Arabians. In the middle of it there is an island, on which stands a priest's house. His name is Beridi, and we understand, that he is visited by all the faithful who pass by, on account of his extreme piety and old age. We were too much taken up with the late misfortune which had befallen our society, to in-

M . indulge

dulge curiosity; and left our Arabs to pay their devotions on the island alone.

We could get no observation at noon. The wind blew very violent the whole day from the N. W. but there is no sea in this bay, though it is two miles across from the rocks to the shore, which is here as mountainous as usual. We caught some beautiful rock-fish in the evening, with our hooks. They were well tasted, and encouraged us to hope for such refreshments, at other places on the coast. The wind increased during the night, and threatens a storm.

SUNDAY, 15th June.

We cannot move this morning, as the wind still remains contrary: the weather is very boisterous without, but we may laugh at the storm, which idly spends its rage on the reef of rocks, that rises up, like the sevenfold shield of Ajax, between us and danger. Never was a coast so provided by nature, with a barrier against the hostilities of the sea or of mankind. The very surge is not permitted to lash it. And all the navy of Europe would be deterred by this formidable outwork, from approaching any fortification which might be erected on the shore. What a pity is it, that the country is not worthy of the disposition, which has been made in its favor! There is no occasion for armies to protect the coast; and it is certain, that Arabia Petrea is not indebted to this line of rocks, for her security. She poured forth myriads of enthusiasts, under her warlike son Mahomet, in search of more fertile lands. Nor does it appear, that her desarts, in that interval, attracted the avarice of foreign invaders.

We amused ourselves during the morning in catching fish, which readily take the bait here. Some of them have a mouth

like.

like a parrot's beak, which our Arabs advise us not to eat. But whether from their unseemly form, or their being really unwholesome, Ibrahim could not discover. At 10 A. M. we saw a boat standing towards us, which we suppose to be bound to Yambo. The people on board descried us, and at eleven o'clock she run so near the reef we were upon, as to be within hearing. We find she comes from Suez, and learn that most of the English vessels have left that port. This was all the conversation that we had with the boat, which put before the wind, and was soon out of sight. We gather this consolation, however, from the intelligence, that it is likely the winds are about to shift in this quarter. We can no otherwise account for the departure of our ships from Suez, so much earlier than we expected. Our voyage may therefore, be more prosperous than it promised to be.

We had no observation at noon, and the wind remained in the N. W. quarter while we lay here. A poor woman waded, and swam through the water to our boat in the evening, and was very thankful for some measures of rice which she took away.

MONDAY, 16th June.

We were awakened at one o'clock this morning, by the boat getting under way. It is impossible for the Arabs to perform this manœuvre, without our knowledge; and though we lost our rest by the noise on board, we were agreeably surprized at their taking advantage of the light breeze, which came from the land. With sail and oar, we made a shift to go at the rate of a knot and a knot and an half an hour, the whole night. At daybreak we saw a vessel to the N. W. standing as we did. Our people say, that she is also bound for Suez, and has been out no
less

less than twenty days from Yambo. At 9 A. M. we discovered two more sail ahead. At ten we perceived a shoal, which they call Morsa, some leagues distant; and at noon, two of the boats appeared at anchor, within a point of land in the N. E. quarter. We stood for them; but the wind had now shifted to the N. W. and it was the work of some hours, to carry ourselves within the reef where the largest vessel was lying. We hooked our boat close by her about 3 P. M. and understand the bay we are in is called Banas. By our observation to-day it lies in the latitude of 24° 30' north. Cape Mahar within view to the northward. We are much disappointed at finding what little progress we have made since we left Yambo; and particularly, after having been at sea to-day no less than fourteen hours. But our voyage bears an intimate resemblance to what the Greeks embarked in of old; and by our mode of coasting alone, we can easily conceive Ulysses to have been ten years rounding the shores of Greece; without the intervention of any enmity, but what the mariner may expect from the winds and waves.

In the evening we went on board the vessel by us. Her burden and accommodations place her far above the stile of our boat; and we could not but repine at our lot, which had thrown us into an open boat, when it is plain that some of them are provided with cabbins. We were received very civilly by her nokidah, who tells us that he is going to Suez. He is sickly, and was very thankful for some medicines we spared him, which we brought with us for the complaint he is afflicted with. These, the Arabians never fail to solicit of Europeans, when they have occasion for them, as they have a notion that we have one and all of us, a smattering in physic. The wind freshened, and blew all night from the N. W. as usual.

TUESDAY,

TUESDAY, 17th June.

The wind is still contrary, and we cannot move this morning. It blew so strong at day-break, that our Arabs made our boat fast with another rope, by a turn round a pointed rock. Where we lie, a man of war might ride in great security. There are several fathoms of water close by the rocks, which break the force of the swell that tumbles down from the N. W. the reef at low water is every where dry, and we then pick up plenty of fish among the crevices of the rocks. While we have this supply, we shall not be at a loss for provisions. We have still a sheep left, and shall reserve a few fowls which we got from the Adventure, for more necessitous times.

At 8 A. M. the nokidah of the large vessel paid us a visit. It was partly to return our compliment, but his principal business was to look at our chart of the Red Sea. Our Arabs tell us that he is one of the best pilots of their nation. On a review of this chart we find it tolerably exact, as to the names of the islands and headlands on this coast. It is our intention, in the course of our voyage, to correct it where it is faulty, and to point out all the reefs and shoals between Yambo and Cape Mahomet. We have the advantage of being with pilots, who are acquainted with every creek and corner of the coast; and may gather such information of the track, as will prove of service to vessels thrown by currents on this dangerous shore. The fellow's surprize was very great, to hear places named by strangers, which only those of his own profession among his countrymen were acquainted with. They have no such thing as a chart; but his natural sagacity quickly made him comprehend the plan of ours. But as we are the first Europeans whom he has heard of in this navigation, he cannot reconcile to himself, how the situation of these islands could have been taken by vessels that dare not approach them. He has not the least idea of the use of the quadrant; and he conceived that we were rather making discoveries in the heavens, than ascertaining our latitude below.

We began to keep a regular watch to-night. Each gentleman and his servant to take two hours in rotation. We shall run no risk, it seems, until we get among the islands; but it is prudent to inure ourselves in time to a necessary habit. There were hard gales from the N. W. all day and part of the night.

WEDNESDAY, 18th June.

We were under way at 6 A. M. with the wind at N. by W. and stood out to sea. But the wind was too moderate to be of much service to us, against the heavy swell which the late blowing weather has occasioned. We tacked therefore at 10 o'clock, and the wind coming round more to the W. we were enabled, contrary to our expectations, to fetch a reef to the northward of Cape Mahar about 2 P. M. There is another boat at anchor about a mile to the northward of us, supposed also to be bound to Suez. Our boat beats better to windward than the two which were in company with us yesterday. The largest of which has run into shore near a league to the southward, and the other within a mile of us.

We were disappointed of an observation to-day by the high lands to the southward, which obstructed our view. Our progress however has been very little. Were not the full moon at hand, we should look for little success in beating up such a coast as this. A few days of a southerly wind would give us a good shove in the short distance we are going; and all our hopes rest on the influence of this useful planet. The gentle light which she now affords us during the night-season, proves a great relief to us after the sunshine of the day, in this sultry month. But difficult as we find it to keep ourselves cool in the day-time, it is no easier matter to defend our bodies from the damps of the night, when the wind is loaded with the heaviest dews that ever fell. To be in readiness for every change of wind in our favor, we are obliged to forego the benefit of the awning I mentioned. We lie exposed to the whole weight of the dews, and the cloaks in which we wrap ourselves, are as wet in the morning, as if they had been immersed in the sea. It is plain, however, that they are not impregnated with the bad qualities, which render people so fearful of the dew in most parts of the world, or our constitutions would have evinced the fact.

The weather was very moderate during the night, and the wind remained in the usual quarter. We relieved our watch regularly, as the night before, and find that a little practice will make it easy to us.

THURSDAY, 19th JUNE.

We got under sail at day-break with the wind at N. and stood out to sea until 10 o'clock. The wind now heading us, we tacked and lay up along shore. Our course was but slow, but we continued gaining ground until 2 P. M. when we ran into a fine bay, and brought to, on a reef within an hundred yards of the beach. We are not at all displeased with the working of our boat. She has run her two consorts out of sight, and beat the boat which was a-head of us yesterday. There was a contest between them the whole morning, and the victory declared in favor of our boat, which has fetched a mile to windward of the other. However contemptible the prize, there is a secret satisfaction in being superior to our neighbors on every occasion,

fion. And I doubt, whether the winner at an horse-race could have exulted more, than we did at our dexterity, in beating a veffel, much worfe found than ours.

The bay we are in, is in the latitude of 24° 36' N. by an obfervation which we took to-day. To the W. it is defended by a reef of rocks, and the high land to the northward and eaftward, would fecure it from a ftorm in thofe points. There is water enough within for the largeft fhips; but it is very uncertain, whether they could gain admittance within the reef that guards this coaft. It is not always that we difcern that reef to the weftward of us; but there is every reafon to imagine, that we are ftill failing within it; and that the rocks are only more funken in thofe places, where the fea is not feen to break upon them. It was accident alone, that brought the Adventure through this reef before our arrival at Yambo; and it would be the fame chance, that would fteer a veffel of her burden into this bay, clear of the dangers which impede the paffage.

To atone, in fome meafure, for the want of exercife in our prefent fituation, we make a practice of going into the water regularly before fun-fet. The coves we lie in, are very convenient for this purpofe; and we find great benefit, as well as refreshment, from the falt water.

FRIDAY, 20th JUNE.

We weighed at day-break, and ftood out to fea, with the wind at N. N. W. At 7 A. M. we faw the ifland of Hafana, bearing about N. N. W. at the diftance of eight leagues. At eight, we ran by a funken rock, above three leagues from the land; and at the fame time we difcerned breakers upon our lee-quarter, a league further in the fea. At ten we tacked with the wind at W. and ftood along the coaft. At eleven we came among a number of breakers,

breakers, that extend three or four leagues into the sea. Our pilot appears to be well experienced in this navigation. He displayed his dexterity to-day, by running us through narrow channels, and almost brushing the rocks to the windward of the boat. This is as dangerous a part as we have seen of this coast; nor would it be possible for a ship, without an Arabian pilot on board, to steer through this net of rocks and shoals, except by a miracle.

We proceeded under an easy sail for some hours. The weather was remarkably hot, and we were exposed, as usual, to all the rage of a vertical sun. But we had the satisfaction to reflect, that we were gaining somewhat on our way. And this served to alleviate the inconveniences to which we are subjected by our situation. The satisfaction, however, was transient. The wind headed us at two o'clock, and we were obliged to run into shore by another boat, which is said to be bound for Suez. We had the mortification still not to keep the ground which we had so happily attained. The pilot did not like the birth, and ran back again to the southward, in search of another. It is impossible to portray the countenances which we exhibited during this manœuvre. We could not contain our vexation, and remonstrated pretty warmly with the pilot, on his sporting with our good fortune, and throwing away the advantages which we so seldom obtained. He lent a deaf ear to our complaints; and went near a league, before we arrived at the bay where he intended to pass the night. Here we came to on a reef, at 4 P. M. and found the water not deep enough to admit vessels of any burthen. Our observation at noon brought us into the latitude of 24° 46′ N. The wind was moderate all night from the N. W.

SATURDAY, 21st June.

We were rouzed at three this morning by the boat getting under way. Our beds take up the breadth of the boat, and were we ever so much overpowered with sleep, the trampling of the mariners' feet upon our bodies, would soon chase away all inclinations of that nature. There was a light breeze from the land, and the moon being at her full just before it sprang up, flatters our hopes of more favorable winds for some days to come. We went easily along until day-break, when the high land of Hasana appeared, bearing N. W. at the distance of six leagues. This island is in the form of a sugar-loaf, and rises like an exhalation from the sea. At 9 A. M. a fine breeze sprung up from the S. E. and at noon we anchored in a small bay, off the northernmost point of Hasana. We were much out of humor at this delay, but found it impossible to prevent the Arabs stopping, for purposes unknown to us. It is an hardship on us, to lose the benefit of a fair wind, with a month's provision and water on board. But we are obliged to consider the resolutions of these people as law, in every thing that respects the management of the boat.

The island of Hasana is a barren rock, inhabited only at particular seasons, when the natives from the continent bring off wood, water, and provisions, for the conveniency of vessels that pass to and fro. They erect temporary habitations for their families, and live chiefly upon the fish with which this coast abounds. This island is not more than two leagues long, and about half as broad. It lies about three leagues from the main, and in the latitude of 25° 3' N. by this day's observation. Here we found three boats, bound likewise for Suez. They mean to join us to-morrow, in order to pass the cluster of islands that lies to the northward of this. This we learn from our nokidah; who assures us that the Buddoos, or wild

wild Arabs, infest those parts, and make no scruple to attack a single boat. It was one reason for his calling here, if we are to take his word; and though we hold ourselves strong enough to venture singly through this sea, all argument and displeasure on our side, are equally vain.

The wind blew briskly from the S. E. the remainder of the day, and continued in the same quarter until we retired to rest. The loss of time did not add more to our discontent, than did the indolence and phlegm of our Arabs.

SUNDAY, 22d JUNE.

Our nokidah and pilot both lay ashore last night, so that it was not practicable for us to have sailed, had our inclinations only been consulted. A land breeze came off from the N. E. about an hour before day-break, and at 6 A. M. we sent Ibrahim ashore to hasten our people. He returned with an answer, that the other boats were not ready, and that it was fruitless to urge the necessity of our affairs, or to expect their departure a moment before their own time.

It is more than probable, that the snow Aurora was wrecked on the back of this island in the month of December; a circumstance which has been already noticed in this work. The captain's journal places the island in this latitude; and we have sufficient proofs of a wreck being in this neighborhood. The beach is covered with a number of * teak-timbers, knees, and bolts of a vessel; and a fine English-built cutter lies upon the strand, which is new, and in good repair.

---

* The teak-tree is a native of India, and its timber resembles oak so much, that it is used throughout the East for ship-building. It is thought to surpass oak in point of duration.

At nine we weighed, in company with five boats, and stood to the eastward, with little or no wind. At ten a fine breeze sprung up from the S. W. and we ran by a number of shoals and breakers to the windward of us, that are four or five leagues from the main. At eleven we passed a sandy island, from which there appears to stretch a connected line of breakers to the island of Hasana. Within this line we have made our run to-day. At 2 P. M. we anchored to the eastward of the island of Harama, which lies about six leagues to the northward of Hasana. We had no observation at noon, but we conclude it from our reckoning to be in the latitude of 25° 20′ N. This is a low sandy island, extending about two miles in length, and half a mile in breadth, and situated about a league from the main. There are a few huts near the place we are anchored at, which serve to shew the poverty of the inhabitants, and that we have little to fear from them, though we perceive that there are boats belonging to the island.

From this day's navigation we are convinced, that no ship can approach this part of the coast of Arabia, with any degree of security; as the sea is all along foul with shoals and rocks, and we frequently saw breakers to windward of us, which could not be less than six or seven leagues from the land. The wind was variable during the night, but blew chiefly from the westward.

MONDAY, 23d JUNE.

We weighed at day-break, after taking on board a couple of sheep, which we purchased here for three dollars each. There was a brisk breeze from the E. N. E. with which we stood along the coast. At seven o'clock we passed the small island of Abumellie, which is surrounded by breakers. Here we discovered an Arab family ashore, and a boat put off with some of the men, to visit

visit our people. This island is bare of every thing but a few bushes, and does not lie half a league from the main. At eight the wind came round to N. which obliged us to stand out more to sea. Our bark is, indeed, a prime sailor, and no vessel which we have met with, can keep pace with her. But this is rather a disadvantage to us, as our pilot daily foregoes the superiority he has gained, to keep company with the other boats. He now inclined more to the westward than was necessary. His intention was evidently to loiter for our consorts. We cannot prevent the delay which this plan must occasion, during our disagreeable voyage. Our Arabs seem resolved to grant their countrymen the protection which our company may afford them; and at the same time, they are not wanting to persuade us, that our security consists in going together.

The run to-day has been very clear, and the coast appears more fertile, than we have seen it on this side of Mocha. At 2 P. M. we tacked and ran into shore. To our great disappointment, we could not weather a bluff point ahead; and the pilot ran back near a league, before he could find a secure birth. At length he came to, on a reef close to the shore before four o'clock, where we were presently joined by two of our fleet. We could get no observation at noon, on account of the high land to the southward; but, by our reckoning, we take the place which we now lie in, to be in the latitude of $25°\ 38'$ N.

We had more exercise for our physical skill this evening. There is a boy lying sick of a fever, on board one of the boats near us; and on application for relief, we sent him some cooling draughts, to be repeated according to the directions which we received. But some bowls of weak tea, which the boy more readily took, produced an immediate perspiration, and seem more likely to promote his recovery. Our success will not fail to recommend us to the Arabs. The wind blew from the S. W. a great part of the night.

TUESDAY,

TUESDAY, 24th JUNE.

We got under fail at day-break, with a fine breeze from the land, in company with the two boats. The other three appearing above a league aftern. We kept about half a league from the fhore, but found the water fo fhallow, that we hold it impoffible the annual Judda fhip fhould go to Suez in this track. There were breakers the whole way, fome leagues without us. Several fandy iflands are fcattered about this part of the coaft, which are laid down in the chart. The fhore is now covered with underwood, and interfperfed with date-trees; but no inhabitants have come into view.

At 8 A. M. the wind died away, and our crew took to their oars and rowed out to fea, in hopes of meeting with the fea-wind. The channels here, in many places, will fcarcely admit our boats between them; and the rocks around us, ftand out of the water, and are covered with the largeft birds which were ever feen. The Arabs call them Meriah. They have a prodigious long bill and long legs, which enable them to catch fifh in near a fathom water. The current feems to be for us, but we have no opportunity to try it. At nine we came up with the fouthernmoft point of the ifland of Naaman, which is laid down in the chart in 26° 6' north; with fands about it. But this we find to be an error. The ifland begins in the latitude of 25° 50' and extends to 26° 6' north; and although at a diftance, it might be taken for a number of different iflands, on a nearer view, it proves to be one continued land, overflown in feveral quarters at high water. We run between this ifland and the main, through very clear and deep water, with a ftrong breeze at W. S. W. Latitude per obfervation 25° 50'.

At 3 P. M. we opened a cove within a reef of rocks, and anchored

anchored close on the Arabian coast, where one of our fleet had already arrived. The rest we fairly ran out of sight to-day, except a boat of our own size, commanded by our pilot's brother; which stopped at Naaman to procure a supply of wood. By our reckoning, we take our anchoring-place to be in the latitude of 26° north. At sun-set our nokidah weighed his anchor, and ran out into deeper water, to prevent a surprize from the wild Arabs, who frequent this neighborhood. The other boat followed our example. There were calms and light airs the whole night.

WEDNESDAY, 25th June.

We weighed our anchor at day-break, with a light breeze from the land. The two boats were in company, and we went under an easy sail for some hours. At 8 A. M. a fine gale sprung up from the southward, and agreeably quickened our course. We ran by several sandy islands, within a league and an half of the main, and in spite of the hot weather, entertained our imaginations with the fairness of the wind, and the novelty of the navigation. We had been a fortnight on board yesterday, and though we were advanced not a third of the distance to Suez, we had the satisfaction to reflect, that we had gained all our ground in the last four or five days. For the first week our progress had been delayed by the misfortune of our companion, and the strength of contrary winds. The winds are now variable, and promise to be so until the change of the moon. It only depends upon our Arabs, to improve the occasion which fortune presents to us.

On some of the islands which we passed, were several birds, larger even than those we saw yesterday. We positively mistook them for men at a distance, wading in the sea; and one

of

of them was so bold, as not to be scared at a shot, which was fired at it from our boat. At 11 A. M. the wind veered round to the westward, and our pilot thought fit to run under the lee of a sandy island, where the other boats soon came to, likewise. With this wind we might have gone a great way further to the northward, were we not in a manner shut up among shoals and rocks, by keeping so close to the shore. By our observation this island is in the latitude of 26° 7' north.

Here our people gathered a quantity of eggs, which the birds lay upon the sandy reefs. They tell us these eggs are well-tasted and wholesome; but we are not driven to such streights, as to be obliged to put up with all kinds of food. The boy is much mended in his fever, and entertains a great opinion of the virtues of tea. There were light airs from the southward, and calms, during the night.

THURSDAY, 26th JUNE.

We got under sail at day-break, in company with the two boats. The wind was at S. E. and we ran easily for some hours, through very foul water, with sandy islands on each side of us. At 9 A. M. we came to, under a small island; where our nokidah tells us we must wait for the rest of the fleet, in order to pass some islands ahead, which are haunted by piratical Arabs. The caution of this man begins to communicate itself to our minds. Were there not some danger lurking near us, he could not be so uniform in his behavior, or so solicitous for the junction of the boats behind us. As the wind freshens from the southward, we have hopes that the rest of the fleet will join us in a few hours. But this is little consolation to persons in our situation, who are anxious to conclude our voyage, and are obliged to forego a fair wind in a contrary monsoon. This

island

island is about four leagues from the main, and by our obſervation, is in the latitude of 26° 8′ N. There is a prieſt dwells upon it, called Morbeck, to whoſe cell our Arabs are gone, to pray for a fair wind, at a time that they are trifling one away! To the ſouth of this iſland there is a remarkable rock, which appears at a diſtance, like a lion couchant. One of the boats is anchored by us, the other is gone to the continent to cut wood.

At noon we diſcovered two boats to the ſouthward, and before 2 P. M. we were joined by all the fleet, except one boat which is a bad ſailor, and lags behind. We immediately got under ſail, and ſtood to the N. W. with a fine ſea breeze. We ran briſkly through deep and clear water, until paſt four o'clock, when the wind coming round to the northward of weſt, the whole fleet ſteered into ſhore, and anchored cloſe on the Arabian coaſt. The hindermoſt boat came up within a mile of us, ſo that we are now ſix ſail in company. This place, by our account, lies in the latitude of 26° 16′ N.

We had ſcarcely come to an anchor, when we diſcovered camels and a number of women moving towards us. They proved to belong to a wandering tribe of Arabs, who are wont to come down in a friendly manner, to ſell ſheep and water to veſſels that touch on the coaſt. Their appearance was truly miſerable; and we could perceive but little difference between the human and brute creation, whom nature had bred in this deſart region. Their wants, their appetites, and their inſenſibility, bore an intimate reſemblance together. And they were as much below our envy, as above our compaſſion. Light airs from the weſt all night.

O   FRIDAY,

FRIDAY, 27th June.

We were disturbed in our first sleep, by the fleet of boats getting under way at one this morning. There was a light breeze from the land, and with the help of our oars, we made a shift to go between two and three knots an hour. Our run was through very foul and shallow water. At 11 A. M. we passed a sandy island, which is lofty, and makes like the ruins of a castle standing in the water: the sides perpendicular and appearing like walls, and at one end, the face resembling a decayed tower. The rocks in this sea are often thrown into fantastic shapes. Some we have seen like boats under sail, and some like animals and men.

A fine breeze now sprung up from the S. W. and at noon we ran by another island, sandy like the former, and lying within four leagues of the main. By our observation, this island is in the latitude of 26° 26' N. From hence we continued our course through clear and deep water, until 3 P. M. when the wind heading us, we stood into shore, to fetch our pilot's brother, whose boat got the start of us to-day, and had come to an anchor under the land. This was the boat that went for wood yesterday, and we were astonished to see a fine timber on board, which she had picked up ashore. It is of teak, and being about 30 feet long, we conjecture it to be one of the beams of the unfortunate Aurora, which the sea has cast up again.. The Arab thinks to get a good price for it, at some of the ports in this sea.

This place, by our reckoning, is in the latitude of 26° 36' N. Here we found an opening in the land, which disclosed a very deep and romantic valley, where the sea, at times, appears to flow in to a considerable depth. The same chain of mountains

still

ftill continues within land, that we have traced from Yambo. They only vary in the line, which in fome places, approaches nearer to the coaft than in others. Four of our fleet not being able to reach us, bore away for anchoring-ground, which is not in fight. This is no fmall mortification to us, who will be under the neceffity of waiting for them. The wind blew from the weftward during the night.

SATURDAY, 28th June.

There was a fine breeze fprang up from the land before day-break, but we did not weigh, in expectation of being joined by the other boats. At 5 P. M. they came in view, but the force of the wind was fpent, and we failed with little or no wind. At 8 the wind came round to the N. W. and began to blow fo frefh, that our pilot was fain to run under a reef of breakers, which lies more than three leagues from the main. Here our pilot's brother was already arrived, but none of the reft of the fleet could come up. Our fituation is very eligible. We are here defended from the violence of the weather, and are ready to flip out, fhould the wind veer again to the eaft or fouth quarters. As we advance on our voyage, we have daily frefh matter of furprize, and behold the intricacies of a navigation, which we had no idea could exift in any corner of the globe. By our obfervation, this reef is in the latitude of 26° 40′ N. Cape Sellah bears due north, at the diftance of fix leagues.

This fea abounds with the large mother-of-pearl oyfters; and our nokidah to-day gave us a proof of his agility, by jumping out of the boat when under fail, and bringing up one of thefe oyfters in two fathom water, in time to catch a rope from the boat's quarter. Thefe fellows' dexterity in fifhing cannot be fufficiently admired; and wherever we are, we may depend upon

upon our mafter for a difh of excellent fifh. At low water the reef appears fome feet above the level of the fea, and our table was not unprovided with its ufual fervice. This circumftance is very favorable to this coafting voyage; as, whatever other hardfhips they may endure, the want of provifion is not felt by the mariners.

There were hard gales all day from the N. W. fo that we could not quit our ftation. As the moon enters into her laft quarter to-day, this contrary wind betides us no good, and we apprehend there will be no change until the new moon. We are become very fkilful in the influences of this planet; but how are they to be pitied, whofe fuccefs depends upon fo inconftant a power! The weather was more moderate during the night. The wind in the fame point.

SUNDAY, 29th June.

At half paft fix this morning a light breeze came off the land, and flattered us to leave our ftation. We weighed in company with the other boat, and ftood to the N. N. W. but the wind fhifting fuddenly to the W. N. W. and an ugly fwell being againft us, before we had got a league, both the boats were obliged to tack, and run back to their former birth under the reef. Here we were joined by three more of our fleet at 9 A. M. They had luckily made fuch a ftretch to fea, as to be able to reach this reef, when the wind changed to the weftward. There was now but one miffing boat, and at 10, we difcovered her at anchor upon the reef, about a league to the fouthward. Our fears of the weather are now confirmed. We muft look for delays for fome days to come; which, joined to fome circumftances of our fituation, call forth all our fortitude to combat with cheerfully.

The

The weather was very tempestuous, and there were frequent gales from the N.W. during the day. The night was more moderate; but we had a disturbance of another nature on board our boat, which alarmed us at first, but turned out to be a ludicrous, rather than a serious adventure.

Besides our nokidah and pilot, there is another Arab on board, as I have said before. The rest of the crew are Abyssinians. During the first watch at night, which it was my turn to keep, this Arab, who was talking with his companions, suddenly fell upon the deck in the stern of the boat, and to all appearance, was seized with a convulsive fit. We were immediately in motion, and offered to administer such relief to him, as we had seen practised in the same cases. But our astonishment was great, when we found the Arabs would not permit any assistance to be given him. They declared, that he was only disordered in mind, and that an evil spirit possessed him, who could only be expelled by the force of prayer. Accordingly the nokidah began to pray over him aloud, while two men held the unhappy creature down, to prevent, as they said, the ill effects of the temporary influence which over-ruled him. They told us stories of men in this situation, who committed murder, and every other act of desperation. This idea appeared so extravagant to us, that we treated it with ridicule; and could not but pity the ignorance of a people, who were such slaves to superstition. The notion was certainly imbibed from the demoniacs of Palestine, who are mentioned in the New Testament. We have scriptural authority to believe their existence at a certain period. But to suppose they have still liberty to enter into human bodies, and that man has the same power, as our Saviour possessed over supernatural beings, are tenets worthy of a weak and unenlightened mind. We were much surprized, however, at the length of the fit, which continued between two and three hours;

and,

and, from the strong agitations of his body, left the Arab in a state of imbecillity for the rest of the night. But the devil was at length exorcised, and the nokidah remarked to us with triumph, the great efficacy of prayer!

MONDAY, 30th JUNE.

We weighed at six this morning, in company with the four boats, with a light breeze from the N. N. E. The other boat stood after us at a distance. Our run to-day was through very deep and clear water, and, by the long and ugly swell which tumbled in upon us from the N. W. we conjecture there is no reef of rocks without this part of the coast, and that a large vessel might stand in, without danger. Latitude, per observation, 26° 44′ north. At twelve o'clock the wind hauled round to the N. W. and the whole fleet tacked and stood into shore. At 1 P. M. we ran into a small inlet, defended from the sea by a reef, and hooked ourselves to a rock, within two fathoms of the beach. Here we were joined by the rest of the fleet, except one boat which cannot keep up.

As we came in here, our nokidah told us to prime our fire-arms, and prepare ourselves for the reception of the wild Arabs. He had scarcely spoken, when our old pilot leaped into the water and swam ashore, and with all the agility of youth, ascended an eminence that juts into the sea, to learn if there was any immediate danger. This inlet opens into a valley, on each side of which we have planted a centinel. The country has resumed its barren appearance, and yields only a brush-wood, with which our fleet have supplied themselves. This place is called Jebul, or Mount Lebel, and by our reckoning, lies in the latitude of 26° 46′ north.

About half an hour after our arrival, a man and woman came

came down to us in a friendly manner, and assured us we had nothing to fear, as there were no buddoos in that neighborhood at present. But our Arabs pay little attention to this information; and are so suspicious of this station, that we doubled our watch during the night, and perhaps, would have made an enemy repent of an intrusion at such a season. The weather was moderate during the night, but the wind still remained in the N. W. quarter.

TUESDAY, 1st JULY.

We got under way at half past one this morning, with a light breeze from the land, in company with the four boats. We stood along shore with sails and oars, until 7 A. M. when the wind heading us, we made a stretch out to sea. At eight we tacked with the wind at west, and stood to the northward. At nine we passed a little sandy island, about two leagues from the main. At ten we ran close by a reef of rocks, about half a league further in the sea. There was no swell to-day, which we attribute to our being within shoals and reefs, and we saw a rock some leagues without us. But this may be owing to the nature of narrow seas, where a swell soon rises, and as soon subsides, as the wind freshens or moderates.

We fetched as high as we could on the Arabian shore, and at noon anchored in smooth water, where three of the boats soon joined us. The pilot's brother is a better sailor than we, and is anchored at least a league ahead. By our observation we are in the latitude of 26° 56′ north. The coast is not so hilly here, and our people are less apprehensive of a surprize. The wind remained at N. W. during the rest of the day, but so moderate, that we have great hopes of variable winds, if not a total change, at the new moon, which now approaches. We have only run

half

half the diftance between Yambo and Suez; but a few days of a foutherly wind would do our bufinefs. There were light airs from the land in the night.

WEDNESDAY, 2d July.

We weighed at day-break with a breeze from the land, in company with the three boats. We ftood clofe in with the fhore, and went through fmooth and fhallow water until 9 A. M. when the wind coming round to the N. W. we made a ftretch out to fea, tacked, and weathered a fandy ifland ahead, where our pilot's brother lay to his veffel for us. This ifland, by our reckoning, lies in the latitude of 27° 1' north, and has a reef of breakers, extending fome leagues beyond it to the N. W. It is only inhabited by birds, of which we faw an amazing number on the fhore. At eleven the wind heading us, we ran into the Arabian fhore, and at noon anchored in a cove, furrounded by high mountains, which rife perpendicular from the fea. Here we found the pilot's brother, and were foon joined by the three other boats. Our fleet now confifts but of five boats, the other having been totally feparated from us.

This cove is called Maraut by the Arabians, and by our obfervation, lies in the latitude of 27° 3' north. We have reafon to think that Ras, or Cape Sellah, which is laid down in the charts in 27° north is twenty miles to the fouthward, and the land in 27° does not form a cape. We have our pilot's authority, as well as our own obfervation, for this remark.

Towards the evening fome natives came down, with about a dozen camels loaded with water. We were at too great a diftance to be in danger of a furprize, and fent our people afhore to replenifh our cafks, which, with all our care, began to be low. Here we likewife provided ourfelves with firewood; and are told there

there is a spring of water near the beach, which is the first we have met with on this coast. It is, however, so very brackish, that nothing but necessity could induce any one to drink it. Our nokidah returned, with a branch of a very fragrant shrub. It grows wild among the rocks, and differs in appearance and smell, from any species that we know of. The vicinity of the natives made us double our watch during the night, which was calmer than usual.

THURSDAY, 3d JULY.

We got under way at day-break, with little or no wind; but with our oars, we made a shift to creep on at the rate of a knot an hour. The four boats in company. At 9 A. M. the wind came from the N. N. W. with which we made a stretch out to sea. We soon found that we could make nothing of it, and at ten we tacked and stood into the land. We saw an island ahead about four leagues to the northward, which we take to be the island of Sufcha, as our chart names it, though our pilot calls it Shaur. By our observation at noon, we were in the latitude of 27° 9' north. Our run to-day has been through deep and clear water, and as we have not observed any reefs or shoals without us, we have reason to think a ship might stand close into the Arabian coast in this latitude. This is, in fact, but a matter of opinion, founded upon such evidence, as the reader has before him. We are neither masters of our time, nor the motions of our vessel, and our remarks can only arise from a superficial view of things.

At 1 P. M. we anchored under a point of land on the main, which we take, by our reckoning, to be in the latitude of 27° 12' north. From hence we saw another island, bearing to the westward of Shaur. We are now approaching to the scenes of danger,

ger, with which we have been so long amused by our Arabs; and have some hopes that we shall not be awaked to the reality of our apprehensions. We were soon joined by the rest of our little fleet. The wind blew from the N. W. during the day, but very moderately.

Towards the close of the evening, we discovered a couple of women and some camels in the country, with the help of our glasses. This was sufficient to put us more upon our guard, to prevent our being surprized by these roving tribes. There were calms and light airs from the northward, for the first part of the night.

FRIDAY, 4th JULY.

We weighed at one A. M. with a light breeze from the land, in company with the other boats. At six a fine breeze sprung up from the S. E. with which we stood along the Arabian coast. At eight we ran by the island of Shaur or Sufcha, whose shores are very steep, and resemble decayed walls at a distance. This island is about two leagues in length, lies about two leagues from the main, and by our reckoning, is in the latitude of 27° 20′ N. A reef of breakers extend from the island to the N. W. on which we saw the wreck of the annual Judda ship, said to have been lost here in a gale of wind in the year 1774, on her way to Suez. Her stem and stern, and many of her ribs, still appear above the water, and pronounce her to have been of prodigious magnitude. Indeed, the accounts of this Arabian galleon's burden, are so extravagant, that it might seem to offend credibility to repeat them. I shall only observe, that she sails from Judda in the month of March, and by following the track which we have gone, as near as possible, she is generally fifty days, or two months, on her voyage to Suez: and, as it has happened this year, from some accident or other, she sometimes gets no further than

than Tor. To fail in the performance of so short a voyage, in the most favorable season of the year, would be an inexplicable circumstance to a mariner, unacquainted with the navigation of this extraordinary coast. To us, who are no strangers to the course, the wonder is, how a vessel of her great burden and unwieldy structure, can accomplish the passage at all.

At 10 A. M. the wind hauled round to the westward, and we stood N. N. W. until eleven, when all the fleet bore away for the land. After we had passed the island of Shaur, an ugly swell came tumbling upon us from the N. W. Our run to-day was through shallow water, until we reached Shaur; but we found very deep water between the island and the main. At noon we anchored under a reef of rocks, above two miles from the Arabian coast. Latitude, per observation, 27° 28′ N. There is a prodigious high mountain inland, some leagues to the northward of us, on the top of which are two remarkable spires, that resemble a bull's horns. We saw a fire ashore, but no people. The wind was W. all day, and part of the night.

SATURDAY, 5th JULY.

We weighed before one this morning, with a light breeze from the land. The other boats were in company. At day-break the wind came round to the S. E. with which we stood along the shore. There was an heavy swell from the N. W. which considerably impeded our progress. Our run to-day was through clear and deep water. We looked out ahead for Mount Sinai, and stood on until noon, when the wind shifting to the westward, we tacked, and the whole fleet stood into the land. Our latitude, per observation, was 27° 49′ N. We now discovered a large town ahead, which our Arabs call Moilah. There is little doubt but it is the same place, which our chart erroneously lays down in 27° N. about 50 miles

miles to the southward. We saw an island to the N. W. which our pilot tells us is Sanafir. At 1. P. M. we plainly discerned the high land, which we take to be adjacent to Cape Mahomet, bearing W. N. W. At three the wind veering round to the W. the whole fleet anchored within a reef of rocks to the northward of Moilah, and about one league and an half from the shore.

The mountain mentioned yesterday with the remarkable top, lies behind this town, which appears through our glasses to be a regular fortification, of a square figure. Our nokidah gives the inhabitants a very bad character, and tells us a story of their recently seizing, and plundering a Judda boat, which put into the road through stress of weather. At sun-set, the shore to the N. of the gulf of Akaba bore W. by N. Cape Mahomet we take to bear due west, as we have entered the gulf. By our reckoning, this reef is in about the latitude of 27° 58′ N. The wind continued at W. the remainder of the day.

When the evening closed in, all the boats run out into six fathom water, on account of the vicinity of Moilah, of which placed our Arabs have a very unfavourable opinion. After it was dark, we saw many fires on the Arabian shore, but every thing remained quiet during the night. The wind inclined towards the southward.

SUNDAY, 6th July.

We got under way at two this morning, in company with the other boats, with the wind from the S. S. W. At day-break we saw the island of Sanafir, bearing W. by N. at the distance of four leagues and upwards. There are breakers without us, which probably extend, with little interruption, from the island of Shaur to Sanafir. At 10 A. M. we came up with the latter island, and came to, under it, to wait for some boats which sail worse than ours.

ours. This island is nothing but a high barren rock, and lies in the latitude of 28° 3′ N. We saw a turtle-shell on the beach, but could not procure a turtle here, or in any of the islands we have passed. At half past ten we stood to the northward, in company with the whole fleet, and on opening a strait that divides this island into two parts, we discovered two boats at anchor under the land. On their perceiving us, they immediately got under sail, stood towards us for a time, then slackened their sail, and after having amused us for an hour and more, ran back into their former station. By these manœuvres we concluded them to be pirates, which was confirmed by their not answering the signals, which were made them by the rear of our fleet. Our numbers only prevented their engaging us, and our Arabs bade us expect to fall in with more vessels of this kind. The shore of Sanafir is very bold, and would admit of a large ship running close to it.

At noon we saw the island of Tiran bearing due west, and the island of Barkan N. W. The wind was still at S. S. W. when we bore away for the island of Barkan. These islands are both laid down too far to the southward in the charts, as is the coast adjacent to Cape Mahomet. Latitude, per observation, 28° 7′ N. At 2 P. M. the whole fleet anchored in a cove at Barkan. By running so deep into this gulf, we could not stand with this wind for Cape Mahomet, which must bear S. W. of this island. We have here obtained a convincing proof of the necessity, which boats are under to sail in fleets on this coast. Not more than five months ago, four boats from Suez to Judda, were plundered at this very island of Barkan by pirates, and some Greek and Turkish passengers cut off by these barbarians. This story was confirmed by the testimony of some of our servants, who were ashore, and saw quantities of wheat and coffee scattered about the beach. The wind hauled round to the S. E. at sun-set, but we did not move, the passage to the Cape being too hazardous, we find, to risk in

I the

the dark. We were induced, from concurrent circumstances, to double our watch during the night; the best part of which the wind was from the southward.

MONDAY, 7th JULY.

We weighed at four this morning, in company with the other boats, with a light breeze from the S. E. At day-break saw a vessel some leagues to the southward, standing as we did. At ten o'clock passed an island within three leagues of the main, which our pilot tells us, is Tiran. This information much surprized us, as in our chart, Tiran lies some leagues to the southward of Cape Mahomet, whereas, by our reckoning, this island lies in 28° 15′, which is considerably to the northward of the given latitude of the Cape. There is indeed an head-land to the northward of this island, which we took for Cape Mahomet; but our pilot tells us, that the Cape bears S. W. of us, at the distance of seven or eight leagues. By our run yesterday and to-day, the coast from the Cape to the top of the gulf of Akaba, runs nearly N. and S. though our chart lays it down two points more westerly. This is not the only mistake. This gulf is twice as broad as the chart makes it, or we have been sailing on dry ground the whole day. Latitude, per observation, 28° 14′N.

At 1 P. M. the wind hauled round to the S.W. and all the fleet bore away to a reef of rocks that we had before past, and anchored under them, within 3 or 4 leagues of the main. It is a mortification to us indeed, to be baffled in doubling the cape with a wind, which we have so anxiously wished for, and which is become foul instead of being fair, by our having run up so high into this gulf, when we might have stood over direct from Moilah to Cape Mahomet.

At

At fun-fet the wind, to our great joy, came round to the E. S. E. as it induced the whole fleet to get under fail, which we had never before done at night. In weighing her anchor, the largeft boat among us was near driving upon the rocks. The wind bl w frefh upon them, and it is probable fhe would have been ftranded in a few minutes, had not one of our people fwam off to her in time with a rope, with which we towed her out of the danger that threatened her. By the advice of our nokidah, we primed our fire-arms anew, and fate up the whole night, to be the better prepared for the reception of the pirates, who, he affures us, are accuftomed to lurk in great numbers about Cape Mahomet. This was doubtlefs a troublefome circumftance, but our minds were fo taken up with our approach to the Gulf of Suez, that there was not room left for difagreeable reflections. With the prefent wind we were in hopes of making the harbour of Tor fome time to-morrow, and if a chance then appeared of our having a tedious paffage by water, we refolved to proceed by land to Suez, as captain Dibdin's officers had purpofed to do, which the removing of the cargo of the Judda fhip would, in all likelihood, afford us a good opportunity of effecting. The night was ferene, and we ftood on with the coaft under an eafy fail.

TUESDAY, 8th JULY.

About two this morning the wind fhifted to the N. N. W. and we ftood to the weftward, at the rate of three knots an hour. We have left the reef of rocks behind us, or our Arabs would not go on fo boldly on a foul coaft. Juft before day-break we laid down, to take a fhort nap after our watching. By 7 A. M. we were awake, and upon enquiring for Cape Mahomet, were much furprized when the pilot pointed it out to us, bearing to the fouthward of us at the diftance of twelve or fourteen leagues. Our
disappointment

disappointment was great at this information. We expected to have rounded the Cape before this, and had recourse to our chart, which only plunged us into fresh perplexity. We could only solve the difficulty by supposing, that we had gone much higher up the gulf of Akaba than we imagined; and were now obliged to stand to the southward, in order to double the Cape. At eight we opened a gulf, which they tell us, is the gulf of Akaba, and the head-land which we have come round, and took yesterday to be Cape Mahomet, must be the true island of Tiran. This coast has been bolder than any other we have passed; and what is remarkable, we did not see a shoal or breaker, the whole morning.

Our latitude, per observation, was 27° 42' N. We were above half a degree to the southward of yesterday, and this tended to convince us, that we had been much deeper in the gulf of Akaba than we suspected. We stood W. and sometimes W. by S. as the wind permitted. At 1 P. M. we saw two sail to the southward, one of which our pilot supposes to have been the large boat, which parted company with us long since. At two the wind shifted again to the southward, and all the fleet bore away for the land to the westward of us. At five we anchored under a rocky island, within a league of the main, where we found a strange boat at anchor. None of the fleet, but the pilot's brother, fetched this island besides; but we are told they will easily join us when the wind changes. Our vexation is infinite, that our situation will not admit of our taking advantage of a southerly wind. When we have doubled the Cape, we may look for this wind in vain. The pilot points it out to us, at the distance of three or four leagues, and talks of getting to Tor in the morning.

Just as the sun set behind the coast we were upon, the mariners of the strange boat observed a couple of turtles, swimming from the reef we lie on, and immediately rowed out to sea after them.

them. It is common to turn thefe animals upon their backs, when they are afleep on the furface of the water; but it was a new thing to us, to fee them taken when awake, in their own element. We could not but laugh at the attempt, but we had foon reafon to condemn our own incredulity. The dexterity of the Arabs was equal to it. One of them jumped out of the boat with a rope in his hand, purfued, overtook, and after a ftruggle under water, faftened a hook to the head of the largeft turtle in four fathom. It was, with equal facility, run up into the boat, and brought in triumph on board our veffel. This creature weighs about two hundred weight, and will furnifh a plentiful meal for the whole fleet. The wind kept to the fouth moft of the night.

WEDNESDAY, 9th JULY.

The other boats came up to us at two this morning, when we weighed with a fine breeze from the N. W. At three the gale encreafed fo much, as to fend us at the rate of fix knots an hour. This made us uneafy, as we doubted the poffibility of doubling the Cape. When the day broke, we faw high land to our right, which we ftill took to be the Arabian coaft; as we had not, to our knowledge, parted with it. But as the fun rofe, we were not a little aftonifhed at his fituation, which was quite the reverfe of what it ufed to be. We loft no time in calling upon the pilot, to explain this phenomenon. He replied without emotion, that we had paffed the Cape during the night, and that Tor itfelf was a confiderable way behind us. We had no compafs on board, but from the fun's pofition, we were certain that we were going to the fouthward. We could not divine the reafon of this, except that the bay in which Tor lies, was deeper than the chart defcribes it. This idea fatisfied us for awhile; and under this delufion we ftood on at the fame rate, fometimes doubting the fidelity of our Arabs, and fometimes hoping that we were in the right courfe.

Q But

But we were at length awakened to a conviction of our suspicions. By our observation at noon, we found ourselves to be in the latitude of 26° 35′ N. which is above a degree to the southward of what we were yesterday. The deceit was too glaring, to be further concealed from us. We had been looking out the whole morning for the Egyptian shore, as the gulf of Suez is not reckoned to be ten leagues in breadth. We were instantly ascertained that we were upon the Egyptian shore. It now struck us, that our boat was originally bound for Cosire, and that the vizier of Yambo had put us on board of her, for the sake of reserving the major part of the freight to himself, which he actually did reserve, by the confession of the nokidah during the passage. So that we got to Cairo, he did not care by what route. He had performed the Xerif's orders, in dispatching us from Yambo, and as there is a frequented track from Cosire to Cairo by the river Nile, it is a sufficient reserve for the conscience of an Arab. The vizier had often pressed us to go by the way of Cosire, which we had as often rejected, from the idea of its being a more uncommon and dangerous road, than that by Suez; and as we were not compliant, he had thus tricked us into what we had determined to avoid.

In this persuasion, we charged our nokidah and pilot with perfidy, and informed them, to their utter astonishment, that the shore before us, was the Egyptian, and that we were not many miles distant from Cosire. Their ideas of navigation are entirely confined to the headlands and shoals, which lie upon the coast; and to obtain a knowledge of our situation from the quadrant, was as new, as it was unintelligible to them. Their fear, however, of our resentment, made these fellows at first persist, that we were bound for Suez; to which falshood they attested by swearing by their beards; an oath the most sacred to Mussulmen. But what perjuries will not fear lead mankind into? Their notions of

"Europeans

Europeans taught them to dread a detection of their behavior. Their ignorance gave them hopes of imposing this place upon us for Suez; and they apprehended that their lives would be the forfeit of a premature discovery. It was now plain, that they had taken the advantage of the night before last, to run over to the Egyptian coast. They had never before sailed in the dark, and they artfully contrived to deceive us, under cover of the night. All our difficulties were now solved. We had been led to mistake the gulf of Suez yesterday, for that of Akaba. It was directly astern of us when we awoke; and we did not discover that we had made a new shore. We had not at that time, the most distant imagination of the treachery which was intended us. We were puzzled, indeed, to account for the course we kept; but the situation of the coast might oblige us to change our direction; and the assurances of the Arabs of our being near the Cape, perfectly lulled us into a fatal security.

The pen would convey but a lifeless picture of our feelings in this important crisis. A thousand circumstances crowded upon our minds, to evince the cheat which had been put upon us. Several boats had left Yambo for Cosire, preceding our departure; and we had been informed, that all boats bound for Cosire, were obliged to make Cape Mahomet at this season, before they stretched over to the Egyptian shore. The boats that we had joined, were actually those bound for Cosire; and we had sailed with them for above three weeks, under the belief of their being destined for Suez. It is not so wonderful, that incidents of this nature should have escaped our notice. We mixed but little with the Arabs, and were such strangers to their language, that there was no occasion for their being upon their guard when they conversed before us. But Ibrahìm, our interpreter, had no such excuse for his want of discernment. Moments there doubtless were, when he might have suspected their design, if they had address enough to conceal it partly from him. We have no doubts of his honesty; but from the simplicity he has betrayed in this matter, draw but a bad omen of his services in the enterprize before us. It is too late to hesitate upon the step we are to take. Resistance is equally absurd and vain. Necessity, with all the force of a vortex, impels us forward. We cannot pretend to carry the boat to Suez, contrary to the inclinations of our mariners, and against the northerly monsoon. We know Cosire to be under the Turkish government, and immediately dependent on Cairo; and we have the vizier's pass, to afford us a safe-conduct to that place. We have no doubt of the virtue of this pass, however we have been deceived by the person who gave it. He had the Xerif's order to forward us to Suez; and after he has so materially benefited by our purses, we give him credit for an inclination to serve us, by the means of his master's signet, which we know to be respected in all Mahometan regions.

Our minds were somewhat relieved by these reflexions. We partook of the turtle at dinner with apparent cheerfulness; and even went so far, as to adopt their own measures, and express to the Arabs our indifference, in regard to the port we were going to. In this disposition we made the mosque of Cosire, without any other emotions, than what disappointment naturally excites in the human breast. The toils and dangers which we had undergone, envenomed the stings of that disappointment; and after a month's endeavors, we found ourselves nearly in the same situation, as when we set out from Yambo: not, indeed, so far removed from Suez, but infinitely in more uncertainty and distress.

At 7 in the evening we anchored in the harbor of Cosire; and find by the distance which we have run, that the island we remained at last night, was that of Shadwan, well known to the

English

English vessels which trade from India to Suez. As soon as it was dark, the nokidah went ashore, to advise the commandant of our arrival; and to interest him, as he assured us, in our behalf. To confess the truth, we had not the prospect of passing the most agreeable night. Our fortune was wrapped up in doubt, dark as the shades which enveloped the creation; and we anxiously looked for the returning light, to dispel the obscurity of the scene!

Thus, Madam, have I at length conducted you to Cosire, instead of the promised port of Suez. In pursuing the course of this narrative, you have been subjected, like the principal characters, to the inconstancy of fortune; who, in imitation of the light ones of the sex, finds a pleasure in deceiving those the most who aspire to the favor of her smiles. I have frequently had occasion to dissent against the well-known proverb of the Romans, "Fortune favors the brave," though I am far from pretending, that the undertakers of this voyage, are an instance of its fallacy. The fatigues that we have endured in a month's cruize in an open boat, during the hottest season of the Eastern year, and the dangers that we have ran in exploring a wild and piratical coast, were well encountered for the end we had in view. True fortitude is exalted by opposition, and, like the fabled Antæus, rises with fresh vigor from successive overthrows. The present moments, when our reception at this place, nay, our very safety, is precarious, are critical indeed, and teem with events, that may awaken curiosity, and excite the susceptible breast to regret the unseasonable interruption of this narrative.

If the foregoing sheets have the good fortune to meet with your

your approbation—if they are adjudged to contain the unstudied touches of nature, and interest the public in the fate of three unlucky travellers—I shall be tempted to renew the thread of our adventures, and recount the most remarkable occurrences of our journey from Cosire to Alexandria. The novelty of the track will engage the reader, where business is deficient; nor can he wholly be at a loss for amusement, in a region so untrodden, on a river so celebrated as the Nile!

It is a received maxim, that there is no incident in a man's life, but from which he may derive some instruction. If I have reaped any advantage from the late scenes I have been engaged in, it is a stock of philosophy, which has cost me no little pains in the acquisition; and will, I trust, prove sufficient to support me in any trial, to which the lot of humanity may hereafter subject me. But to my own sufferings may my indifference be confined! When I separate my concerns from those of my fellow-creatures; when I become deaf to the call of distress; or behold, unmoved, the tear of contrition, may I be rejected by the more enlightened class of society, and chiefly by her, who is one of its first and brightest ornaments!

I have the honour to be,

MADAM,

Your's, &c.

Cosire, in Upper Egypt,
9th July 1777.

A SERIES

A

SERIES OF ADVENTURES, &c.

IN THE YEAR M.DCC.LXXVII.

IN LETTERS TO A LADY.

LETTER II.

MADAM,

TO prove as good as one's word is the province of every honest man, but more particularly will it be expected where inclination and duty go hand-in-hand. Whatever may be the fate of my former letter, the specious name of honor will insure the performance of my promise, and lead me into error under a mistaken notion of things. The man of honor submits his better judgment to the opinion of the multitude, and sacrifices his friend's life or his own, to extend his reputation. In like manner, the author is betrayed by the secret impulses of vanity, and is so tenacious of the empty applauses of the croud, as to be still risking what little fame he may have acquired, in the pursuit of more. But you, Madam, have to answer for this transgression, and, though innocent of the intention, are unhappily the cause of a poor author adding to the number of his sins. There is doubtless matter enough in the pages which he has the honor to submit to your perusal; but in respect to the manner, he only wishes that he was possessed of your talent to excuse it to the world.

There

There is a regret mingled with the pleasure I feel in retracing my progress through a land, which has been renowned from the earliest times, and is replete with the noblest ruins of antiquity. Which gave birth to Cleopatra, and contains the ashes of Alexander! From whence music boasts its divine origin, and on whose mythology Homer formed the grounds of his immortal work! The parent of science! the nurse of heroes! and the monument, alas! of decayed greatness! Too severe, O Egypt! has been thy lot; too severe an example dost thou afford of the instability of human glory. It is in thy school that the proud should learn humility, the atheist religion; more instruction will he gain in the review of thy fortune, than from the dreams of philosophers or the lessons of divines. Here will he see the invincible Sesostris vanquished in his posterity; the public works through which he meant to hand down his name to latest ages, yielded to the conqueror, Time; and his once potent empire divided by the sword of infidels!—The sublime imagery of Shakespear rushes to my mind on the contemplation of this awful scene,

" The cloud-capt towers, the gorgeous palaces,
" The solemn temples, the great globe itself,
" Yea, all which it inherits, shall dissolve,"
&c. &c.

The fairest productions of art here bear the marks of barbarous rage, and ignorance usurps the fields, where learning reared her column to the skies. The far-famed Nile now rolls his stream through lonely plains, and sullen laves the shores, where freedom smiled; which Love and which the Muse were wont to grace!

For the sake of a more familiar stile, I have preferred the form of a diary in the following narrative. I detest formality, and would sacrifice a well-turned period for the appearance of ease.

ease. The reader who looks for connected accounts, Ciceronian epithets, and polished expressions, in these rambling pages, will be greatly mistaken in the intention of the author; whose highest aim is to amuse the curious, and to touch the humane. Loose hints, concise descriptions, and unstudied details, sum up the chief parts of a work, which is merely published to promote the interests of humanity, and to afford a caution to the unwary traveller. There is one thing which he has most reason to fear will be objected to it, and that is, the want of the marvellous and surprizing, in a region so involved among the fables of antiquity.

THURSDAY, 10th JULY.

Cosire is situated in 26° 20′ north latitude, and is the southernmost port on the coast of Egypt. It has been a place of great note, and is still considerable for the exportation of grain to Arabia, which is brought in the caravan from the Nile. There is a prodigious high range of mountains behind it, which are an exact counterpart to those on the Arabian side; through these mountains is the road to the Nile. The harbor is defended to the northward by a reef of rocks, which stretch about a mile into the sea; and to the southward and westward, the land forms it into the shape of a crescent. Here is water for ships of burden; but without a pilot, they could not venture into the bason. The fort of Cosire stands upon a rising ground; and is a square building of about four hundred yards in circumference. It was formerly strong enough, to have withstood a regular attack; the walls being of stone, and raised to a considerable height. But at present, it is in a defenceless state; the breaches which time has made in it, being repaired with mud-work, and not more than three dismantled pieces of cannon left to protect it. The town

town itfelf is in a more miferable condition. Of all the numerous houfes which once reared their heads here, nothing but their walls are ftanding; and of the mofques, which good Muffulmen efteem beyond all other edifices, but the remains of two now can be difcerned, and one of thefe bowed almoft to the ground. The reader is here prefented with a view of a place, fo new to obfervation. It is a matter of conjecture whether, in fifty years hence, there will be any traces of habitations on a fpot, which at this moment exhibits only the outlines of them. But if the town difplays fo unfavorable an appearance, it falls infinitely fhort of the dreary afpect of the country around it. So far from a tree being in fight, the eye cannot catch a verdant fpot, whether it furveys the mountains within, or the plain that ftretches along the fea-fhore. And this defart is the barrier to the celebrated and fertile land of Upper Egypt!

At 7 o'clock the principal Turk and two Arabs came on board the boat, to invite us afhore, and to acquaint us that there was a houfe provided for our reception. We had paffed but an uncomfortable night, and were overjoyed to be relieved from our fufpence, by fo polite an invitation. We readily accepted of it, and ourfelves and our baggage were conveyed to the houfe appointed for us; which, though the beft in the town, was little better than an Englifh barn. Here we were received by an Arab of diftinction, whom we found to be the fon of the Arabian fhaik or prince of the diftrict, who was abfent on an excurfion to the Nile. Though the garrifon of the fort of Cofire is under the command of a Turkifh officer, appointed by the bey of Cairo, the government of the city and the commerce of the port, are entirely in the hands of the Arabs; to the chief of whom we are recommended by the vizier of Yambo. This is a piece of intelligence which we have learnt from the nokidah of our boat, and indeed, the vizier could do no lefs, to atone for his treachery

treachery towards us. The young man very politely supplied his father's place, and informed us, it was his intention to accompany us to the Nile, as soon as the caravan, which was daily expected, should arrive from thence. This he considered as the least dangerous and expensive mode of travelling; as a few camels would require a guard, and run more risk of an attack from the banditti which infest the mountains of Upper Egypt. With these plausible reasons we are obliged to acquiesce, though the delays we undergo are not the smallest mortifications we meet with. Our room was crouded the whole day with visitors, whose curiosity led them to view us. Europeans they might have seen here in disguise, but the habit which we wore was evidently new and surprizing to them. Among these people there were two Christians, who appeared much rejoiced to see us, and presented us with a dish of rusks, which were very light and palatable. They are clothed in the Arabian dress, which we likewise intend to assume when we set out on our journey, not only to avoid the inquisitive and illiberal temper of the natives, but for the sake of coolness. The loose and light vestments of the oriental nations are admirably adapted to the nature of their climate; and the numerous folds of the muslin turban, are the best invented defence against the burning rays of a vertical sun.

FRIDAY, 11th JULY.

We had company, as yesterday, to pay us their compliments this morning, for which we are as much indebted to the indolence of temper, as to the politeness of the Arabs. If we except their hours of devotion, they have no other way of passing their time than in visits of ceremony. Books are entirely neglected by them, except those of a religious turn; and which are more calculated to infuse the gloom of superstition into the mind of a Mussulman, than

than to afford amusement. Poetry itself, which seems to have sprung from the pastoral regions of Arabia, is no longer courted nor acknowledged by this degenerate race; and the names of their poets are more honored and known in Europe than in Asia. Strange as this assertion may appear, there is nothing more certain than the truth of it; and it cannot be disputed; that the propagation of a novel and bigotted faith, has been always attended with the same melancholy effects in every part of the globe. The blindness of zeal destroys every thing that is not intimately connected with the object of its pursuit; and the high-priests of a new-fangled doctrine, are the Goths and Vandals of the age, who overturn the altars dedicated to the arts and sciences.

Another Christian accompanied those who paid us a visit yesterday, and we learn, to our great satisfaction, that they are waiting for the caravan which is to convey us to the Nile. There is an inexpressible pleasure in meeting with those of our own religion in a foreign land, and especially where the difference of opinion is sufficient to occasion the worst of treatment to a traveller. But it is universally acknowledged, that Christians have greater privileges, and experience better usage in Egypt, than in any other part of Turkey. Governed by her own beys, and but nominally dependant on the Porte, she deviates wholly from the false system which subsists in the Ottoman politics; and studies her own interest in the favor she shews to Christianity. Too supine for study, and too proud for labor, the Mahometan resigns the pen and plough to the industrious Christian. But for this despised tribe, the wheels of government would stand still, and the Nile would yearly fatten his banks in vain. The mechanics, as well as husbandmen, are of this persuasion; and the secretaries, as well as most of the confidential officers of the great and petty princes of Egypt, profess the Christian tenets.

The Turkish commandant has just sent to acquaint us, by our nokidah, that it is customary to search the baggage of travellers, that the duties of the port may be levied on any merchandize they possess. Though we assured them that we were fitted out, not as merchants, but as travellers, we could have no objection to a practice so usual in all places. In the evening, therefore, we were visited by some of the principal people, to whom we opened our trunks; and can say, that the scrutiny was less rigid, and conducted with more decency, than in many of the custom-houses of Europe. While these gentry were drinking coffee with us, at sunset intelligence was brought us of the caravan's approach, which afforded us no inconsiderable pleasure. The young shaik was informed of his father's arrival, and hastened to receive him. We soon learnt that only a part of the caravan was come with the Arabian shaik; who sent us his compliments, and excuses for not waiting on us, being fatigued with the journey. He promised to visit us early in the morning, to provide us with camels, and to adjust the œconomy of our expedition by the return of the caravan, which would certainly be here in a few days. If we encounter no further delays, we shall not repine at being betrayed into this route, which is new, and may afford us matter of curious speculation. As the wind also continues to blow from the N. W. quarter, we can the more easily give credit to our nokidah, who assures us, that our boat would not have gotten to Suez this month to come, and that the season alone prevented our being carried to Suez agreeably to our desire. As this fellow seems very earnest to serve us, and has promised to remain here until we depart for the Nile, we the more readily forget the trick he played us, which the apprehensions of the vizier's resentment might induce him to commit. That titled villain has principally benefited by our misfortunes; and, were this last evil necessary to fill up the measure of them, instead of paying the enormous sum of 650 dollars for

our

our paſſage to Coſire, we might have been tranſported here at a trifling expence, on any of the numerous boats that trade between Yambo and this place.

SATURDAY, 12th JULY.

We were ſurprized this morning with an early viſit from the Arabian ſhaik, attended by the chief people of the town. He is an elderly man, of a good countenance and a polite addreſs, and in every reſpect anſwers to the idea which an European would form of one of theſe leaders. He confirmed the tenders of ſervice, and promiſes of protection, made us by his ſon; and ſeemed willing to diſpatch us immediately to the Nile with the few camels he had here, provided we were content to leave our baggage behind, to be ſent after us by the great caravan. Though our living on the Nile until our baggage came up, would be more agreeable in reſpect to the ſituation, and the cheapneſs of proviſion, when compared with this place, we determined to wait for the caravan, which we now found was not expected theſe eight days. And this not only on account of ſecurity, but as it appeared to be the wiſh of the ſhaik, who declared his intention of accompanying us himſelf, or putting us under the protection of his ſon during the journey. When this point was ſettled, we requeſted the ſhaik to furniſh us with a camel to carry a letter to the Nile, from thence to be forwarded to the India Company's agent at Cairo, that he might be adviſed of our arrival in theſe parts. To this the ſhaik chearfully conſented, and we addreſſed the following letter to Mr. Baldwin, and delivered it to the Arab.

To

To GEORGE BALDWIN, Efq.

" SIR,

" We take the liberty to acquaint you of our arrival at this place on the 10th inftant. A concurrence of accidents has obliged us to undertake this uncommon route, although it was our intention to have proceeded to Cairo by the way of Suez. As we are charged with difpatches of the utmoft confequence from the prefident of Madras to the Court of Directors, we flatter ourfelves, that this circumftance will be a further inducement to your humanity, to intereft yourfelf with the bey of Cairo in our behalf, that he may immediately iffue paffes to Ghinnah and Jirje, for our better fecurity in going down the Nile. We have a protection from the vizier of Yambo to the Arab fhaik of this diftrict, who has treated us with great civility, and promifes to fend us to the Nile, under charge of his fon, by the return of the caravan, which is expected here in a few days. It is with his affiftance that we are enabled to forward you this intelligence of our fituation. When we have the pleafure, Sir, of feeing you at Cairo, we fhall do ourfelves the honor to deliver the letters we are charged with to your addrefs, which we confider of too much importance to you to be trufted to this conveyance.

" In the hopes of meeting with you in a fhort time, and of expreffing our fenfe of the fervices which your influence in this country may afford us, we remain,

SIR,
    Your very obedient, &c."

" Cofire, on the coaft of Upper Egypt,
    12th July, 1777."

When the fhaik and his courtiers had taken their leave, we had a continual levee the whole morning, and the durbar of an eaftern prince

prince could not be more crouded than our apartments. We treated our vifitors with coffee only, as it is the cuftom of the country for every one to carry his principal entertainment about with him, which is the pipe. It fupplies the place of meat and drink, and even thought itfelf; though they tell you here, that the pipe is the beft friend imaginable to meditation. Be this as it may, the Arabs do not feem to benefit by it in this refpect; though never did I fee a paffion carried to fuch excefs as this.

At noon the young fhaik accompanied us in a walk about the town, and as we paffed the fort, we were faluted with one gun : a compliment for which we made a fmall donation to the gunner. In this excurfion we gathered nothing, but a nearer view of the poverty of the people, and the dreary face of the country. At our return home we had another vifit from the fhaik, to acquaint us, that the carriage of a letter to Cairo would be very heavy, and that we might as well omit fending it. When he named 60 dollars for the trouble, we were not a little ftartled at the fum, and fhould have been well inclined to drop the matter, had we not held it of great moment to our concerns. We declined, however, giving fuch an extravagant price, for what we told the fhaik was of little confequence in itfelf. He was called away by fome bufinefs in the midft of this conference, and our nokidah offered to follow him, and to bring him to reafon in his demand. The fellow accordingly went on this embaffy to the fhaik, who confented at length to take 20 dollars for the difpatch of the letter. The money was immediately advanced, and the camel was that night fent off to the Nile, if any reliance could be placed on the word of an Arab. The attempt to impofe on us in a charge of this kind, was only confidered by us as an effay on the ftrength of our purfes ; and we are in hopes, from our having lowered them fo confiderably in their prices, that we fhall be the lefs liable to impofition, in our future dealings with the natives of Egypt.

Our

Our evening, as usual, was passed in receiving company, among whom we saw several people who were to be our fellow-travellers. There was a merchant, in particular, who was very intelligent, and offered to accommodate us with his house, on our arrival at Ghinnah, a large city on the Nile, to which the caravan is to carry us. He tells us, to our great satisfaction, that we shall find no difficulty in procuring boats for our passage down the Nile; and that at the easy expence of 25 dollars. So that our money holds out to Cairo, we must be content to pay for every inch of the road, through this strange and remote country. We have been obliged to make several little presents to the great people already; but these have been confined to pieces of Indian handkerchiefs, and bottles of European liquors. These the Turkish commandant carried away under his garment, with all the gravity peculiar to his nation; and, to heighten the joke, he was pleased to let the spirits pass under the denomination of physic.

The weather here is remarkably pleasant for this time of the year. This must be owing to the prevalence of the northerly winds, that blow across the Red Sea to this coast. Neither are the dews so heavy and troublesome, as we found them on the shores of Arabia. A lucky circumstance to travellers, who have been so long accustomed to the magnificent and spacious canopy of the sky, that they cannot sleep within doors, or be confined beneath the low and contracted roof of a chamber. We have a good yard belonging to the house, where we pass the nights.

SUNDAY, 13th JULY.

Our charges are considerably augmented by the price of water, which is become so scarce, that we are at times at a loss for a draught of it. The people here drink of a bad sort, which they bring

bring from a spring at above a league's distance, it not being in their power to pay a quarter of a dollar per skin, for so considerable a necessary of life.

The northerly wind continues to blow so strongly, that we have great reason to think we should have been much longer beating our passage to Suez, than we shall be in getting to Cairo by the route we have stumbled upon. The character of our nokidah begins to be again doubtful. After all his promises to stay by us until our departure, and to see us provided with good camels, he came to us this evening with the shaik, and, after a parade of his attachment towards us, pretended to regret the necessity which called him away. He even persuaded the old man to declaim in his behalf; to acquaint us that the letter which the vizier of Yambo had sent by the nokidah, was of the utmost moment to our interest; that we were thereby entitled to the shaik's protection, as far as his life would afford it; and that he hoped we would remember him, now he was about to leave us. Notwithstanding our indignation was rouzed at the prevarication of this fellow, we did not hold him worth our attention, nor did we chuse to let the shaik into the reason of our desiring his stay. It was our business to appear to place an unlimited confidence in the man, whom chance had made the master of our fates. And indeed he acted very impartially on the occasion, and concluded his harangue, with intreating us to consult our inclinations only, when we fixed on a recompence for the nokidah's services. We thanked him for his goodness, and carelesly added, that we would think on this subject in the morning. There is no doubt but the nokidah's waiting our motions, might be prejudicial to his affairs which summon him to Yambo; but it was our declared intention to have made him a very handsome consideration on this account. To have sent advices to our friends in India of our safety, and of our departure

ture for the Nile, was a matter which we had much at heart. This very fellow had promised to accomplish it. He has undoubtedly forfeited all further pretensions to our favor, so that the present which we give him will be very trifling.

MONDAY, 14th JULY.

The greatest part of the morning was spent in a conversation with the nokidah, and in writing a letter to the vizier, in testimony of this fellow's good treatment of us. His conducting us to this place appears to have been more the vizier's crime than his; and, in spite of his recent abuse of our confidence, our distresses had not deprived us of the principle of forgiveness, so far as to permit us to deny him a request of this nature. The safety of his family, who were in the vizier's power, depended, as he assured us, upon our word. The address was extraordinary enough, to a man who had been the primary cause of our misfortunes; and it may be expected that we did not miss the opportunity to give a vent to our indignation. But, irritated as we were against the minister, we disdained even to expostulate with him on his unfair proceedings. We were determined not to afford him matter of triumph, and concealed the effects which his detested policy had been attended with. The letter was expressed in general terms; and we bore witness to the conduct of the nokidah, as far as regarded his attention and respect towards us. With this he seemed better satisfied than with the present we made him. We assigned but ten dollars for himself and the pilot, of whom I have made such frequent mention in the journal of the boat. This was a sufficient mortification to people, whose expectations had been raised by the rewards we promised them on our safe arrival at Suez, and whose ideas of our wealth were so extravagant. The several trifles we had left in the boat amounted to no inconsiderable sum; but the value of these were already forgotten. We were more liberal to the boat's crew, who came at the same time to take leave of us; as they had been the innocent instruments in the execution of the plot, which was devised against us in the town of Yambo.

We perceive a jealousy subsists between the Turk and Arab on our account, which we have no reason to be concerned at. As the presence of the former will prove an infallible check on the motions of the shaik, we shall rather be desirous of fomenting the difference, by paying an equal attention to these chiefs, than, by attaching ourselves to one, run the chance of incurring the resentment of the other. The government of the district is undoubtedly in the hands of the shaik, who holds it from the mandate of the bey of Cairo; and to his influence we must commit ourselves in our journey to the Nile. But the ostensible dignity lies with the Turkish officer, who commands the fort of Cosire in the name of the bey, and is placed here as a spy on the conduct of the shaik. They never meet at our house but by accident; and then nothing but common civility passes between them. The Arab, in particular, is uneasy at the frequent visits of the other, and it is no longer ago than this morning, that he cautioned us to trust to him alone for the supply of our wants. While the Turk, on the other hand, let us this afternoon into the knowledge of every thing that we wanted to be informed of. The customary price of camels to the Nile will be but trifling, and we hope, by his means, to escape the impositions which we should otherwise incur from the poverty of the Arabs, who, in many respects, are of no unamiable character. We have found them to be decent in their manners, and temperate in their diet; addicted to no warmth or levity of temper, respectful in the last degree to their parents, charitable in their dispositions, and

humane

humane to their dependents: ſtrictly attentive to all the forms of their religion, and wholly unacquainted with the unnatural vices which originated in the Eaſt, and have long diſgraced the Chriſtian empire. But this aſſemblage of good qualities is thoroughly tainted by the luſt of lucre, which no bounds are forcible enough to reſtrain. Their command of mind is applied to facilitate the baſeſt purpoſes of gain, and their pretended ſanctity often ſerves to cover ſome ſcheme of fraud. It muſt be owned, the neceſſities of people, who almoſt live in a ſtate of nature, muſt bear hard on the innate principles of goodneſs which they may poſſeſs; and when the prejudices of their religion, which inculcate the practice of deceit towards Chriſtians, are thrown into the balance, it will not be ſo much wondered at, that the ſcale of injuſtice prevailed againſt us: that we were ſo maltreated in Arabia, or that we ſhall be obliged to win our way through the deſarts of Thebaïs to the Nile, by dint of gold.

The young ſhaik, after his father had left us, took a liking to a very good ſpying-glaſs which we had brought with us. As he is likely to be our fellow-traveller, we begged his acceptance of it. At the ſame time our nokidah came to take his leave; and we parted on good terms, notwithſtanding what had paſſed between us.

TUESDAY, 15th JULY.

This morning a jar of water was brought to us from the ſhaik, which had juſt arrived from the mountains. He had heard us complain yeſterday of the want of ſweet water, and very politely ſent this jar to our houſe, which had come for his own drinking. We were content to pay three dollars for the carriage, as we ſet an higher value upon water, in our preſent circumſtances, than if it were wine. We had an early viſit from the old man, to
whom

whom we prefented a piece of Indian chintz for his women. Had we been apprized of our going this road, we might have brought numberlefs trifles from our veffel, which would have appeared of fome eftimation in the eyes of a people, to whom all foreign articles have the charms of novelty. This man however has feen more of the world than the generality of his countrymen. He has been twice at Conftantinople; and at Alexandria, he tells us, he went on board an Englifh man of war of fixty guns, from which he feems to have derived an high idea of the power and dignity of the Britifh nation. He has been comforting us with the hopes of the caravan's not exceeding the time appointed for its appearance; which now approaches, to our great fatisfaction. There is nothing to be feen here but fea, mountain, and fky; and we long to be coafting the banks of the Nile, and to become eye-witneffes of the fertility and beauty of a country, fo celebrated by hiftorians, and confirmed in our admiration by the teftimony of the people here, who are never tired of repeating its praifes. We learn that our boat, and four others, failed this morning for Yambo; and that three larger ones remain here to receive their lading from the caravan. The paffage to Yambo can be made with eafe in four or five days. What a contraft to the long and tedious voyage that we experienced to this place!

Nothing is a greater proof of the warlike difpofitions of the Arabs, than the pleafure they take in the infpection of arms of all kinds. Our fwords, guns, and piftols, have undergone a thoufand examinations; and been honored with a profufion of applaufes, not, we fufpect, without hopes, on their fide, of profiting by our politenefs. Were a fword or fpear to be put into the hand of an Arab, whatever difguife he might be in, his bent of mind would as quickly betray itfelf, as did Achilles', when he handled the arms which Ulyffes placed before him. He is always

ways armed as if going to battle; and we never fee any one, whofe profeffion allows of it, unprovided with a pair of loaded piftols in his girdle, a fabre and a dagger by his fide, and a fpear of about fix feet in length in his right hand. In his left he always carries a pipe, which, moderately fpeaking, is not five minutes together from his lips in the courfe of the day. Though this general practice of carrying fire-arms on peaceable occafions, is totally repugnant to the ideas of civilized minds, there is nothing but what may be reconciled to us by the force of habit; and we now view this threatening apparatus of war without the fmalleft emotion. In the evening the fhaik brought us a plate of unripened limes, which, indifferent as they were, we underftand have come from the neighborhood of the Nile.

WEDNESDAY, 16th JULY.

We are very fortunate in refpect to the owner of the houfe we live in. He is an old Arab, of a civil demeanor and a quiet temper; and if ever a mortal paffed away an inoffenfive life, it is this hoft of ours. His worldly cares extend not beyond the little œconomy of an humble roof, and the fale of a few articles, with which he makes fhift to provide for the calls of nature. The only luxury he taftes of, is his pipe of tobacco and his cup of coffee; and his fole enjoyment, is the tendance of a milch goat, that follows him about with the docility of a dog. The milk of this animal he kindly referves for our ufe; and, indeed, it is ferviceable to us, in a miferable place, where milk is not to be procured. In the courfe of fuch a fimple life, it is not likely that he fhould imbibe the errors which higher ftations are apt to betray their poffeffors into; and there is no doubt but the prayers of this poor Arab are acceptable to the Almighty difpofer of all things. Content carries along with it the afpect of every virtue;

and

and not to repine at the destiny which Heaven has allotted us, is certainly of more solid importance to mankind, than the attainment of a thousand dazzling talents, which, by fitting us to the admiration of this world, too often render us indifferent to the acquisition of a more glorious recompence.

The shaik and the commandant are become very regular in their visits to us. By this particular attention we conceive hopes of the caravan's approach, as we do not think they would thus court us through mere form. The Turk is by much the more modest of the two, which must be attributed to a more general knowledge of the world. He has asked for nothing but the liquor before mentioned; and has received nothing from us, but a piece of muslin handkerchiefs, which we presented him with last night. The Arab does not maintain this decency in his conduct, though he is by no means open in his demands. He is continually asking us, through the channel of our interpreter, of the things we possess; and this morning desired to look at a curious pair of pistols of mine, which I had carefully concealed from his knowledge. Though I could not learn in what manner he had discovered them, I was obliged to promise them to him on our arrival at the Nile; when we fondly flattered ourselves to be delivered from the necessity of standing upon our guard. These pistols have a stop upon the cocks, which must render them safer to an Arab, who is accustomed, on a march, to sleep with them in his girdle.

The weather was hotter to-day than we have before experienced it, which we attribute to an alteration in the wind, that has blown from the land, though very faintly. Were it not for the constant gales which prevail in these seas, the coasts would be intolerably hot, as the soil is nothing but rock and sand.

THURSDAY,

THURSDAY, 17th July.

The fhaik brought us this morning a bottle of cinnamon-water under his cloak. We were prevailed on to tafte it, out of compliment to him, who fhewed us the example, but we heartily repented of it. Whether owing to the ftill, or whatever caufe it might be, there was a copperas tafte in the liquor, that did not agree with our ftomachs. This will be a caution how we make free with foreign liquors, among a people, whofe ignorance may be impofed on by the venders of thefe articles.

We have difcovered an amiable trait in the character of the old man, which has confiderably heightened our opinion of him. He has a paternal regard for his fubjects, and feems to fhare in any innocent recreation they can take. It was no longer ago than laft night, that a flave-boy, belonging to our company, was playing on the fiddle for the entertainment of the fhaik. The novelty of the found brought a crowd about the gate of the yard, where we were fitting on carpets to enjoy the cool of the evening. The old man perceived them to be pleafed with the mufic, and afked our permiffion to let them come in. This was no fooner granted, than the yard was filled with people of all ranks, who expreffed great fatisfaction and furprize at the fkill of a boy, who might be put on a footing with the blind fiddlers that fet a country wake in motion. The ideas of the better fort of a fimple people, cannot be expected to be more refined than thofe of the lower clafs of a polifhed nation. Nature is the fame in every climate, and betrays its want of cultivation, by an undiftinguifhing tafte in the feveral degrees of perfection to which the arts and fciences may be carried. The notes of a violin or flute may touch a rude ear with fenfations of delight, although not regulated by the paufes of time; or how can we pretend to receive pleasure from the wild notes of the wood-lark or nightingale? The truth is, we look not for any excellence in the bird, but what nature has afforded. The sweetness of his pipe makes ample amends for the irregularity of the measure; and we drink the melody, without feeling the want of correctness.

We had a visit as usual from the Turk, who watches his time, and comes always after the departure of the shaik. He informs us, that he has just had a messenger, who brings advice of the immediate departure of the caravan from the Nile. If this account be true, it must arrive within two days at furthest. The Turk shewed us a chop or signet, that he received from Ibrahim Beg, the bey of Cairo, nominating him to the command of the fort of Cosire. He is a very obliging and good-humored man; and it will be our inclination, as well as interest, to cultivate his friendship.

It is not often that we venture out of the doors of our gateway, except by moon-light, when we stray down to the seaside, which is the only prospect from this place that can bear observation. There was doubtless some appearance of cultivation, when the country was better inhabited, as the most stubborn soil cannot resist the efforts of industry. But as the power of the Turks began to decline in these parts, commerce failed apace; the inhabitants of this populous city removed by degrees to the more fertile banks of the Nile, and have left it a prey to poverty and desolation!

FRIDAY, 18th July.

We received very disagreeable tidings this morning relative to the caravan. The road is so infested with Buddoos, or wild Arabs, that its progress is delayed, until a reinforcement arrives from the Nile. It seems that a shaik of the mountains, through which

which the caravan paffes, has lately difappeared; fo that the fecurity which the country was in from his influence, no longer fubfifts. It is cuftomary for the caravan to pay a tribute to thefe chiefs, for a paffage through their diftricts. They are only robbers of a larger growth, and openly fet their protection to fale, to defend the traveller from the rapine of their tribes.

Diftreffing as this circumftance is, we are habituated to difappointment, and are arrived at that happy temper of mind, which rejects complaint in things unavoidable. As foon as a fufficient number of camels arrive, to tranfport ourfelves and baggage to the river, we are determined to fet out, in company with the fhaik or his fon; our number and fire-arms being fufficient, in our opinion, to put any band of robbers to flight. We fhall, at leaft, make up fifteen camels; not to mention the Chriftians and others, who might be glad to join us on fuch an expedition. But it is likely we fhall not be reduced to take this ftep, which, at any rate, muft be attended with rifk. The caravan may come before any further intelligence, as it only waited for the difperfion of the Buddoos, who are between it and this place; and the practice of giving notice of its approach, by lighting fires on the hills, has been difcontinued, fince the arrival of thefe troublefome neighbors.

The boats that waited for grain by the caravan, are now refolved upon failing, as its appearance is fo uncertain. The mafter of a boat belonging to Judda, came to us this morning to know our commands. As he feems to be a good fort of man, and this is the only opportunity we may have of advifing our friends in India of our fituation, we are determined to write by him, to the care of Mr. Horfeley at Mocha, who has his letters very punctually forwarded to Suez *per viam* Judda.

The Arabs are beggars from the higheft to the loweft. Indeed, fo facred is the ftate of poverty among them, that they hold its votaries

votaries as under the peculiar direction of Providence. And this humane notion is the source of that charity, which is the most general virtue they possess. It is not, therefore, to be wondered at, that an Arab feels not the shame which overspreads the cheek of an European petitioner. He asks, without scruple, for what he thinks his poverty entitles him to; and intrudes himself in his rags into the presence of his superiors, from which he seldom or never experiences a repulse. A son of a shaik of Yambo is about to return thither on one of the boats, and came to-day to demand a present of us. As we were at a loss what to offer him, the old shaik stood our friend on this occasion, and gave him two gold pieces in our name, called mauheboops, of the value of one dollar and an half each. These we are to give him credit for when we settle accounts with the shaik. In the evening the man came for our letters, which we delivered to him.

SATURDAY, 19th JULY.

The air was so bleak during the night, that we were glad to retire into the house, though the place we sleep in is defended from the wind, by the height of the walls. This is one of the finest climates under the sun, the air serene and wholesome, and the sky always unclouded. The rays of the sun are tempered by the refreshing breezes from the sea, which constantly blow during the hotter months of the year. The southerly winds prevail only in December, January, and February; and at the changes of the moon, they are sometimes felt for a day or two in the other months. From our experience of this sea, we do not think it practicable for a vessel to get up to Suez later than March. But then she may always reach Cosire, whence her packets, and even her goods, may be conveyed at an easy expence to the Nile. Ghinnah, a city of Upper Egypt, is situated about 130 miles W. N. W.

of

of Cofire; thither the caravan goes, and there boats may be had in great plenty for Cairo, which is 500 computed miles from thence. This route can be only recommended to a packet-boat with difpatches from India, or to a veffel that lofes her paffage to Suez; as the expence of boat-hire down the river, and the cuftoms of this port, would prove a confiderable draw-back on the profits of the voyage. But in fuch a fituation, we doubt not that veffels would find their account in coming here, inftead of repairing to Judda, as the fnow Adventure had orders to do, to the great lofs of her owners. A treaty of commerce might as readily be effected with the princes of Upper Egypt, as with the bey of Cairo; if the India Company do not confider this trade as prejudicial to their interefts. It is not my intention, at prefent, to enter into a difcuffion of this matter, as I acknowledge myfelf but an incompetent judge of it. But if the fpecies of goods which are carried to the Cairo market, and the channels into which they are afterwards thrown, be confidered, it does not appear, that the eftablifhment of this commerce would operate materially to the Company's lofs. The cargoes for this track are chiefly of the fineft affortment, and their circulation confined to the ports of the Mediterranean; fo that it is not to be feared they will interfere with the fale of the Company's merchandife [*].

The Arabs here are much lefs referved in converfation than in Arabia. The fhaik himfelf has mentioned his wives to us more than once, though it is a fubject on which his countrymen at home preferve the ftricteft filence. But in proportion as they are removed from the land of their Prophet, it would feem that they throw off the aufterity which is infeparable from bigotry. Their features are confiderably relaxed here, of the folemnity that they

---

[*] It is not unlikely that this queftion will be decided by the Turks themfelves, whofe ficklenefs and rapacity may lead them to overfet an infant commerce, by means more forcible to thofe engaged in it, than the authority of the legiflature itfelf.

affect

affect at Yambo; and the old man relishes a joke with as much glee as ourselves. He has juſt now gained much upon our confidence by an inſtance of forbearance, which beſpeaks him somewhat diveſted of the rapacious ſpirit of his tribe. My European ſervant was imprudent enough to venture out in the duſk, into the quarter of the town where the *filles de joie* reſide. He was diſcovered by the patrole, and after having ſuffered ſome indignities, was hurried away to the guard-houſe, whence he was releaſed by the ſhaik's order, as ſoon as the report was made to him. This happened two nights ago, and was kept from our knowledge. The old man was very backward to mention the ſubject to us, which he did at length, on account, we believe, of the miſchief that might enſue to the fooliſh fellow, were he ever caught by the natives in ſuch a place again. Had this incident occurred at Yambo, or even at Mocha, where ſtrangers are leſs liable to impoſitions, there is no doubt but the ſervant would have been detained in priſon, until his liberty was purchaſed at the price of three or four hundred dollars.

The ſhaik brought us word this evening, that he had juſt received certain intelligence of the caravan having left the Nile. While he was ſitting with us, an expreſs arrived, intimating that a party of Buddoos were in the neighborhood, and had ſeized a camel and four aſſes belonging to the town, which had gone out this morning to fetch charcoal. The old man immediately ſignified his reſolution to ſally forth with a few attendants, and obſerve their motions. For this end he borrowed the pair of piſtols belonging to me, which he had long fixed his eye upon, and which I had promiſed to preſent him with on our arrival at Ghinnah. Fires were now lighted on the different eminences which overlook the town, and the drum beat to arms. Nor were theſe precautions uſeleſs, in ſuch a defenceleſs place as this, which might be plundered with great eaſe by a reſolute and well-accoutered

accoutered band. But thefe robbers are reported not only to be indifferently armed, but to be void of all fpirit when they meet with refiftance. The third part may be furnifhed with matchlocks, and the reft with fpears and fwords. A miferable race, wandering from hill to hill, and fubfifting on the pilfer of ftraggling paffengers. We prepared our fire-arms for their reception, fhould they venture to affault our caftle; and there was little occafion for our keeping a regular watch, as it was not poffible to obtain a found nap during the night, whofe "dull ear" (as Shakefpear denotes it) was deafened by the rattling of the drum, and the chorus of a war-fong. Thefe the Arabs continued until the morning dawned, and, delivering them from their fears, permitted us to take an hour's repofe.

SUNDAY, 20th July.

We find that the Turkifh commandant had every thing in readinefs in the fort, to have done execution among the Buddoos. The gunner this morning was fpunging the few pieces that are mounted on the walls, having drawn, we fuppofe, the charges of powder, which may ferve on a future occafion. The Turk breakfafted with us, and magnified, with the rhodomontade of his nation, the ftrength of his citadel, and the valor of his troops; both of which, however, we muft confefs, might withftand the attack of an army of fuch vagrants, as thefe have been reprefented to us!

Even in this remote corner of the globe the character of the Turks ftrongly difplays itfelf. Sufpicious of ftrangers, and jealous of obfervation, they endeavor to conceal their weaknefs under an oftentatious language. Though he has never invited us into his fort, the commandant frequently talks of the importance of his charge; and though the contempt which the fhaik entertains

entertains for him is too visible to escape our notice, he is willing to inspire us with an idea of his own superiority. Conscious that his power is daily mouldering away in these parts, the Turk grows more and more distrustful of the Arab; while the latter can no longer suppress the rancor which he has conceived against his tyrannical masters. To what lengths this mutual aversion will carry them, time alone can discover. But this appears probable: should a favorable conjuncture present itself to the Arabs, to recover the territories of Egypt, it will not pass by unheeded. This conquest of their Prophet's family may return into their hands, and then, by a natural course of things, revert to the dominion of the original possessor. Thus, by a retrograde motion, the chains of bondage may be unloosed, and the rights of the native be restored to him.

One of the present subjects of our apprehension is, that the house we live in will not last our time, should the caravan meet with further delays. The rafters are of the date-tree, and instead of plank or tiles, the floor is composed of rushes laid close together. On this loose sand is placed, and over all the coarse matts of the country. Materials of this sort must have a wonderful elasticity in them; and every step we take, is attended by an universal tremor of the house. Neither would a stranger imagine that we were better provided in regard to the roof. This is formed of nothing stronger than rushes, on which stones are heaped, to prevent their being scattered by the winds. But in this settled climate the native requires no defence, but against the rays of the sun; thunder and lightning being almost unknown to him; and even rain a very uncommon visitor. By the accounts of the inhabitants, no rain has fallen at Cosire for these three years past; nor does it ever exceed a shower or two, when it comes. Of this the structure of their remaining houses is an unquestionable proof; for being rebuilt with mud, and half

thatched

thatched with rushes, one day of rain would mix them with their mother earth.

MONDAY, 21st July.

Old and desolate as this town is, cats are the chief and almost only nuisance which we have found here. But we are infested with these vermin to such a degree, that no provision can be secured from their talons during the night. It is to no purpose to lock the door, when the roof is so unable to withstand their assaults. A droll adventure happened last night, in consequence of the voraciousness of these animals, which may not be unworthy of remark. We had been presented with a dish of nice cakes by one of our Christian acquaintance, which a servant, out of his great wisdom, hung up in the room where one of our companions slept. Though the doors and windows were flung open on account of the heat, he thought the cakes would be safer here than in any other place; and for the greater security, suspended them over the gentleman's bed. But the very reverse fell out. When all was quiet, the cats, which had been attracted in great numbers by the savory smell of the cakes, rushed in at once from all quarters, and, without the least respect to the intended guardian of them, and directed by instinct to their booty, flew in a tumultuous manner towards it. Our companion was awakened by the growling of two of these ferocious creatures, who were disputing for a prize on his pillow; and, finding by the noise which assailed his ears, that the combat raged with equal fury on all sides, he ran to a stick that stood near him, and with an activity equally new and surprizing, laid about him with such success, that his persecutors made off at length with the remains of the plunder. We, who took up our lodging in the yard, were disturbed by this uncommon tumult, which did not continue

continue lefs than a quarter of an hour. It immediately recalled to our minds an adventure of Don Quixote's, with this difference only, that the prefent was not a preconcerted one. It was perhaps happy for our friend, that the cats had fomething forcible enough to draw their attention from him, or his face and body might have fuffered equally with the knight's of facetious memory. Our mirth was increafed however according to the innocence of the diftrefs, which deprived him of his fleep during the whole night. This was every moment broken by the mewing of thefe animals, that hovered around the fcene of action until the day broke, and difclofed to the unfortunate hero the caufe of his perplexity.

Should we remain here much longer, we fhall not have wherewith to fupply the cravings of thefe people, who are continually importuning us for powder, ball, flints, and every article that they fix their eyes upon. Empty bottles are particularly acceptable to them; and the fhaik himfelf did not difdain to requeft a dozen for his own ufe. Even fuch trifles as thefe have given rife to jealoufies in this fimple place: nay, one of the fhaik's guards has gone fo far, as to throw out threats of vengeance againft our fervant Ibrahim, becaufe the preference of a few bottles was given to another. To punifh his infolence, we took upon us this morning to forbid this fellow the houfe. Since our firft arrival he has been remarkably officious, and profufe of his tenders of fervice; but as we have always confidered him in the light of a fpy, we did not regret the opportunity which permitted us to rid ourfelves of fo troublefome a vifitor.

TUESDAY, 22d July.

A boat arrived laft night from Tor, in the gulf of Suez, which brings intelligence that there are four Englifh veffels ftill

at

at Suez. We may therefore flatter ourselves with the hopes of relieving our friends in India from their apprehensions for our safety: the accounts we have hitherto sent being unsatisfactory, and their conveyance uncertain. Our shaik likewise informed us, in the course of his visit this morning, that two Europeans had arrived in a boat at Tor, and had set out on camels for Suez without any escort, about a month ago. These we know to be the gentlemen already mentioned to have touched at Yambo, and who had the charge of the packet which Captain Dibdin brought from Madras. We could not but congratulate ourselves on being carried by this road instead of that by Tor, which would infallibly have been the furthest port that our boat could have reached in the Red Sea, at this season. Our situation appears to us in every respect more eligible than theirs. The country between Tor and Suez is esteemed the most uncivilized in all Arabia. There is no regular caravan, and we cannot but tremble for the security of these adventurers. Their appearance indeed is a powerful circumstance in their favor; and it might be better for us, if we were as bare of baggage and money as they are reported to be.

The shaik informs us, that another camel and some asses have been taken by the buddoos, which occasioned his sending an express last night to meet the caravan, and warn it of the danger. The alarm which these robbers have spread through the country, has certainly been the cause of its extraordinary delay, which is so grievous to the inhabitants of Cosire, that the Turkish commandant just now told us, he has dispatched a camel to Ghinnah, to request that an additional guard may be sent after the caravan, to conduct it hither. A scarcity of every article of life has been felt here for some time, and famine itself can only be warded off for a few days longer.

There is a trait in the character of the Arabs, which is very disgusting;

difgufting; but no more peculiar to them than to Muffulmen in general. They are fo dirty in their linen, that though they take great pains to adorn themfelves in gay apparel, this habitual uncleanlinefs cannot be concealed. Their fhirt is of the coarfeft linen, and much refembles the Englifh fhift. Their drawers are loofe, and ufually of filk, and their under garment of dyed linen, except on particular occafions, when it is exchanged for a more coftly one of filk. Over this they throw a cloak of broadcloth, which is edged with fattin or fur. They wear flippers on their feet, and turbans on their heads, of much lefs magnitude than the other followers of Mahomet. The drefs of the women varies little from that of the men. Their fhirt and drawers are the fame, but their whole habit confifts of a loofe gown, which is gathered up and faftened at the breaft. They take the greateft pride in their hair, which falls down their necks in numerous plaits. But this is concealed when they go abroad by a part of their vails, with as much care as their faces. The vail is divided into two pièces, and joins by a clafp on the forehead, which is either of gold or of precious ftones: fo that the forehead and eyes are entirely expofed to public view. The complexions of the females are much fairer than thofe of the men, which muft be attributed to the care which is taken to preferve them from the fun. In this particular they feem to be a diftinct fpecies from their fwarthy mates; and are really fo in refpect to the neatnefs of their drefs, and the liberality of their principles. This encomium is but due to their merit, and falls fhort of the affiftance which we experienced from them in the hour of our greateft diftrefs.

WEDNESDAY,

WEDNESDAY, 23d JULY.

We were agreeably ſtruck this morning with the appearance of three camels, which were haſtening to the town. They brought the news of the caravan's approach. It left the river in three diviſions, and travels by eaſy ſtages towards Coſire. The firſt diviſion fell in with the wild Arabs who were lately in this quarter, and was attacked by them, and plundered of forty camels loaded with merchandize. It happened to be the ſmalleſt, and unprovided with a proper guard. The two larger diviſions will not be here before to-morrow, and are ſaid to conſiſt of one thouſand or twelve hundred camels. But the danger we learn is now over, as theſe banditti are gone towards Suez, which is the road to their own country. This is the intelligence which we received from the Turk at breakfaſt, and it was confirmed by the ſhaik, when he came to wiſh us joy of our ſpeedy departure.

By theſe camels there is little come beſides wheat, and we are ſtill diſtreſſed for good water. We have been obliged to drink the water of this place for theſe two days paſt: it is very brackiſh and unpalatable: but we take the precaution to boil it for our uſe; and this has probably prevented its diſagreeing with us.

One of the plagues of Egypt ſeems to be renewed to-day, to our extreme annoyance and regret. We had been quite free from the inſects which are continually engendered in hot climates, when a warm ſoutherly wind has brought ſuch a ſwarm of flies along with it, as to prevent the poſſibility of obtaining our cuſtomary nap after dinner. The whole houſe is filled with them, and not a moment's ſatisfaction is to be found within doors. This is the firſt time that the wind has been in the ſoutherly quarter ſince our arrival at Coſire; and conſequently is the firſt fair wind that we ſhould have met with, had our boat purſued her voyage to Suez. The gulph of Suez is ſo narrow, that the wind muſt be very favorable to carry up a boat ſo badly fitted out as ours; and all attempts on our part to beat up the channel, muſt have proved fruitleſs. Though the charge of duplicity againſt the vizier and the nokidah of Yambo, remains unrefuted, this prevalence of contrary winds is no impeachment of their experience of this ſea. The weather is confiderably changed by the alteration of the wind; and had we a thermometer to announce it, I am convinced that it is hotter by many degrees, than it was yeſterday. We are the more incommoded by the heat, as our houſe has not a window towards the ſea.

THURSDAY, 24th JULY.

The ſhaik this morning propoſed to us a ſcheme of getting expeditiouſly to the Nile, though he could not but take notice of the heavy charges that would attend it. We had been repeating our complaints of the delay of the main body of the caravan, and of the detriment which our ſtay here, would be of to our affairs. This was a fine opening for him to benefit by our neceſſity, which he judged was too preſſing, to admit of heſitation in point of expence. He offered to procure us as many camels, as would tranſport us and our baggage, from thoſe which arrived yeſterday. For theſe, however, we were to pay double the price of camel-hire to Ghinnah, on account of the ſcarcity of theſe animals at preſent. To this meaſure we would readily have ſubſcribed, had not the price he demanded, exceeded trebly what it ought to have done from his own calculation. When he even reduced it, at our remonſtrance, to eight dollars per camel, we were ſtill at a loſs how to act. We found that we could not manage without eighteen camels, for the accommodation of ourſelves,

selves, the ſhaik, and an eſcort of ten ſoldiers, which he thinks is the ſmalleſt we can have, and for whoſe attendance we muſt pay ſixty dollars. As it is impoſſible for us to aſcertain the charges that we ſhall incur on the way to Cairo; as the impoſitions that we may meet with on the Nile may equal, if not exceed thoſe which we have already experienced, it was but prudent to have an eye to our purſes, which may be exhauſted before we find a friend to repleniſh them. But our deliberations on this head, were put an end to by the advice of the other principal people of the town, who came upon us at this critical moment. They repreſented to us the danger that we ſhould run, in travelling with ſo ſmall a body; that the caravan's delay was certainly occaſioned by alarms on the road; and that, at all events, it was better for us to wait for intelligence from the caravan, before we attempted to proceed. Nay, they even went ſo far as to reprobate the conduct of the ſhaik, which, in this reſpect, favoured of temerity, and an inattention to our intereſts. Though we gave not an entire credit to the inſinuations of theſe people, whoſe jealouſy of the ſhaik's good fortune was palpable enough, we had heard too much not to be guided by reaſon, which pointed out to us the ſafeſt path to purſue. Rejoiced as they would have been, to have enjoyed the opportunities which the old man had to pillage us daily, their malice confirmed our reſolution, which began to waver, of waiting for the caravan.

To our great relief, ſome aſſes which we ſent to the mountains, are returned this morning, with ſix ſkins of water. This we may drink without fear, as its quality is good; but it is rather more unpalatable than that we have been uſing of late. The taſte is oily, from the ſkins having been newly ſoaked in that diſguſtful liquid, to prevent their leaking. We have the agreeable proſpect before us, of being furniſhed with this beverage during our journey through the deſart; as the Arabs, whoſe

whose business it is to keep the skins in orde., are too lazy to attend to the cleanliness of the inside of them.

FRIDAY, 25th JULY.

This morning the shaik brought the master of the Tor vessel to pay us a visit. It seems, that he went in company with the European gentlemen from Tor to Cairo, where he carried his own coffee for sale. We have the pleasure to be eased of our fears on their account, by this intelligence of their safe arrival at that capital. It is rather extraordinary, that we should have remained so long ignorant of these circumstances, and that the adventures of our countrymen should have been related to us by halves. But this has been more the effect of accident than design. The Arabs give us credit for the *sang-froid* which is the principal ingredient in the composition of their own minds; and were careless of the communication of an incident of such little importance to us, as the safety of these strangers. Great events are sometimes exhibited to mark the character of an individual; while a trait like this will suffice to fix that of a nation!

From the master of the vessel we enquired several particulars of a journey, so new to our experience, and so similar, in our idea, to the one which we were about to undertake. But little could be gathered from a man, whose imagination was wholly engrossed by self-interest, that could contribute to our instruction or amusement. The road, he tells us, lies through a continued desart, on which they travelled for fifteen days; and, to their agreeable surprize, they met not with any interruption or alarm. In the course of the conversation we learnt, that this man's vessel is the property of the shaik's brother, who is a merchant of Cairo. This connection of his may be a bond for the old man's good usage of us; as, over and above his dependence on the bey, his brother might

dearly

dearly anfwer any complaint which we might prefer on our arrival at Cairo.

At noon a camel arrived, with intelligence of the caravan's long-expected approach. It had halted during the heat of the day in a valley about two leagues diftant, and will be here in the evening. The fhaik confirmed this news in a vifit in the afternoon, and gave us afiurances, that we fhould fet out the day after to-morrow at furtheft. At fun-fet about 200 camels came in, and the reft are expected during the night. We fent a meffage to the fhaik, to defire he would provide us with camels, and give the neceffary orders concerning our departure. This brought him to our houfe again. But the prologue to the fcene was the demand of a loan of twenty dollars, which he was in want of to purchafe coffee. As he was to accompany us to the Nile, an adventure of this kind would make it the better worth his while, and give him fome employment during his abfence. Thefe were arguments not to be contefted; at leaft, we fhould have been willing to keep the old fellow in humour, had it been at the expence of double the fum in queftion. For as to any difcharge of the debt, it was the laft thing we looked for. We had been too long acquainted with the genius of the Arabs, to confider fuch a demand in any other light, than a new fpecies of begging. The crafty veteran received the money with many profeffions of gratitude; and while he promifed to expedite our journey, we obferved a fmile of exultation on his countenance, which feemed to portend us no good.

SATURDAY, 26th JULY.

The morning was ufhered in by a vifit from the fhaik, who was attended by the principal Arabs of the town. We foon difcovered the errand they came upon, which was, agreeably to the national maxim, to fee what they could ftrip us of before our departure.

Every eye appeared enlivened with expectation, and devoured in idea the contents of our baggage, which was piled up in one corner of the room. Whatever might be their diffenfions in other matters, they were evidently unanimous on the prefent occafion. We were determined to bring them to the point at once, and demanded of the fhaik the fum total we were to pay for getting to Ghinnah. This, after fome hefitation and wrangling among themfelves, they fixed at 205 dollars. The paper which they delivered to us to explain matters, will evince the knavery and extortion of this race: efpecially when it is known, that the ufual hire of a camel is but two dollars, and that money bears ten times its original value, in a country where fpecie is fo fcarce. The tranflation is literally as follows:

To the government of Cofire for its protection	Dollars 100
To twelve camels from hence to Ghinnah - - -	80
To pay for two afkaries or foldiers, to guard you - -	10
To a prefent to the fhaik for his company - - -	15
	Dollars 205

This fum, added to our other expences, will occafion our being fufferers to the amount of 500 dollars fince our arrival here; which may alfo be placed to the account of the vizier of Yambo. We paid it down, however, on the fpot, and difmiffed our vifitors, who appeared to be well pleafed with the fuccefs of their negotiation.

While we were employed in packing up our baggage, and preparing for our expedition, a man of a good mien, and a creditable appearance, entered the room without ceremony, and requefted a private audience on bufinefs of moment to ourfelves. He was of the race of the Seids, who pretend to be the defcendants of Mahomet, and, as fuch, are univerfally refpected among the followers

ers of that successful impostor. The generality of these Seids tread in the footsteps of their founder, and have as slender a title as himself to the homage which they demand from the deluded multitude. But so prevalent is the blindness of man, that the shadow shall outweigh the substance in his sight; and these hypocrites, under the garb of a specious name, shall obtain pensions from Mahometan princes, who were never guilty of rewarding merit or virtue during their reigns. I have myself known more than one instance of this kind, while I resided in India; and was once told by a Seid, who came to solicit charity of me, that he had rejected with scorn a purse of 300 rupees, or 40l. which was offered him by the nabob of Arcot, who was fain to purchase his prayers at a larger price! With such a confidence, which would lead him into every secret, and such a protection, which would secure him from any chastisement, it is no wonder that the man who now visited us, should have become acquainted with the intrigues of the Arabs, or that he should have had resolution enough to warn us of them. After asking pardon for my digression, to this man we will now return.

When the servants were dismissed, and the door was shut, the Seid professed to us his concern at finding us in that inhospitable region. That he had heard of our former adventures with surprize, and was filled with admiration to conceive, how we should surmount the dangers which now encompassed us. That as our foes were numerous, our conduct could not be too circumspect; and that, above all things, we should decline, to the utmost of our power, any proposal to travel in a body distinct from the main caravan: for, as he was convinced there were designs formed against us, the only chance to frustrate them, was to keep our persons and baggage with the croud. However bitter and alarming this communication was, we could not but pay our hearty acknowledgments to the author of it. We considered him as a good

spirit,

spirit, who had assumed this form to assist in our preservation, and we promised to hold his friendly caution in faithful remembrance. The yard was full of people, who were sewing up our trunks in bags, and the shaik himself was sometimes among them to give directions. This circumstance obliged the Seid to shorten our conference, who took his leave for fear of observation; but not before he had recommended us to the protection of his Prophet, whose votaries, at the very moment, were plotting our destruction.

Scarce had our humane monitor left the room, when the shaik came in to excuse himself from accompanying us. He lamented that some affairs of importance required his presence at Cosire, because he should be deprived so soon of our company. But as to our convenience and safety, they would equally be consulted by his son, who would attend us on the road. He found no difficulty in persuading us of the truth of this conclusion. Our present views were to get, in the best manner we could, to some civilized place, whose extent would screen us from notice, or whose government would secure us from further depredations. In the immediate temper we were in, the services of the son seemed to promise us full as much sincerity as those of the father.

SUNDAY, 27th July.

We were employed the whole morning in preparing for our departure, which is fixed for four o'clock this afternoon. After all the money we have paid, the principal article of our journey is yet to be provided at our expence: and this is water. Ten new skins, that hold from three to four gallons each, were accordingly purchased for the use of ourselves and servants. And this stock stood us in no contemptible sum, in a country where good water is dearer than any other necessary of life. We furnished ourselves

with

with a kind of bifket to fatisfy the calls of hunger, and added to the ftore a mutton-pye of our own making: for cookery was a knowledge to which we had been indebted more than once, for a comfortable meal, fince we left the fnow Adventure.

Our old hoft is almoft the only reafonable being we have met with here. While the reft of his countrymen are racking us to the utmoft, he is very well contented with a gratification of fifteen dollars, for the time that we have refided in his houfe, which is upwards of a fortnight. We take a pleafure in beftowing on this good man the little trifles we leave behind us, fuch as chefts, beds, and old linen, in gratitude for his fervices, which were not the flighteft to people in our fituation; impofed upon as we fhould have been in every neceffary of life, but for his timely interpofition. We were obliged, however, to obferve great fecrecy in this donation; which, mean as its intrinfic value may appear, might have excited the attention of his fuperiors, and induced the fhaik himfelf to difpute it with him after our departure.

At four o'clock we put on our Arabian dreffes, which we had provided for the journey. As we have fuffered the hair to grow upon our upper lips for fome months paft, we are each provided with a tolerable pair of whifkers; and as our complexions are by this time pretty well tanned by the fun, we hope the more eafily to efcape obfervation. But there is a peculiar characteriftic in the individuals of every nation, that will diftinguifh them through the difguife of drefs and language. This is exemplified daily amid the neighboring ftates of Europe, whofe habits and manners are nearly the fame; and cannot fo much excite wonder in our cafe, where the whole temperature of our minds and bodies was fo contrary to that of the people, whom we endeavored to perfonate. Our landing on this coaft, it is true, was known, and our progrefs was every where preceded by the herald of rumor. But neither of thefe caufes confpired towards

the

the difcovery of our origin, however they might have operated in the feizure of our effects, and the detention of our perfons. Every eye immediately pronounced us to be aliens to the land, and did not require any further fupport of this opinion, than its own penetration.

The Turkifh commandant had been very fparing of his vifits of late, which we had imputed to his fhame of feeing us, after the fcene of extortion he had been concerned in. Though we gave him credit for a principle which the Arabs are wholly devoid of, it appears, that we did him great injuftice in our conclufion. In the divifion of the fum demanded of us for the ufe of the government, the Arabs had not only excluded him from a fhare, but had kept the whole tranfaction from his knowledge. This we learnt from his own mouth, in a farewell vifit that we now received from him. Whether he really was our friend, or was over-reached by the fhaik and his adherents, we cannot pretend to determine; and if we thought favorably of this Turk, it arofe from his perfonal civilities towards us, and could not be juftified by the general deportment of his nation towards Chriftians.. This Turk, and an Arab merchant, were the only people in whofe profeffions we trufted; though it happened, that their good wifhes were all they could beftow on us. The merchant was a refident of Judda, and was here on a commercial fcheme. He had contracted an affection for the Englifh in his native place, and cautioned us frequently againft the knavery of his countrymen, though he was afraid to difclofe his good-will towards us openly. To him we entrufted letters directed to the care of Mr. Horfeley at Mocha, advifing our friends in India of our departure to Ghinnah.

The fhaik's avaricious difpofition feems to equal that of his countrymen in general. He has thrown off at laft the mafk of diffimulation, and acts in his native character. While it an-

fwered

fwered his purposes, he affected the humane patron; and now he plays the unfeeling tyrant with as good a grace. Our departure is deferred until the morning, on account of the caravan's not being in readiness; and the fhaik has taken this opportunity to infinuate to us, that the camel-drivers are not fatisfied with the price we have paid them! Gracious Heaven! of what latitude is the confcience of an Arab, which is not content with three times the value of his beafts' labor! for three times are we already charged, to what the native pays for the hire of a camel. We are bent upon not complying with this further impofition, unlefs this man fhould be bafe enough to obftruct our departure. The old fellow and we parted for the night on bad terms; and he was particularly irritated at our declining to accept of a centry to guard our baggage, which was piled up in the yard. This was done by the advice of our venerable hoft, who told the fhaik, that his walls were a fufficient defence for our property. This diverted the fhaik's attention from us, and he let drop fome words fignificant of our reliance on a foolifh dotard, who might not be able to protect our effects from the attempts of the town's people. We paid no other regard to this fpeech, than by fpreading our carpets around the baggage, and taking our pofts on the ground, ready to defend it againft the defigns of fecret or avowed enemies.

MONDAY, 28th JULY.

"All's well that ends well," fays the old proverb; and this, if ever, was verified with us. The fhaik came early in the morning, and looked gloomy. His ordinary falutation was even omitted, and convinced us, that his difcontent was great, and not to be removed, but by a compliance with his humour. When a Muffulman fails in the modes of politenefs, the worft is to be apprehended from his power, which will carry by force the point which his addrefs address was unable to accomplish. All ceremony was now laid aside, and he told us in plain terms, that he must have more money. He condescended, indeed, to place this requisition to the account of the people of the town and country, who had been pestering him for buxies, or presents, from us. That it was our misfortune to be considered by these people as men of vast wealth, whose trunks were filled with gold, precious stones, and rich merchandize, on which it was their custom to levy a tax. It was in vain that we remonstrated against this demand, which was as wanton as unjust. It was in vain that we referred to the shaik's own knowledge of our effects and profession, neither of which subjected us to the taxation imposed upon merchants and their goods. It was in vain that we appealed to the government of Cosire for its interposition in this matter, as we had paid so largely for its protection. The dependants of the shaik were yet to receive their mite, and he declared in a determined tone, that he could not pretend to send us in safety to the Nile, until he had received orders from the bey of Cairo, unless we satisfied the hill-people with a donation of twenty-five dollars. Hard as the extortion was, we panted too much for a return to our friends and country to hesitate long about it; and the shaik was content with the sum of twenty-three dollars, which we had kept about our persons for the extra expences of the road. And lucky it was for us that this money was reserved from our baggage, which, in its present situation, could not have been opened for a supply, without exposing our real treasure, which was not inconsiderable, to the eyes of the shaik. Suspicion of our concealed money was the only ground on which he proceeded in his demands; but a conviction of it might have operated more materially to our detriment. The cloud which had loured in the countenance of the shaik, was in a moment dispelled, and, with a tone of infinite good-humour, he ordered the camels to the door to take up our luggage,

gage. The hopes of our departure were now for the firſt time certain, and while we gave orders to the ſervants in what manner to diſpoſe of the things, our ſpirits inſenſibly returned to us, and chaſed all ideas of animoſity and complaint. It appeared that during our altercation the caravan had left the town, but was to halt in a valley at a ſmall diſtance, to be joined by all ſtragglers. To avoid the impertinence of the mob that ſurrounded the houſe, the ſhaik adviſed us to quit the town, and wait for our camels at the weſt angle of the fort. After a very cordial and moving ſeparation with our good hoſt, we reſorted to the houſe of the Judda merchant, and partook of a breakfaſt which he had prepared for us. Having embraced him, as a friend who had been raiſed up to us from the tribe of our enemies, we haſtened to the appointed ſpot. Here, as we ſat beneath the wall, our other friend, the Turk, appeared on the ramparts, and bade us adieu! At this inſtant the camels came up, and we found that they had only provided us with ten inſtead of twelve, for the eighty dollars. Nor was the ſhaik preſent to rectify this wilful miſtake. To increaſe my own hardſhip, my companions happened, as luck would have it, to be beforehand with me, and to poſſeſs themſelves of the two only riding camels that were in our train. I was, therefore, fain to put up with one of the beaſts which carried the baggage; and not finding my ſeat ſo eaſy as I could have wiſhed, I conſoled myſelf with beſtowing an hearty malediction on the ſhaik, for this parting proof of his kindneſs. Soon after we had moved onwards, we were overtaken by the young ſhaik and the two guards, who were to be our eſcort on the road. They brought us the compliments of the ſhaik, who had grace enough left to ſhun an interview, after this laſt ſcene of his political farce. The young man endeavoured to palliate the offence, by aſſuring me it was a miſtake, which ſhould be rectified when we joined the caravan. Beſides the aforeſaid Arabs, our company conſiſted of Major Alexander,

Y

ander, Mr. Hammond, and myself, my European servant, two slaves belonging to the major, our interpreter Ibrahim, an Arab servant named Abdul Ruffar, whom we had hired at Cofire, and an Indian fakeer, whom we permitted to ride on a baggage-camel, to affift him on his route to Cairo, where he was bound on a religious penance. We had a couple of mufkets, as many blunderbuffes, and two pair of piftols among ourfelves, with plenty of cartridges which we had prepared. The fhaik's fon and his attendants were much more completely armed, as were the cameldrivers, who followed us on foot. At two o'clock in the afternoon we joined the caravan, which we found in a valley two hours journey from Cofire. The diftance I computed to be five miles, as, by the beft obfervation I could make now and during our journey, a camel goes at the rate of two miles and an half an hour. Here a fcanty ftream waters the thirfty foil, and about an acre around is covered with date-trees. Under thefe we made a delicious repaft, upon the mutton-pye which we had brought with us. The water is brackifh in this fpring, and is what the inhabitants of Cofire generally ufe.

In this valley we had a glimpfe of the friendly Seid, and it was the laft we got of him. Some of the camels were in motion long before ours, and he paffed us on one of them. At three o'clock, we moved off the ground, and were not a little ftartled to find that our whole collective force did not exceed forty camels. The caravan had departed, it feems, when the Seid went by, and the conviction of this brought his vain precautions to our minds. We could not help expoftulating pretty feverely with the young fhaik on this neglect of his, which might fubject us to rifk. But as he laughed at any idea of danger to fuch a body as we were, and talked of overtaking the caravan before it reached the next ftage, we were under the neceffity of becoming quiet, to avoid the appearance of fear,

which

which would have funk; us in their eftimation. It was our intereft to conceal, as much as poffible, the real motives of our apprehenfion, and to appear to place a confidence in the man, who was become our conductor. Our party was the fourth of this little company, and we kept in as compact a body as the road would allow of, to fecure us the better againft the effects of treachery or furprize. We continued our way through the valley, which foon became defart and ftony like the hills above it. At fix o'clock we halted to drink coffee, and to feed our cattle. This ftage was three hours, or feven miles and an half. At eight o'clock the fignal was given for marching, but juft as we had mounted our camels, an alarm was fpread of the approach of the wild Arabs: In the confufion which this naturally occafioned, we immediately difmounted, and affembling our fervants, marched directly to the quarter where our Arabs had fet up a war-cry, and whence the difcharge of feveral matchlocks had reached our ears. On the road we met with the young fhaik and his attendants, who were feeking us out, and feemed not a little furprized at our alertnefs, and the good countenance we affumed in this ugly affair. This we underftood from an expreffion which he dropped in the hearing of our Ibrahim; which, joined to the fudden ceffation of the tumult, convinced us that he was at the bottom of it. But whatever he and his affociates intended, the trick failed of any other purpofe, than that of letting them fee we were ready to repel any infult. They gave fome trifling reafon for the buftle, which they told us was owing to the unexpected appearance of one of the hill-people, who had threatened to pillage us while at Cofire. As we neither faw this man, nor received any fatisfactory account of the matter, we attributed it to a defign to try our mettle, and to make what advantage they could of our fears. But we lent a deaf ear to their demands of buxies or prefents, which we mortified them in

Y 2 faying,

saying, were not due to the timidity that they had betrayed. When all was calm we mounted again, and moved on;' our only light the stars, which shone very bright. We continued to traverse the same valley as before, until two o'clock in the morning, when we halted beneath the hills, and spread our carpets to take such repose, as our time, and the peculiarity of our circumstances, would admit of. The last stage was six hours, or fifteen miles, and by our reckoning, we are twenty-seven miles from Cosire.

TUESDAY, 29th JULY.

At five o'clock the Arabs rouzed us to get ourselves ready. We were soon mounted, and began our march; fasting, and not recovered from yesterday's fatigues. We were very solicitous for a junction with the caravan, but from the last evening's manœuvres, and our disappointment at night, we are by this time ascertained that our separation had been intended, and consequently, that a meeting would be unlikely before our arrival at Ghinnah. In this uncomfortable situation, our only hope rested upon the knowledge which the caravan had of our being in the desart, which we flattered ourselves would deter our conductors from any open outrage. Besides, we numbered the camels and merchandize of a merchant of Ghinnah among our body, which we considered as a kind of protection; though whether we owed this union to accident or design, we could not determine. This merchant, by name Mahomet, travels with us; and we understand, that we are to be lodged in his house during our short stay at Ghinnah. He is the brother of one Ally, who professed a great regard for us at Cosire; and who is the cause, we suppose, of the invitation which the merchant has given us.

The country as we advance, still wears the same barren face.
Here

Here and there a dwarf date-tree appears, and the trufle-bush is frequent on the road, to the great delight and benefit of the poor camel, who devours it very greedily. Among these bushes we found several deer, who must necessarily live many days without water in the depth of this desart; except that, like the rein-deer, who digs with certainty for provender beneath the snow, they supply themselves with water from a similar practice. The Arabs find springs in particular spots, and I doubt not but nature has implanted in these poor animals the instinct to satisfy one of her loudest calls. We likewise saw numbers of quail, and several earths of an unknown animal; probably of the hare and gerbua, which are common in the desarts of Arabia, but did not come within our view. This country would be truly romantic, were it covered with verdure. The variety of slopes and declivities with which it is interspersed, the frequent vistoes which the openings between the hills afford, would present the beautiful scenes of nature, were the soil fertilized, as they do the sublime, in their rude and sterile state. The mountains contain both alabaster and marble, of which many pieces lie scattered upon the road. We made a long and fatiguing march, and at eleven o'clock halted in a pass between the mountains, where the Arabs dig for fresh water, and find it very good. They have nothing indeed to do, but to remove the dirt with which the spring is choaked up; and as the water is drawn before its transparency returns, we strained it through a cloth to take off the foulness. The mountains here are so perpendicular, and approach so close together, that at noon there is a shade on the south side for travellers to repose under. We had centinels on the heights during our slight repast, as this place has the character of being very dangerous. The last stage was six hours, or fifteen miles. At one o'clock we moved onwards with a plentiful supply of water, and went near a mile through this pass, which winds about like the entrance of an Indian fortrefs; and where an handful of men might check the progrefs of a large army, were the country worth difputing for. The wind was very hot from the vicinity of the rocky mountains, and this day's journey proved very laborious to us, who had led a fedentary life for fo many months paft. Our minds indeed had been fufficiently exercifed, but our limbs were enfeebled from eafe and inactivity. We had no refrefhment, but fome bifcuit and water, during the day, though our conductor, who was well mounted, pufhed on frequently before us, and had his cup of coffee with his friends, beneath the fhade of fome projecting hill, that afforded fuel for a fire. This our camels would by no means admit of our doing; and though coffee would have been the beft recruit which our fpirits could have received, we could only repine in filence at the young man's neglect. At five o'clock we halted on a plain to refrefh ourfelves. This ftage was four hours, or ten miles.

At feven o'clock in the evening we mounted again, and for the firft time afcended an eminence by a very eafy approach. We quickly regained the level country, and advanced at a fafter rate than by day, through the vallies in which we are conftantly buried. The night was as bright as the laft, and we fhould think it a lucky incident were we to lay by in the day, and to travel only by night. At two o'clock in the morning the moon rofe, which was the fignal for us to halt. And much indeed did we ftand in need of repofe, after a journey of fuch a continuance. Befides, we fuffered greatly from the uneafy motion of the camels, which nothing but habit could reconcile to a man. For my own part, I am fo particularly aggrieved by the faddle of the camel on which I ride, that the fmall of my back is ftripped of its fkin. This arifes from my ftill being furnifhed with a baggage-beaft, notwithftanding the fine promifes of the young fhaik. Authors are much miftaken in their particular ideas of this animal.

mal. His being able to go from 100 to 150 miles in the twenty-four hours, is a very fable. Perseverance and hardiness are the qualities which distinguish him above all other quadrupeds, and peculiarly adapt him to the barren countries, where he is found in the most vigorous state. His common pace does not exceed three miles an hour, at which rate he will go sixteen hours out of the twenty-four, for a journey of a month and upwards. But put him beyond his usual speed, and he soon tires. For a day indeed it may be quickened to five, and even six miles an hour; but he shortly grows obstinate, and refuses to proceed at a rate so disproportioned to his abilities. He is however very docile, and when trained to a caravan, requires neither a rein to guide, nor a whip to forward his motions. To a stranger nothing can be so ineligible as this mode of travelling; tedious and fatiguing to the last degree, and especially in these parts, where we could not provide ourselves with litters, to defend us from the scorching rays of the sun. Our course yesterday and to-day was generally to the northward of west, and sometimes west and by south, and due west. The last stage was seven hours, or eighteen miles, and by our reckoning we are now seventy miles distant from Cosire.

WEDNESDAY, 30th JULY.

At five o'clock this morning we were wakened from our sleep, which had been very sound, notwithstanding the suspicious company we are in. We got up more assured of the good faith of our conductor, seeing that no attempts had been made to surprize us, at a season when exhausted nature had left us at his mercy. At a moment of such alarm, there was something particularly aggravating in our situation. Worn out with the labors we had undergone, sleep insensibly stole upon the most determined eye; and the common satisfaction of keeping a watch at least upon the motion motions of an enemy, was denied us. Short as our nap was, it gave us spirits to pursue our journey. But this might not long have proved the case, if we were to obtain but two hours repose out of the twenty-four, in travelling to any considerable distance.

Before we had gone far, my European companions and myself began to find our bowels greatly affected by the water which we got yesterday. This, at all times, is an alarming complaint; and nothing but our supposed vicinity to Ghinnah, could have administered consolation to our distress. We entered, after an hour's march, upon a large plain, sterile and stony like the mountains which we now left behind us. It is a circumstance worthy of remark, that we never crossed any considerable acclivity in our passage through this desart; though at every point of view, the traveller supposes he has a laborious height to ascend, and that he must make his way good, by conquering the stupendous precipices which continually present themselves before him. But indulgent nature has accommodated the country to the necessities of the native. Throughout the hilly region, which extends itself from the Red-Sea to the Nile, she has scooped out a line of vallies for the passage of the caravan. The soil is a mixture of stone and sand, which, beaten down by the constant tread of the splay-footed camel for many centuries past, affords an even and firm pavement to the beasts that travel over it. The road is wide enough in some places for an army to pass in a line; and in others, will not admit above two or three camels abreast.

This country must have experienced a sad reverse, were it ever so fruitful as the antients have represented it. For the last fifty miles we have not met with any tree but the hawthorn, or any verdure but what the sweet-scented shrubs faintly afford the sight; and now that we are within a few leagues of the Nile, the prospect is not mended for the better. At eleven o'clock we halted under a spreading hawthorn to breakfast; but had not as yet

yet a glimpse of the Nile, or any token of our being in the neighborhood of so fine a river. The last stage was six hours, or fifteen miles. Here, to our great astonishment, we found that our water was expended. This must have been owing, as much to thefts in the night, as to the impudence of the camel-drivers, who, as we go along, draw water from our skins in despite of us, though depending from the beasts on which we ride. The insolence of this tribe is surprising. Though their camels are hired by us, they pretend to a right of mounting them themselves, when they are weary of walking. Thus, do the poor baggage-beasts groan, at times, under the additional burden of a man's weight. It was as much as I could do to keep my camel-driver from getting up behind me; and my friend, the major, was not so fortunate, whose driver once effected a seat on his camel, in defiance of his remonstrances, and threats, to deter him from such a piece of assurance.

At one o'clock, the young shaik moved forward, to procure us a supply of water from some springs which lie out of the road; and we proposed to remain here during the heat of the day. But we presently discovered something that made us hasten our departure. There was a certain Arab, whom I have already mentioned to have rendered himself very disagreeable to us, during our abode at Cosire. This fellow had been appointed by the shaik as one of our guard; and was at this very time under the shade with us. By his assiduity on the road, he had tried to efface the unfavorable idea we had of him; and as our friend, he now insinuated to us, that it was better for us not to trust ourselves at Ghinnah, where the inhabitants were professed rogues, and would plunder our effects. Nay, he went so far as to propose to conduct us to Banute; a town a few hours higher up the river, where he could ensure us the best reception, and a choice of boats to transport us to Cairo. This circumstance was too

barefaced

barefaced not to alarm us, and we determined to push on, through an almost insupportable heat. But our conductor was absent, and we were left in the hands of our guard and the camel-drivers; a force which indeed we did not fear, but would have been glad to be quit of in a solitary and inimical place. This resolution was confirmed by Abdul Ruffar, our Arabian servant, who was entitled to credit from his past behavior. He advised us by no means to listen to, or remain with these rascals; but to follow the young shaik, whom they had the confidence to tell us was a foolish youth, who did not know our interests. Accordingly, at two o'clock, we mounted our camels, in spite of their importunities to wait until the evening, and moved on, in the most sultry day I had ever felt in the East. We soon rejoined the merchant's camels, which had taken shelter under a thorn-tree at some distance, and were ready to attend us. While united with this body, we did not fear going astray; and pursued our course, under a full security of being on the road to Ghinnah. We had no water, but what our earthen guglets contained; and this was soon expended. It is impossible to describe what we suffered from heat and thirst during this stage. A mouthful or two of dirty water, which one of our guards gave me, made me forget for the moment his recent insolence; and all our former apprehensions were insensibly swallowed up in the more painful idea of falling victims to thirst. Our tongues actually became parched to our palates; and we were obliged to wet them every now and then, with spirituous liquors, to prevent suffocation from the clouds of dust which continual whirlwinds threw around us. This expedient was but transitory, and served indeed to encrease the rage of thirst. It was our common misfortune also to labor under a violent complaint in our bowels; and to the want of the bad water that occasioned it—a want which we had lamented in the most earnest manner—our preservation

servation was probably owing. I was so afflicted myself with this disorder, that I could scarcely sit my camel through excess of pain. The wind and dust had equally affected our sight, so that we wandered on in agony and darkness. There is no doubt that our Arabian companions partook in some measure of our sufferings; but they were too much accustomed to the sun, to feel all the effects of his fury; and we had some reason to suspect, that their stock of water lasted long after ours had failed us. To crown this scene of distress, we at length overtook the shaik, who, we learnt, had been disappointed in replenishing his skins, by the appearance of wild Arabs about the springs. This news sounded like the knell of death in our ears; not from the neighborhood of these robbers, who were once so formidable to our fears, but from the absence of a fluid, on which we supposed our lives to depend. Faint and spiritless, therefore, we toiled on until eight o'clock at night, when we halted, without having encountered any foe in the way. But far different was this halting-place from any other we had come to. Without a draught of water to moisten our throats, it was impracticable to force down a morsel of bread; and the pain and weariness under which our bodies labored, were too extreme to admit of a momentary repose. Overwhelmed with hunger, thirst, and fatigue, we sat ourselves upon the ground, and revolved our melancholy situation in silence. Every skin was alternately ransacked by us for water, and not an article left untried that was likely to produce the least moisture. My companions and I had unluckily recourse to raw onions, which were among the baggage. But no sooner had we tasted of this potent root, than we repented of our rashness. The effect was quite contrary to our hopes; and our drought was irritated to the highest degree. This stage was six hours, or fifteen miles.

At nine o'clock the word was given to resume our march. The doubtful light of the stars, and the evils we endured, prevented our seeing clearly what was going forward. But our Arab servant soon alarmed us with the intelligence of our having left the merchant's camels upon the ground; and by some words which the drivers had let drop in his hearing, that they had but a bad opinion of the shaik's intentions respecting us. The scene was now become very critical, and a catastrophe not very happy, appeared likely to ensue. We rode up immediately in a body to our fraudulent conductor, and charged him with treachery towards us. We instanced his first having parted company with the caravan, and then with the merchant's camels, which being both bound for Ghinnah, plainly indicated his unfriendly design of carrying us to another place. To our great surprize, he acknowledged the charge of deceit towards us in this particular, but endeavoured to divest it of any sinister motives. That it was his father's opinion, as well as his own, that our departure might be retarded at such a city as Ghinnah, from the rumor of our riches, which would induce the officers of government to visit our baggage. That he had it in command from him to leave the caravan at the first stage, and to carry us by another route, without awakening our suspicions, which he must confess his countrymen had given too much cause to be directed against them. That the merchant's camels, from which we had just parted, would reach Ghinnah in a few hours; and that we should arrive about the same time at Banute, a village somewhat higher up the Nile, where we might embark secretly, and without molestation for Cairo. There was something as plausible in the substance of this defence, as engaging in the delivery of it. That coolness of temper, and ready eloquence, for which the Orientals are so conspicuous, were fully exerted on this occasion. From the former declarations of our guard, and the present confession of the shaik, we were assured there was a combination against us; but whether it had any ill tendency, we could not so easily determine.

mine. In truth, we were now in the power of our guides, and our deliberations could only terminate in a resolution, to sell our lives as dearly as possible, should they attempt to play us false.

There was but little variety in the scene during the remainder of this stage. The night was too dark to favor our observation of the objects around us, if our misfortunes had not extinguished every spark of curiosity within our breasts. Hour succeeded hour, without a vestige of fertility appearing, to announce a speedy period to our troubles; and we were almost sunk into a fit of despair, when the sight of a camel, bearing two skins of water, raised us in a moment to the pinnacle of joy! Colors would be faint to express the transports of wretches half-dead like us of thirst, at such a change! We owed this supply to the good-nature of the shaik, who pushed on before us to the river, to relieve our distress; and I must do him the justice to own, that no service could have been more material than what he rendered us on this occasion. Nor did it pass unrewarded. It restored him to our good graces, and we renewed our promise of an handsome donation on his putting us into a boat. Before I ventured to drink, I had the precaution to wash my mouth, and to gargle my throat several times. I recommended the same method to my companions, and I do not believe it was unserviceable, as the extreme dryness of our palates would otherwise have obliged us to swallow a quantity that might have proved fatal to us. But still we drank with great eagerness and pleasure. And it is not to be wondered at, considering the goodness of the water, and our long abstinence. We were now within a mile of the Nile, and at three o'clock arrived at a village composed of tents and huts. We made no disturbance in unlading our baggage, and having stretched our carpets upon the ground, betook ourselves to a short, though sound, repose. The last stage was six hours, or fifteen miles; so that we travelled yesterday no less than eighteen hours, or forty-five miles; an amazing

ing stretch, if our calamitous situation be considered. This part of the Nile, by our reckoning, lies 115 miles to the west of Cosire.

THURSDAY, 31st JULY.

We awoke this morning long after the sun had risen, and, upon looking around us, had the pleasure of seeing the Nile, which now began to be gilded with his early beams. We were near a quarter of a mile from the river, and could only obtain a view of the water through different openings in the bank. Here the borders are adorned in several places with the date and other fruit-trees; though the country around wears the same dreary aspect as before. In one of these verdant spots lies the village of Banute; the place we are in, being lonely and uncultivated, and consisting of a cluster of cottages, the property of some camel-drivers. Nothing can more evince the magnificence of this celebrated river, than its breadth at this distance from the sea. It appears to our eye not much less than a mile wide; though, with its windings, it cannot run a course of less than 700 miles, from its leaving Banute, until it discharges itself into the Mediterranean.

The young shaik was absent some hours, and brought us the disagreeable tidings, that no boat could be procured in this neighborhood. We were now reduced to the indispensable necessity of seeking one at Ghinnah; and the shaik left us, to get fresh camels to carry us to that city. We are again inclined to doubt the errand on which we came here; but whatever may have been the view of our conductor and his associates, a solution of their odd conduct cannot be very remote. While our patience is thus exercised in respect to our minds, it is not less so in a case of equal importance to our bodies. Though we have fasted, in a manner, for three days past, we are afraid to send to Banute for a supply of

meat

meat and fruit: the inhabitants, we learn, are impudent beggars, who would not wait our beftowing alms upon them, fhould they happen to be apprifed of our fmall number. A pretty fpecimen, indeed, of a place which has been recommended to us by our guard! But the humble diftance which the fhaik keeps, fhews plainly his opinion of it. A pair of pigeons which this place afforded, ferved juft to allay the appetites of our company; and as we had no money at hand, the fhaik lent us a couple of dollars to pay for them and fome dried dates, which we took with us to eat upon the road.

At three o'clock in the afternoon we quitted this miferable village, and fet out for Ghinnah, in tolerable health and fpirits. Whether we owe our recovery to the falubrious water of the Nile, or to a ceffation of fatigue for the laft twelve hours, we arofe this morning with a perfect freedom from our late complaint. Our faces were now turned to the north, and we went for the moft part of this ftage in the fame direction. This was no unpleafing circumftance, as we thereby prefented our backs to the fun, which had fo dreadfully annoyed us yefterday. At four we entered a fandy valley, where we faw an herd of deer. When we mounted the hills beyond it, we had a glance, for the firft time, of a cultivated country. The Nile appeared about two miles to the weftward, wafhing the foot of the mountains by which it is fkirted on that fide. To the eaftward, the whole fpace between us was laid out in plantations of grain, which were watered by inlets from the river. There was as extraordinary a contraft in the profpect before us, as could poffibly occur in the wantonnefs of nature. The fcene to our left, verdant, and crouded with clumps of ftately trees, which were bounded by a fine river; while that to the right was barren as before, and offered nothing but fands and ftony mountains to the eye.

Our

Our company was reduced by the abſence of our guard, who had got the ſtart of us on the road by the ſhaik's orders, ſo that we could not muſter above ten camels, had we been in the way of danger. At five o'clock we paſſed by the ruins of a large village, which our guides tell us has long been abandoned, on account of robbers, who were continually plundering the property of the inhabitants. Here we were alſo deſerted by the ſhaik, who gave us notice of his intention to puſh on to the city, to prepare an houſe for our reception. He aſſured us, that he could anſwer for our ſafety on the road, and at Ghinnah, where he would introduce us under cover of the night, and previouſly provide for our embarkation. Whatever reluctance we might have towards this ſtep, it was impoſſible to fruſtrate it, and he put his camel on at ſuch a trot, as made us loſe ſight of him preſently. We were even worſe provided with cattle than before, and on our endeavoring to mend their pace to keep up with the ſhaik, we received remonſtrances from the owner againſt hurrying his camels. This fellow attended us, and was as ſurly a dog as I ever met with in my life. When he found that my companions and I paid little regard to his words, he had the impudence to make Abdul Ruſſar, our Arab ſervant, and the poor Hindoo, alight, and trudge along on foot, under pretence that the beaſts they rode, were overladen. When we were appriſed of this circumſtance, we rated the owner ſoundly for his inſolence. But he remained inflexible, and I know not to what a pitch our difference would have ariſen, if Abdul Ruſſar had not wiſely urged us to acquieſce in a thing, which he now pretended was a matter of choice. He had great merit for his prudent interference, at a time when we were about to forget the reſtraint we were under in this Mahometan region. And happy would it have been for the Fakeer, if he could have yielded to circumſtances with equal temper. But his ſpirit was so wounded at the indignity which had been offered him, that he took the first opportunity of remounting his camel, unobserved by the owner. We were at this juncture some hundreds of yards ahead, and were not a little surprized to hear the most lamentable outcries in our rear. These proceeded from the unfortunate Fakeer, whom we beheld under the discipline of the Arab's stick, but urging his beast forwards, without betraying the least design towards quitting his seat. As we approached him, his confidence seemed to redouble, and he began to pour forth the vilest abuse on his antagonist in the Moor language. It was perhaps conducive to his safety, that the Arab did not understand him, who, at our instance, not only desisted from the assault, but left him in quiet possession of the camel. This so elevated the spirits of the Hindoo, that giving more credit to his own vociferation than to our support, he descanted largely on his own courage and rank in life, which he averred was formerly a Subedar, or commander of Sepoys in the English service. As this man had hitherto kept a centinel on his lips, we did not regret the rude manner in which they had been put off their guard; as the many stories which now fell from them, served, in some measure, to banish painful reflexions. But, indeed, the scene which now disclosed itself, quickly absorbed our attention. After a six months confinement in a ship, and in barren countries, it was not without an exquisite satisfaction that I beheld the earth cloathed again in green, and adorned with her fairest ornaments of wood and water. The captive, who has long pined in a gloomy dungeon, could not experience more joyful emotions at the sight of day, than animated me on this occasion. I looked about me with sensations unknown before. I called to my camel-driver to gather every blossom that the bushes afforded, which my imagination supplied with fragrance; and this part of the Nile, which would appear contemptible when opposed to the rudest banks of the

A a   Thames,

Thames, was to me fraught with numberless beauties. We now, for the first time on our journey, beheld the marks of agriculture. The people were in some places tending their cattle, and in others following the plough. The river discovered itself at various breaches in the banks, about two miles to our left; and we saw wells that were worked by * pacotahs, as in India. Water-channels now intersected the road, to supply the country to the right of us, which here began to be cultivated. At these channels our poor camels halted, and drank with the eagerness and perseverance of creatures unaccustomed to quench the heaviest call of nature, which I may safely pronounce to be thirst. I can truly say, that, during the last three days, I have not eat an ounce. Meat we had not, and I could never get down above a mouthful or two of bread. My companions were nearly in the same situation; which can only be attributed to our stomachs having been overcharged with the quantities of water, which the heat and dust obliged us to swallow.

Between the time of our seeing the ruined village and sun-set, we counted not less than a dozen desolated towns, which we were given to understand had been unpeopled on the same account: some large, and the houses still standing; and others defended by walls and towers, whose remains are still respectable. Were a traveller allowed to indulge a conjecture on a cursory view of things, I should rather suspect that these ruins were of far greater antiquity than the modern inhabitants of Egypt imagine; and that time, the grand destroyer of all human systems, had depopulated these parts, and not the dread of the roving Arabs. When the

---

* A pacotah is a machine of a very simple construction. By the means of a long bamboo, fixed across a mast, a single man will raise water from the depth of ten or twelve feet, by walking up and down the bamboo. During this leisure movement, the man above encourages himself with a song, in which he is accompanied by his fellow, who stays below, to distribute the water as it comes up in the bucket.

Saracens

Saracens over-ran Egypt, whole cities muſt have yielded to the deſtructive tide; and while the bloody conteſt ſubſiſted between them and the Turks, the reſt were involved in the general wreck of this country's grandeur. I particularly remarked the ruins of one town, ſituated on two hills to the right of the road, and joined together by a wall which runs acroſs the valley. The front of this town ſtill extends itſelf a mile, and its towers and hummums, which are of ſtone, are many of them in tolerable repair. Our guides had, indeed, names for this, as well as ſome of the reſt of theſe places; but being of Arab derivation, they could throw no light on the ſubject of our enquiry.

The night was very bright, from the countleſs hoſt of ſtars which are wont to ſhine with unclouded luſtre in this ſerene hemiſphere. A full hour before we reached Ghinnah, we left our northern direction, and travelled due weſt. The many gardens and plantations that we paſſed, announced our vicinity to the city, where we arrived at nine o'clock. At our entrance we went by a large moſque, which was illuminated, and full of people, who were attending divine ſervice. We ſaw many good houſes and ſtreets, before we reached the lodgings that had been provided for us. Here we were houſed at half paſt nine, without having met with any adventure that could tend to a diſcovery of our perſons. The manſion ſeems large and commodious, and belongs to the merchant whoſe camels accompanied us the greateſt part of the way. He welcomed us with great cordiality, and, having ſeen our baggage carried up ſtairs, lighted us himſelf to our apartment, where ſome new bread and freſh dates were ſerved up to us. During our repaſt the merchant Mahomet, his brother Ally, and the ſhaik, attended us, and on their wiſhing us a good night, we reminded them of our anxiety to be gone. The laſt ſtage was ſix hours, or fifteen miles, ſo that we have come 130 miles ſince we left Coſire, though the direct diſtance muſt fall ſomewhat ſhort of that number.

number. While we were going to bed, we were thrown into some confusion by Major Alexander missing his Indian sabre. The baggage was rummaged for it in vain; so that we were obliged to call up our host to lay the complaint before him. The major now remembered having left it below stairs, and, as it could not be found, the suspicions of our host immediately fell upon the soldier, who had been so long the object of our aversion. This soldier he now sallied forth at this late hour to seek; and bidding the major to be of good cheer, assured him that the sword should be recovered, if still within the precincts of the city.

FRIDAY, 1st August.

I awoke at day-break to-day after a very sound repose. One night's rest had perfectly restored me to myself, if I may except a languor upon my limbs, which so laborious a journey might occasion to a constitution that is none of the strongest. When I had got on my Arabian habit, I perceived a pair of stairs that led to the top of the house. As I conceived myself to be sufficiently disguised, I made no scruple to ascend them, in order to take a view of the city. Ghinnah, or Cana, as the antients called it, is pleasantly situated on the eastern banks of the Nile, in that district which is known by the name of Upper Egypt. By our nicest observation of its bearing from Cosire, it lies in the latitude 26° 40′ N. which brings it considerably lower down the river than we find it, either in the old or modern maps. Its length extends from east to west, and its principal streets run in a parallel line, and ascend by a gentle acclivity from the river to the center of the city. This situation seems adapted to the neighborhood of the Nile, which, in the time of the floods, must lay the adjacent parts under water. Its appearance is truly romantic, as every house is surrounded with an inclosure, and partly concealed from view by the lofty date-trees, that every here and there mingle their tufted heads with the spiral mosques and swelling domes, as if ambitious to rival their proudest heights. I was proceeding in my observations, when our host came up to bid us good-morrow, and hearing that I was above, he called to me in haste to descend. I was rather surprized at this abrupt command; but when he pointed out the offence which his neighbors might take at having their women overlooked, I bore with the reproof, though my curiosity had not been awakened from that quarter. I was well acquainted with the jealousy of the Mahometans in this particular; and therefore did not consider the conduct of our host as any way unreasonable. To the great satisfaction of the major, he produced the sword, which he declared had been taken on the thief he mentioned. He demanded, however, eight dollars for the hire of two men, who had assisted him in the pursuit of the soldier some miles from the town. The money was paid to him without hesitation, as the weapon was of value to the owner; but our ideas of the justice which prevails here, became very unfavorable, when we understood that the loss of his plunder was the only punishment which the knave was likely to experience.

We feasted this morning at breakfast on cow's milk, to which we have been long strangers, and on the first good bread we have tasted in Egypt. Indeed, we learn, that this place is plentifully supplied with every necessary of life, situated in a serene climate, and far removed from the turbulence and intrigues of the capital we are hastening to. A picture, pretty in speculation, and what we flatter ourselves we shall find just in the practice. The shaik and our host joined us at our coffee, and we expected to have heard something of the boat; but their errand was to get such presents for the camel-drivers and guard, as are usual for travellers to give. We were content to be quit of them for a dollar each;

each; though it went not a little againſt our inclination to include the roguiſh ſoldier among the number. Scarce had they left us, when we had a viſit from the guard themſelves. The offender came without a bluſh into our preſence, and had the effrontery to make a jeſt of taking the ſword, which he pretended he only meant to have kept as a pledge, for the preſent that was due to his comrade and himſelf. He added, that they were now come for that preſent, which they had ſo juſtly deſerved at our hands, by the protection they had afforded us on the road. We were inclined enough to have diſputed their merits in this caſe, had it not been in the power of theſe fellows to publiſh our arrival at Ghinnah, and expoſe us to the rapacity of the government. Their demand, therefore, met with a civiler reception than they expected, and we aſſured them that it had been already gratified. We were now witneſs to one of the moſt ſtriking inſtances of the unlicenced tempers of the Arabs that ever occurred in hiſtory. For no ſooner was the ſpokeſman certified of the ſhaik's having received his quota, than he caught up his ſabre which lay by him on the carpet, and half-drawing it, told us with a reſolute air, that if we would diſcloſe but the ſum which the ſhaik had preſumed to take without their knowledge, he would force it from his throat with the point of his ſword. This language from a ſoldier, of his ſuperior, did not ſuit our notions of military diſcipline; and we diſpatched Abdul Ruſſar to ſeek for the ſhaik, and acquaint him therewith. He ſoon came, and ſuch a ſcene paſſed between the prince and ſubject, as baffles all deſcription. An hundred times did they catch up their ſabres, and challenge each other to inſtant conflict, and as often did they revile each other in the bittereſt terms. But our friend had the greateſt juſtice in his reproaches, as he ſtigmatized the ſoldier with having betrayed his truſt, in reſpect to the major's ſword. This breach of truſt ſeemed to both of theſe warriors the principal crime in the robbery;

and

and the quarrel waxed to such a pitch, that finding it impossible to soften their fury, we looked to our arms, in order to intimidate the soldier. His comrade had sneaked off in the beginning of this dispute, and wisely informed the people of the house of what was passing above. This intelligence, together with the noise, brought up the host and his family, just at the nick of time, that our apartment was about to become the scene of bloodshed, in a populous and civilized city, on the trifling subject of a few dollars! This company soon accommodated the matter, and the soldier was dismissed, with a promise of obtaining his dividend of the sum in question.

Our distaste for the people we are among, was so heightened by this late transaction, that we now pressed the shaik, very seriously, to discharge the obligation he was under to embark us in a boat for Cairo. We found ourselves at greater liberty, and under less apprehension, when committed to the wide waves in an Arab boat, than now when we are upon Arab ground; and I doubt if there was one among us, who would not have undertaken the pilotage of a boat to Cairo, though the current was the only guide he could depend upon, in preference to staying at Ghinnah a day longer. The shaik saw our anxiety, and assured us solemnly of his intention to keep his word, as soon as a boat could be got ready. Our host, and his brother Ally, offered to pledge themselves for the shaik's sincerity, and the latter proposed himself to accompany us to Cairo. They left us to sit down to a meal of wheat, boiled in mutton-broth, which had been delayed by the strange business of the day.

SATURDAY, 2d August.

We are doomed to be the sport of fortune, to achieve adventures which we never aspired to, and to find our situation more dangerous

dangerous than ever, at the moment that we are foolishly expecting the period of our troubles. Though the night was close, and I had not rested well, from the dust which incommoded the terrace we sleep upon, I was up, according to custom, at day-break, and in going down stairs to the back-yard, in order to wash me, was met by a servant of the house, who took me by the arm, and, with a significant gesture, hurried me up again in apparent agitation. When he could make a shift to explain himself, by the means of Ibrahim, we understood, to our great concern, that the vizier of the city was in the house, and locked up in close conference with our host. This early visit had a very unpromising appearance, and as we had remained within doors since our arrival, we attributed this discovery of us, to some treachery in those who were in the secret. My companions posted themselves on the stair-head, to learn, if possible, what was going forward, and I was ruminating in an inner apartment on the consequences of Arab duplicity, when they came running to me, with an account of the street-door being besieged by a body of horse. Our host himself followed them into the room, and, with the utmost shew of terror, desired us to load our fire-arms quickly, and assist him to defend the house, which he expected would be assaulted every moment. It was some time before we could get him to interpret the meaning of this alarm. We were not a little surprized at last to learn, that the horse at the door belonged to the shaik of Banute, and were sent with injunctions to carry us before their master, who had been apprized of our having passed his residence, without paying him the usual compliment. As improbable as this story appeared, what imposition was there which could not have been practised with success on people, who were utter strangers to the customs and language of the country? We were well informed of the independence of the Arab shaiks, and their propensity to extort money from travellers; and though the sending

an

an armed force into a commercial town was incomprehenfible to us, yet we did not know but it might enter into the fyftem of their politics, where one party was fuperior to another. In order, we fuppofe, to terrify us into their meafures, our hoft told us, that there was no regular government at prefent in Ghinnah; that every man was the protector of his own houfe, which he would defend, on our account, againft all invaders. From one of our windows, which in this country more refembles a pigeon-hole than any thing elfe, we beheld a number of horfemen, who paraded the ftreet, but did not betray any intentions to proceed to violence. On our obferving this matter to our hoft, he pretended that it difcovered an inclination to treat with us; and immediately went down to the gate, to make, as he faid, the beft terms for us in his power. Thus were we, on a fudden, fhut up in a beleaguered place, and either on the point of being put to the fword, or being obliged to deliver ourfelves up prifoners of war. The caftle was befieged in form, and the treacherous governor about to forego his truft. We remained, during this interval, under arms in our apartment, and had centinels pofted on the ftairs, to apprize us of any danger. After this farce—for a farce it was, though of a very ferious nature to us—had been kept up for two hours and upwards, our hoft at length came up. He told us, that he had fo far fucceeded, as to get us excufed from our vifit to Banute for a pecuniary confideration, and that the fum of 150 dollars would free us from thefe troublefome guefts. From the vizier's vifit, and the ftrange conduct of the hoft, we fufpected there was a collufion between them and the cavalry at the door, and that we had already fallen within the gripe of the government of Ghinnah. Under this perfuafion we fubmitted with a good grace, to what we judged was unavoidable. We paid down fifty dollars in advance, though we loudly protefted againft the impofition, which we declared would leave us almoft deftitute of money. To moderate our vexa-

B b   tion,

tion, and to revive the pleasing ideas of our departure, our host very artfully shifted the subject, and reminded us of putting him in cash for the boat, which the shaik and his brother were gone in pursuit of. His demand was forty dollars, which we readily deposited in his hands, on his solemn declaration, that he received them for the hire of a boat, which should be ready for our reception at night.

In a short time after our host had left us, he returned to advise us of the vizier's approach, who followed him into our apartment, attended by a number of officers of state. They came, as they informed us, to enquire into our business, and our reasons for travelling through their country. Tho' they had taken us rather unawares, we put the best face we could upon the matter, and declared ourselves travellers, whom ill fortune, and not our own inclinations, had led among them. On their demanding our pass, we produced the one from the vizier of Yambo; and we thought it fortunate that we could shew them letters from Captain Bacon, and the supercargoes of the snow Adventure, to Ibrahim Beg, the bey of Cairo, to convince them that our journey was not a secret to the bey. The vizier put the pass into his pocket, and we remarked, that he eyed the letter to the bey with great attention, and whispered with apparent earnestness to some of his followers before he returned it to us. We gathered the most flattering presages from this incident; and as he had preserved the utmost politeness and moderation in this interview, we saw the vizier and his train depart, in the fullest confidence of having found protection in our letters, against the government, which were so well inclined to have persecuted us.

When these people were gone, we partook of a repast which the family had provided for us. It was simple, but well-drest, and consisted of meat and vegetables, both stewed and roasted. We had not seen the young shaik all day, and were uneasy at his absence.

fence. When he made his appearance, he affured us that he had been employed in our fervice fince we faw him laft, and that he only wanted the money, to fecure the boat which he had engaged for us. But this information feemed chiefly to be a prelude to his own demands, and we difcovered that he was come, like the reft of his countrymen, for a prefent. Though we had promifed him a gratuity conditionally, yet as we placed too much reliance on the oath of an Arab, we hoped to bind him more ftrongly to us, by an act that favored of confidence, as well as of bounty. We therefore prefented him with twenty dollars; and Mr. Hammond gave him a fhaul to which he had taken a liking. He appeared fo much ftruck with this generofity, that he fwore by his Prophet, he would not leave the houfe until a boat was provided for us. We then fent for our hoft, with whom we had entrufted the boat-hire; but underftood from him, that he had juft paid it away with the reft of the money to the Banute cavalry, who, on this prompt payment, had relinquifhed their firft demand. Tho' this ftory was rather ftrange, it carried not a fufpicious air on the face of it. We faved fixty dollars by the manœuvre, and readily proffered to advance the boat-hire anew. A reys, or nokidah, accompanied the hoft, who, after fome altercation, agreed to let us have a large, commodious boat, to carry us to Cairo, for fifty-five dollars. As the price was confiderably increafed, we affected to run fhort of cafh, in hopes to imprefs them with a notion of our being too poor to be worth detaining. Accordingly we produced feveral Indian coins, both of gold and filver, which we defired might be weighed, to make up the fum. Though we let them underftand that thefe were pocket-pieces, which we had preferved through curiofity, I fear this expedient was the means of awakening the avarice of thefe robbers, and teaching them to expect a hoard of this treafure. On receiving the amount, with five dollars befides, to provide bread and two or three fheep for the

voyage,

voyage, the fhaik, our hoft, and the nokidah, fwore in conjunction to the immediate performance of the treaty. But they think, as the poet fays of lovers, that " Jove laughs at *Arab* perjuries," and they can fwallow the moft facred oaths, without the fmalleft intention to keep them. And this we found more ftrongly verified than ever.

On the faith of their promifes we had packed up our baggage, and difpofed ourfelves for our removal. Nine o'clock was the appointed hour, and we waited for it with all the impatience of a bridegroom, who looks forward to the moment which is to crown his fondeft wifhes. But our watches announced the hour, and no Arabs appeared. We, however, accounted eafily for the delay; efpecially as the natives muft find it difficult to afcertain time, in a country where clocks and watches are unknown. Ten o'clock came, and brought no intelligence of them. Our fufpence now began to be cruel; and we fent Abdul Ruffar down ftairs, to enquire what was become of the hoft and his companions. He returned without having obtained any other tidings, than their being ftill abroad. It is impoffible to give the reader an idea of our fituation during this interval. We were affembled on a terrace that was open to the air, and had no other light than what the ftars afforded us. The worft interpretation was put upon their abfence, by fome of our company. Ibrahim began to defpair; and Abdul Ruffar himfelf could not account for the conduct of his countrymen. Tired out with fruitlefs expectation, we ftretched ourfelves upon our carpets, and endeavored to compofe ourfelves to reft. In the midft of our difordered flumbers, we were fuddenly alarmed, about midnight, by a noife at the outward gate of the houfe. We heard the door open, and the found of a man's feet haftily afcend the ftairs. Hope hung upon his fteps; and when we beheld our hoft enter with a light in his hand, we called out, as if with one voice, that we were ready to attend him.

him. Judge ye, who have ever experienced the fallacy of appearances in matters nearest to the heart—judge of our emotions, when we found, that, instead of a boat being in readiness to carry us away, the vizier and his train were below! The late hour, our recent disappointment, and the surprize which this news threw us into, operated together to render us very unfit to receive these unwelcome visitants. But we had not even time to enquire into the meaning of this intrusion, when the vizier entered. He was accompanied by all the officers who were with him in the morning; but his retinue was now enlarged by a number of soldiers, each of whom bore a torch in his hand. They seated themselves, without waiting to be asked, on the carpets which we had risen from; and calling for our interpreter, the vizier desired him to tell us, that he was come to levy a duty on the goods and jewels that we had with us: that he and the council of state had formed a resolution to demand no more than 4,000 dollars; and if we refused to pay so moderate a sum, they must send us to their master, the Shaik-Ul-Arab, who was then on the frontiers of his dominions, to answer for our refusal. The exorbitancy of the demand made us treat it in a light manner; and as to our taking another journey upon camels, we declared it was better to die here, than to fall a sacrifice to the fatigues of the Arabian method of travelling. We told them our baggage lay ready for their inspection, and they might soon satisfy themselves of our poverty. Whether this confident behavior impressed them with an idea of our sincerity, or that their designs were not ripe for execution, we cannot pronounce; but the vizier declined the search. He however politely insinuated, that a shaul or two would be very acceptable to him. I had two fine ones belonging to my Turkish dress, which had stood me in 100 dollars. These I produced without hesitation, tho' I declared truly they were all I had, when I presented them to the vizier. On receiving them, the minister

nister begged us to be easy, as he now considered us to be under his protection, and would give us a pass in the morning for our safety down the river. When he had taken his leave, we reproached our host for the failure of his word. But he shifted the blame from himself to the vizier, who, he assured us, had put a stop to our voyage for this night. He repeated his former assertions, that the boat was ready for our reception. In short, he drew so flattering a picture of the vizier's good intentions towards us, and expressed such a zeal for our service, that he obtained his ends of getting a shaul himself from Major Alexander, and of lulling us once more into a transient security.

SUNDAY, 3d August.

The morning came, only to furnish us with fresh instances of the perfidy of these people. Instead of the vizier's pass, or any signs of our departure, we were left to our own reflections, and we saw nothing of the young shaik, of our host, or of his brother. Nay, to such a pitch was their neglect carried, that at noon we found there was no dinner provided for us in the house. In this embarrassment we sent out Abdul Russar to purchase us some provision; and as we understood the city abounded with Christian merchants, we directed him to apply to them for their opinion of our detention, and for their advice and assistance on this alarming occasion. Too strict a watch was kept upon the motions of Ibrahim, to admit of his negotiating such a matter for us. It was rarely that he was suffered to stir out of doors, under pretence that the people of Banute were once more in search of us, to tax us in another present; and when this liberty was allowed him, he was attended by the host, or some of the family. We were yet in the dark, therefore, in respect to the form and nature of the government under whose extortions we groaned. But we gave the absent

sent prince, whoever he might be, full credit for a principal share in our sufferings.

In about an hour's time our faithful domestic returned, with a couple of fowls and some greens, which he immediately set about to dress for us. But, to our great concern, he had met with no success in the more material part of his errand. No admittance had been given him at the Christian houses, because it was the hour of dinner; an hour sacred to privacy among the Oriental nations. While we were waiting for our humble repast, we were not a little surprized at the sight of the vizier, who came to pay us a visit, attended only by his servants, who remained below. It was about two o'clock, and long past his time of dining. Nevertheless, on our victuals appearing, he sat down to a single dish with us, and partook with much seeming satisfaction of the fare which was put before him. He called for spirits, which he jocosely said the Christians were the most choice in, and drank several coffee-cups of rum, both during and after our meal. The vizier's name is Mahmoud. He is a young man of about thirty years of age, tall and well made, of a pleasing aspect and insinuating address, lively and entertaining in his discourse, and void of the reserve which marks the generality of his nation. It appeared to us that he was come *incog*, with an intent to unbend himself with the novelty of European company, and with the charms of a liquor which is forbidden by his law. But strong as these motives might be, we had quickly cause to be convinced, that there was another more prevalent in his bosom, which induced him to honor us with this visit. He began his attack in complimenting the knowledge and sagacity of our countrymen, and in passing the highest encomiums on the manufactures of our country. He dwelt in particular on the beauty of the fire-arms, and, by an easy transition, expressed a desire to possess a pair of English pistols. I had one pair left, very handsomely mounted with silver,

which

which I immediately presented him with. These had been seen by our treacherous host the preceding morning, when we had taken up arms to defend the house, and as I perceived that the vizier had got an item of them, I parted with them in the best manner I could. Not satisfied with this compliance, he now cast his eye on the major's sword. But its master had too great a value for an old and trusty servant, to give it up so easily. He had already redeemed it from the hands of a robber, and, perhaps, on that account, prized it more than ever. But the vizier's inclination for the sword seemed to increase, in proportion to the reluctance of the owner to resign it. In such a situation as ours, I could not see the use of with-holding any article from a man, who, by his rank and authority, might apparently dispose of us as he pleased. In my experience of these people, I had never found the good of resistance, in cases of this nature; and cannot take any shame upon myself for advising conciliating and pacific measures, in a country where a successful opposition would prove fatal to us. We had arms to defend ourselves, and I believe skill to have repelled superior numbers; but it must be allowed, that we should dearly have abided a recourse to them. Under this conviction, I endeavored to soften the vizier's disappointment, by tendering him a creese, or dagger, in lieu of the sword he wanted. Its handle was agate, studded with small rubies and emeralds; and as it belonged to my Turkish dress, was a very proper present to an Arab. This creese, with the pistols, cost me seventy dollars at least; but the sooner we are divested of our valuables, the nearer will be the hour of our departure. The meaning of this interview was too obvious to escape our notice; and we should have been content to have purchased this minister's friendship at the price of our baggage. Though every request he made could only be construed into a demand, he never exceeded the bounds of good-breeding in this piratical visit; and it must be acknowledged, that there

never

never existed a more polite robber than the vizier of Ghinnah. He had the art to shift the discourse to something flattering or amusing to us, whenever we attempted to touch on the subject of our departure; and notwithstanding we perceived his drift, he had the address to evade the question, and to lead us from the point we had always in view. In short, he laughed with us, rallied with us, and drank with us; and, as a particular compliment, obliged us in our turns to smoke of his pipe. He lengthened his visit until eight o'clock in the evening, and, during the whole time, displayed all the skill and education of a professed courtier. We were absolutely foiled in our attempts to sound this politician's mind; and, at the end of the interview, had not obtained the least insight into the extent of his designs upon us. When we lamented our confinement in a private house, and complained of the deceitful conduct of our host, he affected to take a part in our troubles. But his language was ambiguous, and left us to conceive something more than it conveyed. At his departure, however, he assured us with a smile, that he intended to renew his visit on the morrow; but that he should insist on standing our caterer, and sending us a dinner more suitable to our condition. To this he added, that he hoped it would be the last meal we should eat in Ghinnah. Inconclusive as these words were, we were somewhat assured by them, and thanked the minister very cordially for his good intentions.

MONDAY, 4th August.

What with the anxiety of our minds, and the closeness of our apartment, we pass our nights in a very uncomfortable manner. The weather is very sultry, and the high walls which surround us on all sides, seem calculated to prevent a free circulation of air. But we had more important cares to engage our attention. From the wreck of our fortunes, we were intent to save a sufficiency to carry us to Europe, should it please God to deliver us from this rapacious tribe. I had about 100l. left in venetians and guineas, which, with a gold watch, and a ruby ring of some value, I concealed in an handkerchief about my waist. My European servant contrived also to carry about him some pictures and trinkets set with jewels, of mine, in his sash and turban. Mr. Hammond and the major made use of similar contrivances, to preserve their treasure. But the abundant riches of the latter became a grievous burden to him. He had lent the supercargo of the Adventure 1000 pagodas, or 400l. respondentia, to be paid at Suez. At our departure from Yambo he had received this sum, and what with pagodas and rupees that he had besides, he could not at that time be in possession of less than 1000l. in specie. A large capital, and though somewhat lessened by our former travels, still considerable enough to put him to great difficulties in the disposal of it. An heavy bag of 500 venetians was suspended about Ibrahim's waist, and afforded us no little trial of the honesty and attachment of this Indian. The major's slave-boys were likewise encumbered with gold and silver; and a prodigious handsome sword, which he had hitherto secreted in his bed, was now, for greater security, hidden in a hole under the stair-case. The handle and scabbard were of silver, highly wrought, and doubly gilt. This sword was valued at 100l. sterling, and was once the property of an eastern prince. These measures were adopted, from a suspicion that our trunks would undergo a scrutiny to-day, and that nothing but this ceremony having hitherto been omitted, obstructed our departure. It was our original misfortune to be lumbered with too much baggage, and it had been better that we had committed every thing to the waves at Cosire, than to have brought any packages but papers with the caravan. Its appearance almost warranted the exaggeration of the vulgar; and the approach of the English travellers, loaded with gold, precious stones, and merchandize, was every where published.

published. As they had no idea of people being led by curiosity or accident to visit their country, it was very natural for them to place our journey to the desire of gain, and to consider us in the light of merchants. Instead of coming here with privacy—as we had foolishly believed on the word of our conductor—it now appears, that we were expected with impatience by the principal inhabitants; and that our persons and our goods had only been transferred from one hand to another. To the blessing of God only can we now attribute the moderation of the shaik of Cosire, and our preservation on the road hither. Our lives and property had been at the disposal of him and his dependants, and we could not but shudder to reflect on the company we had travelled with. But to be exposed to pillage in a large and populous town, to which merchants of different countries resort, is only to be explained by the strange ideas they entertain of our baggage, which they will not search, though we press them to do it, and will not seize, though inclined to possess it. Thus kept in a struggle between avarice and fear, our journey is delayed, our apprehensions awakened, and our lives possibly endangered, until the conflict shall be decided in the breasts of these spoilers!

We have seen nothing of the young shaik since he received his present, nor of our host Mahomet, since he made us the fine promises of a speedy departure. Ibrahim watched an opportunity this morning to slip out unobserved, and to accompany Abdul Russar to some Christian houses. They were directed to sound these people, respecting the protection they were inclined to afford us. To know whether they could harbor us in their houses, in case we effected an escape from our prison; or at least would assist in procuring us a boat, to accomplish our flight under cover of the night. This negotiation was as fruitless as all the others we had undertaken. Neither their desires to serve us, nor the hopes of a good reward, were forcible enough to command the interposition of these Christians, confident as they were that we labored under the persecution of the government. To fill up the measure of our distress, the very boatmen, whom Ibrahim spoke to distantly on the subject, positively declined to receive us on board without a passport. Once more then must we give up the flattering prospect of liberty, and attend with patience the issue of our misfortunes.

It has been remarked by some philosopher, that in every trial to which humanity is put, how numerous soever the illusions of hope, there is still a succession of causes to revive this active principle, and to preserve the mind from the influence of despair. It is a pleasure to me to subscribe to a sentiment, which holds out so comfortable a truth to mankind, and which ascribes so benevolent a property to the divine ordination of events. Various had been the turns of our fortune, but never had we lost sight of an happy sequel. Even now, when all immediate succour is denied us, we look forward to a distant promise. The Indian Fakeer, whom we had not seen since our arrival here, and whose absence we could only attribute to his having pursued his journey, followed Ibrahim into the house, and offered to carry a letter to Cairo. He informed us of his having been frequently denied admittance to us, and urged us to dispatch him with all possible speed, that he might depart unnoticed. The gratitude of this poor Indian excited our admiration, and we delayed not a moment to take advantage of his unexpected offer. We penned a short but pathetic letter to Mr. Baldwin at Cairo, acquainting him of our alarming situation, and begging his interest with the bey to demand our release of this government. We had every reason to believe that our letter from Cosire had not reached Mr. Baldwin, but we had a better foundation for the success of this, as the bearer had evinced himself our friend, and was in a character that would render him unsuspected. But to ensure the delivery of

it,

it, as much as lay in our power, we prefented the Fakeer with five dollars, and on the back of the letter defired Mr. Baldwin would pay him as much more, as a reward for his fidelity. The Indian was very thankful for this kindnefs, and after concealing the letter in his turban, took leave of us with no little emotion. He luckily went out of the houfe unqueftioned by the porter; and we prepared ourfelves to receive the vizier, in a better temper of mind than we had been in for fome time paft.

At two o'clock the minifter came, accompanied only by the rafcal Ally. We were glad to find that he was not unmindful of his promife; and indeed he exceeded our expectations in the fumptuous dinner he had provided for us. It confifted of thirty covers, wherein various kinds of fifh, flefh, and fowl, were ferved up to our table. We had not feen fo plentiful a meal for many a day, and were not backward in doing honor to it. The vizier was particularly attentive in recommending the beft difhes to us, and feemed much pleafed at the appetite with which we ate. He relaxed entirely of his ftate, and when the victuals were removed, he and Ally fet in for ferious drinking. It was impoffible for us to efcape a dram or two, which he forced upon us. But he would take no excufe from Ally, who being a Muffulman like himfelf, was called upon to keep him in countenance. The rum was old, and confequently potent, and did not require a great quantity to intoxicate thefe boon companions. The vizier's head however was much the ftrongeft; and while the liquor only rendered him more talkative, its effects upon Ally were mifchievous and alarming. He acted a thoufand extravagancies, and at length pulled one of the vizier's piftols out of his girdle, and fired it in the air. In this ftate of frenzy the piftol might as well have been directed at one of our breafts, and we were very glad, in a few minutes after, to fee him fink upon the floor in a fit of ftupefaction. This afforded matter of great triumph to the minifter, who began to

conceive

conceive an infinite affection for us, talked of carrying us home to an house more eligible for our reception, and in the fulness of his heart, offered us horses and guards to conduct us through the city. He was very desirous to play a game of chess with me, when he understood I was conversant with it, and we were entertaining hopes of being benefitted in some shape or other by this paroxysm of kindness, when he was suddenly overcome by sleep. He stretched himself upon the carpet on which he had been sitting, and all our airy notions of relief vanished with his waking thoughts.

He had been upwards of an hour in this situation, when a messenger brought a letter, the delivery of which was too important to be dispensed with. We therefore ventured to wake the minister, who I believe was ashamed to be found in such a manner. On perusing it, he said the contents concerned us. That the shaik of Banute had sent two boats to pursue us down the Nile, under a supposition of our having pushed on for Cairo, and that they were now returned to seek us here. He bade us however to rely on his protection, and to keep ourselves quiet until these people had left the city, when he would dispatch us with safety. He then took his leave, not empty-handed, as during the visit he had wheedled the major out of a shaul, which appears to be the chief object of his desires. We had gained no ground in this interview; and held the revival of the Banute story, as a mere feint to renew our apprehensions, and to conceal the real motives of our detention.

TUESDAY, 5th August.

The prospect begins to grow darker and darker, and our departure seems to be more distant than ever. We are utterly neglected

lected by the family, and, in a manner, forsaken by the world. We had sent Abdul Ruffar to search for them in vain, when about eleven o'clock he returned with Ally. He was just risen from his bed, and the fumes of the liquor were scarcely evaporated from his brain. We were not sorry to see him in a situation, from which we had a chance of procuring some material intelligence. But he was a traitor in his cups; and gave the lye to the notion that good liquor will make a rogue honest. For my own part, I had been so mortified at the depravity of human nature, which, in the shape of our landlord and his associates, had not only violated the rights of hospitality, but repeatedly broken the most tremendous oaths which could be taken in the sight of a just God, that I was tempted at times to disown my alliance to such a race. Oppressed by one part of it, and unassisted by another, whose religion should have enforced their compassion towards us, it is not surprizing that we beheld them with an eye of abhorrence and distrust. We had experienced that there was no safety among them, and to the interposition of the divine Power alone, could we look for our deliverance. But the simplicity of Ibrahim led him to renew a confidence, so often misplaced. He gave more credit to the word of a Muffulman, and was the last to see into their falsehood. He took great pains to worm out of Ally the secret intentions of his brother. Repeatedly did he demand what they fought for from us, and as often did he proffer in our name to leave our baggage to them, provided they would convey us and our papers to a boat. Shame frequently appeared in Ally's face during this interrogation; and it was not without the hesitation attached to a guilty conscience, that he acknowledged they wanted more valuables. On this the major produced a silver mug, which he promised to deliver to the brothers at the river-side. But Ally would not be satisfied without a diamond-ring, which he had seen on the major's finger at Cofire. This

was

was a ring of no inconsiderable value, and had been imprudently exposed by the major, at a moment, indeed, when he did not suspect the mischief which was hatching against us. It would have been impossible, perhaps, to have waved this demand, if the major had not luckily been in possession of a paste ring of nearly the same size, which he imposed upon Ally for the diamond one. This ring and the silver mug were to be his, when he performed his engagement of putting us into a boat. The sight of them seemed to rouze the fellow, and to animate his zeal in our behalf. He left us on the instant, with a design to seek his brother, and to see what could be done for us. As an earnest of his good intentions, he left word with Abdul Ruffar below, that he would provide a dinner for us, which we were likely to have gone without before. We saw nothing of him however until two o'clock, when he brought us a very scanty and indifferent dish of fish stewed in oil. We could not help murmuring at our condition, and the rascal apologized, as well as he could, for the badness of the victuals. We were now left to ourselves for the rest of the day, to solve if possible the intentions of our enemies, and to deliberate in vain on the best measures to guard against their malignity.

In the evening, Ally brought his brother to us, whom we had not obtained a sight of for the three last days, though supposed to be under the same roof with us. Nature had been very just to this man, as the villainy of his disposition was written in legible characters in his countenance. He was in a manner dragged up to our apartment, and his present appearance would not have discredited a king's evidence at the Old-Bailey. He hung his head, though possessed of an infinite stock of assurance, and the frivolous reasons which he assigned for his absence, were the plainest proofs of his guilt. He now joined with Ally in seeming earnest for our departure, and which he assured us nothing delayed but the search of our baggage. This ceremony he understood

stood, was to be performed in the morning, and he fully discovered his principles, by desiring us to suffer him and Ally to inspect our baggage before the vizier came to do it. There was a time when this proposal would have been treated with the contempt it deserved; but our immediate dependence on these fellows, obliged us to listen to it with complacency. We were aware of their knavish designs, but we considered our effects as the clog which impeded our course; and a livelier picture cannot be exhibited of our situation, than the readiness with which we accelerated the hour, which might leave us destitute of the common necessaries of life. Our operations were now confined to the obtaining of our enlargement. We thought only of resuming our journey. The means of accomplishing so arduous an undertaking, were entirely left to the direction of chance.

WEDNESDAY, 6th August.

This is the sixth day of our arrival at Ghinnah, and we are as perfect strangers to the place as the hour we came here. Our view is limited to the street in which we live, and which we peep into from our windows, that are very small and very high. Here our faces engage the attention of passengers, many of whom are brought by curiosity to view us: the detention and ill usage of European travellers having made no little noise about the city. But compassion is the only medicine they can afford us. Although our case is known, we have little chance of relief under so precarious a government, where the ruling maxim seems to be, that the weaker side must go to the wall.

It is our fortune once more to excite the pity of the fairer part of the creation, and to find tenderness and humanity among the members of an Arab tribe. Exactly opposite to our prison is the haram of a man of some consequence, if we can judge of him

D d   from

from the number of his women. It was but two days ago that we discovered we were the objects of these females' regard; who, when the sun goes down, come tripping by pairs to the front of their terrace, and, by signs and salutations, enquire into our welfare, and lament their inability to relieve our distresses. Some of these women are beautiful, and all well made; and they make no scruple to appear before us unvailed, at no greater distance than the breadth of a narrow street. It would be an easy matter for us to discourse together, with the help of our interpreter, were we not afraid, in our critical situation, of incurring suspicion and danger. We find satisfaction, however, in this dumb intercourse. Unavailing as their sympathy must prove, our vanity is not the less flattered by it. We have retorted upon our oppressors without design, and triumph over them in the tenderest point!

Before we had breakfasted, our host and his brother visited us, to make the proposed search. We readily opened our trunks to them, and they were not a little surprised to find nothing but linen and cloaths, where they expected at least to light upon piece-goods, jewels, and money. They took, however, two handsome china bowls, a box of cut Trichinopoly stones, half a dozen sheets, and a Turkish habit from the major; and from me a Turkish coat only. Mr. Hammond's trunks escaped their hands. We were much astonished at this moderation, but suppose an apprehension of the vizier's catching them in the fact, occasioned their hasty retreat. As they were going away, Ally staid until his brother was out of hearing, and then asked the major in a whisper, to let him secrete the silver mug which was promised him in the boat. It unluckily stood on the window-seat with the remains of the major's breakfast, and without waiting for an answer, Ally took it up, and marched with it down stairs.

We had scarcely got rid of these plunderers, when the vizier
and

and his train made their appearance. They were very rigid in their scrutiny, until they came to a box belonging to me, which contained a packet and letters of consequence. The manner in which this box was secured, with nails and wax-cloth, gave them hopes of being well rewarded for their trouble. But when the lid was taken off, and the contents were displayed, never was such surprise seen, as was betrayed in the countenances of the vizier and his adherents. They seemed to awaken as from a dream, and after conferring together with evident marks of disappointment, they precipitately retired, notwithstanding our remonstrances, that they would finish the examination, and permit us to depart, though at the expence of our baggage.

We had sent Abdul Russar abroad to procure intelligence, and he returned with the news, that a boat was on the point of setting out for Cairo. He had sounded the nokidah, to know what he would do in our behalf; who, in defiance of bribery, would only venture to convey a letter for us to that city. As nothing could be effected towards our escape, we were content to address another letter to Mr. Baldwin, relating the new troubles we had met with, and the necessity of his immediate assistance, to deliver us from the perils which environed us. This letter Abdul Russar carried with great secrecy to the nokidah, who, in consideration of a present, undertook to deliver it to Mr. Baldwin.

In the afternoon the vizier repeated his visit, under pretence of taking down our names, and making out the pass for our departure. The conduct of this man towards us had been truly singular. He had courted us for his own views, and he had deceived us without any apparent motive. He had taken indeed many things from us in a polite way, but when he had an opportunity of satisfying his avarice with the choice of our moveables, he shrunk back, as if ashamed or afraid to persevere in his intentions.

intentions. This palpably shews that there is a ruling authority to which he is accountable, and to which we are indebted for our security to this hour. He positively told us that we should go at night, and our host as positively promised us his camels, to transport us and our baggage to the river-side. At six o'clock our host came, but it was only to inform us, that the young shaik had ran away to Cosire with the boat-money. We could not at first think so ill of our conductor, but our host assured us, that we had seen our last of him. More money was now demanded for the hire of a boat, but we had so long persisted in the story of our money being all expended, that we could not have produced any, without confirming their opinion of our wealth. This fellow, however, had the address to obtain the sword from the major, which had been refused to the vizier, and had been redeemed, with such trouble, from the clutches of the soldier. This sword he now demanded upon the footing of a former promise; and the major thought proper to gratify his wishes. He has been a material sufferer during the transactions of this day.

THURSDAY, 7th August.

We were at breakfast upon ripe figs and bread, for which we were indebted to the attention of Abdul Russar, who is our caterer at such times as our host neglects us, when two of the vizier's people entered the room, accompanied by our host and his father. The last is an old man, and not only privy to the iniquitous conduct of his sons, but a tormenting solicitor himself for any thing that comes within his view. The trite tale of the Banutecavalry being returned for money, was once more attempted to be imposed upon us; but we had learned to parry the attack, by desiring them to convey our baggage to the horsemen, who were welcome to dispose of it as they thought fit. This liberal offer did

did not suit their defigns. It was the fpecie which they looked for, and it seemed as if they began to fufpect that we did not keep it among our baggage. From 1000 dollars, which thefe mock agents at firft demanded, they fell at once to 100, then to 80, 60, 40, and at length to 20 dollars! The vizier's adherents foon retired, when they found themfelves treated in fo cavalier a manner, and left us to difcufs the matter with Mahomet. This is the Cerberus whom we are to gain over, if the door to our efcape is to be opened to us. We have tempted him with many a fop, but his price is yet to be reached, if it be in his power to permit of our departure. We condefcended to affure him, that we had not the money to fatisfy this demand; but that, to oblige him, we would give up our filver fpoons, which we ufed at our table, and which were equal to the value of twenty dollars. He appeared to liften with great attention to this propofal, but fuddenly recollecting himfelf, he paufed for a moment, and told us, that without a letter from us, fpecifying that he had received no money from us, he could concern himfelf no further about our affairs. The effrontery of this Arab exceeded, if poffible, his depravity. He talked as if his endeavors had been exerted for our good; and held the language of friendfhip amid the daily practice of injuftice. We were, therefore, not a little rejoiced to find, that our hoft did not quietly enjoy the fruits of his villainy. On inquiring into the neceffity of giving him fuch a letter, we learned that the town's people threatened to pillage his houfe, and to fhare with him the 1000 venetians which he was reported to have obtained from us. A declaration under our hands of its falfity, would ftifle the report, and preferve his property from being left to the mercy of an enraged populace. We had been fo little accuftomed to truth in this country, that we were become fceptics in every thing, which did not immediately fall under our own obfervation. This fellow, however, had evidently fome reafon

for

for his fears, and, in order to difcover their origin, we difmiffed him with a promife of furnifhing him with the paper he wanted.

'Ibrahim informed us, that he had been frequently preffed by Ally, to go abroad with him at unfeafonable hours. This behaviour awakened our fufpicions, that fome foul play was intended to this faithful domeftic; and we accordingly cautioned him not to truft himfelf in Ally's company. But by a ftrange infatuation, he neglected this admonition; and by venturing out of doors, when we had laid down to take our afternoon-nap, fell into the net which was fpread for him, and very nearly involved us in the danger we were moftly to apprehend. He returned about five o'clock in a ftate of intoxication, and could hardly find words to explain the caufe of it, when he became quite befide himfelf. We gathered, neverthelefs, from him, that Ally had met and inveigled him into a coffee-houfe, under pretence of treating him with a difh of coffee. That he had tafted fomething particular in the coffee, and would not be prevailed upon to ftay, when he found his head begin to grow giddy. That villain Ally had doubtlefs introduced an opiate into the cup; and whatever his view was, it was baffled by the refolution of Ibrahim, who forced his way home in that condition, and difplayed a conduct we did not give him credit for before to-day. The major's bag of venetians was ftill about him; but it was impoffible for us to know, what intelligence might not have been drawn from him in fuch a fituation. He was by no means addicted to liquor; and though he would not refufe his dram when on board the Adventure, he had fo long abftained from fpirits, that we were convinced he had not been affifting to his own intoxication. We had the greateft confidence in his honefty and attachment, but we dreaded the difcoveries which he unknowingly might have made. We were anxious to fuppofe that no harm had yet been done, and hurried him

him to bed in an inner apartment, where we watched him like a child, that he might not get down ftairs, or hold any converfation with Mahomet or Ally, until he was fobered again. Thefe blood-hounds followed the fcent which the latter had hit off, and came up repeatedly, under pretence of talking to Ibrahim about our departure. But we were aware of their intentions, and hindered their waking or getting any accefs to him. It would not have been fo eafy for us to have prevented the intrufion of the vizier, and we trembled for his appearance at this moment. I can declare for myfelf, that I have not experienced the poignancy of diftrefs until this accident; by which we find ourfelves brought to the brink of deftruction, through the fimplicity of one of our own attendants. The morning, we hope, will reftore him to a fenfe of his folly, and difpel the cloud which thickens around us.

FRIDAY, 8th August.

The occurrences of this day have been fo crouded, fo ftrange, and fo affecting to humanity, that the reader will doubtlefs offer a plea to himfelf for the irregularity of a narrative, which was taken down late at night, and while our fates were ftill in all the horrors of uncertainty. The defire of being held in the memory of mankind, even awaits us to the mouth of the grave; and however hideous the danger, a liberal mind cannot bear the idea of going out of the world by an obfcure and unknown track, while there is a chance of tranfmitting its fufferings, its fortitude, and its refignation, to the regard of pofterity. And fhould it pleafe God to permit this journal of our diftreffes, to furvive the general wreck which threatens our lives and property, it may have the merit of difclofing to others, the perils which attend the traveller through this favage clime; and to warn him by our examples, of the little credit he fhould repofe in the fanctity, the hofpitality of

the

the Arabs; for which virtues they have been falfely celebrated by uninformed hiftorians!

The morning had paffed as ufual, in fufpence and diftruft of thefe people's intentions, nor did any thing occur to fweeten our daily potion, but the repentance of Ibrahim, and the behavior of the poor women whom I before mentioned to have taken notice of us. Immured in a fimilar confinement, they felt for our fituation, and partook of our troubles. The tale of our difafters had certainly reached their ears, as they enquired by figns whether we had cloaths left, or victuals to eat. Actuated by our melancholy geftures to fuggeft the worft, thefe tender-hearted creatures brought fruit and fugar-canes, all they could probably lay their hands upon, and threw them by ftealth acrofs the ftreet to our terrace. This humane tafk they were employed in for half an hour and more, when they difappeared, on our advertifing them of the arrival of vifitors.

The alarm was falfe, for it was only Abdul Ruffar, who was returned from reconnoitring the motions of the enemy. In his walk he had been encountered by fome Chriftian merchants, who now recommended to us, to get a letter privately written to the Shaik Ul Arab, complaining of the ufage we had met with, and imploring his protection. They not only advifed this expedient, but promifed to forward the letter for us, in the fuccefs of which they implicitly confided. We could not do better, we thought, than follow the opinion of thofe of our own perfuafion; and we had actually difpatched our agents to them upon this errand, when the fcheme was unknowingly overfet by the major. We had all along confidered ourfelves as clofe prifoners; and the major refolved to make an effort to get into the ftreet, to be certified of the worft of our fituation. He found the door locked, and knocking to get it opened by the porter who conftantly attended without, the family were alarmed, and came

in

in numbers to prevent his forcing this passage. A struggle ensued, which the major thought prudent to desist from, and returned up stairs with our servants, who were detained at home by this untoward accident.

While we were consulting on some remedy for this disappointment, a body of people came up to our apartment, ushered by our host. The principals were an old fat man, and one dressed in a scarlet robe, who told us that he was the hakeem or governor of the town, and had been commanded by the Shaik Ul Arab, his master, to take us under his protection; to enquire into the particulars of the injuries which we had sustained; and to transmit a faithful account of us to the shaik, who would see justice done to us, let whosoever be the aggressor. Our spirits had long been in want of a cordial to revive them, and this speech operated very powerfully upon them. The appearance of these officers, and the authority which they took upon them, gave credit to their words. We considered ourselves as distinguished by the compassion of the shaik, though we could not discover by what providential accident the tale of our disasters had come to his knowledge. But elated as we were by this sudden change in our affairs, and consonant as the hakeem's offer was to our hopes of revenge, we were too well aware of the unstable state of an Arabian government, to be led astray by a false emblem of power. The event proved that we did not judge much amiss; and that it is dangerous to make enemies in a body, where we are not assured of friends.

Before the assembly had well seated themselves, the vizier arrived, and took his place among them. He betrayed a downcast and irresolute countenance, and I observed him to look often at us, to guess I suppose at our intentions. I endeavored to clear his doubts with a smile. In reply to the hakeem, we declared our scruples to prefer complaints, strangers as we were to the country, and unassured of protection. On this we were urged by

E e   most

most present to a plain recital of facts, which they said was but due to the honor of their master, whose character would suffer by the mal-treatment of strangers, who were suffered to leave his dominions without redress. Ibrahim on this advised us to give a general statement of our losses, without specifying the names of our oppressors; which would irritate no one, and still obtain us the protection of the government. Had this counsel been followed, it might have turned out better; though it is impossible for human judgment to determine it. The examination began under this restriction, and Ibrahim expressed sundry sums of money and articles of value we had been deprived of, by the arts and menaces of persons unknown. The vizier sate in the circle like a private man, and listened in silence to the account of the robberies; in which he seemed satisfied not to be declared an accomplice. But the zeal of Abdul Ruffar quickly altered this peaceable scene. I had observed him sitting in a corner, with indignant looks and restless postures, when, unable to bear with the villainy of his countrymen any longer, he started up, and pointing to his own neck as a pledge for our safety, he went up to the hakeem, and pronounced aloud, that our doubts of protection prevented the truth from appearing in its proper colors. That, to his knowledge, our host Mahomet had forced money and effects from us; and that the vizier himself had defrauded us of shauls and other things to a considerable amount. But the integrity and courage of this poor fellow met with a very unworthy recompence. He had built more than ourselves upon the regal authority, which could not, in the persons of the shaik's officers, shield him from danger and disgrace. The vizier rose abruptly from his seat, and half drawing his sabre, would have stopped his countryman in his tale, had he not been luckily prevented by those near him. The assembly broke up in confusion, and we could not but

be alarmed for our own safety at such a moment. No sooner
was Abdul Ruffar delivered from one enemy, than he encountered others more bitter in the host and his family, who fell furi-
ously on him in the presence of the hakeem, and it was with
much difficulty that we rescued him from their hands, at the expence of some heavy blows. But the scene did not conclude here.
To make good our host's assertion, that every one is absolute in
his own house, he turned the vizier, hakeem, and all the shaik's
officers out of doors, and told them deridingly, to go and consult
elsewhere. Our faithful domestic would fain have followed them,
but he was prevented; which so intimidated him, that dreading
the resentment of the family, he came unobserved to our terrace,
and dropped himself thirty feet at least, from a perpendicular
height, into the street. He escaped; but not, we apprehend, without some sprain or contusion, from so desperate a leap.

This tumult had scarcely subsided, when one of a more serious
and insulting nature ensued. Apprehensive of a discovery, and
perhaps weary of carrying about such a load, Ibrahim had deposited the bag of venetians which he was charged with, in the corner of a dark room which held fire-wood. The major was apprized of this step, and might very well be satisfied of the security of
his treasure. But the prying disposition of the family surmount-
ed our precaution. Ibrahim had been met coming out of this
room by Ally, before the arrival of the hakeem and his company. Suspicion is ever on the watch, and gives a motive to
every action that falls under its observation. The late dispute,
in which he had borne so active a part, had not driven it
from this fellow's mind; who, when all was quiet again, stole
up softly to the room which had excited his curiosity. Ibrahim by good fortune saw him enter it, and crying loudly for assistance, ran towards the place which concealed the money.
He was heard and followed by the major and my European
servant,

servant, who found him at the room-door struggling for the bag, which Ally had secured, and would have retreated with. Numbers however prevailed, and the bag was presently redeemed from the rascal's gripe, who retired, muttering vengeance against us.

We had soon reason to lament this unfortunate discovery. It awakened a new spirit of avarice in our host, and confirmed him in his exaggerated ideas of our wealth. He came up stairs, attended by the informer Ally and his servants, armed with swords and spears, to demand the contested treasure. We had expected this, and in the interval, the major had time to change the bag of venetians for one of rupees, which was not a twentieth part its value. The gold was again committed to Ibrahim's waist, and the silver was carelessly thrown into one of the trunks. The deception succeeded; and, after some altercation, the bag was produced from the trunk, and imposed upon Ally for the one that he had seized upon. The bulk was nearly the same, though nothing but the confusion he was in, can account for his not distinguishing the difference between the weight of the gold and silver. Though this action was nothing less than a robbery, these Arabs were willing to give it a more favorable term, and said, that they took it on condition of providing us with a boat, and accelerating our departure. There was something too gross in this behavior to amuse us with expectation; but we were as ready as themselves to save appearances, and to conceal our mortification at being subjected to such violence. Some of our company had proposed manual resistance; and a musket was actually taken up on the occasion, which was laid down upon a conviction of the folly of opposition, where our lives were not concerned, in a country so inimical to Christians, and so severe in its decrees against those, who, however justly, have dipped their hands in the blood of a Mahometan. We adopted a middle course, and so far maintained our dignity, as to insist upon the host's dismissing

missing his servants before we would treat with him. This he easily complied with, and received the bag containing eighty-seven rupees, with many assurances of fidelity, and promises to effect our deliverance from this city.

Our host justified the opinion we entertained of him. So far from keeping his word, and endeavoring to serve us, in return for the money he had extorted, he only left us, to contrive some method to make sure of our remaining treasure. In less than half an hour he returned, accompanied by two villains, who called themselves the servants of the Shaik Ul Arab, and who produced a paper, which they termed his order to search our baggage. Though we could not but doubt the authenticity of this paper, we were far from opposing a measure which we had so often solicited; and which we hoped would deliver us from further persecution on this head. It is too cutting to my reflection to recount the particulars of this scrutiny, which was conducted rather with the violence and indecency of a robbery, than with the forms of a search. Not a single thing escaped the hands of these fellows, that was of the least value. Mr. Hammond, among other articles, lost a pair of silver-mounted pistols, which he had hitherto preserved, and they plundered the major of his silver spoons, a silver urn handsomely chased, and weighing above fifty ounces, which he had in vain concealed within some kitchen utensils, besides a quantity of linen to a considerable amount. From me they took a silver hookah, a set of gold buckles, two pieces of Indian hankerchiefs, a gold brocade waistcoat, and a Turkish gown, which, at the lowest calculation, were worth 200 dollars. I left the room while this scene was transacting, as it was to the last degree grating to my nature, to behold, unrevenged, so daring an outrage against all divine and human laws. They retired about eight o'clock in the evening, loaded with their spoils, and we threw ourselves upon the floor, to endeavor to get

some

some repose, after a day spent in uproar, altercation, and fatigue: insomuch that we had not leisure to take a proper refreshment. It is no wonder if our rest was disturbed, and our imagination haunted with gloomy ideas, under such peculiar circumstances. We could observe from our windows a strong guard to be posted about the house, with camels ready saddled at the door, but for what purpose we knew not; whether to take us to the boat, or to any place more suitable to their black designs. We were deprived of our servant, who used to provide us with the necessaries of life, and were to trust to chance for the morrow, should it ever dawn upon our eyes, after the unparalleled treatment we had suffered. Guilt might possibly be touched by the stings of distrust and fear; and to quiet these monitors, it was uncertain how much further our persecutors would plunge themselves into the abyss of wickedness. In the variety of this distress, life was still dear; and, divested as it was of ease and enjoyment, we slept with arms in our hands, to preserve it from violence!

SATURDAY, 9th August.

The dawn relieved us from our apprehensions, but found us in all the agitations of suspence. We were chiefly distressed at the absence of Abdul Russar. We knew not what mischance might have befallen him, in his attempt to escape the death which was intended him; and we were at a loss to furnish ourselves with provision for the day. There was a risk attended the going abroad of Ibrahim, after the adventure of yesterday; and we had not much dependence on the charity of the family, who had already forfeited every pretension to humanity in our estimation. We had luckily a little coffee left, which we boiled, and made out a breakfast with the stale bread of yesterday. About an hour

after

after this, a servant of the house unexpectedly brought us up some milk mixed with water, with a scanty allowance of bread. We understood that we were indebted to our host for this meagre repast, but we neither saw him, his brother, nor any living creatures but at a distance, during the whole morning. Among these were our kind friends in the opposite house, to whom only we now appear to be of the least consequence. These compassionate females had been alarmed at the tumult in our apartment on the preceding evening. I had observed them, at the time, frequently peep over their wall, to see what was going on, and seemingly anxious about the consequences. Nor had they exhausted their attention towards us. At the still hour of noon, when the streets are deserted by the people, they came to their terrace, and with sympathizing looks would have consoled our sufferings. Often did they wipe their eyes which were suffused with tears, and as often did they inquire, by the most significant signs, whether our lives had been endangered during the transactions of the past day. Notwithstanding our forlorn condition, we should have little deserved the name of men, if this behavior had failed to make a suitable impression upon our minds. Like the cordial which is administered to the dying patient, it served to revive our spirits, though we were sensible its effects were temporary and insufficient. Their generosity was equally extended to our wants. Naturally supposing that we were stinted in our nourishment in such an inhospitable house, these affectionate souls threw over loaves of bread and boiled eggs, tied up carefully in their vails, which came safely to us, and would have proved a plentiful supply, if something extraordinary had not disturbed them while taken up with this charitable act. We are apprehensive that they were discovered assisting us by their keeper; and, as they did not appear to us again, that they are doomed to stricter confinement, for exerting an impulse of benevolence to

their

their fellow-creatures in diſtreſs! No breaſt but a Muſſulman's, could harbor a jealous thought on ſuch an occaſion, or confound a principle of compaſſion with an amorous inclination towards perſons in our ſituation.

About two o'clock the ſame ſervant whom we had ſeen before, brought us a wretched compoſition of eggs and oil, which, for my part, I found it was impoſſible to touch. I was content, therefore, to adapt my meal to our priſon, and dined upon bread and water. At this moment we had notice given us, that the hakeem and his train were below ſtairs, and that he purpoſed to remove us in the evening from this hateful habitation. He preſently came up to us, to confirm this agreeable intelligence, and received our cordial acknowledgments for his humane intentions. We had experienced many reverſes of fortune ſince our arrival in this country, but none ſo ſudden, ſo unlooked-for, as the preſent. From the circumſtances which attended the hakeem's expulſion yeſterday, we little expected to ſee him re-enter the houſe in triumph, and reſcue us from the force which had ſo ſucceſsfully oppoſed him before. But it ſeems that he comes armed with new powers from the ſhaik, to take us immediately under his own protection. It is not eaſy to unravel the politics of this ſtate; but the deciſive behavior of our hoſt laſt night, is a preſumptive evidence of his authority being about to draw to a concluſion. He has plundered us of all he could lay his hands upon, and he wiſely abſents himſelf at a period when he either cannot, or does not, think it worth his while to detain us. We found from the hakeem, that Abdul Ruſſar is ſecurely lodged in his houſe, tho' his legs and feet are violently contuſed by the fall. We are happy in his ſafety; but the damage which this faithful adherent has ſuſtained in our cauſe, cannot but ſtrongly affect us. The hakeem now bade us farewell until ſun-ſet, when he promiſed to return with a camel and an eſcort, to convey us and our baggage to a

dwelling

dwelling of his own. To prevent the family from giving us any further disturbance, he left a servant at the door of our apartment, whom he directed to keep watch during his absence.

There was no danger, however, of our being molested in the smallest degree. The house appeared to be abandoned by its inhabitants; and this solitude luckily afforded the major an opportunity of recovering his costly sword, from the hole in which it had been deposited. This he once more sewed up in his bed; and we had packed up the remains of our baggage, long before the appointed hour of our removal. We waited with great patience until the day closed, and it was quite dark before any of us betrayed the least uneasiness at the hakeem's stay. But as the night waxed old, we relapsed into the dreadful state of uncertainty which we had so repeatedly known. We had not a doubt of the veracity of the hakeem; but we began to suspect that our enemies had prevailed against him, either by secret intrigues or open violence. We were apprized of their animosity, and we had every thing to dread from their success. It was ten o'clock before this gloomy prospect was dissipated, by the arrival of the hakeem. He came attended by a party of soldiers, and a camel to transport our baggage. The villain Ally had now the assurance to shew himself, and to superintend the removal of our things. Before we went out, the hakeem obliged us to prime our fire-arms anew, and dropped certain expressions which seemed to Ibrahim to imply danger on the road. Had we been convinced of an ambuscade being laid for us, we should rather have preferred to encounter it, now we were patronized by the government, than to have remained in an house, which had been a scene of mortification and deceit to us. The die was cast, and we were to abide by its decision; which we did, by marching after our camel and servants, who helped to carry the baggage, accompanied by the hakeem and his guard. Each of the servants took a lighted taper in his hand, and,

and, to heighten the scene, we were enjoined profound silence. In this manner did we traverse a number of streets, each of which we found secured by a gate; and after going above half a mile, arrived at the place of our destination about eleven o'clock, without having met with any interruption. We were introduced by the hakeem to our lodging, and after passing through a large court, were carried up stairs to a small, but airy, bed-room. Our baggage was also brought up, and deposited in a back-room, where the servants are to sleep. The friendly hakeem now took his leave of us, and fixing a centry at our door to protect us, left us to enjoy almost the only sound rest we had known since our departure from Cosire.

SUNDAY, 10th August.

Here are we, after all our difficulties and dangers, safely pounded within the precincts of an haram. Such, on our awaking this morning, did we find the house we were got into. It is an antique structure, much injured by time, and stands upon a spacious foundation, though the apartments are small, and huddled together after the mode of these eastern piles of lasciviousness. Around our chamber the floor is raised about two feet from the ground, which serves us to eat upon by day, and to sleep luxuriously upon by night. Hence we have a fine view of the river, from which we are but two or three streets distant. It is here seemingly less than a mile in breadth, and discovers itself through different openings in the gardens, with which this city is adorned. The wind from the north-west now prevails, and meets the current, which runs with the utmost rapidity towards the sea. This produces a fine effect. The town lines this side of the Nile, and the opposite bank is bordered by a mountain, which at one place breaks off abruptly, and discloses a large plain, covered with enclosures

closures of grain, and here and there embellished with groves of date and orange trees. While we were indulging ourselves with this prospect, we had a visit from the friendly hakeem, who seemed alarmed at our exposing ourselves to public view, and hastily shut our windows. He excused this check to our curiosity, from the necessity there was for us to remain in privacy until the arrival of his master, or of further orders from him respecting our concerns. We could not but acquiesce in this measure; and after bidding us to rely on the justice of the Shaik Ul Arab, he left us to partake of a meal of good bread and milk, which his domestics had provided for us. Our breakfast was scarcely over, when the hakeem sent for Ibrahim, to attend him at his own house. We expect this interview will determine something positive about our fate.

When we left Cosire, we laid our account that our troubles would end with our journey to the Nile. Who could have dreamt that after escaping the perils of the desart, we should be reduced to despair in a populous city! It were better that our baggage had been sunk to the bottom of the Red Sea, than that it should have afforded us a trifling part of the uneasiness we have suffered. Prisoners for ten days in a private house, where each moment was impoisoned by the uncertainty of our destiny, we were now, perhaps, in a more honorable confinement in the hands of government, which we shrewdly suspect asserts our cause, rather from a desire of recovering the plunder for itself, than of doing justice to us. But we are content if our departure can be purchased at so low a price.

We were anxious to see Abdul Russar, whose ankles we find are much more strained by his fall, than were at first reported. But he is not to be moved here until the evening, when we shall be able to administer such relief to him, as is in our power to do. At one o'clock Ibrahim returned to us, and we understand that the hakeem has got out of him all our losses, not excepting the other night's pillage, which he had at firſt determined to conceal. And with ſome reaſon, as the villains threatened our lives if we divulged it to any one. But Ibrahim ſays, there was no one preſent at the examination, but a Chriſtian ſecretary, who took it down, and the hakeem privately aſſured him, that his maſter would give orders to ſeize the robbers, and make them reſtore their booty. God only knows the termination of this matter; but, for our parts, we would compromiſe to eſcape with our preſent damages. We now ate heartily of a plentiful meal, which Ibrahim had provided for us. Mutton, fiſh, and vegetables, are very cheap here, and no European could complain of their manner of dreſſing their food.

We ſaw nobody during the evening, but the ſervants belonging to the houſe. But we received a complimentary meſſage from the hakeem, with notice of his maſter's approach, who is expected here immediately. Theſe are welcome tidings to us, who have no idea of getting away, until the arrival of this great man. It is our plan to be rid of this place as ſoon as poſſible; and we propoſe to make a tender to the ſhaik of all he may recover on our accounts. Happy, if we have the luck to eſcape without further pillage.

In order that we might enjoy the benefit of a cool wind, and a moon-light evening, we went to bed very early, as we had been deſired not to open our windows until the lights were extinguiſhed. And now an adventure occurred, which was romantic to the laſt degree, and bore a reſemblance to thoſe feigned ones, portrayed by the inimitable pencil of Cervantes. I was awakened out of a ſound nap about ten o'clock, by a loud knocking at the gate, which ſecures the upper end of the ſtreet we live in. I found my companions had been diſturbed by the ſame noiſe, and were equally ſurprized with myſelf at the ſtrangeneſs of it. Preſently after the gate was opened, and a number of people aſſembled before

fore our houfe, whom we could difcern by the light of the moon, difpofing themfelves in different fituations on the ground, and converfing with great earneftnefs and vociferation. While we were pondering on the iffue of this bufinefs, which had an alarming appearance at fuch an hour of the night, when we knew our refidence was meant to be kept fecret, and that our lives might be fought by the villains whom we had informed againft, I went out on the back terrace to awake the guard, which was ftationed to protect us, when fuddenly a band of mufic ftruck up without, and recalled me to the fcene of action. This band was compofed of ftring, wind, and parchment inftruments, and though the harmony was none of the beft, it could not fail to have a fingular effect upon our imaginations, haunted as they were with doubts and apprehenfions. A fingle voice fometimes accompanied the mufic, which was in general of a melancholy ftrain. This ferenade lafted until midnight, and when the moon went down, it was continued by torch-light. But the intent of it we are utterly at a lofs to difcover. Whether to celebrate a marriage, or a funeral, or whether it was performed by the hakeem's guard, to divert their mafter or ourfelves. It was one o'clock before the night was reftored to its ufual quiet; at which time I fell afleep, but had my repofe difturbed by the extravagance of fancy, which brought a motley jumble to my mind, of mufic, harams, arms, captivity, and impaffable waftes!

MONDAY, 11th August.

This day was the moft barren of incidents of any that we have long experienced. Not a meffage, nor the leaft intelligence from the hakeem, in regard to our affairs. This has at leaft a good appearance. He means, perhaps, to wait the arrival of his mafter, inftead of deceiving us with the hopes of his own interpofition, and obtaining prefents from us on that fcore, like the vizier and

and the people into whose hands we at first fell. We learn from Ibrahim, that the rude concert last night was intended for the hakeem's entertainment, who is our neighbor, and who sate smoking and drinking coffee with his women the greatest part of the night. This is a favorite diversion with the Arabs and Turks, who keep themselves still during the heat of the day, and enjoy the cool hours of the night, and the serene light of the moon, with a relish unknown to the inhabitants of the inclement north. Those only who have partaken of this enchanting scene, under a sky still unclouded, can form an idea of its luxury; where the very dews are genial, and the night-breeze carries a temperate coolness on its wing. And this season favors more the bringing of their women into view; when silence and solitude prevail without, and afford them the selfish satisfaction of beholding beauty, without the intrusion of a rival, and tasting of its charms with the avarice of misers.

At four o'clock we had a visit from the hakeem, who only staid to enquire after our healths, and to reassure us of his protection. We had determined on making this man a present, to secure his further good offices, and finding that he was averse to taking any thing but money, we sent him twenty-one venetians by Ibrahim, with an apology for the smallness of the donation, which had been bounded by our poverty. To our great joy, our domestic, Abdul Russar, returned with Ibrahim from the hakeem's house. He was obliged to be moved in the arms of the servants, though we are pleased to find that his hurts do not portend any ill effects. One of his ankles is quite reduced, and the other promises fair to admit of his getting abroad in a few days.

TUES-

TUESDAY, 12th AUGUST.

The indisposition of Abdul Ruffar has already proved very inconvenient to us. Our silver is expended, and we are at a loss to exchange our gold for dollars, or to gain any intelligence of what is passing without doors, during this poor creature's confinement. He often cautions us against trusting any of his countrymen in matters of such importance; sensible as he is of their want of charity for Christians. As for Ibrahim, he is as much a prisoner as ourselves. The hakeem tells him, that he cannot answer for his safety, until the shaik returns, should he fall in the way of our old host and his gang. We are too well ascertained, from ocular proof, of the little order which subsists here in the absence of the chief, to doubt it. We learn that his return is anxiously expected by the whole city, and cannot be very distant, if we may trust to the information of Abdul Ruffar, who says, such is the temper of this people, and such the instability of this government, should the shaik remain for any length of time in another place, the inhabitants of Ghinnah would throw off all submission to his officers, and fall to cutting each other's throats. What a blessed land have we dropped into! What a race are we amongst! who are only to be ruled by the sword, and to be taught humanity at the expence of their blood!

We had scarcely breakfasted when the hakeem entered our apartment, accompanied by a man whom we had frequently seen at Cosire. He had been assiduous in his visits to us there, and had proffered us the use of his house during our stay at Ghinnah. This the shaik of Cosire prevented by his intrigues, and the man arrived here yesterday in the caravan. We find he is a merchant of this city, and though, agreeably to the mode of

Arabian

Arabian travellers, he was wont to assume a poor habit at Cofire, we now saw him in a creditable dress, and seemingly on an intimate footing with the hakeem. He lamented our misfortunes, which were the common topic of conversation, and reproached us for not having accepted of his offers of assistance. Though he must have been sensible that we did not merit this reproach, while our conduct was directed by another, and though we have cause to be on our guard against the professions of an Arabian, there is little doubt but we should have fared better under this man's protection, than in the vile hands we fell into. Our present situation is far from being disagreeable. The hakeem is civil and attentive to us, and at the same time does not pester us with his company, or solicit us for presents. From this conduct we draw more favorable omens, than from any incident since the change of our situation; and as he confirms the report of the shaik's approach, we endeavor to resign ourselves with patience, for the accomplishment of that desirable event. It may be, that our release will be at last owing to the interposition of Mr. Baldwin at Cairo. We have great expectations that our letters are both safely delivered to him. The reward of five dollars, which is to attend the receipt of each, is the strongest incentive that could be devised to secure the fidelity of the messengers. But fortune has been so much out of humor with us of late, that we cannot promise ourselves a return of her smiles, until they beam upon us.

Just as we had laid down to rest, there was a knocking at the outward gate, which we found to be made by the hakeem, who came to borrow one of our fusees. He was mounted on a fine horse, which I observed from the window, and was accompanied by a party of armed men on foot. He sent us word, that he was going about the town to preserve peace and good
order;

order; which is a neceſſary practice in cities better regulated than Ghinnah.

WEDNESDAY, 13th August.

We are obliged to be early riſers, in order to receive the company that wait upon us during the cool of the morning. We have generally finiſhed our breakfaſt by ſeven o'clock, and at that hour to-day we were ſummoned by our ſervants to the back terrace, which commands a noble view of the river, to ſee a number of boats under ſail. Theſe we learnt were the Banute fleet, which arrived here two days after us; with the ſoldiers of which our hoſt, the vizier, and others, had alarmed us, and forced us to pay down a ſum of money, which was falſely charged to their account. They are going down to Jirje, and being chiefly gallies, painted, and gilt, and adorned with ſtreamers, they cut no contemptible appearance in falling down with the ſtream, to the amount of twenty boats. We deſcried armed troops on the poop of each galley, and heard the drums beating to arms on board. There is a myſtery in the accounts of theſe Banute people, which we cannot unravel. Immediately after their departure, we had a viſit from the hakeem, who threw open the windows of our apartments, and told us with a chearful air, that we had now nothing to fear, as the Banute people, who are a ſet of thieves, and apt to plunder defenceleſs veſſels on the river, were ſailed for Jirje. This deſcription neither anſwers the ſtay which theſe people made here, nor the good condition of their boats, which is far from beſpeaking them to be a needy race. We therefore enquired of the hakeem of the origin and government of Banute; and were told, that it formerly belonged to his maſter, the Shaik Ul Arab, but had lately been taken poſſeſſion of by the Turks. This confirmed us in a vague report

port we had heard, of Banute being really in the hands of Ibrahim Beg. It might consequently be, that the hakeem wished for his master's return, that justice might be done us ere we proceeded to Cairo; and was willing to conceal us from the Turks, whom he artfully represented as robbers, to prevent our applying to them for a passage. So strongly had this prepossession taken hold of our minds, that some among us were not wanting to lament our ignorance of this circumstance, and to consider the departure of the Banute fleet, as a preclusion to the escape which we had so long meditated.

At five o'clock the hakeem paid us a second visit, in which he was accompanied by two considerable merchants of the town. They all produced letters from the shaik, which they told us respected our losses, and his coming to redress our wrongs. When the merchants took their leave, the hakeem asked us, whether we were inclined to take a walk with him to the river-side. This agreeable invitation my companions were obliged to decline, as the rascals who plundered our trunks, had not left them a Turkish gown: but I readily accepted of it, as I had a gown that luckily escaped their search. It is easy to conceive the joy I felt at being restored to the freedom of the air, after our perilous confinement; not to mention the good face which our affairs assumed by this step, as the people's intentions must appear to be honest, who exposed us to the eyes of the town. I accordingly arrayed myself in the best manner, and followed the hakeem, attended by my European servant and Ibrahim. As we walked towards the river, we were accompanied by a croud of people, who behaved themselves very respectfully; awed, perhaps, by the presence of the hakeem and his guard. We soon left the town, and ascended a dyke which is thrown round it, to prevent it suffering by the inundations of the Nile. I had the good fortune to be witness to the commencement of this periodical phenomenon,

menon, by mere chance. From the dyke we descended to the river, by a pier that extends itself to the natural strand, and measures some hundreds of yards in length. At the extremity of this pier we seated ourselves on carpets, which were spread for us on the ground, and I had full leisure to survey the objects around me, the novelty and beauty of which equally engaged my admiration. The Nile is originally of a tolerable breadth here, and at other seasons would not disappoint the traveller in his expectations of so celebrated a stream. But two days ago it began to assume a grander aspect. The kitchen-gardens which supply the town, and stand in the low grounds, are already overflown; and several channels are opened in the bank, through which the waters rush with great rapidity, and promise by to-morrow night to spread themselves to the dyke, which is at least a quarter of a mile distant. The same effects seem to have been produced on the opposite side; where I observed the country to be overflown even to the mountain's edge, and the rising lands to appear like islands in the waters. In mid-channel the stream runs with amazing force; carrying down rushes, bushes, and fragments of trees, which the floods have swept away with them from the heights, and will in a few days discharge into the Mediterranean. The sun was fallen behind the hills on the western banks, from whose burnished tops a dazzling radiance played upon the ruffled waters. The boats glided along their curling surface: the date-groves rung with the amorous cooings of a thousand doves, and the cattle lowed in the distant dale. The charms of this lovely evening are beyond my art to depicture, but they will be ever faithfully imprinted on my imagination. At dusk we returned homeward, and I could obtain but a very imperfect sight of Ghinnah from this point of view; as it stretches towards the river like the end of a Turkish slipper, and is screened by the dyke from the eye. We passed by a bridge on our way back, turned on a single arch over a creek where the boats lie,

lie, and which appears to be a modern work of no elegant design *.

* It may not prove unpleasing to the reader, to compare the observations of other travellers on this place and its neighborhood. As we passed over the desart between Cosire and Ghinnah, we can confirm the assertion of Captain Norden, that there are no remains of the antient canal mentioned by Herodotus and others, to have been dug for conveying goods from the Nile to the Red-sea. Ghinnah and its environs are still noted for manufacturing the best earthen-ware in Egypt; in the bottoms of which, the same peculiarity subsists as related by Dr. Pococke.

"At two o'clock in the afternoon there came on a calm, which obliged us to land on the same side, a little below *Giene*, or *Kiene*, a town, which is not at present very considerable, but which has, however, a mosque. There was formerly in this place a great commerce; for they had made a road which led to *Cosire*, a port of the Red-sea; and in three days they crossed the desarts of Thebais. But at present this route is not secure, on account of the robbers.

"I had been told much of the antiquities of this place, which engaged me to go thither; but I found nothing there. The inhabitants themselves of the place could give me no account of them. In vain did I seek for the antient canal that was dug for conveying merchandizes to the Red-sea, and for bringing others from thence by this means. I did not perceive the least mark of it, neither in the town, nor in the adjacent places. It is in this town they celebrate every year the great festival, at which the Bey of Girge is commonly present; but not without having first obtained permission from the Arab princes or Schechs.

"I perceived that all the neighboring places of *Giene* were covered with all sorts of plants, such as pompions, coloquintidas, and others, which were, for the most part, unknown to me. As I did not see any corn there, I imagined that they had cut it; and that the plants which I perceived, were the second product of the ground.

"There were in the neighborhood of the town divers ponds, in which water was preserved after the inundation; but it was not good for drinking. It had a brackish taste, which it takes from the soil itself; and indeed the inhabitants do not use it for any other purpose than watering their grounds, and giving drink to their cattle." Norden's Travels in Egypt, &c. vol. ii.

"We now pursued our voyage with a fine wind, and passed by the canal that goes to the city of Coptos, which is at present remarkable for making the best earthen-ware in Egypt, it being very light and much esteemed; but they could never be prevailed on to make the vases with broad bottoms, that they might stand without danger of falling; so that the people are obliged to set them in wooden frames." Pococke's Travels, chap. vi.

I found myself rather fatigued from my walk, and was glad of the approach of our hour of repose, which, for want of candle-light, we are obliged to anticipate as soon as the day is closed. But we were awakened from our first sleep by the sounds of tinkling instruments, accompanied by a chorus of female voices. I looked out of the window, and saw a band of thirty damsels at least, come tripping towards us, with measured paces, and animated gestures. The moon shone very bright, and we had a full view of them, from their entering the gate of our street, until they reached our house: Here they stopped, and spreading themselves in a circle before the door, renewed the dance and song with infinite spirit, and recalled to our minds the picture which is so fully given of these dancing females in holy writ. After they had favored us a few minutes with their lively performance, they moved on to the hakeem's house, and serenading him with an air or two, this joyous band quitted our quarter, and went, as the dying sounds informed us, to awaken the other slumberers of the town, to melody and joy! These are certainly the descendants of the women of Israel, whose beauty and skill gladdened the heart of the sapient king. The dancing girls of India are not to be spoken of at the same time: they are but an illegitimate race, were their excellencies to be compared with those of the nymphs of the Nile. Had these figures presented themselves to me in a vision, I should have concluded that they were the fair inhabitants of our mansion, who were come to demand the restitution of their late possessions!

THURSDAY, 14th August.

We were impatient to know the cause of the agreeable disturbance we met with last night, and learnt from one of our guard, that the dancing girls observe the ceremony we were witness

ness to, on the first visible rise of the Nile. It seems that they took our house in their way to the river, where they went down to bathe at that late hour, and to sing the praises of the benevolent Power, who yearly distributes his waters to supply the necessities of the native.

It is designed, to all appearance, that we shall meet with no friends in this inhospitable region, or immediately lose the protection of those who have displayed a ray of humanity for us. We were but this morning congratulating ourselves, on having fallen into the hands of a good man, who has not only rescued us from the house of a villain, but has even sheltered us under his own roof. He had yesterday admired a couple of carpets belonging to Mr. Hammond and me. We had sent them to him after breakfast, when he paid us a visit to thank us for our attention. He came escorted by a large train, little dreaming how shortly his glories would set, which now shone forth in meridian lustre. The change in his fortune was announced to us about five o'clock in the afternoon, when several strange servants came to our house. Their errand was to advise us of the approach of a new hakeem, who was sent by the shaik to displace our friend, and meant to take up his quarters for the night, in the back part of our habitation. While we were forming conjectures on this sudden event, several of the principal merchants of the town visited us, to confirm the news. They assured us, that the shaik had particularly charged this new officer with our affairs, and had dismissed the old hakeem from his employment, for having suffered European travellers to be plundered, and detained within his jurisdiction. In our own minds, we would readily have dispensed with this severity, to a man who had rendered us the most material services. Moreover, we could not but suspect, that the interest of the vizier, and others who had benefited by our arrival, had prevailed against the more honest

character

character that had exerted itself in our behalf. This reflection wounded us deeply, as the truth of it might reduce us to our former desperate situation. Considering the bad treatment we had met with, it is not strange that we should be jealous of any innovation in the protection which had been lately extended to us; and, in our experience of this tribe, that we should doubt of finding a second man of moderation among the officers of government.

About sun-set the new hakeem arrived, and sent us word that he was ready to receive us. This is the first visit we had paid to another. We found him seated upon a carpet on the back terrace, with a crowd of people about him. He is an elderly man, tall, thin, and of a mean appearance; distant in his behavior, and seemingly full of his own consequence. This may possibly arise from the lowness of his origin, which is that of an Abyssinian slave. His deportment was so different from that which distinguished his predecessor in office, that we could not but look upon him as an arrogant upstart, who promised to abuse the favour of his lord. He condescended, however, to tell us, with a smile, that his master had recommended us to his good offices, and had directed that the strictest justice should be rendered to us. While we staid, a number of persons came to pay their compliments to him, among which was Sauker, one of the rascals who had assisted the two brothers to pillage our baggage. By this effrontery he perhaps expects to escape suspicion; and to intimidate us by his presence, from bringing a charge against him. We soon retired to our apartment, and found that the vizier, among others, made his court to this new magistrate. Nothing can be a more direct implication of the arbitrary government we are under, than the promotion of this Abyssinian to one of its first dignities. When Charles of Sweden, the most despotic monarch of his age, wrote to the senate of Stockholm, that he would send his jack-boot to preside over them; ungrate-

ful

ful as the idea was, it surely was less humiliating, than if he had threatened to dispatch a Turkish slave from Bender for that purpose. And yet we were now witness to the universal homage that may be paid to such a character. The suddenness of his arrival, and the respect which he commands, no doubt bespeak, that he is charged with some important business; but we should be pleased to depart, without waiting the issue of his errand, though it prove to be the restitution of our losses. The shaik, it seems, is but a day's journey hence: but we fear we shall be necessitated to wait his arrival, which the critical situation of his affairs still renders uncertain.

We have not seen our old friend since his disgrace, but we sent Ibrahim to make him our acknowledgments and good wishes. He seemed much flattered with a mark of attention, so new to a person in his condition; and returned us assurances, that he will represent our story in its true colors to the shaik, for whose court he is to set off to-morrow or next day. This kind interposition may serve to advance our suit; and we understand that we shall then get rid of the company of our new guest, who goes into the house of his predecessor, on the latter's departure. His servants let off some paltry fire-works at night behind the house, for which they demanded a gratification. They were cunning enough to call that a compliment to us, which was more likely intended for their master; and we were glad to be released from their impertinence, at the expence of a few silver pieces, of the value of a penny apiece.

FRIDAY, 15th August.

We do not find that we are likely to be as soon quit of our guest, as we at first expected. There is no talk of his moving
this

this morning, and as it appears to depend upon the departure of his predeceffor, we may have the pleafure of his company for fome days longer. This is a fad reftraint upon us, who are confined to the front of the houfe, which confifts of two fmall apartments for ourfelves, and one, more roomy, for our fervants. Nor are we free from apprehenfions, left fome difcovery fhould be made to our difadvantage. The hakeem's fervants are continually mingling with ours, and may draw inferences of our abounding with money from our manner of living, if not from the imprudence of our people, whofe fimplicity may betray us, notwithftanding the cautions we have given them on this head.

Juft as we had dined, an order came from the hakeem to clear the room which our fervants were in, for the reception of fome travellers. This, at the time, was a very difagreeable command to us, though it may turn out as much to our benefit, as any thing which has occurred fince our arrival here. The travellers prove to be a company of Turks, on their return to Cairo, from an excurfion into this country. There is a man of confequence among them, who, on notice of our being here, immediately fent fome of his attendants to enquire into our bufinefs in this quarter. It may be fuppofed that we were very particular in the narration of our troubles, and the ill ufage we had met with. The politenefs and humanity of thefe Turks were very ftriking to us, who had fo long experienced nothing but rudenefs and barbarity from the human race. They regretted the impoffibility of having our company on the road, without the permiffion of the Shaik Ul Arab; and were hurt at the thoughts of leaving us among a people, whom they feemed to have no opinion of. But they promifed to reprefent our cafe to the bey of Cairo, and to exert all their intereft with him to demand our releafe from the fhaik. They acknowledged, however, that the reafons for detaining us until the fhaik's arrival, may be very good, as the river is at prefent fo infefted with pirates, that they are obliged themselves to go by land to Cairo. There is a Christian among them, who has charged himself with a third letter, which we have addressed to Mr. Baldwin from this city. He is a confidential domestic, and, by his influence, has prevailed upon the Turk his master, to write to the shaik in our behalf, to state our uncomfortable condition, and to advise him to dispatch us forthwith to Cairo, as we are content to leave the punishment of our oppressors to his discretion. Heaven knows what effect this kind mediation may have with the shaik; but we have long suspected that our release can only be accomplished from Cairo; and are stocking ourselves with a fund of patience to support us in the tedious interval. The journey by land, we are told, is from ten to twelve days, and the Turks propose to set off at day-break. Allowing, therefore, three days for obtaining an order from the bey in our favor, three weeks at least must elapse, before the return of the answer which is to set us at liberty. But Hope, the deceiver Hope! sometimes whispers better things in our ears; and as we are importunate in our desires to be sent away, we are inclined to expect the shaik will not detain us after his arrival at Ghinnah.

SATURDAY, 16th August.

The Turks have deferred their departure until night, which, on account of our reliance on their good offices at Cairo, and their delivery of our letter, has given us more vexation than the matter may deserve. The itch of avarice appears to have infected the mass of the people we are among, from the highest to the lowest. The new hakeem, though an Abassee, and a slave to the shaik, cannot resist the disease, and is already fingering, in idea, the gold and valuables which he conceives us to possess. He sent for

for Ibrahim at midnight, and queftioned him clofely touching our circumftances, and the prefents we made to his predeceffor: and, laftly, if we had any offering left for himfelf. Ibrahim, in conformity to his inftructions, reprefented the poverty we were reduced to, and which utterly difabled us from tendering any thing worthy the hakeem's acceptance. He difclaimed all knowledge of our having given either money or goods to the *quondam* hakeem, though he found that this man had got an item of the removal of our carpets. It is a bitter comfort to us to obferve, that the man who was fent down by the fhaik to protect us, fhould be the firft to attempt our property. The fubftance of this mercenary interview we received from Ibrahim, while we were at breakfaft.

We had vifits to-day from feveral of the Turkifh gentlemen, who are in the fuite of the grandee. They repeated their tenders of fervice on their arrival at Cairo. A very fine Georgian boy is in the train, whofe beautiful features and fair complexion eafily diftinguifh him from the Turks. He is a flave, and, we underftand, is in high favor with his mafter.

As the hakeem had offered us the liberty of going abroad, whenever we pleafed to apply to him for a fervant to protect us, at five o'clock Mr. Hammond, who was now equipped with a cloak, accompanied by myfelf, Ibrahim, and the hakeem's fervant, fallied forth. We directed our fteps to the bazar, or market-place, and entered a caravanfera, which attracted our curiofity. Thefe buildings are receptacles for travellers, and are either erected at the public expence, or by the donations of private people. The one we faw was a very large ftructure. Its entrance was through a ftone gateway, which led into a fquare court, furounded by apartments of two ftories. The ground-floor was open in front, and thrown upon arches, and divided into different rooms, by a baluftrade of ftone. The back part was clofed, and appropriated for warehouses for the merchant. Beneath one of these arches we found a Turk sitting, whom we had left at Yambo, and who had once put it into our heads to come by this inauspicious route to Cairo. We immediately recognized one another, and were very hearty in our congratulations on this unexpected meeting. He took us into his apartment, and placing coffee before us, very kindly condoled with us on our misfortunes, which had reached his ears. We find that he remains here, on account of the dangers on the river. After pressing this Turk to visit us frequently, we took our leave, and walked without any interruption to the river. Here we went on board a boat, which waits for a lading of coffee for the Cairo market. This boat is one of the most convenient I ever saw. She has two cabbins, besides an awning of matts, that extends to her main-mast. The roof is high, and, with the sides, handsomely carved and painted. We were politely received by the nokidah, who said he hoped for our company to Cairo. We should rejoice much to be accommodated in this manner in our voyage down the Nile. It was from this boat that the view of Ghinnah, which is annexed, was taken. At sunset we returned home, and found our good friends the Turks were preparing to decamp. At nine o'clock they mounted their camels to the number of twenty, well armed, and went off with the benefit of a fine moon, which renders travelling at night very delightful in these serene climates. The chief of the Turks rode on a fine dun camel, and was followed on another by the sprightly Georgian, well accoutered with a scimitar and a matchlock.

SUNDAY, 17th August.

The hakeem has actually fixed his residence at our house, and means, we suppose, to take good care of us and our baggage. When the Turks went away, he took possession himself of their
apartment,

apartment, which was before occupied by our servants. We are now reduced to an uncomfortable situation, and cannot enjoy a moment's privacy, but during the hours of meals and repose. But we are determined to suffer no further inconvenience from the vicinity of the hakeem. We have accordingly directed our servants to take up their lodgings at night on the terrace which extends itself over our apartments, and which we often ascend in the evening, to obtain a view of the country.

We were surprized with an early visit from the Turk, whom we had encountered at the caravansera yesterday, and were much pleased with this mark of his attention. He now gave us the particulars of some transactions at Yambo, which nearly concerned us, and which proved very satisfactory, in respect to the measures which we had taken with Lt. * * *. The reader will remember our separation in the Red-sea, and the melancholy circumstances which reduced us to the necessity of returning him to Yambo, on a boat bound to that port. On his arrival at Yambo, it appears, that his madness broke out with more violence than ever. Instead of waiting for the boat's coming to an anchor, he jumped overboard at the entrance of the harbor, and swam to the beach below the town; and would have made his way into the country, had he not been pursued by some of the mariners, who overtook him, and carried him before the vizier of Yambo. This was the second time he had been brought to this minister in this extraordinary manner, and within the compass of a few days. His misfortune had been more than suspected on the former occasion; but it was now communicated to the minister by the nokidah of the boat, who was charged with our message, to request that Lt. * * * might be sent on the first vessel to Judda. On his coming into the vizier's presence, he gravely demanded to be made a Mussulman, and to be entertained in the service of the xerif. This request luckily could not be complied with by the Mahometan

law,

law, which does not admit of converts, who are deprived of the faculty to judge between right and wrong. Neither does it now establish its faith by the means of the sword. So different are the principles of the same sect, when the flame of blind zeal has abated of its ardor. It happens, however, that the unhappy victims of madness meet with an attention in this country, that is not paid to rational beings. They are considered as inspired, because hurried beyond the precincts of reason; and though they still serve as a butt of ridicule to the shafts of the vulgar, they are secured by their situation from the shadow of an injury. On this principle the vizier acted. From his own wardrobe he gave the turban and Arabian dress to our unfortunate companion, to humor his frenzy, and sent him safely to Judda, full of the idea of having become a follower of Mahomet. Poor youth! to what joy and satisfaction wilt thou hereafter awake, should it please God to restore thee to thy senses. What will thy sensations be, to consider the past as no more than a dream; to reflect on the dangerous abyss that thou hast escaped, by the interposition of the Divine hand! It must occur to every human mind, that the news of his safety was the most pleasing music to our ears. Driven by stern necessity to a separation with him, when his condition was truly deplorable, we could not but admire at the happy turn which matters had taken. We had acted for the best in sending Lt. * * * back to Judda; and could not but rejoice at the intelligence which now reached us, of his being gone thither under proper protection: Had he less fortunately remained with us; had he been exposed to a month's sun in an open boat; had he visited the coasts of Egypt; toiled with the caravan over the desart, and experienced the oppression we have met with at Ghinnah, it is impossible that his intellects could have withstood the complicated shock, and a confirmed madness, or perhaps death, would have ensued! Whereas every good consequence is to be expected from the step we took;

took; every assistance will be given him by the surgeon of the Swallow sloop, which was luckily at Judda; and we can promise ourselves that he was hospitably received by our friend Captain Bacon, and even accommodated with a passage to Bombay, should the Adventure be bound to that port *. We also learn from this Turk, that the nokidah of our boat was more to blame than the vizier of Yambo, that we did not attempt to get to Suez. He went to the vizier while we were at anchor at the mouth of the harbor, and told him that he could reach no port but Cosire!

In the evening the major sallied out in an Arabian dress, which he made here, accompanied by Ibrahim and our usual guard. He returned with two Christian merchants, whom he had got acquainted with. They are persons of credit here, and very civilly invited us to repay their visit.

MONDAY, 18th August.

We were disturbed at midnight by a knocking at the door, which proved to be the hakeem and Ibrahim, whom he had called up to attend him. This was the first visit he had paid us, and was as disagreeable as unexpected. We at once guessed the purport of it. He is a plain man, and did not use much ceremony in introducing what he had so much at heart. But we were at a loss what to offer him, that could be acceptable. Money he pretended to decline taking, and we, with equal artifice, pretended that we had none. There were two sets of silver buttons, and two silver chains, which belonged to the regimentals and swords of the major, and which had escaped pillage. These we produced, as the only remains of our goods which were of value;

* The humane reader will rejoice with us, to know, that our designs respecting our unfortunate companion were fully answered. That he found Captain Bacon at Judda, and returned in the Adventure to Bombay, recovered of his frenzy.

though

though we promised to acknowledge his services in a better manner from Cairo, should he procure an order from the shaik for our immediate departure. The weight of these toys attracted his notice, though he did not seem to admire their workmanship, which was none of the best. He however put them into his bosom, and desired to look at some of our cloaths. But so particular was this fellow, that he could not be prevailed upon to peep into our trunks; and so scrupulous, that he would not receive a single thing, until we put it into his hands. A pretty salvo truly, for his conscience, which grasped at all in our possession! Besides the silver articles, he carried away three broadcloth coats of different colors, and two silk tambour waistcoats—for the purpose, we imagine, of covering his pipes, and the scabbards of his swords—and half a dozen cambric handkerchiefs for his own use. In consideration of this present, he has undertaken to write to his master, for permission to send us away by land, which is the only safe track at present. It is not without extreme compunction that we forego the ease and pleasure of a voyage down the Nile, to encounter the dangers and hardships of the desart. But we foresee no end to our detention here, while we depend upon the river for a conveyance; and readily acquiesced in the hakeem's proposal, who about one o'clock left us to finish our repose.

Before we were up we had a visit from the friendly Christians, who brought us a present of fine milk, and made us an hearty tender of their services during our stay here. There is an honest simplicity in these men, that affords us infinite satisfaction; and we suppose it was the apprehension of immediate danger to themselves, which with-held their good offices, when we stood so much more in need of them.

Behold the justice of divine Providence! which often punishes the iniquities of mankind, by their very accomplices in guilt. A
retribution

retribution the more dreadful, as the villain who breaks through every tie himself which links man to man, is not yet so hardened as to be proof to a breach of confidence in another. The blow which is given by the public executioner, is weak, when compared to that which comes from the hand of a friend. There is intelligence just arrived from Cofire, that the merchant Mahomet, who invited us to his house to plunder us, and who had returned in the last caravan to that place, is so desperately wounded, that his life is despaired of. The quarrel arose between him and some of his confederates, touching the division of our spoils. His brother Ally and his father were this day examined before the hakeem, on the subject of their ill usage of us. The result we have not learnt; but it cannot be very dangerous to them, as we find Ally has obtained leave to attend his dying brother.

In the afternoon the hakeem, and two merchants of the town in the confidence of the shaik, came to our apartment to take a list of the things we have lost. This they advise one of us to carry to the shaik, and to make him a formal tender of the whole. This errand would be readily adopted by us, had we any thing fit to present to him, agreeably to the Eastern custom. These people looked into our trunks for this purpose; but finding us bare of valuables, they gave us hopes of being dispatched without paying this great visit.

TUESDAY, 19th August.

Some further particulars relative to the misfortune of Mahomet, were communicated to us this morning. We learn, to our surprize, that the young shaik of Cofire, and the soldier who stole the major's sword, were the principals in the assault. They went in company with Mahomet to Cofire, and were constantly soliciting of him a proportion of the money which he had obtained from us. This he had the imprudence to decline; and on their finding he was deaf to their arguments, they one day took an opportunity to seduce him from the caravan, and attacking him jointly, they cut him desperately with their swords. There is no doubt but he defended himself manfully; but his strength and resolution could not avail him against this cowardly proceeding. The assassins have escaped to Cosire, but the soldier's relations, who live here, have been seized by the order of the government. In case of Mahomet's death, however, we find a pecuniary mulct will preserve the murderers from the punishment due to their crimes.

This story affords a truer picture of the dispositions and manners of the Arabs, than volumes could portray on such a subject. We reflect with horror, on the connection which subsisted between us and the delinquents in question; and consider our escape from them, as altogether unexampled and miraculous. It is now plain that they could meditate the plunder of our baggage; and we might have fallen a sacrifice in the desart, with much less danger to them, than the deceased Mahomet, whose family will exact revenge.

We had another visit from our Turkish acquaintance at the caravansera. From him we have obtained a very extraordinary and alarming piece of intelligence. Since our arrival here, we had received confused accounts of Ibrahim Beg's absence from Cairo; but we could never get to the bottom of the story. It now appears, that for this month past, Egypt has been the seat of a bloody and obstinate civil war. Ismaul Beg took on him to assume the government of Cairo, by the connivance of the Porte; but the late Bey Ibrahim disputed the usurpation, and appeared in arms to maintain his own title. The matter was contested in a desperate battle without the walls of Cairo, and ended in the defeat of Ibrahim Beg, who retired up the Nile, and is

now

now in a province not three days march from this place. Instead of pirates infesting the river, we understand, that the danger arises from the soldiers of Ibrahim Beg, who are raising contributions upon it. The Turk tells us, that the gallies which fell down hence some days ago, were commanded by Muſtapha Beg, who is in the intereſt of the depoſed Ibrahim, and is gone to join him. But it is not poſſible, that the fugitive chiefs can long withſtand their ſucceſsful opponent; whoſe army is already ſtrengthened by a large detachment of the Grand Signior's forces. We underſtand too, that the Shaik Ul Arab has acknowledged Iſmaul Beg, which accounts for the bad character that was given us here of the Banute-people, who are of the other party. It alſo ſtrikes us forcibly, that the letters which we produced for Ibrahim Beg, were one cauſe of the ill treatment we experienced from the vizier and his aſſociates. The ſhaik was out of reach of our complaints, and Ibrahim Beg, our only friend beſide, not in a ſituation to redreſs them. We had a contrary idea when we boaſted of theſe letters; and muſt acknowledge the uncertainty of human conjecture, which errs in matters apparently the moſt obvious.

This ſudden revolution creates no ſurprize in a country unſettled in its government, and divided by the jarring intereſts of a number of petty princes. But to us it is a matter of ſerious reflection. We hear, indeed, that the European factories are undiſturbed at Cairo. But how far the influence of Mr. Baldwin will prevail with the new bey, or how we ſhall reach the capital, through the diſorders of a country, agitated by oppoſing factions, and laid waſte by the ſword of rebellion; we are at a loſs to determine. Danger beſets us on every ſide. Public commotions are united to private perſecutions, to compleat our diſtreſs; and the moſt alarming circumſtance of our affairs ſeems to be, that we are at the mercy of two ſimple though honeſt Muſſulmen, our domestics. They have hitherto preserved their fidelity to us; but such is the frailty of human nature, that a long residence here may have a bad effect on their morals; exposed as they are to the artifices, and obliged as they are to mingle in the society of this fraudulent tribe.

WEDNESDAY, 20th AUGUST.

We had an early visit from the hakeem this morning, who brought us a plate of raisins of the sun, which are produced in Lower Egypt. He came, seemingly full of the scheme of one of us going to the shaik, and proposed sending a boat up to-day on this service. We readily fell into this measure, which, notwithstanding the objections that were made to it yesterday, I have long considered as absolutely necessary to our immediate release. Little can be done with the ministers of Eastern princes, whose hands are tied by the awe which they stand in of their masters, or whose minds are so habituated to the receipt of presents, that nothing short of the whole substance of the petitioner, can satisfy their avarice. I made a tender of my services on this occasion; not more from a principle of curiosity, than a desire of hastening our departure; and was happy to find that they were accepted of by my companions.

In the afternoon we had a visit from the *quondam* hakeem, whose advice we have constantly solicited since his disgrace. As he can now have no selfish interest in our concerns, we are inclined to place more confidence in him, than when we were at his discretion. He has business with the shaik, and has kindly promised to accompany me on this embassy. He is well acquainted with our story, and if he is as much our friend as we take him to be, he may quicken the dispatch of our business, by a candid representation of facts. He tells us, that the place of the fhaik's prefent refidence, called Ghofe, is but feven or eight hours journey by water, and that we fhall be abfent but two days from hence.

The day paffed away without another meffage from the hakeem, or any preparation for my journey.

THURSDAY, 21ſt August.

There is no end to the prevarication of thefe people. The more earneft we are to go in perfon to the fhaik, the lefs willing they are to admit of it; and it is likely, after all, that we fhall be juft where we were before the new hakeem arrived. He told Ibrahim this morning, that he was looking out for a boat to convey me to the fhaik, but it was uncertain when he fhould procure one. This excufe, from a man who can certainly command every boat belonging to Ghinnah, is next to waving the vifit altogether.

A funeral proceffion paffed our houfe about noon, which was very folemn and numerous. The corpfe was preceded by troops of women, who went vailed, and at certain intervals, uttered a choral cry, which was accompanied by expreffive action. The coffin was borne by fome of the friends of the deceafed, and feveral little flags of different colors were carried around it. A body of priefts clofed the proceffion, who recited aloud paffages from the Alcoran, as they walked along. Muffulmen never neglect to fhew their fenfe of thefe fights; and perhaps it would prove of no detriment to Chriftians, to imbibe fome of their cuftoms on thefe occafions. There was an Arabian merchant on a vifit to us, when the funeral went by; and though in company with ftrangers, he was not afhamed to run to the window, and to join audibly in the devotions of the train. It is true, that the obfervance of thefe forms, makes not the Arabs better members

of

of society; that it neither checks their propensity to fraud, nor instils one benevolent idea into their breasts, towards the votaries of a different persuasion. But still it throws a decency into their discourse, a sobriety into their manners, which is very persuasive. They possess, what may be called, the graces of religion, which would better adorn a good Christian, whose temper is charitable, and whose heart unknowing of deceit!

Just as we sate down to dinner, the hakeem sent for Ibrahim, and told him, that he expected an answer from the shaik to-day or to-morrow, which, perhaps, would save me the trouble of waiting on him. This is what we dreaded; but I fear, there is no rebelling against this man's will; and we must endeavor some way or other to fix him in our interest. In the evening Mr. Hammond and I went to the caravansera, to pay our compliments to our Turkish acquaintance. He received us with his usual civility. The chance of proceeding to Cairo by the Nile, seems to be much against us, on account of the disturbances. We should, therefore, be very happy in the Turk's company in our journey by land, as his knowledge of the language and customs of the country, would be a great defence to us against the inconveniences of the road. His circumstances, however, will by no means afford the expence of five camels, which the coffee he has would require; and he is content to wait the issue of the disputes upon the river. We could not converse on so delicate a subject in a public place, and have therefore desired the favor of his company in the morning, when we shall propose to pay for his camel-hire, should he consent to make one of our party. This is to be kept a profound secret. Though fifty dollars can be no object to us, when compared to the services we are likely to reap from his presence, we must, at all events, conceal a circumstance from the hakeem, which would sufficiently denote the strength of our resources.

As we were going to bed, we had a visit from the hakeem, who is very mysterious in his hours of communicating with us. To our great joy, he did not touch on the usual string of presents; but came, as he said, to satisfy our minds of his intentions to send us under a safe conduct to Cairo, when he received the shaik's sanction for such a step.

FRIDAY, 22d AUGUST.

The hakeem sent for Ibrahim at day-break, and sounded him respecting the valuables in our possession, which might be worth his acceptance. We have already promised to send him a remnant of broad-cloath, and some India goods, on our arrival at Cairo, by the return of the guard which he is to give us for our protection. But the native disposition of these people renders them suspicious of the professions of others. He, who does not hold himself bound by a promise, will not give another credit for the performance of one, which may be broken with impunity. The hakeem, therefore, wants to absolve us of this distant obligation, provided we come down immediately with something of equal value. Generous man! how he consults the interests of persons immediately under his protection! What humane endeavours he daily exerts to render justice to distressed strangers, whom he came here professedly to console and to relieve! Two of the gang who were leagued against us, have been twice brought before him. The vizier has been as often summoned to his tribunal. Examinations have been taken of the facts; but as the accusers and the culprits have never been brought together, nothing is likely to ensue from this extraordinary mode of trial, that can tend to the recovery of our property, or the punishment of the offenders. Smaller crimes, however, are corrected with severity, when they are offered to Mussulmen;

an inſtance of which occurred to-day before our door. A Chriſtian and an Arabian were convicted before the hakeem, of ſtealing a ſmall quantity of ſilver plate from a caravanſera. This act of delinquency was puniſhed by a ſevere baſtinadò on the ſoles of the feet, which we underſtand is the general method of correction.

This being the Mahometan ſabbath, the hakeem went in great ſtate to the moſque. But the furniture of his horſe was not of a piece with the diſplay he meant to make. It was very antique, and conſiderably the worſe for wear. Neither did his beaſt do much credit to his keeping. The horſes in Upper Egypt ſeem to labour in common under this neglect. They are very ſprightly animals, though of a ſmall ſize; and yet they cut no figure, where corn and ſugar-canes are in great plenty; which muſt be attributed either to the unſkilfulneſs of the groom, or the penury of the owner. Indeed, proviſions of all kinds are ſo cheap in this country, that the natives live well, for little or nothing. We, who neceſſarily pay for things at double rates, provide for a family of ten or twelve people, at the moderate expence of one dollar and a half, or ſeven ſhillings *per diem*. In this are included fruits of various kinds, of which we eat ſo heartily, that they often conſtitute a quarter part of the coſt. Bread is at leaſt thrice as cheap as in England, and fine mutton ſells uſually at two pence *per* pound. But what avails the plenty that reigns here, when freedom has fled the land, and taken up her abode in northern climes? Inſecure in the enjoyment of their property, which is the ſport of every inteſtine commotion, the natives rather drawl out a life of uncertain tenure, than exiſt with the ſpirit of human creatures.

A ſervant belonging to our houſe brought me a piece of copper money, which I immediately knew to be Roman. On my giving him a ſilver dewanny for it, value a halfpenny, he
produced

produced three others, all Roman coins, and found, as he tells me, among some ruins here. To spur his activity in procuring me more, I gave him two dewannies apiece for the rest, with which he seemed much delighted. I can only regret the critical situation we are in, which prevents our beating up an ample field, that undoubtedly abounds in every species of antique rarities.

SATURDAY, 23d August.

The *quondam* hakeem sent for Ibrahim early this morning, and proposed my accompanying him to the shaik this evening. We very readily closed with this scheme, and sent our compliments to the hakeem, desiring his permission to go. This was a request which he could not flatly refuse; but Ibrahim says he appeared much chagrined that we would not trust to the letter he had sent, and to which he daily expected a favorable answer. We are so tired out with evasions, that any state seems preferable to that we are in; and I have accordingly prepared myself to embark with the *quondam* hakeem and Ibrahim for the shaik's court at sun-set.

While we were at breakfast, we had a visit from the Turk, who was accompanied by a friend that is likewise going to Cairo. He opened to us a design which we much approved of, and doubt not to bring it to bear, in case of the shaik's permission. He tells us there is a boat ready to sail for Cairo, on which we may embark at my return, provided we are willing to give their passage to some camel-drivers, who are waiting for a conveyance to Cairo. He is acquainted with a company of these people, who want to transport their coffee thither. They will save us the expence of a guard, as every man carries a matchlock, and, in defence of his property, will form the best protection we can desire for our boat. We esteem ourselves very lucky in having found an adviser, whose

K k interest

interest will prompt him to be sincere, and whose journey depends upon our success.

I had a message about eleven o'clock, to prepare for my voyage immediately after dinner. This meal is served up at noon in this country, and we were in the height of it, when Ibrahim was sent for by the hakeem. We did not like this summons, and were the less surprized, when we learnt that the hakeem dissuaded us from going to the shaik. This he did, under the pretence of the trouble it would give me, and the little consequence a visit would be of, unfurnished as we were; with a present to smooth the introduction of our suit. To this we replied, that nothing could be accounted a trouble which would effect our departure; and in respect to the want of a present, the gentleman who went, proposed to lay the paper, which contained our losses here, at the shaik's feet; and to request him to recover the whole for his own use. And that this could not be considered as a trifling gift, which amounted at least to 1,200 dollars. But he was deaf to these arguments; and at length told us he would write again by his predecessor in office, urging an order for our safe conduct to Cairo. But that he could not admit of my visiting the shaik, and falling into a thousand difficulties, from an inability to satisfy the demands of the shaik's secretaries and domestics. There was some shew of reason in this remonstrance. We were well acquainted with their craving disposition; and though we had money enough to have scattered among them, our situation is so precarious, that we dare not pretend to it. The fact is, we are in his power, and cannot act contrary to his inclination. We therefore submitted with a good grace, and sent Ibrahim to the *quondam* hakeem, to remind him of our story, and to bespeak his influence with the shaik in our behalf. Ibrahim attended him to the boat, and brought us back assurances of his utmost services, which the poor man delivered with tears in his eyes. This is too uncommon an
expression

expression of sincerity among the Arabs, to make us suspicious of its not coming from the heart *.

We walked to the caravansera in the evening, to acquaint the Turk of our disappointment, and to tender him camels for the conveyance of his coffee, should the shaik think it safer for us to go by land. He received the offer with gratitude; but still gives us hopes of hearing better news concerning the troubles on the river.

SUNDAY, 24th August.

The Turk came to us this morning, with a face full of something important. After the first cup of coffee, he delivered himself of his burthen, which was at all events to dissuade us from going by land. He told us, that he proposed setting off in a few days for Jirje, to wait till the river was clear, and pressed us much to accompany him. We were rather startled at this proposition, after what had passed between us the night before; and, willing to know his sentiments fully on the matter, we repeated our intention to proceed by land, in case the passage by the Nile should remain still perilous. Now it was that we learnt the desperate situation we were reduced to. The dangers which encompassed us appeared in their proper colors, and required not the touches of art to give them a formidable appearance. Armies of contending parties obstructed our progress by water; and a band of robbers threatened to pursue our footsteps by land. In short, we discovered that this Turk was tender of the characters of Mussulmen, until he began to suspect we should suffer by their treachery. He therefore informed us in confidence, that we should be mad-

---

* Thus were all my hopes of viewing the antiquities of Luxor and Thebes, dashed in a moment, by the caprice of a slave, who is become our master, and detains me from accompanying this Arab to the shaik, who is in that neighborhood.

men to trust ourselves over the desarts of Thebais, when our departure could not be kept a secret. That, allowing the hakeem to be sincere, and that he dispatched us agreeably to the shaik's order, there would not be wanting rogues in this town, who, confident of our carrying away money and jewels with us, would secretly collect thirty or forty light camels, and although we had got two days start of them, might easily overtake, plunder, and murder our whole body. To illustrate this observation, he related to us a story of a Turkish gentleman of his acquaintance, who was treated in this manner about two years ago, in a journey from Cosire to Ghinnah. A report universally prevailed, as in our case, that he was possessed of great wealth, and he was followed by a select band into the desart, and surprized while he was taking some refreshment beneath a thorn-tree. His party was too weak to resist the robbers; and the Turk was shot through the head at the first onset. This anecdote naturally led him to reflect on our late situation, which had been so similar to the unfortunate traveller's, and to congratulate us on the issue, which had been so different. He was ascertained that the same fate had been intended us, from which we had escaped by a signal intervention of Providence. On the other hand, our friend pointed out the probability of our shunning the dangers of the river, by the taking refuge in any town we might be near, on an alarm of enemies; not to add the chance of steering clear of them by night, and our ability, in a stout boat, to make a manful resistance against an hostile attack. We were quickly convinced of the propriety of this advice; and it is resolved that we wait for the shaik's answer respecting our departure. Should it so happen that he direct our being sent by land, we are to inform the hakeem that we are content to run all risks by water, rather than encounter the fatigues of another camel-journey: And, moreover, that our purses will not afford the expence of it. In the mean time, the Turk is to se-

cure

cure a boat, and to hold it in readiness for us. This is a plan which has been reared on the most plausible foundation, but, like the rest of our airy schemes, may be demolished by the changes of the morrow.

I know not whether I should lament or rejoice at my not being possessed of the true spirit of *virtù*, which, overlooking all obstacles and perils, leads the possessor to hazard every thing for the acquisition of an antique medal or seal. Were I one of the number whom Pope says, " Sighs for an Otho, and neglects his bride," I might indeed add to the list of the curiosities which I have picked up, but at the same time endanger our very liberties, by a shew of enquiry into the smallest matters. To procure these reliques, money must be produced, the mere rumour of which might awaken the avarice of the people, at whose disposal we lie. These reflections were suggested by a present, which I received this evening from one of the Christians, of seals taken up both here and at antient Thebes. The impressions, it must be confelt, discover no great elegance in the engraving. But their antiquity is not to be doubted, from the remoteness of the quarter in which they were found.

MONDAY, 25th AUGUST.

News is at length arrived of the death of the merchant Mahomet at Cofire. The persons who communicated it to us, had the confidence to warn us of going abroad immediately, lest the relations of the deceased should revenge themselves upon us, whose money they consider to have been the cause of his murder. A pretty inference, truly! worthy of the subtle intellects of this diabolical tribe! But whether the danger exists or not, we intend to make a plea of it to the hakeem, to hasten our departure, as we do of the murder itself, to excuse our going by land. Indeed,
when

when we are ascertained of the villainy of the Arabs, who are lawless enough to take away a Mussulman's life in the middle of a caravan, what security can be given to Christians, for their safety with a small body? Our Turk paid us a morning visit amid these determinations, and again confirmed us in them. He proposes our getting away to Jirje as soon as possible, and remaining there, until an opportunity offers to convey ourselves to Cairo. He describes Jirje to be a large and well-regulated city; where we may keep ourselves private in a caravansera, and be two days nearer the capital, to obtain intelligence. We are too tired of the oppression and deceit of the people of Ghinnah, not to wish earnestly for a change of the scene; which, at any rate, cannot prove less agreeable and eligible to us.

The fall of villainy occasions as great lamentations in this town, as would the demise of integrity in an honest land. The tragedy which was lately acted near Cosire, gave birth to a mournful procession of females, which passed through the different streets of Ghinnah this morning, and uttered dismal cries for the death of Mahomet. In the center was a female of his family, who carried a naked sword in her hand, to intimate the weapon by which the deceased fell. At sundry places the procession stopped, and danced around the sword, to the music of timbrels and tabors. They paused a long time before our house, and some of the women made threatening signs to one of our servants; which agree with the caution we received to keep within doors. It would be dangerous enough to face this frantic company; whose constant clamor and extravagant gestures give them all the appearance of the female Bacchanals of Thrace, recorded of old.

As our Turk came up stairs this evening, he was stopped by some of the hakeem's servants, and we were obliged to send Ibrahim to obtain him admittance. The little man was much nettled at this usage, nor could we account for it. The bustle

below

below stairs had occasioned an enquiry into the cause, and Ibrahim was summoned by the great man, to explain it. The Turk insisted upon accompanying him, and returned to us very well satisfied. He told the hakeem that he was an acquaintance of long standing; was known to our consul at Cairo, and purposed to attend us to that city. We are very well pleased that this matter is broken to the hakeem; who politely apologized for the affront, which had been offered to a friend of ours, through the ignorance of his servants.

The meanness of this Abassee is shocking to a liberal mind, which must be reduced indeed to accept of the trifles which he greedily solicits. He suspects us to be bare of money, and is willing to ease us of our remaining cloaths. He even takes apparel which can be turned to no use; and the very sheets from our beds have not escaped his rapacious hands. Daily are the inroads which he makes into our baggage; and we are content to have it reduced to a small compass. Among all the bad qualities this fellow possesses, pride cannot be included in the number.

TUESDAY, 26th August.

The times of Yambo seem to be once more revived, and our patience fated to be put to the severest proof. Three days are elapsed since the last letter went to the shaik, and no answer is yet arrived. It is a mystery to all, that no notice has been taken of the various accounts, which have been transmitted to the shaik, relative to us. He doubtless knows of our detention; but we greatly apprehend, that he is still a stranger to the principal circumstances of our story. Were it not for the confidence we repose in the former hakeem, we should not expect any orders in our favor, until the shaik's return, which every one says is near at hand. This morning we saw his nephew pafs towards the river, where he embarks in a boat to meet the fhaik. Four or five hours of a fair wind, will carry him to the place to which his uncle has lately moved.

We had a long vifit from the hakeem this forenoon. He tells us that advices came yefterday from Cairo, which afford hopes that a ftrong force will foon be fent up the river, to clear it of Ibrahim Beg's parties. A large detachment of Ifmaul Beg's army has fecured an important poft about fifty miles below Jirje; fo that the communication is open from thence to Cairo; and Muftapha Beg's gallies are thereby detained at Jirje. A very fhort interval may occafion a revolution in matters; and the rebels who obftruct our progrefs, may be driven back to the upper parts of the Nile. We alfo find that Ifmaul Beg, by thefe advices, has invefted the Shaik Ul Arab with the fovereignty of four more provinces of Upper Egypt. A refined ftroke of policy in the Bey, to confirm him in the intereft of the government; and to oblige him to defend thefe very provinces againft the fugitive chiefs, who might acquire a fupply of men and money from the conqueft of them.

In the courfe of our converfation with the hakeem, we difcovered his predilection to our going by land. On our pointing out the obftacles which might deter us from fuch an undertaking, he endeavoured to obviate them, by the ftrongeft affurances of his care and protection. He went fo far as to declare, that on our fetting out for Cairo, he would feize upon Ally and the fellows who had robbed us, and detain them in cuftody until our fafety was known. That he would alfo affix chops or feals, upon the warehoufe-doors of the camel-drivers, until they returned with the intelligence of our arrival at Cairo. Thefe promifes are encouraging enough, and might induce us to venture at laft upon camels, if an example were made of the rogues who plundered us, to deter others from attempting the like. The camel-drivers who went with the company of Turks to Cairo, are expected back in four or five days. They will, perhaps, bring us an anfwer from Mr. Baldwin, and we have the good fortune to be furnifhed, by his means, with a recommendation to the fhaik from Ifmaul Beg. But there is little chance of our being obliged to determine on this point, during the abfence of the fhaik. The government is likely to reap no little advantage from our coming here. The murder of Mahomet has given it a pretence, to fecure the property of the camel-drivers belonging to that caravan. We faw a fecretary pafs by with a party of foldiers this afternoon, and were told, that he had been affixing chops to the different warehoufes of their caravanfera, which contained coffee to a confiderable amount. This would partly go towards fatisfying the family of the deceafed, but the moft confiderable portion be confifcated to government.

I went up to the top of our houfe in the evening, to obferve the progrefs of the inundations of the Nile. The frefhes now are at the greateft height; and there appeared a prodigious alteration in the fcene fince my laft view of it. The waters are fpread to the very extremities of the town. The ftream is greatly agitated and difcolored, and runs down with the force of an headlong torrent.

WEDNESDAY, 27th August.

I was awakened before day-break by the fame troop of women, which paffed our houfe the other day in honor to the memory of Mahomet. Their difmal cries fuited well with the lonely hour of the night: and I underftand that this relic of the Grecian cuftom lafts for the fpace of feven days; during which interval the female relations of the deceafed make a tour through the town, morning and night, beating their breasts, throwing ashes on their heads, and displaying every artificial token of sorrow.

The general rumor of the town is, that the shaik will be here to-morrow. Some of his domestics are arrived, which in a manner confirms it. It is time for us to be relieved from the restraint we are under, as every hour teems with the danger of discoveries. From the frequent inspection of our baggage, we still hold it expedient to carry our money and valuables about us. Besides the irksomeness of such a charge, accidental occurrences have often brought us to the brink of betraying it: and more than once, to my great confusion, has the hakeem himself sate down so close to the place where my watch has been concealed, that he must infallibly have heard it going, had we not strained all our invention to engage his attention. God grant that the shaik was once come among us! when the worst which can happen will be, that we shall know the utmost malice of our fate.

We took a walk this evening along the banks of the Nile, to see the revolution of things in that quarter. The deluge extends itself daily on every side; and we remarked many places where the river has formerly made inroads into the town itself. A face of business diffuses itself around the country. The husbandmen have prepared their grounds for the reception of the manure, which the floods will leave upon them. Nature assists them in a point, the most laborious and expensive to the farmer in other * countries; and to this account, the cheapness of grain may be imputed in Upper Egypt, more than to the quantity which the land produces, which is only cultivated on the banks of the Nile. When the waters retire, the seed is immediately sown, and a

---

* The author must except the kingdom of Bengal, which is watered by that noble river the Ganges; whose operations and effects bear an intimate resemblance to those of the Nile.

crop

crop is reaped within the short space of four months. The most astonishing instance of the quickness of vegetation that the world can afford. As we had encountered some intelligent fellows on the road, I enquired into some of the natural curiosities, which have so long distinguished this region. I learn that the ostrich is too common, to be much regarded by the natives. That the crocodile is a most formidable tenant of the Nile, and held in great dread by the fishermen; one of whom told us, that he was present at the death of a crocodile a short time ago, in whose belly were found the gold rings and ornaments of a dancing-girl, who was devoured by the monster, as she was bathing in the river. The hippopotamus, or river-horse, is likewise yet, though rarely, met with, between this place and Jirje. I have an exact resemblance of him in an antique seal which came from the ruins of Thebes; but I must add, that he is often found to be twelve feet and upwards in length. His skin is so hard as to resist a musket-ball; and he is so cunning, as seldom or never to be seen ashore, by day-light. Among the various reasons that induce my preferring to travel by water, the desire of beholding this rare production of nature, is not the least cogent: and I cannot but anticipate the gratifications which are in store for us, whenever I meditate on a voyage down the Nile, disturbed as it is by the commotions of war.

THURSDAY, 28th August.

The morning was ushered in by the arrival of a great man, who came immediately to our house, accompanied by the hakeem, who went to the river-side to receive him. He is a Turk, and was lately governor of Ghose, a town some hours distant up the Nile, from whence he was removed on the revolution at Cairo. He is going by land to that city, and on hearing of our situation,

situation, very politely sent a message to request the favor of our company. A better opportunity could not have offered itself for our proceeding by this route; and we must undoubtedly avail ourselves of it, if no good intelligence reach us touching the passage by water, before the shaik's return, which this Turk assures us will be to-morrow evening, or the next morning at furthest. It will be with the utmost regret, that we forego the verdant prospects, the romantic scenes, which the banks of the Nile abound with, to traverse stony vallies and a dreary waste. We cannot with any degree of patience, compare the ease and convenience of a boat, to the labor, fatigue, and heat we shall experience, in journeying upon camels. But so hearty is our aversion to the people we are among, so wearied out are we with the delays we have met with, that we are ready to encounter the horrors of the desart, provided we encounter them under a safe conduct, rather than remain here a week longer, to wait the issue of the disputes upon the river.—But our resolutions are the sport of fortune, and catch their hue from the aspect of the day. It is with some concern, that we shall separate ourselves from our little Turkish acquaintance, whose good-humour and attention have greatly preferred him in our esteem. But it would be folly to reject the protection of this great man, who travels with a strong guard, for the uncertain and dangerous prospect of getting down by water.

We were warmly solicited by the hakeem to-day, for various articles, which he had overlooked before. This is a strong intimation that his master is at hand, to deliver us at least from his importunities.

FRIDAY,

FRIDAY, 29th August.

A woman came to our door to-day, who ufed to afk charity of us at Cofire. She is juft arrived with the caravan, and brings fome fhocking accounts touching the death of Mahomet. It appears, that he was left in the defart by the villains who affaulted him, and remained there three days without any affiftance whatever, when he was accidentally taken up by a party of a few camels, and carried to Cofire. There he lingered three days more, ere death relieved him from the pains he endured. The tortures which were referved for this poor wretch, from the rankling of his many wounds, are really affecting to humanity; but the horrors which muft have haunted his confcience in this dreadful interval, are too formidable to conceive. The deceit which he had practifed towards ftrangers, the breach of hofpitality beneath his own roof, and the perjuries that he had committed in the prefence of a juft God, muft in thofe moments have recurred with double force to his imagination, and ftruck him with a full conviction of his guilt. Even the Arabs themfelves, who are feldom reftrained from evil from the contemplation of a future ftate, acknowledge the interpofition of the divine hand in the fate of this man. Unhappy victim of prejudice and paffion! may thy fins have been expiated by the anguifh of thy exit! And may the eternal pardon which is promifed to repentance, meet thee as fully, as what I beftow upon thy offence!

Our hopes of going in company with the Turkifh officer, are cut off as foon as formed. He purpofes fetting out this night, and we are immoveably fixed here, until the prefence of the fhaik breaks the fpell. We cannot but fecretly reproach the hakeem for this difappointment. Had he permitted of my embaffy to the fhaik, there is little doubt but we fhould have obtained

tained permiffion to accompany this Turk to Cairo. But we have not been wanting to effect the utmoft. We have written a fourth letter to Mr. Baldwin, ftating our uncomfortable fituation; which we have committed to the care of one of the Turk's domeftics, through the means of Ibrahim.

The Turk and his party departed at midnight, which we obferved from our windows, that almoft face his lodgings. He had given out that he fhould not go until the morning. Thefe precautions were taken by the former travellers who went by land; to deceive, we prefume, the thieves who lurk in this neighborhood.

SATURDAY, 30th August.

We had fcarcely breakfafted this morning, when advice came of the long-expected approach of the Shaik Ul Arab. We immediately went to the top of our houfe, to fee the ceremony of his landing. We had hitherto reftrained our joy at an event, which was too defirable to be credited, without the evidence of our fenfes. The reader may therefore judge of our emotions, when we beheld a large fleet of boats, falling down with the ftream. We found the fhaik to be in the headmoft, from the pendant and enfign which were difplayed on board; and he foon entered the creek, which is a fhelter for boats from the violence of the frefhes, both fides of which were lined with people to receive him. But by the ftrength of the current his boat was forced upon a bank, mid-way in the creek, and not without great difficulty, difengaged. The watermen on the Nile do not feem to underftand their bufinefs, like their fraternity on the Thames; or they would not have left their monarch fo long in perplexity. Several ropes gave way in drawing the boat from the bank; and two hours elapfed before fhe was brought to the landing-place, though affifted by fome hundreds of people.

It

It was pleasant enough to behold the terraces crowned with women, on this occasion. Their keepers were probably abroad, to pay their compliments to the shaik, while the birds flew to the tops of their cages, to taste of the momentary sweets of liberty. I never saw so numerous a shew of females, some of whom, in our neighborhood, proclaimed themselves proficients in the arts of coquetry, by withdrawing their vails to attract our notice, and dropping them again, when our eyes were fixed upon their faces. Many were the salutations we received from these good-natured creatures; whose freedom of behavior to us, I attribute to the rigid confinement in which they are kept. Restraint is the bane of modesty in female bosoms; and I will venture to say, that there are more women of loose inclinations in the Turkish dominions, than in all Europe beside. So just is the advice of our countryman Prior, in regard to our treatment of a fair companion:

> " Be to her faults a little blind,
> Be to her virtues very kind;
> Let all her ways be unconfin'd,
> And clap your padlock on her mind!"

At four o'clock we were summoned to the presence of the shaik, whom we found alone in a lower apartment of his palace. We were much elevated by his arrival, and perhaps, could not have appeared to better advantage before our protector; whose cordial reception of us bespeaks him to be such, in the truest sense of the word. He seated us on the same carpet with himself, and after a few compliments, which were interpreted to us by Ibrahim, he directed coffee and fruit to be placed before us. Here for the first time we saw grapes, which were very fine, and a peculiar date, which surpasses every thing of the kind I ever met with.

with. While we were partaking of this repast, I had leisure to take a full view of the shaik, and cannot resist the inclination of introducing a character to the reader, of which I flatter myself he will have reason to be enamored hereafter.

Isman Abu Ally, the great snaik of the Arabs—for such we would render the Shaik Ul Arab—is a short fat man, of about five feet two inches high, and turned, as we learn, of seventy-five. His eyes are grey, and his complexion very fair; but what at once gives him a singular and more youthful look, his beard, which is very bushy, is colored of a bright yellow. This exterior may not seem the most promising, and might create distaste, if the benevolence that beams from his countenance, were not foremost to secure the heart of the beholder. Neither can the shrillness of his voice, which is harsh and dissonant, destroy the beauty of the sentiments, which it is insufficiently made use of to convey; as the elegance of the words may sometimes atone for the demerits of a tune. He is still active, for a man of his size and age; and his spirits are so good, that were it not for the ravage which time has made among his teeth, he might pass for a younger man by twenty years at least. Except the viziers of Yambo and Ghinnah, whom we had found to be villains by sad experience, we had hitherto dealt with the dross of the nation. It was reserved for this moment, for us to meet with the polite gentleman and the honest man, comprized in the person where they ought to be found, in the representative of his people. Happy the subject of a virtuous land, who at once possesses and imitates so rare an example! But how sunk in the abyss of infamy are the race, who wholly deviate from the standard of rectitude; and though daily reproached by the life of their monarch, are not to be reclaimed by the tone of authority, or the elocution of active virtue!

We had quickly cause to find, that we had not given the shaik too

too much credit for his integrity. His impatience to acquit himself in our opinion, of any connivance at the conduct of his servants, could scarcely be restrained by the forms of civility, which precluded business during our repast. But no sooner was it ended, than he shifted the conversation, and came directly to the point which we were so much concerned in. He lamented the treatment which we had undergone, and which could only have happened in his absence; and he vehemently reprobated the behavior of his officers, which he was determined to punish in the most exemplary manner. After a few leading questions, which tended to confirm the report that had been made to him touching our story, he professed, that his return to Ghinnah had been hastened on our account. That he had come purposely to do us strict justice on our persecutors, and to dispatch us under a safe conduct to Cairo. As a proof of his sincerity, he ordered Ally, the brother of the deceased Mahomet, to be brought before him. He had been previously taken into custody, and was waiting without, to be examined. With this fellow, came Sauker, one of the rogues who had assisted to plunder us, and who of his own accord, produced the things which had fallen to his share, in the division of the spoils. He laid them at the shaik's feet; and with the greatest effrontery declared, that he had taken them, only to secure them from the thieves of the house: and that his truth might be deduced from his care of our property. Though his offence was palpable, this step was sufficient to skreen him from punishment in a country, where retribution is all that is required by the prosecutor, and where justice is generally to be appeased by pecuniary fines. But the ill-advised Ally did not escape in this manner. He boldly denied having robbed us of money or valuables, and was loudly exclaiming at the injustice of the accusation, when the shaik raised his voice, and a dozen Abyssinian slaves suddenly seized

seized on the culprit, and hurried him out of the room. We were in pain for the fellow, and were meditating on the consequences of his arrest, when he was brought into our presence again, bound hand and foot, with a chain about his neck, by which he was held. He was on the point of receiving the bastinado on his knees, when he confessed the charge, and promised to return all that he had taken from us. The shaik was inclined to inflict the punishment on him; but by the interposition of those about him, in which we joined, he remitted it for the present; and directed Ally to be led home, that he might produce the goods. Our triumph was complete. One of our antient enemies had atoned for his crime, in a manner that outwent the most sanguine idea of revenge. The other was humbled at our feet. He survived indeed: but it was only to abase himself before us, and to depend upon our moderation for his security!

In about half an hour Ally returned, and produced a few of the least valuable articles. He earnestly requested until the morning to deliver up the rest, and to repay us the money that he had cheated us out of. This was granted him at our desire, and the prisoner committed to his own house, under the custody of a strong guard.

Several of the shaik's courtiers had come in during this examination, among whom were his nephew and the *quondam* hakeem. We found the latter was in disgrace, and endeavored to make his peace, by expressing to his master, the many obligations we lay under to his care of our persons. The good old man only shook his head in reply, and waved the subject, by desiring us to attend again at seven o'clock the next morning, when he had summoned a full court of justice to punish our aggressors. He dismissed us, with fresh assurances of his protection; and, as an earnest of what we might expect, he directed our servants to carry home the recovered goods in triumph before us.

SUNDAY, 31st August.

We breakfasted betimes, and at seven o'clock went to the shaik's house. The court were already assembled in an open spot before the house, which was shaded by an high wall from the morning sun. Here we found the shaik encompassed by his great men, with a number of soldiers and attendants at some distance in their front. Carpets were spread in the intermediate space for our reception. Here we seated ourselves, after making our obeisance to the shaik, and waited in silence the issue of the trial. Next to the shaik's right hand was placed his nephew, and, as we understand, his declared successor in the government. He is a comely and good-humored looking man, seemingly between thirty and forty years of age; and by his behavior, appeared to be less our enemy than any other of his uncle's counsellors. So unhappy is this upright and humane prince in the lot of his servants.

Just before we came in, the culprit Ally had undergone a severe bastinado, on again proving refractory; and the hakeem was sent to search his house for the stolen goods. This occasioned a pause in the proceedings, which were interrupted by the sudden appearance of the vizier, who, to our great astonishment, took a seat which was vacant next to the shaik's nephew. This confidence was unexpected, and filled us with unfavorable prognostics of the event of our suit. But our doubts were of short continuance. He had entered unregarded by his master, and was talking with great ease to those about him, when the shaik turned about, and in a solemn tone, asked him for the shauls and things, which he had received from the English gentlemen. The whole frame of this gay courtier was evidently discomposed by this question. He had probably

bably laid his account with our suppressing the part he had taken against us, after the high hand with which he had once stopped the accusation of Abdul Ruffar, and was unprepared with an evasion. His countenance instantly was disrobed of its pleasantry; his limbs trembled, and his tongue faltered in framing a reply, the substance of which was, that he was a stranger to the matter with which he was charged. We were ashamed of the meanness of a man of his rank, but the wrath of the shaik was wound up to the highest pitch at the hearing of this falsehood. He was confirmed of the guilt from the symptoms which the offender displayed; and without calling any fresh evidence to corroborate it, he proceeded to decide. But he could hardly find utterance for his orders, which were to arrest and flog the vizier immediately. A number of slaves started from the croud, to execute the pleasure of their lord. The astonished minister could not believe his ears, and would fain have persuaded himself that the affair was a jest. He was presently convinced of his mistake. The officers of justice laid violent hands upon his person, tumbled him from his proud seat, and in a rude manner hurried him away, in spite of his outcries and fruitless resistance. This behavior served only to exasperate the shaik. His eyes flashed with the honest indignation which lighted his bosom; his strength could scarcely support the agitations of his mind; and after some effort, he raised himself from his carpet, and repeated his commands in a voice, that struck terror into the breasts of all present. He was immediately surrounded by a croud of his courtiers, who kissed his hands, embraced his knees, and interceded with him for the pardon of the vizier. These nobles took no share in the passions of their monarch, and were only attentive to exculpate one of their body, though at the expence of honor and justice.

I must own that I was concerned at the fearful situation of a man, who had never been guilty of any actual violence towards us, and whose

whose greatest trespass was the receipt of presents, on his assurances of protection, when he permitted of our being plundered by our inhospitable host and his adherents. These, however, were crimes of the deepest dye, in the eyes of the good old shaik. When we directed Ibrahim to plead for the inoffensive conduct of the vizier towards us, he would not hear of any apology for a villain, who had so little the honor of his country at heart, as to injure its character by winking at the maltreatment of strangers. He could the less overlook it in a servant of his own, and added, that it was at our instance only, he would remit the punishment due to his enormity. The mortification neverthelefs was reserved for the vizier, that he should be brought before us, disarrayed of his gay apparel, his hands bound behind him, and a chain fastened about his neck. In this miserable plight, he was told of the obligation he was under to our generous application; and led home by a guard, to produce his ill-gotten acquisition, as his only hope of safety. We observed a general murmur among the grandees, at the compliment which was paid us on this occasion. The disgrace of one of their body excited no friendly sentiments towards us; and not a few menacing looks were thrown upon us from the circle. On the other hand, the shaik harangued them in a sensible and pathetic speech, on the honor of their nation. He cast the most just and severe reproaches on the character of the absent minister, and warned them in future, against such inhuman practices towards Christians and strangers. He then turned to us with the kindest aspect, and re-assured us of his protection. He thanked us for the confidence which we had reposed in him, in venturing through a country, so remote and unknown; and lamented anew, that his absence from his capital had given room for our repenting the experiment. He supposed that no society, however enlightened, was free from the class of reptiles by which we had suffered; and the law provided a just retaliation for the

offence.

offence. But he attributed the commiffion of the offence to the neglect of the hakeem of Ghinnah, who had flumbered like an unwary centinel on his duty. For this he had been difcharged from his office, and a flave of his own been fent to take care of us until his arrival. All that was now wanting to complete our fatisfaction, was the recovery of our loffes, which he would fee effected; and our journey to Cairo, which he fwore fhould be accomplifhed without an injury being offered to an hair of our heads.

As virtue as well as vice is magnified by comparifon, it will not appear extraordinary, that our encreafing regard for this great man began to border upon enthufiafm. Reader! if thou art of the yielding kind, if thy mould is fufceptible of tender impreffions—fay, when furrounded by a croud of homely females, did thy heart never beat high at the approach of tranfcendant beauty? So, from the cloud of mifcreants that encompaffed his throne, fhot forth the glories of the Egyptian king! So bright, fo peerlefs did he rife from the contraft. So unworthily ftationed, and yet fo worthy of the ftation in which his birth had placed him! Nurfed in the lap of ignorance and barbarifm, like another Peter, he had triumphed over nature. Nor opinion could warp, nor habit could bind him. He nobly fpurned the prejudices of education, and, without any guide, fave the impulfe of innate goodnefs, he foared to the fuperior heights of virtue. She feemed the miftrefs of his inclinations, rather than of his election or intereft; and, befide him, the world may afford but few fubjects of fuch an influence. It is true, that his endeavors were not crowned with the fuccefs that diftinguifhed thofe of Peter, the Great. But Peter attended more to the aggrandizement than the morals of his people; and, with all the great qualities of the hero, funk infinitely below the Egyptian, in the feelings of the man. The latter was fit to have ruled over an enlightened empire.

While

While the former, after all his victories, was, in many respects, an example unworthy of imitation!

Our ignorance of the Arabian language obliged us to have recourse to our interpreter, for an acknowledgment of these favors. But at the same time, it saved us the confusion of appearing at a loss for a suitable reply. We sheltered ourselves under this fortunate circumstance, which, in a great measure, left our patron to conceive a gratitude, which words would have but poorly expressed.

A messenger now arrived with two shauls and my creese, from the vizier. The other shaul, he said, he had parted with; and the pistols he had given to Ally. Once more, therefore, was the wretched Ally produced before the court; and on denying the receipt of them, the bastinado was again inflicted on him *. Besides the articles which had been restored, there were still a silver urn, a pair of gold knee-buckles, and a quantity of valuable linen to be accounted for. Not to speak of the money which they had obtained from us, under various pretences. But these were said to have fallen to Mahomet's share in the division; and his robbery and death were made a plea of by the family, to satisfy us for our loss. The shaik would not hear of this apology, which he termed false and evasive. And sooner than we should suffer by that family, he declared, that he would first order their substance to be disposed of, and if that would not repay us for our losses, Ally and the rest of them should be sold as slaves, to make up the sum. It was now time for us to interfere. The matter was exceeding the bounds to which we meant to push it; and policy, as

* This is a very novel as well as fearful punishment. The prisoner is placed upright on the ground, with his hands and feet bound together, while the executioner stands before him, and, with a short stick, strikes him with a smart motion on the outside of his knees. The pain which arises from these strokes, is exquisitely severe, and what no constitution could support for any continuance.

well

well as humanity, prompted us to drop it. Our principal aim was to get from Ghinnah, under a proper protection. Our persecutors had been chastised, and it was preferable for us to put up with some inconvenience, rather than run the risk of being detained here, in the pursuit of full redress. On this account we listened to the mediation of the hakeem, and some of the courtiers, who beseeched us to withdraw our claim to all but eighty dollars of the remaining debt, which Ally might raise from the camels he possessed. Our acquiescence in this proposal gained us credit with all present, and drew a particular compliment from the worthy shaik; who protested, that he could not but admire our generosity, though it was exercised at the expence of their national character. The reader, perhaps, may agree with us, that we ought not to have subscribed to this insinuation, as such a man as was then before us, was enough to redeem his nation from obloquy.

"The court now broke up, and we were dismissed, not a little pleased with this mode of administering justice. The punishment inflicted upon robbers in other countries, suppresses the growth of them in the general opinion. But when we reflect on the frequent robberies that are committed in our own, it seems doubtful, whether the severity of the sentence answers the expected end. For a traveller, at least, who has his own interest most at heart, the satisfaction which we received was infinitely more eligible, than any that could have been made us of a sanguinary nature. We had recovered what we had lost all expectation of seeing again; and to our haste and good-will only, is to be attributed our not obtaining the unconditional benefit of the shaik's decree. As a small token of our respect, on our return home, we made up such a present as we judged would be most acceptable to a man of his turn of mind, and sent it to the shaik by Ibrahim. It consisted of a couple of fine shauls, an Indian carpet and palampore, and an

handsome

handsome sabre and case of pistols. The sabre and pistols, tho' articles of the greatest value, he returned, and sent us many thanks for our remembrance of him in the rest, which he said he would keep for our sake. He also told Ibrahim, that he had directed a merchant to furnish us with camels for our journey, as the river was too perilous for us to venture on. This last instance of his attention served to rivet in our minds the character of Isman Abu Ally, who is indeed a pearl thrown to the swine of Ghinnah.

MONDAY, 1st SEPTEMBER.

Our whole thoughts now are turned to our departure. The merchant attended us early this morning, in company with the hakeem, to settle the price of our camels. The common price is from eight to ten dollars each, and it is not surprizing that we pay the highest. But the number of camels which they obliged us to take, was what vexed us the most. We want but nine for ourselves and servants, and they insist upon our providing six more for the use of our guard. These are our camel-drivers, who, in our late journey, were wont to ride two upon a camel; but in the longer one we are about to enter upon, are to have a beast apiece. These additional camels will greatly encrease the expence; but were the demand an imposition, we are determined to submit to it with a good grace, rather than trouble the shaik any further upon our score. We wish not to add to the number of enemies we have in this town, and mean to quit it with the utmost dispatch. We desired the hakeem, therefore, to advance the merchant the eighty dollars which he was to levy upon Ally, as an earnest for the hire of his camels.

A thought struck me during our examination yesterday, which I would not have had verified for the treasures of Egypt. The shaik is old and very corpulent; and had it so happened that he had

had burſt a blood-veſſel in the heat of his paſſion, I was revolving the probable conſequences in my mind. There was not a man of rank preſent, whom we could conſider in the light of our friend. Even the nephew was neuter; and there is no certainty of the part he would have taken, had ſuch an accident befallen his uncle. In truth, there is little doubt but we ſhould have paid for his favor with our lives. Such a backwardneſs had been ſhewn before his arrival to bring the offenders to juſtice, and ſuch a forwardneſs in his preſence to ſkreen them from puniſhment, that the ſhaik ſaw through the partiality of his officers, and reprehended them for it. One particular circumſtance that betrayed their bent, is worthy of remark, and eſcaped me in the relation of the buſineſs of yeſterday. The gold buckles which had been taken by Ally were put down in the liſt of our loſſes, at what the Arabs imagined an exorbitant value. They could not ſlip ſuch an occaſion of gratifying their malice, and lowering our intereſt with the king. They boldly taxed us with exaggerating our loſſes, and endeavoring to profit by their maſter's clemency. They demanded that a jeweller might be ſent for, to aſcertain the truth of their charge. To this the ſhaik was averſe, as, perhaps, conceiving we might have erred through miſtake. But at our inſtance a jeweller attended, whoſe evidence defeated the malice of our enemies. He weighed them in the preſence of the court, and pronounced the gold to be equal to the value affixed, independent of the workmanſhip, which was ſo rare and ſo curious, that he ſuppoſed it muſt have enhanced the price of the buckles more than one half. It muſt be obſerved, that this jeweller, like the other mechanics of this country, was a Chriſtian, and knew the ſhaik too well, to be afraid of ſpeaking the truth, to the great confuſion of our accuſers, who were completely creſt-fallen at this retort.

We

We had a fresh proof in the afternoon of the shaik's concern for our welfare. It seems that the camels which went to Cairo with the company of Turks, luckily returned this forenoon, and as they belong to the shaik, he is determined to accommodate us with them. This intelligence is just brought us by the hakeem, who has sent to the merchant for our money to pay to the shaik's people. We are not a little rejoiced at this change, which will add not only to our security, but ensure us good treatment from the camel-drivers on the road. At five o'clock they came to pay their respects to us; and we have promised the head-man, who we find is the chief of the camel-drivers of Ghinnah, and an officer of no small consequence, a present of a dress on our arrival at Cairo. His camels are to be ready to-morrow evening, when we are to set out on our journey through the wilderness. We shall, in all likelihood, fall into the track of the children of Israel, when they fled from the verdant banks of the Nile, and took refuge on the shores of Arabia. We are to strike into the road to Suez, to shun the parties that hover about the river; and it was not far below that city, that the Israelites were supposed to have crossed the Red-sea. I cannot, however, suppress my regret, at losing this opportunity of going down the Nile. Had I been a man who travelled for his amusement, I should not probably have experienced this disappointment. I would have waited here, agreeably to an offer which the shaik made, or have gone to Jirje, as the little Turk proposed, until the troubles on the river were subsided. No obstacle should have deterred me from exploring the course of so celebrated a stream, but my being charged with business of a public nature, which will not admit of delay. The importance of this charge has been the rule of conduct of, at least, Mr. Hammond and myself. It induced us to commit ourselves to an open boat in the Red-sea, in the hottest and most unfavorable season of the year; and it now prompts us to embark

chearfully

chearfully in a journey through a defart, unknown even to the inhabitants of the country; and which, except in the inftances I have recited, has not been traverfed for this century paft, by any but the outcafts of the human kind!

In the afternoon we were vifited by three Chriftian merchants, who live at Dundara, a town about three hours, or twelve miles diftance down the river. They are come here to compliment the fhaik on his return, and are the moft creditable people of the mercantile clafs whom we have feen. They had turbans of a blue checkered pattern, to diftinguifh them from Muffulmen; and no native Chriftian is allowed to wear them of other colors, though this reftriction is not enforced with ftrangers. Thefe merchants inform us, that there is an Italian gentleman, who has refided at Dundara for thefe thirty years paft, and who is a painter by profeffion. But we find that he has exercifed his art rather for his amufement than profit; and that his own houfe alone is adorned with the productions of his pencil. We are curious to know the adventures which brought fuch a character to fettle in this obfcure corner, and, did our time permit, we fhould readily accept of thefe merchants' offer to bring us together. Notwithftanding the unfavorable difpofition of his fubjects towards them, every thing confpires to prove the fhaik's affection for Chriftians. All his principal domeftics, and particularly his fecretaries, who enjoy his unlimited confidence, are of this perfuafion. Indeed, all ranks of them join to found the praifes of the prefent fhaik, who ftands between them and the oppreffion of the Arabs. He has been their guardian for forty years and upwards; and I fear there will be a great change in their fituation at his death.

TUESDAY, 2d SEPTEMBER.

We were furrounded this morning by a croud of fervants belonging to the fhaik, who expect money from us. Though we might

might have got rid of them, by threatening to complain of their insolence, we chose to avoid the odium of such a measure; and called upon the hakeem to accommodate the matter for us. Those who assisted to punish the offenders, we agreed to gratify with a piece of gold each: and the hakeem dismissed the rest, as not being entitled to our bounty.

At eight o'clock we had a message from the shaik to attend him. We found him, as before, encompassed by his principal courtiers; and he obligingly desired us to seat ourselves upon carpets beside him. He told us, that he had solicited our presence, to give us into the charge of the master of his camels, who is dignified with the title of a shaik. This man was accordingly called before us, and the shaik addressing him by the name of Hadgee Uttalah, informed him, that he was to convey us and our baggage safe to Cairo; and that should we prefer the least complaint against his conduct, his head should answer for it. Nothing could be more satisfactory to us, than a charge like this, so publicly delivered; and of the weight of which, Hadgee Uttalah himself appeared to be so fully sensible. It not only tended to secure us from the danger of treachery on the road, but the warmth with which the shaik espoused our cause, was, in our opinion, the strongest bulwark we could have against the secret malevolence of our enemies. The good old man became very familiar with us, and asked a thousand questions concerning the natural and artificial productions of our country. He admired a china bowl which belonged to the major; but declined taking it, as common earthen-ware was full good enough for him. From this, however, he took occasion to mention an European, who had been long in his service, and had the ingenuity to imitate china very closely. He called for a specimen of this fellow's skill; and we were surprized to see a couple of vases delicately wrought and painted. We were desirous to behold.

hold the artift, but were informed by the fhaik, that he was left behind at a town up the river. We now heard many droll anecdotes of this Englifhman, as he called himfelf. That he delighted in high-feafoned difhes, and drank fuch a quantity of fpirits, that it was a wonder his infide was not confumed by fire. This intemperance fuited but ill with the fimplicity and fobriety of the Arabians. But the fhaik was polite enough to fay, that the report which had been made to him of our mode of living, had effaced the difagreeable impreffions which he had received of our countrymen. He would venture to add, however, that one article of luxury, which he obferved to be in ufe at our table, had given rife to the ideas of our wealth, and fingled us out as a beneficial prize to his covetous fubjects. And this was the filver, of which our cups and fpoons were compofed. To a people who were accuftomed to wooden utenfils, that glittering metal was a bait, which had allured them to an unjuft though tempting purfuit. Far as it was from exculpating the conduct of the Arabs, we could not but feel the force of this oblique reproof. The modeft manners of the antient Romans, when in the meridian of their greatnefs, recurred to our imaginations. We blufhed for our deviating fo much from their example, in the prefence of a man, who trod in their footfteps without a mark to direct him. And perhaps, for once in our lives, we defpifed the fymbols of oftentation and the effeminacy of fafhion!

While we were thus engaged, the relations of the foldier who murdered Mahomet, together with the camel-drivers of the caravan, were brought before the fhaik. They were accompanied by the father and brother of the deceafed, who appeared as profecutors. The witneffes for the culprit making little or no defence, the trial was foon concluded; and fentence of death was paffed upon him by the fhaik. Although the murderer came a

prifoner

prisoner yesterday from Cosire, it is remarkable, that he was not present on this occasion, nor allowed to offer any thing in bar to his condemnation. If, however, the salutary laws of our free constitution are wanting here, the loss would not be felt, could this country continue to boast of its present equitable judge. But those laws were provided to guard as much against the encroachments of the crown, as the machinations of the subject. Happy the soil in which they flourish! Thrice happy the people who bask beneath the sunshine of freedom; and depend not upon the uncertain character of a chief magistrate; upon the virtues or vices of a king!

As the name of the young shaik of Cosire has not been mentioned in this trial, we suppose that he was wronged by report, or skreened by interest from the charge in which his comrade was involved. It had come to the Shaik Ul Arab's ears, that this young man and his father had extorted money and effects from us. The accusation had been framed by his courtiers, who were perhaps, jealous of the advantages they had derived from us; and every persuasion was now used to make us acquiesce in it. Had we given scope to our resentment against this treacherous pair, it is likely, that we should have supported the accusation; which opened a way to redress for their impositions at Cosire, and their inhumanity in betraying us into the hands of such villains at Ghinnah. But one good action which they performed towards us, outweighed the multitude of their misdeeds in our minds. We remembered that our lives and property had been at their mercy, both at Cosire, and in the road to this place. The first had not been attempted by them; and when the last could not have been with-held from them, we acknowledged a merit in their forbearance, when the principle which excited them to extort a part, could have put them in possession of the whole. Weak as this reasoning may appear to the sticklers for justice, it had

force

force enough with us to operate in favor of the delinquents. We knew the unlicensed tempers of the Arabs, and it was but fair to judge of them by their own rule of action. We declined, therefore, the shaik's kind offer to call these fellows to account; and professed an ignorance of their being any otherwise accessary to our misfortunes, than by their fatal recommendation to the family now before us.

We had no latent meaning in this application, but the venerable shaik did not let it pass unnoticed. He pointed out the certainty of the detection of villainy, either sooner or later. He deduced it from the instance which was now before him; where, without a friend to take our part, the wrongs which we had suffered had accidentally come to his knowledge, and the authors thereof had been punished according to their deserts. He called upon the father of Ally to own, that the hand of Providence was to be seen through the whole of this transaction. That his sons were but the instruments of our safety, though avowedly our enemies; and under the notion of enriching themselves at our expence, had prevented our falling into the lurking perils which awaited us on the river. But that their intentions had been justly rewarded. While we were sheltered under royal patronage, one of his sons had fallen in a contest, about the very property of which he had deprived us; and the other was crippled with blows, and covered with disgrace on the same account. The confusion of Ally and his father was not to be concealed at this incident. They seemed to be sufficiently humbled by the melancholy end of Mahomet, but this pathetic exhortation of the shaik's had an evident effect upon their feelings; and the heart must be corrupt indeed, that was not amended by it. For my own part, I never was so edified by the discourse of a divine, as I have been, by listening to the sentiments of this unlearned Mahometan. And it is not to be wondered at. His language

guage was that of the heart, and his opinions breathed the fragrance of truth. His doctrine was a reflection of his life, and both equally bright and unsullied. When he admonished, he directed himself to the consciences of his audience; and he never failed to convince, though it is plain he failed to reform *.

At ten o'clock we took our leave of the shaik, but are to see him again before our departure, which is fixed for ten o'clock at night. On our return home we met a man carrying a red flag, and uttering aloud some proclamation. His head was crowned with a chaplet of bays, and the croud were very attentive to his words. We enquired into the purport of his business, and were told, that he was an herald, who daily gives notice of the rising of the Nile. We understand that it is now near its greatest height; and expect, when we get into the flats of Lower Egypt, to find the country entirely under water.

We

* From a passage which I have lately met with in Dr. Pococke's Travels through Egypt, I am induced to think that he encountered this amiable personage, and was indebted to him for letters, which procured him both civility and protection during his voyage up the Nile. Isman Abu Ally was, from our information, possessed of his present dignity in the year 1737, and, of all the Arabians, was the most likely to extend his humanity to strangers. The passage is this:

" On the 3d of January, the wind not favoring us, we stopped at a place about three miles from * Furshout. Here resides the great shaik †, who is governor of all the country on the west as far as Assouan. I waited on the shaik's secretary, with a present of five or six pounds of coffee; in return, he sent a live sheep to the convent to entertain me with, and introduced me to the shaik, who was in an Arab dress, sitting in a corner of a room. He rose on my entrance, and my servant brought in my present, which consisted of two boxes of prunellas, two of other sweetmeats, and some glass vessels. He asked where I intended to go? I told him, to the Cataract. He replied, with a good-natured smile, that a boat of Franks ‡ lately went up; and that the people said, they came to discover the way into the country, in order to return and take

* Furshout is in the neighborhood of Ghinnah.
† The literal meaning of the Shaik Ul Arab.
‡ In this boat was Capt. Norden, well known for his accurate accounts of the antiquities of Egypt.

We have been employed the whole day in preparing for our expedition. Bread, biscuit, and flour were brought us in the afternoon, sufficient to serve us a fortnight; and with the beans provided for our camels, run us up a bill of eighty dollars. But in this account are included a sheep and an half, which are fried down in clarified ghee or butter, and twenty new skins to carry our water. With this stock, we trust at least to keep famine from our heels, in this journey through the inhospitable wild which divides us from Cairo. We had paid the balance of our camel-hire, which amounted in the whole to 150 dollars; and were in readiness to attend the shaik, previous to our departure. But the camel-drivers are either superstitious, or have something to detain them until to-morrow night. They came to us about eight o'clock, and told the hakeem it had just occurred to them, that to-morrow was the new moon; a time above all other the most lucky to commence a journey. He appeared very angry at their having adopted such an idea at so late an hour; and finding that no arguments could conquer their desire to remain here to-night, he referred them to the shaik for an answer. The good old man was vexed at the delay they intended us. But his good-nature inclined him to their side. He sent for Ibrahim, and directed him to tell us, that though the request was absurd in itself, the humoring their prejudices would be the readiest way to ensure the regard of these people. We submitted without a murmur to this irksome detention; and the more so, as the shaik has added to his former kindness, by giving a camel to our conductor Hadgee Uttalah, to save us that expence.

We

take it; and then desired to know what I wanted to see? I told him the ruined cities. He observed, that we had no such ruins in England, and asked, whether, if they should go into our country, we would permit them to see every thing; adding, that he would give me letters, and a man to go with me; so that I might be assured I should travel securely." Chap. 6 Pococke's Travels.

We have just heard that the shaik has changed the sentence of death which was passed on the prisoner this morning, to a long imprisonment. It seems, that an execution has not been known during his reign; and he means to continue this ill-judged lenity. But this will be but of little avail to the assassin, provided one of his family does not fall a sacrifice in the interim, to the relations of the deceased. This kind of retribution is exercised with impunity in this country; and one life will glut the vengeance of the prosecutors, though the offender himself escape. But this is only in respect to each other. Should a Christian but accidentally spill the blood of a Mussulman, an hecatomb of his persuasion would scarcely suffice to expiate the offence.

WEDNESDAY, 3d SEPTEMBER.

It now appears likely that none of our letters have reached Mr. Baldwin. The camels are returned that carried the company of Turks away; and we were surprized that no answer was come to the letter, which we entrusted to the Christian domestic. But on discoursing with Hadgee Uttalah, we find that they did not go to Cairo. The Turks were formerly in the service of Ibrahim Beg, and though they purposed to have deserted to the party of Ismaul Beg, their hearts either relented or failed them, and they halted at a town on the river, two days short of the capital. We have, therefore, the greater reason to congratulate ourselves on the generosity of the Shaik Ul Arab; as no application could have been made to him in our behalf, until our misfortunes reached Mr. Baldwin. By his influence, we are in every respect better provided for a journey, than when we left Cosire. We can depend more upon the goodness of the camels, and the honesty of the drivers. We have provisions in plenty, and are furnished besides with limes, to assist in quenching our thirst. We have dried

dried dates with us, to vary our meals. This fruit, when dried, is much preferable to that fresh from the tree; and when eaten with bread, is both a pleasant and nourishing food. We expect to be but nine or ten days on the road; and as we go by ourselves, we are in hopes to persuade the Arabs to follow our directions—to travel the greater part of the night, and to lie by during the heat of the day. This mode of action will preserve us much from the sufferings, which we underwent during our late journey. But we must trust to chance for a shelter from the sun at our different halting-places, as there is no such conveniency as a tent to be procured here.

As we are on the point of leaving Ghinnah, it may be expected that I drop some observations on the customs and manners of the inhabitants. But in a narrative of this kind, the reader will gather more information from the conduct of the actors themselves, than from an author's description of them. Their general treatment of us is the best glass from which their pictures can be reflected; while the particular behavior of one or two individuals, is a convincing proof, that virtue is the common inheritance of mankind, and is confined to no enlightened spot. It remains then only for me to say a few words on points, too unimportant to have come into view before. No people are plainer in their dress, which in the lower class is generally of blue linen. Those of the higher rank endeavor to ape the fashion of the Turks. They are arrayed indeed in silks and woolens, but without lace and embroidery. They are universally modest in their behavior, decent in their conversation, and sober in their way of life. Gaming is unknown to them; and strong liquors in such little request, that we found but few Arabians, who broke through the precept of their religion, which forbids the use of them. But the vices they possess, are sufficient to eclipse the lustre of these good qualities. Were it not for the cheapness of provisions, the po-

verty

verty of the people would bear hard upon them. But for the value of a penny, each man can provide for the day. Beside meat and poultry, which are in great plenty, the river supplies them with fine fish at the lowest rates; and eggs are sold at a penny the dozen. These things we can declare from ocular demonstration; and from our window we can see the menial servants of the shaik receive their daily pay, which, we are assured, does not exceed the value of a penny. Water is their only drink, except it be mixed with coffee; enough of which may be procured for a penny, to treat a company of visitors; a fact of which we had frequent experience. But the simplicity of this race is best to be deduced from the figure which their head makes. The Shaik Ul Arab is very abstemious in his diet, and plain in his equipage. There is nothing magnificent about him; and he generally appears in a black gown, which is very fine, and resembles our bombasin. His turban is of muslin; and the only finery about him, an orange or straw-colored shaul, which is carelessly thrown across his shoulders. He carries no arms about him; which we observed to be the case of all the old men, to proclaim, we suppose, that war is no longer their province.

There is no trust to be reposed in the word of a cameldriver. We sent to the shaik at five o'clock in the evening, to request our final audience; and found to our surprize, that Hadgee Uttalah was with him, to demand our journey to be postponed until the morning. Ibrahim remonstrated in our name against this proceeding, and the shaik was enraged at its insolence. But his anger was of as little consequence as our regret. There was no prejudice now to be removed, but an obstacle more insurmountable. The camels are not ready, and there is no help for the delay.

THURS-

THURSDAY, 4th September.

It is a matter of the greatest surprize to a rational being, to perceive mankind given to falsehood, without a beneficial end in view. And no where, as I have had occasion elsewhere to observe, is this practice so frequently to be met with, as among the Arabians. By telling one lye, the camel-drivers have reduced themselves to the necessity of adding an hundred to it. On their coming to us this morning, we reproached them with their duplicity in the presence of the hakeem; and demanded to depart immediately, as the only recompence they could make us for our many disappointments. On this the whole mystery was unravelled. We found that some of their camels had been so much fatigued in their late expedition, that they were not able to travel before. But it is their genius to disguise the truth at all times; and they made use of a thousand shifts to evade our departure, rather than disclose the real state of the case. Our displeasure, is, therefore, rather directed at their folly, than their villainy; and now we have got to the bottom of the affair, our chagrin is considerably lessened at this unexpected detention. We have even consented, by their advice, to postpone our departure until night; when our movement will be more private, and not interrupted by the croud of mendicants which await our charity. This step was enforced by the hakeem's report, who recommended, by all means, that we should set out after dark.

At nine o'clock we attended the hakeem to the shaik's house, to receive our pass, and to take our leave of our benefactor. We arrived there in the midst of a trial of the camel-people, for a robbery on the deceased Mahomet. After sitting about half an hour in a kind of lobby, we were advised to send in our names. On doing this, we were ushered into the room where the court
was

was held, and after the usual salutations, we were seated on a raised place to the right of the shaik. His politeness dictated a few questions to us, after which he proceeded to the trial. We were not sorry to have our curiosity satisfied in this particular; and we attended with great patience to the process. There is no jury in this court of justice, nor any judge but the shaik, whose will is the law of the realm. When the evidences have been given by the witnesses, they are cross-examined by the grandees, who compose the council. The shaik listens attentively to all that passes, forms a judgment of the fact, and at length pronounces the final sentence. At eleven o'clock we made a motion to take our leave, and were dismissed by the good old man with an hearty benediction, and very cordial wishes for the success of our journey. In our hearing he repeated the charge to Hadgee Uttalah, to put us down at the English factory at Cairo; and not to return, without a letter under our hands and seals, to advise him of our safety, at the peril of his life. To secure his fidelity beyond the reach of temptation, the shaik also directed, that the family of Hadgee Uttalah should be placed under a guard, as the surest hostages for the integrity of his conduct. Our hearts were full enough at the idea of parting with this amiable character, but this last proof of his more than paternal care of us, had such an effect upon our feelings, that we were glad to retire, and conceal the ebullitions of our gratitude. The uniform greatness of soul which distinguishes this Mahometan, will encourage strangers to enter his country without fear. And it is not unpleasing to us to reflect, that our misfortunes may contribute to the security of future travellers. They called forth the virtues of this prince from the shade of obscurity; and will be a lesson to his subjects, ever to respect the rights of humanity.

As we returned home we were joined by the little Turk, who

was so assiduous to engage our company by water. We are concerned to separate from him, but he declines our offer to accommodate him by land. He confesses, however, that he is under no apprehensions for us, though he does not chuse to risk his property in the desart. There is something inexplicable in this; but our confidence in the shaik is too firmly rooted, to be shaken by the suspicions of others. We observed that the Turk was much dejected at our approaching departure; and partly guessing at the cause, when we got home, with the concurrence of my companions, I slipped twelve dollars into his hand, to bear his expences down the Nile. His countenance instantly brightened up at this present; and he resumed his facetious disposition during the day, which he dedicated to us. We had already been indebted to his assistance in preparing for our journey; and the major now gave him the charge of his china bowls, which were to be delivered to Mr. Baldwin at Cairo. We also obliged the Turk with many odd things, which were superfluous to us. But he had some trouble in conveying them out of the house, from the vigilance of the domestics, who were doubtless directed by their master to have an eye to his motions.

Now we have seen our last of the shaik, the hakeem intimates that he cannot part with us, without a further gratification. This Abassee! this slave! who cannot sit down in the presence of his master, though raised by his favor to the government of this city, has the assurance to assume airs of consequence, and to trust to our moderation for putting up with them. Besides our former gifts, he came in for one of the shauls which we recovered from the vizier, who, in our opinion, was as much entitled to it as himself. He is now desirous of my silver hookah, though Ibrahim has informed him of its being packed up. Its value chiefly lies in the workmanship; and it is more curious

than

than useful to me. To prevent further importunities, I have sent it to this fellow, though it gave me the trouble of unpacking a trunk. I am sensible that he would be degraded from his office, were the shaik acquainted with his behavior. But he too much confides in our former concealment of his meanness, to be afraid of the consequences: and builds upon our generosity to repeat the offence. The shaik has already been put to so much trouble on our account, that we would overlook a great many impositions, sooner than disturb his repose with fresh complaints. We have already caused some changes in his administration; and it would be in us but a bad requital for all his favors, to foment differences between him and his favorite servants, on light occasions.

We quickly experienced the good effects of our compliance with the hakeem's humor. He sent for the camel-drivers, to remind them of the treatment which they were to give us on the road; and settled the œconomy of our journey, and other points, which they had disputed with Ibrahim. When the sun sets, the camels are to be brought to the door to take up our baggage, which is now reduced to half of its original bulk. After supper we are to bid our long-wished-for adieu to Ghinnah; which it must be remembered, we owe to the virtue of one man!

At sun-set Hadgee Uttalah came hastily to our house, and told us, that as we had paid ten dollars apiece for the other camels, he expected fifteen to be paid him, for the prime beast he was to ride himself. We were congratulating ourselves before we were quit of this griping cast. We knew the shaik had presented him with the price of this very camel, but the fellow had timed his application so well, that we were fain to comply with it. We were about to set off, and neither our haste nor the late hour, would have admitted of our communicating the affair to the shaik. We had no money remaining that the Arabs knew of; but

P p the

the old fox got over this difficulty, by offering to take our note of hand, payable at Cairo. We were the more reconciled to this expedient, as it seemed to interest our conductor in our arrival at that city.

Our baggage was placed upon the camels, and we took our leave of several people who had been civil to us; particularly the *quondam* hakeem, in whose behalf we had ineffectually exerted ourselves with the shaik. At nine o'clock we mounted our beasts, with the same number of attendants as when we left Cosire: an Arab related to Abdul Ruffar, supplying the place of the Indian Fakeer. We directed our way towards the great mosque by which we entered the city, where we are to take up our water; accompanied by the hakeem and a party of horse, who paid us this compliment by the order of the shaik.

When we came to the watering-place a new matter was hatched, more scandalous than any they had yet attempted. We had paid for fifteen camels, and given a promissory note for the hire of another. Now it was that some of the owners of the camels, (of which there are three besides our conductor) applied for three additional beasts, under pretence of lightening our baggage, which they did not conceive would have turned out so heavy. Much altercation now ensued. We were justly nettled at a demand which had all the appearance of an imposition; and loudly called upon the hakeem to take us back to his house. We threatened to acquaint the shaik in the morning with their ill usage. Nay, we even pretended to have changed our minds touching the route; and declared that we would rather hazard ourselves on the river, than among people, who presumed to treat us in this manner. This resolution seemed to alarm them. They prevailed upon the hakeem to vouch for their honesty. They declared that the proposal was meant purely for our interest. To prevent our baggage from being left among the mountains,

and

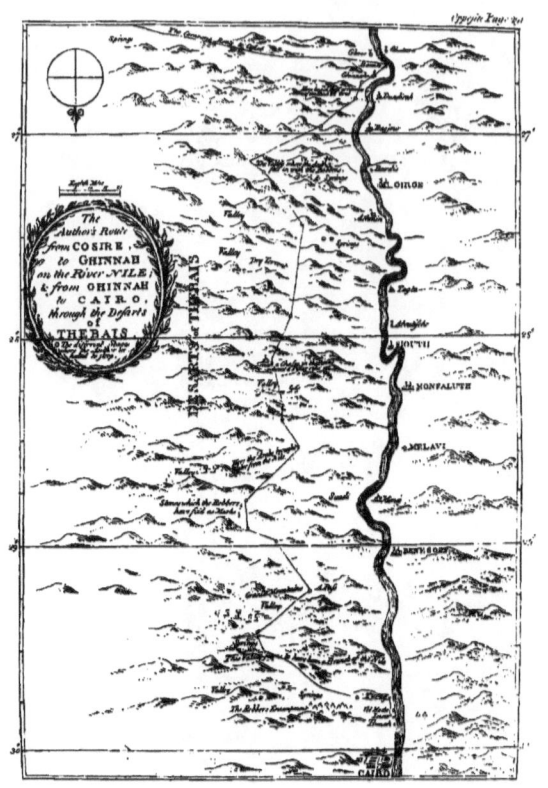

and to secure our lives in case of an attack, it was necessary for us to travel with light camels. That we knew not the arduous undertaking in which we had engaged; or we should scarcely hesitate to consult the only means, to smoothe the difficulties before us. Their application had indeed been too late. But to demonstrate their sincerity, they were content to be at half of the expence, rather than be in want of the camels; and to take our note for the fifteen dollars, payable at Cairo. The candor of this offer reconciled us to the expence; and we had experienced too many delays to contend any further about it. One of the owners returned to the city to collect the additional camels, and bring them after us. At eleven o'clock we moved on, and were still accompanied by the hakeem, whom we strongly suspected to be concerned in the last manœuvre of the camels. He preceded us for about a quarter of a mile on the road; when the troop faced suddenly round, and, after paying us a complimentary salute, went off at a full gallop towards the town. We continued our march in a chearful mood, and going to the north, soon left the trees and the river behind us. Our way lay through a stony and uneven soil; and the moon is too young to assist our camels to pick out their road by night. At two o'clock we halted, and spread our carpets upon a very rugged and uncomfortable place. We were three hours in motion, but find that our distance from Ghinnah does not exceed five miles. I have here affixed a map of Upper Egypt, where the reader is presented with the course of the Nile, and may pursue our route through the deserts of Thebais.

FRIDAY, 5th SEPTEMBER.

I awoke at day-break with my eyes much inflamed and disordered. I have felt a weakness in them for some time, which proceeded from a cold in my head; and after sleeping under cover for this month past, it is natural that the night air should have a bad effect upon my eyes. I dread the journey a little on this account, and shall not be surprised to have a confirmed humour in them before our arrival at Cairo. We are prevented going forward, by the additional camels not being come up. At eight o'clock Hadgee Uttalah set off for Ghinnah in search of them, and was accompanied by his son. As this movement presented us with a prospect of remaining here the greater part of the day, we erected a kind of tent with a cloth stretched over our baggage, beneath which we made a shift to creep, to shelter us from the sun. But we had but a disagreeable time of it. What with the suspence, the heat of the weather, and some suspicions which were propagated among us, of the honesty of our camel-drivers, the hours passed very heavily. It was whispered to us by Ibrahim, that these fellows were not prepared for our expedition; and had only brought us out here to deceive the shaik, who was enraged at their delay. As a proof of this, he told us at ten o'clock that the camels were about to leave us. We sallied out of our nest on this alarm, and found on enquiry, that the camels were only going to the Nile, to fill up the skins with water. But the folly of Ibrahim and the rest of our servants, was very near being productive of serious consequences. They were of opinion that we ought to return with the camels to Ghinnah, and to apply to the shaik for a more trusty conductor. Never, until this moment, had the notions of Ibrahim deviated so much from propriety. But the honesty of his intentions gave them a weight, which I am convinced they would not otherwise have had; and it was actually debated amongst us, whether we should return or not! So precipitate and ill-advised a step, would not only have betrayed our unconquerable jealousy of the Arabs, but in all likelihood, have sunk us in the esteem of the shaik.

It was happily over-ruled; and the camels were permitted to go quietly on their neceſſary errand.

At two o'clock the camels returned; and on numbering the water-ſkins, we found them to amount to thirty. This is a great ſtore; but, from our former experience, may prove little enough for our wants, before we reach the next watering-place. We would not break upon our proviſion, as our journey was not commenced; and made a ſhift therefore to dine upon dates and bread. At four o'clock we were agreeably ſtruck with the appearance of Hadgee Uttalah, and the Arab who went laſt night in queſt of the camels. They brought but two, and Hadgee came without his ſon. On enquiring into the reaſon of this diminution of our guard, we learn that the ſhaik has detained the ſon, as a pledge for the ſincerity of the father. We infer from this, that the ſhaik was not pleaſed with our delay here; and has therefore exacted this new hoſtage from our conductor, to expreſs his diſſatisfaction.

Our baggage was now replaced upon the camels; but a full hour was loſt in diſputes among the owners, touching the burdens to be aſſigned to their ſeveral beaſts. Theſe were, however, at length adjuſted; and at five o'clock in the evening, we left the ground with eighteen camels in company. Our way ſtill lay through a ſtony plain; and about ſun-ſet we mounted a craggy hill, from whence we were agreeably ſurprized with a ſudden view of the river below. The land continues barren until within a mile of the banks; on which, buried in a romantic wood, we diſcerned the buildings of Dundarah, a town of which I have before ſpoken *. The want of population can

* According to the learned Dr. Pococke, there is a temple of Iſis in good preſervation at Dundarah, but no remains of that of Venus, ſo much celebrated of old. The peculiarity of their ſituation, prevented the author and his companions from indulging their curioſity at that, or any other place in the neighborhood.

be

be the only reason, that a desart should extend itself to the vicinity of the finest river in the world. And to the genius of a Mahometan government, must that want be alone attributed. As we descended the hill, we lost sight of the wood and water; and must bid adieu for some time, to such a regalement to our senses. At seven o'clock we halted for the night. The Arabs tell us, that the roads are too rugged and dangerous to travel over in the dark. This is a mortification to us; but we must put up with having come but ten miles in two days, which is our present distance from Ghinnah. Our course has, however, been northerly, and we are so far in our route to Cairo.

SATURDAY, 6th SEPTEMBER.

At half past five this morning we resumed our march. My eyes are still bad, and I have suffered great anguish from them on the road. The heat particularly affects them, though I defend them as well as I can from the sun. As we went along we started several deer; but they are too wild to admit of our getting a shot at them. The road still continues rugged, and we ascended several hills, but could not procure another peep at the river. It is not likely that we are far from it by the course we keep, though it will behove us shortly to maintain a respectable distance, to avoid the parties of Ibrahim Beg, which are said to hover about its neighborhood. At half past eleven we halted to the eastward of a projecting hill, under whose friendly shade we ate an hearty meal of bread and meat. Our last stage was six hours, or fifteen miles. As we came up to this place, we disturbed a poor deer, that had sheltered itself here from the sun. These animals abound in this desart; and as we have not met with, or even heard of, any wild beasts, or venomous creatures in our peregrinations, I conclude Egypt to be free of them, notwithstanding the fables of antiquity.

In

In India we confider it as a thing almoft certain, to find tygers near an herd of deer, which they are always obferved to follow as their ufual prey. When our dinner was ended, we laid down to take a nap. The hour was inviting thereto, and the ftay we were to make here, admitting of the fweets of repofe.

When I awoke in the afternoon, Hadgee Uttalah perceived my eyes to be much inflamed, and very kindly proffered me fome relief. The Arabs generally carry a medicine about them, for the cure of a diforder to which they are fo fubject, from the duft and heat which incommode their country. Experience muft have proved the efficacy of the medicine; and I was fo remote from any hopes of affiftance, that I even ventured to fubmit my eyes to the hands of this quack. The medicine is of a black thick confiftence, and, on his introducing it with an inftrument into my eyes, occafioned a momentary fmart. At four o'clock we purfued our journey, and keeping the fame direction, without varying the fcene, at feven o'clock we reached the foot of a prodigious high mountain, which we cannot afcend in the dark. Here, therefore, we took up our abode for the night. The laft ftage was three hours, or feven miles, fo that we compute ourfelves to be thirty-three miles from Ghinnah. Our courfe to-day has been N. N. E.

SUNDAY, 7th SEPTEMBER.

The Arabs have a very good cuftom of drinking coffee, before they leave their ground in a morning. This we have adopted, and find it much more efficacious in taking the chill off the ftomach, than the old Englifh prefcription of a dram, with which we are, perhaps, luckily unprovided. By fix o'clock we had accoutered our camels, and, leading them in our hands, began to afcend the mountain on foot. As we mounted the fteep, we frequently bleft ourfelves that we were not riding, as the path was so narrow, the least false step must have sent the beast down the bordering precipice. But it must be confessed, that the camel is the most sure-footed of all beasts of burden; nor do I recollect in this fatiguing march from steep to steep, that my camel stumbled once. We were upwards of an hour climbing this mountain, and on the top found an extensive plain. But the prospect from hence was obstructed by the adjacent heights, which in some places overlooked the ground we were upon. We travelled about two hours on this mountain, where we found a sensible difference in the sharpness of the atmosphere, and at nine o'clock began to descend. We once more dismounted our camels, which we had rode over the level surface, and hastened down the declivity, in a third of the time which we took to go up. The path winded round the side of the mountain, and to our left an horrid chasm, some hundred fathoms deep, presented itself to our view. It is surprizing no accident befel the loaded camels, whose harness is so bad, that they were frequently stopped in the middle of a descent, to adjust the baggage which had been discomposed by the violent motion of the animal. When we gained the bottom, two of the camel-drivers pushed forward to see if they could shoot a deer. We have but little dependence upon their matchlocks, which must be rested to take a good aim: and though my companions have muskets, they will not risk their reputation by trying their skill, as they have not balls that fit their pieces. We winded through the valley, where we met with numerous thorn-trees in full blossom and fragrance; and after a long march, halted at half past one o'clock to the eastward of an high hill. Just before we reached this place, a ludicrous circumstance enough happened to me. I had loitered about two hundred yards behind, in company with three of the Arabs, who suddenly stopped my camel, and, by signs, forbade me to proceed. This abrupt behavior roused me from a reverie in which I was plunged; and, on my attempting to go on,

they

they still detained me, and frequently cried out, "Huffal, huffal." I looked immediately for my companions, who, I perceived, were treated in the same manner; and I was about to have recourse to my arms, in order to force a paſſage to them, when, behold! a fine buck ran acroſs the road in front of us, which was followed by the report of a piece. The myſtery was now unravelled, and I was in a moment delivered from the greateſt perplexity I had ever experienced. This had ariſen from my imperfect acquaintance with the language. The word "Huſſal," which had appeared to me like a term of command, I now found to be a deer in Arabic. I quickly rejoined the troop, and laughed heartily with them at the adventure. I need not add, that we did not dine upon veniſon to-day. We had recourſe, however, to our potted mutton, of which we muſt be ſparing, as our conductor and the camel-owners expect to partake of it. We did not lay our account with this partition, but will ſubmit to it, rather than put theſe people out of humour. The laſt ſtage was ſeven hours and an half, or nineteen miles.

At half paſt three o'clock we were mounted again, and going through the ſame valley, in about an hour, reached the bottom of another ſteep mountain. We were obliged to lead our camels up, and in about half an hour gained the ſummit, where we found a plain near two miles in length, over which we rode. At ſix o'clock we came to the extremity of the mountain, when our advanced guard alarmed us with the news of a party of camels being in the vale. As it was a ſuſpicious place to encounter any of our own ſpecies, we all took to our arms, and aſſembled on the deſcent, which was ſo craggy, and ſo perpendicular, that, ſmall as our numbers were, we were enabled, by our ſituation, to have coped with a multitude of enemies. The ſtrangers had obſerved our motions, and drew up in a body below to wait the reſult. We counted no leſs than thirty camels, and deduced therefrom, that we should have two to one against us, in case of hostilities. To gain intelligence, however, of the disposition of the strangers, Hadgee Uttalah himself descended into the valley. He ventured himself unarmed, as a token of peace; and we were not a little impatient to behold the interview which was about to take place. We were deeply interested in its event; and, circumstanced as we were, it is not surprizing that we should doubt of its success. But we were happily deceived in our ideas. No sooner had Hadgee Uttalah approached the new party, than he was recognized by one among them, who ran with open arms to receive him. He was presently encompassed by the rest; and we could discern that he was served with coffee and bread. This staggered us in our opinion of these people's profession; and we began to conceive that they might be travellers like ourselves, who, in these critical times, had explored the desart, in preference to the river. And we were now confirmed in this conceit, by the signs which Hadgee made to us to descend. These signs were interpreted to us by our Arabs, who told us there was nothing to fear. We obeyed, therefore, and went down the hill in as good order as the path would admit of. We were met at the foot of it by Hadgee, who conveyed us and our baggage to a spot at some distance from the strangers, and then returned to them. Many were the embraces and congratulations that were exchanged between the Arabs on both sides. The first thing we learned was, that water is to be procured in this valley, which has induced our gentry to halt here, and replenish our skins. We arrived here at half past six o'clock, so that our last stage was three hours, or seven miles.

While Hadgee Uttalah was engaged in an earnest conversation with the leader of the other party, Ibrahim and Abdul Ruffar came to us with looks of surprize, and informed us, that they had discovered the strangers to be what we at first apprehended—a band of robbers. That they had overheard one of them boast, that this band

band took the forty camels near Cofire during our ſtay in that town—an anecdote which I before mentioned—and that on the banks of the Nile, they had plundered a caravan but a few days ago, with the ſpoils of which they were now returning to their own country! It may be imagined that we were not a little ſtartled at this intelligence. The novelty of the circumſtance did not diminiſh its unpleaſantneſs; and our ſituation was as alarming as uncommon. We were turned adrift in a wide deſart, and, in caſe of oppoſition, were to depend upon our arms, and the fidelity of our Arabs. Even conqueſt would not avail us, were we obliged to fight againſt our guides. In the deſart only could we look for ſafety in this hoſtile land; and we had no clue to unravel its mazes, ſhould we be abandoned by our people. Theſe were the firſt reflections which ſuggeſted themſelves; but our minds were preſently relieved by the aſſurances of Hadgee Uttalah, who now joined us. He made no ſcruple to acquaint us with the profeſſion of the robbers; but added, that they had as much regard for their word as other people. They happily knew him, which was indeed the ſaving of an effuſion of blood. For, on the ſcore of friendſhip, they had pledged their word to him, that they would not meditate the leaſt wrong againſt us. We might truſt them implicitly, for the wild Arabs had never been known to break their faith on ſuch occaſions. After this prelude, we were the leſs ſurprized at a propoſition which they had made him, to accompany us to Cairo. Hadgee himſelf recommended to us to accept of it. Our intereſt, he ſaid, was every way concerned in it. They would ſerve us both as guides and protectors, in this unfrequented waſte: and where they once adopted a cauſe, it was their character to promote it at the expence of their blood. Had we diſtruſted this panegyric, it was not for us to diſſent againſt the opinion of our conductor, who was actually the maſter of our perſons and effects. The pledges he has left at Ghinnah will prevent

vent his rifking his charge wantonly, and on this we rely at this juncture. We have fallen into precious company! and it behoves us to be on our guard as much as poffible. Never did heroes in romance plunge into greater perplexities; and were not this narrative well attefted, it might feem here to breathe the air of fiction. But the good genius which prefided over every adventure we have atchieved, will, we truft, conduct us fafely through the prefent.

At feven o'clock the camels belonging to the robbers went on for water, and left their captain and a guard only with their baggage. This was a proof of confidence; but we betook ourfelves to bed, with our arms by us as ufual, and got as much fleep as the cold would admit of. I was fo unfortunate as to be ftripped of my night-cloak at Ghinnah, and have no defence but a chintz coverlid againft the fharpnefs of the wind, which is due north, and as cutting as I ever felt it out of Europe. When we begin to travel at night, the motion will make us lefs fenfible of the cold. This valley is, by our reckoning, fifty-nine miles from Ghinnah. Our courfe to-day has been N. W.

MONDAY, 8th SEPTEMBER.

I awoke at four o'clock this morning, and found that the camels belonging to the robbers were not returned from the fpring. Their baggage lay within view of us, among which I learn there is coffee, fugar, and fail-cloth, which they have lately taken, and are carrying for fale into the neighborhood of Cairo. At day-break our camels were alfo difpatched for water, and left only Hadgee Uttalah and the owners of the camels with us. As there was no hope of our decamping before noon, to amufe myfelf after breakfaft I fat down to tranfcribe an ode, in the compofition of which I was difturbed yefterday by the adventure of the deer. My camel is the lazieſt of the ſet, and affords me frequent opportunities for muſing, by lagging behind the reſt. A pretty place for inſpiration, truly! methinks ſome critic cries. But as gay ſcenes give birth to gay ideas, ſo the verſe portrayed in a deſart, cannot fail to partake of its ſtrong and gloomy coloring. Thoſe readers who are of a diſpoſition to reliſh ſuch a picture, may look to the Appendix; where, to avoid breaking the thread of my ſubject, I have placed this ode. Conceived among the objects it deſcribes, it is chiefly calculated for the penſive, melancholy heart; to which I beg leave to addreſs it.

It ſeems that robbery is no diſhonorable profeſſion among the Arabs, while they confine their attacks to the people of other diſtricts. Their friends and acquaintances may encounter theſe banditti without violation; and it is ſeldom known, that they lay their own countrymen under contribution. Our Arabs have fallen under the former deſcription, and it is to this extraordinary obſervance of faith, that we ſhall be indebted for our eſcape. Their cuſtom is to make excurſions into diſtant provinces, and to return to their own, with all the plunder they can collect. They conſider it rather as carrying on a petty war, than as an infringement of the rights of mankind; and in this reſpect, perhaps, have as much reaſon and juſtice on their ſide, as moſt of thoſe heroes who have deſolated the earth, and whoſe crimes only want to be diveſted of the vain *eclat* of uncommon actions. The government itſelf winks at theſe proceedings, which enrich its ſubjects; and while the delinquents keep beyond the immediate cognizance of juſtice, they have nothing to apprehend from its reſentment. And if it be conſidered, that many of their aſſociates are men who have been guilty of no offence, but have been obliged by the crimes of ſome of their family, to take refuge in the deſart, to ſhun the vengeance of individuals, we ſhould be the leſs ſurprized at meeting with an inſtance of

humanity

humanity and forbearance among them. The cruel policy of their laws has peopled the waste; and driven men of fair character to mingle with the vile, and to prey on the unwary traveller!

The captain of the gang was introduced to us by Hadgee Uttalah at breakfast, and took a cup of coffee with us. He is a bold, laughing villain, of a middle size, but large limbed: and would be well-featured, were not his mouth disfigured by a deep scar, which contracts his upper lip, and betrays the loss of several of his fore-teeth: the effects we suppose of one of his rencounters! There is a freedom in his behavior, which gains him our confidence. Far from being ashamed of his way of life, he talked of his late exploit, and produced two pair of morocco slippers, a Turkish vest, and other articles of dress, for sale. These we readily purchased, to conciliate his good opinion; and necessity must excuse our receiving stolen goods, knowing them to be stolen. Abdul Ruffar bought an Alcoran, and other religious books, the plunder perhaps of some poor priest; and Ibrahim a French horse-pistol, which will be of more shew than use to him. These things we have procured for at least a third of their value: and Hadgee Uttalah has satisfied the robber, for which we are to account with the former at Cairo. We have been careful to instil into our own people the belief of our being destitute of money; or God knows, what mischief the discovery of our real treasures might produce against us. Our fortune is very peculiar. We might have gone this road a thousand times, without encountering these freebooters. Had we arrived at this pass but half an hour later, we should have missed of them, as they were hasting through the valley to get water, and dreamed as little as ourselves, of stumbling upon human creatures in this unfrequented waste. But the event only can decide, whether the meeting be propitious or not. We have often, during

during our journey, had occasion to applaud Pope's celebrated maxim, that "whatever is, is right." And though so flattering to our interests, may we not hope that even this will prove a fresh testimony of it? The dealings which we have had with their captain, shew that he means to act upon the square with us; and we are still encreasing our debt with our Arabs, of which they are to look for payment at Cairo.

At eleven o'clock their camels returned from the spring, and had their intentions been hostile, they could not have found a better opportunity to execute them, than in the absence of a great part of our force. But their ideas were of an opposite nature. In the afternoon they killed a young camel, in compliment to Hadgee Uttalah; and nothing went forward but preparations for an entertainment. This flesh the Arabs esteem beyond all other; and as they presented us with a piece, our stomachs were not pampered enough to refuse tasting of it. Though we had eaten our humble repast, we had sufficient appetite to find the meat tender and well-flavored. It is coarse enough, however, and might be mistaken for bull-beef.

At three o'clock our camels returned, with the skins filled with good water. There is a feast however among the Arabs, which cuts off our expectations of getting away before the evening. Were it not for the delay, we have not spent a disagreeable day in this valley. It is so deep and so narrow, that there is ever a shade to the east or west side of it, and a draft of wind drawing through, which alleviates the noon-tide fervor.

We find, to our great regret, that we do not move to-night. Hadgee Uttalah now tells us, that as the camel was killed on our account, we cannot in decency but stay, until the strangers have dressed and prepared it for the journey. This will take up until dark, and we have another craggy mountain to pass over.

As

As the troubles probably subsist at Cairo, the old man proposed to us a plan, to carry us to the place of these robbers' residence. This is situated near the river, and but a few hours distant from that city, where he will accompany us in a boat. And the reason he gives for this manœuvre, is plausible enough. His camels run a risk of being pressed for the war, should he venture them to Cairo. Notwithstanding it was the Shaik Ul Arab's positive direction, that the camels should set us down at the English factory, and the scheme itself is not wholly to our mind, we must have that consideration for these poor creatures' property, as not to hazard it wantonly at the capital, if we can be conveyed there, though at a little more expence, in a boat. We have, therefore, given our conductor the latitude to act for the best. But not to forget our interest while he promotes his own.

The crackling of fires was now heard on all sides, and the menial Arabs were busy in turning the large joints upon the glowing embers. Some were dealing out their scanty allowance to the camels; while others unsheathed their glittering blades, to portion out the night's repast. Meanwhile the chiefs were assembled apart, stretched upon the hides of some ferocious animal, once roving and lawless like themselves. Their arms were thrown peaceably by them; while from each mouth, a long protended tube dispensed the fragrant fumes of Persia's weed. Deeds of bold hardiment are now retold: and each vain-glorious boaster is hero of the frequent tale. His province, war! and man, his spoil! Thus fleet the hours, 'till languor creeps upon the band, and quick resigns them to the arms of sleep.

TUESDAY, 9th SEPTEMBER.

The night was sharp as usual, which occasioned us to lie longer this morning to comfort ourselves. We did not move off our ground

ground until half past six o'clock, and the robbers then were not ready to accompany us. They desired us however to proceed, and promised to follow soon after. For three hours we winded through the valley we slept in, and about ten o'clock, began to gain the high ground by a regular ascent. The rest of this day's journey was continued over a succession of hills and dales; where the road was so intricate and broken, that nothing but a camel could get over it. The appearance of the road is so frightful in many places, that we do not wonder, why our people have hitherto laid by in the night. The air is so piercing on the hills, that we feel not the least inconvenience from the meridian ray. The sun, indeed, is far to the southward in this month, and we daily hasten, to our great comfort, from each other: add to this, we have turned our backs upon him. We can already pronounce this journey to be of a different complexion from our last. The roads, it is true, are more difficult and dangerous; but the season is so much changed for the better, that we scarce know what it is to thirst, or to suffer any but a partial heat. At one o'clock we entered another valley, which we traversed until half past two, and for want of a breeze, found it comfortably hot. Here we halted, and were not lucky enough to gain the least shelter from the sun. The change was disagreeable enough from our late situation in the high ground. We passed suddenly from the extreme of cold to that of heat. " Extremes by change more fierce." This valley we found to be the proper watering-place : the spring we met with yesterday, being only known to the robbers who haunt the waste. Our camels were accordingly dispatched to replenish the few empty skins, and to drink themselves, against the long thirst they are to experience. We sprang a brace of partridge and several quail in this valley, which has good cover of fragrant shrubs. The last stage was no less than eight hours, or twenty miles, and by our reckoning, we are but seventy-nine miles from Ghinnah. Our course to-day to-day has been N. N. W. We now see that yesterday was absolutely a lost day, and if we travel at this rate, our provisions, as well as patience, will soon fail us.

It was whispered about that the robbers had taken a different route. We had been here near two hours, and there were no signs of them. This made us suspect, that they had amused us with the idea of joining us, and we were rather doubtful, whether the separation would be to our advantage or not, when a little after four o'clock, I saw the captain of the robbers with two attendants, advancing towards us with a quick pace. Shortly after the whole band appeared in sight, according their steps to the tune of a song, and seemingly careless of the sun-beams and of the world beside. They make a formidable figure, and are trebly armed to what our party are. How different is the fact from what was reported of their discipline and arms! Besides his matchlock, which is flung behind his back, each man has pistols in his girdle, a sabre on his left side, and a hanger on his right, while in his right hand he brandishes a spear. They are also in general better mounted than we; and our having out-marched them to-day, must be attributed to the additional load they have carried in the flesh of the camel. The principal part of our force was absent, and they had another fair opportunity of attacking us to advantage. But very amicable was their salutation; and they only thought of sending their camels to the spring, which met our's returning thence. This we find will detain us here until the morning, and is the second delay which these people have occasioned us. We learn that we are to march for three days on the mountains, before we descend towards the Nile, where we are to water next; which argues the necessity of going from hence with full skins.

WED-

WEDNESDAY, 10th September.

We were late as usual in decamping this morning. The Arabs seem not to relish the morning air, and make up for the delay, by marching an hour or two longer during the heat of the day: a circumstance not over and above agreeable to us. But, perhaps, I speak chiefly for myself, whose eyes are still weak, though on the mending hand, and much incommoded by the rays of the sun. Our satisfactions are seldom without their alloys. In a conversation we had with one of the owners of our camels, as we drank our coffee, he let us know how much we were in the power of his countrymen. He had the assurance to laugh at the idea of the Shaik Ul Arab, who he said was nobody here; and added, that were it not for himself and his companions, we should have been stripped by the robbers, and now been wandering about the desart, destitute of food and raiment *. There was something in this picture that did not flatter our imaginations. Our pride was alarmed; and we quickly retorted, that we never would be reduced to such a condition, while we had a hand remaining to wield a weapon. But in spite of this fellow's arrogance, we thought it prudent to retain him in our interest. We commended his fidelity, and appeared thankful for his friendship, which we promised to shew a proper sense of on our arrival at Cairo. His behavior, indeed, is quite the reverse to that of Hadgee Uttalah, who is not only a quiet, civil body, but one, who speaks of his sovereign with deference and respect.

At half past six o'clock we began to ascend a mountain nearly perpendicular. The way was rugged, and one of my camels be-

---

* This very situation has since been the lot of a company of Europeans, between Suez and Cairo. The miserable end of those who perished in this horrid manner, should redouble our sense of our providential escape.

ing skittish, or perhaps uneasily laden, suddenly threw his burden from his back, and disordered the whole body. My trunks pitched from rock to rock, until they got to the bottom; and I am indebted to good luck, that they were not broken to pieces. The contents which such an accident would have published to the robbers, might have awakened the spirit of rapine which lay dormant within them, and tended to disturb the present harmony which subsists between us. Ibrahim was sent down to replace the baggage, and found one of the robbers very kindly assisting the driver in that office. We were near an hour leading our camels from one ascent to another, before we conquered the summit; and for three hours rode over a plain, where neither shrub nor bush was to be seen. At ten o'clock we descended into a valley, where we halted to breakfast. In this valley, we found plenty of provender for our cattle: Rosemary bushes, and other shrubs of uncommon fragrance, which, being natives of the desart, are still, perhaps, without a name. Though these scented plants are the usual food of the camel, it is remarkable, that his breath is insufferably nauseous. But when he is pushed by hunger, he devours thistles and prickles indiscriminately, without the least damage to his mouth, which seems proof to the sharpest thorns. The last stage was four hours, or ten miles.

At half past eleven we mounted again, and traversed the valley for an hour and upwards, when we climbed the mountains once more, by as narrow and craggy paths as human feet ever trod. As we overlooked the precipices beside us, I discovered several channels apparently worn with water, and am convinced in my own mind, from these and other signs, that either the Nile formerly branched into this desart, or rivers ran here whose springs are now choaked up. " Dumb are their channels and their fountains dry." The very neighborhood of the Nile has undergone one of the unaccountable vicissitudes of sublu-

nary

nary things: and the population of Upper Egypt has shrunk to the narrow compass of the river, which waters her extensive domain!

The band of robbers keep in our rear, and have hitherto halted at an agreeable distance from us. This conduct we approve of much, as their mixing with our simple servants might be productive of discoveries, not to our advantage. At half past four, we entered a valley, where we dined luxuriously in the shade. We are much surprized to find that our biscuit runs short. This will soon oblige us to mess with the Arabs, and to eat of their flour cakes baked in the ashes. But while we keep our healths, we shall scarcely complain of our food, whatever it may be. The Arab we hired at Ghinnah, is the person on whom we must depend for the manufacturing these cakes. He is a droll, who plays a thousand antic tricks to divert the company. But I am of opinion, that he has more of the knave than fool about him. Ibrahim was always too indolent, to administer to our wants of this kind. And as to Abdul Ruffar, he has been of little or no service to us, since the leap he made for his life at the house of Mahomet. He has been long recovered of his bruises, but they seem to have cooled his zeal for our interests. The last stage was five hours, or twelve miles and an half. At eight o'clock we moved on with the benefit of a fine moon, and kept winding through the valley until half past eleven, when we stopped at the foot of an high hill for the remainder of the night. The last stage was three hours and an half, or nine miles; and we are by computation one hundred and ten miles from Ghinnah. Our course to-day has been to the eastward of north.

THURSDAY,

THURSDAY, 11th SEPTEMBER.

We decamped in such haste this morning, that we were disappointed of our coffee, and marched away with empty stomachs. We led the camels up the hill before us, and for two hours passed over such a variety of hills and dales, that we could not pretend to mount our beasts. At eight o'clock, we began to descend into a deep valley, by one of the most dangerous roads we had yet beheld. On each side of us were perpendicular steeps, some hundred fathoms deep. But the traveller's attention seems to be purposely diverted from the danger, by the magnificent objects which surround him. Here he sees pointed heaps of the brightest crystal, that dazzle the eye with their glittering lustre: while ever and anon above his head, tremendous to behold! columns of the finest granite, rent from the mountain, seem ready to bury him beneath their tottering weight. On every part is such a wild confusion of hanging precipices, disjointed rocks, and hideous chasms, that we might well cry out with the poet "Chaos is come again." Whoever can tread these rude retreats, without being struck with the sublimest ideas of that Almighty Providence, who presides as well amid the gloom and silence of the desart, as in the noise and gaiety of the city, must be as dead to the emotions of fancy as to a sense of devotion. Yes, omnipotent Father! to thee we trust for our deliverance from the perils that surround us. It was through this wilderness thou didst lead thy chosen people. It was here thou didst manifest thy signal protection, in snatching them from the jaws of destruction which opened upon every side. Though less deserving of thy regard, we despair not of a prosperous issue to our wanderings; and in the hope of thy support, we look with indifference on what may befal us!

At

At nine o'clock we afcended a gentle acclivity, where we mounted our camels, and rode over level ground until half paſt ten, when we halted among fome fhrubs, to feed our beaſts and to breakfaſt. The laſt ſtage was four hours and an half, or eleven miles.

At half paſt eleven we refumed our journey, which ſtill lay upon a plain. As we went along, we ſtarted two or three deer, which were the firſt living creatures we had met upon thefe heights. At two o'clock we came fuddenly upon a dreadful chafm in the road, which appears to have been the effect of an earthquake. It is about three hundred yards long, one hundred yards wide, and as many deep; and what is the curiofity, in the middle of the gulph a fingle column of ſtone raifes its head to the furface of the earth. The rudenefs of the work, and the aſtoniſhing length of the ſtone, announce it to be a '*lufus naturæ*,' though the robbers declared to us, that beneath the column there lies a prodigious fum of money; and added, with a grave face, they have a tradition, that none but a Chriſtian's hand can remove the ſtone to come at it. We could hardly keep our countenance at this tale, and without attempting a labor, which would have been worthy of the fabled Hercules, we rounded this gulph, which is called Somah; and leaving it behind us, we entered a valley where we found a very craggy road. We continued our courfe through this valley until half paſt five o'clock, when we halted under the fhade of an hill to dine. The laſt ſtage was fix hours, or fifteen miles; and a very fatiguing one it proved, during the hotteſt part of the day. The robbers kept nearer to us than ufual, and encamped on the fame ground. Here our Arabs diverted themfelves with fhooting at a mark, at which they are very dextrous. It is neceffary for them, however, to reſt their pieces, which leaves them infinitely beneath our markfmen in fair fhooting. The example of our people

animated

animated thofe in the other quarter: and there was nothing heard but the report of fire-arms, during our ftay here. The robbers were much delighted with a mufketoon belonging to us, whofe execution upon the rocks was more terrible, and whofe report more loud, than they had any conception of. They remarked too with wonder, that a matchlock mifles fire more frequently than a fufee, although the former has a match in lieu of a flint.

At eight o'clock we mounted again, and refumed our courfe through the valley by moon-light, until half paft ten, when we ftopped to take our repofe. The laft ftage was two hours and an half, or fix miles; and by our reckoning, we are one hundred and forty-two miles from Ghinnah. Our courfe to-day has been N. by E. and N. by W.

FRIDAY, 12th SEPTEMBER.

We did not begin our march before half paft fix o'clock this morning, by which time we had broken our faft with a difh of coffee. We directed our courfe to the weftward, to gain on the river; as this is the fourth day fince we filled our water-fkins, which make but a light appearance at prefent. We foon entered upon a very extenfive plain, fcattered over with a variety of odoriferous fhrubs, and bounded on all fides by lofty mountains, whofe tops were loft in the clouds. After the heights we have paffed, it is no pleafing profpect to behold new difficulties to conquer. But alas! fatigues feem daily to multiply upon us. "Hills peep o'er hills, and Alps on Alps arife."—As we went along we perceived the frefh tracks of numbers of deer, which we fuppofe had taken to the hills on our approach. The nearer we go to the Nile, the lefs fterile is the face of the country. The foil in many places is mixed with clay, and feems capable

capable of cultivation. At half paſt eight o'clock we halted in a ſpacious opening between the mountains, which leads due weſt to the river. Here the Arabs tell us we muſt remain, while the camels fetch water from the Nile, which is about twenty miles diſtant. As the war ſtill rages there, they do not think it prudent for us to approach any nearer. The robbers have encamped by us, and diſpatched their camels on the ſame errand. This delay will prolong our journey a day at leaſt, and conſequently the time we are to ſpend with theſe honeſt fellows. They are, however, on their good behavior with us; and as long as they keep their word with our conductor, we are bound to ſpeak well of them, whatever may be their general character and profeſſion. We ſhould have ſpent a diſagreeable day here, had we not fixed up ſuch a tent as we contrived at our firſt ſtage from Ghinnah, to ſhelter us from the ſun. But there was no ſtanding within it, nor any mode of entrance but upon our knees. This inconvenience, however, is not to be mentioned, among others which we have long ſuſtained. Chairs and tables we have been utter ſtrangers to for ſome months; and it is no longer awkward to us to feed ourſelves with our fingers.

While we waited for the return of our camels, we were alarmed about noon by the report of two cannon. It came from the river, and we began to apprehend that there might be troubles in our neighborhood. Remote as we were from the ſcene of the diſpute, the ſight of our camels might occaſion an enquiry from either party, which might end in the diſcovery of our retreat. Theſe reflections were not of a very conſolatory nature; nor did our ſituation call for foreign evils, to render it leſs enviable. But we were not otherwiſe diſturbed, than in our imaginations. Every thing remained quiet during the day; and though the Arabs, as well as our ſervants, repeatedly declared, that they heard the firing of more cannon, we imputed it to fancy or fear, and attended very

S ſ   patiently

patiently to the issue. We were indeed engaged in another matter, which at first had a serious countenance. We found that our coffee and sugar was expended, and that the camel-drivers were in want of more ghee, notwithstanding the large stock which we laid in of these articles. Now it was that we became sensible of some of the good effects of the company of the robbers. What we should have sought for in vain in their absence, their captain has supplied us with, at half the prices which such articles bear at Ghinnah. Hadgee Uttalah has settled with him for the amount, which we are to repay at Cairo. In truth, the conscience of this robber is no less wonderful than his manners. He is easy of access, and yet carries a proper command over his party; and by his own example teaches them to be civil, and even obliging to us. We would willingly make him a suitable acknowledgment for this behavior, but do not think it safe to produce money, or to depart in the least from our professions of poverty. It was with the greatest pleasure imaginable, that I could oblige him in a trifling point: with a couple of razors, which he saw in my servant's hands, and expressed a desire for.

As the night advanced, our anxiety for the fate of our camels encreased. They did not return before eleven o'clock, and were absent upwards of fourteen hours. They went to an unfrequented inlet of the river, but saw a countryman, who informed the drivers, that Ismaul Beg had repulsed the gallies of Ibrahim Beg, and dispersed his forces upon the banks of the Nile. We are probably indebted to the horrors of the desart, that we have not encountered any of the fugitives, who, to shun famine here, have chosen a route more formidable in point of human persecutions. This place, we understand, is nearly opposite to the town of Suadi, on the Nile; and as our stage to-day was but two hours, or five miles, we are, by our calculation, 149 miles from Ghinnah.

SATUR-

SATURDAY, 13th SEPTEMBER.

At half paſt ſix this morning we left our ground, and travelled over a plain until nine o'clock, when we entered a broad valley, and at ten halted among ſome buſhes to breakfaſt. We now began to be in the ſame meſs with the Arabs. Our own biſcuit was out; but it was with no indifferent ſtomachs that we partook of their unleavened bread. This is made of flour to be ſure, but flour in the coarſeſt ſtate: and what with the making and baking, the reader may conceive that the bread is of a tolerable blackneſs, before it comes to our hands. We moiſten this food with ghee, and crown the repaſt with a diſh of coffee, and a draught of water. I declare, for my own part, that I never enjoyed one, at any period of my life, with a better reliſh. So beneficial are exerciſe and ſobriety to the health! and ſo ſucceſsful is neceſſity in overcoming the force of habit! I may ſpeak confidently on the former heads, in regard to myſelf; as my conſtitution is none of the ſtrongeſt, and I have been ever ſubject to head-achs, and nervous complaints. But none of our company bear the fatigues of the journey better than myſelf; or have been bleſt with a greater ſhare of health during our reſidence in theſe parts. The humour in my eyes was but an external diſorder; and, thanks to our conductor, did not much trouble me after the application he made to them. The laſt ſtage was three hours and an half, or nine miles.

At eleven o'clock we mounted again, and purſued our route through the valley, which is pretty thickly covered with ſhrubs. Nothing is ſo diſagreeable as to go for any length of way through a place of this kind. The poor camels will ſtop at every buſh to ſatisfy their hunger; and, did humanity admit of depriving them of this ſcanty ſatisfaction, neither words nor blows could induce them to mend their pace. At one o'clock we gained, by a gentle

aſcent,

afcent, upon a plain, ftony and bare of verdure. We left the hill in our rear, and toiled onwards over the barren flat in an hot fun until four o'clock, when we entered a valley ftored with rofemary and other fcented bufhes. We winded through it until half paft four, when we halted to refrefh ourfelves and cattle. It muft be obferved, that we found no fhelter from the fun at either of our halting-places to-day, which has rendered it the moft irkfome one during this journey. The laft ftage was five hours and an half, or fourteen miles.

At eight o'clock we moved on with a fine moon. The night was very fharp and cold, though I faced it without putting on any additional covering. The Arabs wrapped themfelves up in their cloaks; and, with the affiftance of their pipes, contrived to baffle the piercing wind, which is by no means agreeable to their feelings. Each man is provided with a flint and piece of fteel. To the fteel a bit of leather is affixed, which takes fire on the firft ftroke, and is ready to light his matchlock or pipe. An unlucky accident had like to have befallen Mr. Hammond, from the ufe of thefe flints. A fpark of fire fell unknowingly upon the leather-bag which contained his ammunition; and had he not by chance perceived the fmoke iffuing from it, in a few minutes it is probable he would have felt the fevere effects of the explofion. This alarm occafioned us to change our pofition, and we kept to the windward of the Arabs during the reft of the march. Our road, after leaving the valley, lay over level ground. As it would be next to an impoffibility to find the way over thefe ftony flats, where the heavy foot of a camel leaves no impreffion, the different bands of robbers have heaped up ftones at unequal diftances, for their direction through this defart. We have derived great affiftance from the robbers in this refpect, who are our guides when the marks either fail, or are unintelligible to us. If it be confidered, that this road to Cairo is feldom or never trodden, it is no wonder that

that our Arabs are frequently at a lofs for the courfe. We are
but the third, and, perhaps, may be the laft company of travellers, who have ventured to go by this route, fince the difturbances
have arifen upon the Nile. Our little Turk at Ghinnah was particularly averfe to it; and though both his perfon and merchandize
would in all probability have enjoyed the fame protection as ourfelves, we are well enough pleafed that he did not encounter the
trial. The truth of it is, the Turks are very tyrannical mafters,
and the Arabs feize every opportunity to repay their obligations
in kind. At twelve o'clock we halted to take our repofe in the
open plain; and fenced ourfelves from the cold wind as well as
we could, with our baggage. The laft ftage was four hours, or
ten miles; and, by our reckoning, we are 180 miles from Ghinnah. Our courfe to-day has been N. E. and during the latter
part due N.

SUNDAY, 14th September.

We decamped at half paft fix o'clock this morning, and purfued our courfe over a level country. The river, we are told,
runs within ten or twelve miles of us; but we dare not approach
it, whatever attractions it may poffefs. On the road we paffed
the fkeleton of a camel, which now and then happens in the defart. Thefe are poor creatures that have perifhed with fatigue;
for thofe which are killed for the fuftenance of the Arabs, are carried away, bones and all together. Of the hides are made the
foles of the flippers which are worn in Egypt, without any drefs-
ing, but what the fun can give them. The circumftances of this
animal's death, when his ftrength fails him on the road, have
fomething in them affecting to humanity. Such are his patience
and perfeverance, that he purfues his journey without flagging, as
long as he has power to fupport its weight; and fuch are his
fortitude

fortitude and spirit, that he will never give out, until nature sinks beneath the complicated ills which press upon him. Then, and then only, will he resign his burden and his body to the ground. Nor stripes, nor caresses, nor food, nor rest, will make him rise again! His vigor is exhausted, and life ebbs out apace!—This the Arabs are very sensible of, and kindly plunge a sword into the breast of the dying beast, to shorten his pangs. Even the Arab feels remorse when he commits this deed; his hardened heart is moved at the loss of a faithful servant!—Peace then to thy remains, unhappy son of want and woe! May no rude wind disturb thy bones, no impious hand remove them from the reach of passing eyes! At sight of them the traveller shall drop a pitying tear. Thy force! thy gentleness! thy giant form! thy toiling days! thy hapless end! shall rush upon his mind, and loudly claim this transient tribute! So may he hope to pass secure the horrors of the waste—so may the beast which he bestrides, escape thy fate!

At ten o'clock we halted in the sun to breakfast, among some thistles, which is all that the plain affords our poor camels. The soil here is gravel, intermixed with chalk and stone. The last stage was three hours and an half, or nine miles. At eleven we resumed our march, over one of the most extensive plains in the universe. Not a hill, not a tree appears; and the eye, as on the ocean, is only bounded by the horizon. The sun here was very powerful; and the wind blowing over the chalky soil, proved more troublesome and disagreeable, than we have found it on the journey. We travelled the whole day without resting, though we were obliged to pull in our camels once or twice among some bushes, to refresh them with a mouthful of food. At five o'clock we approached a range of high mountains, which run westward to the Nile. We stopped within a league of them, until the captain of the robbers and some of the Arabs pushed on to survey the

pass,

pafs, which is sometimes frequented by their fraternity. We moved flowly after them, and at feven o'clock overtook them under the hills at the entrance of the valley, and were happy to find there was no appearance of danger. We sheltered ourfelves behind a thick fpreading bufh to fleep, as the north wind blew peculiarly cold. Here my fervant difcovered a fnake under his bed, which the Arabs tell us is poifonous. But it had no tokens of being fo, if I may be allowed to judge from the variety of fnakes which I have feen in India. This laborious ftage took us up eight hours and an half, or twenty-two miles, fo that we are by our reckoning 212 miles from Ghinnah. Our courfe to-day has been to the weftward of N.

MONDAY, 15th SEPTEMBER.

We were in motion by fix o'clock this morning, and advanced towards the hills, to which we judged we were fo near by the light of the moon. But it was a full hour before we entered the valley that divides them. Here we found plenty of provender for our camels, who get but a meafure of beans *per diem* each, befides the food which they pick up in the way. A flender allowance indeed, for fo large an animal! On all fides we obferved the frefh flot of deer, and of another creature, which I take to be an elk from the fize of the hoof, but which the Arabs call a mountain fheep. Thefe mountains are compofed of alabafter, porphyry, and granite; large fragments of which are fcattered about the road, either by the force of a whirlwind, or their fall from an immenfe height. It was doubtlefs from this quarter, that the antient kings of Egypt furnifhed themfelves with the materials of thofe fplendid edifices, whofe remains are yet vifible in the principal cities of this kingdom. Thofe lofty columns which have aftonifhed mankind at Alexandria and elfewhere, and which have

been

been transported to Italy at a prodigious expence, were probably cut from these quarries; as the vicinity of the Nile afforded such an eligible conveyance to the sea. This is, in fact, but a conjecture; but such as a traveller may be allowed to indulge himself in, were it only to rectify the mistakes of some very ingenious writers, who have supposed all this profusion of marble to have been brought from above the cataracts of the Nile, and thence deduce the insignificancy of those celebrated falls *. But to me the premises appear so ill-founded, that I cannot admit of the inference; though it must be acknowledged, that accident alone could have led a stranger to the discovery of a quarry, which is unknown or unattended to, by the natives of the country. We winded through this valley 'till ten o'clock, when we halted among some thorn-trees to drink coffee. This stage was four hours, or ten miles.

At eleven o'clock we resumed our course through the valley, which is well stocked with thorn trees that are large enough to throw a shade. Our nostrils were saluted with a fine odour, as we passed by the snowy blossoms that whiten the vale. On the road we started an hare, and saw many earths, which this poor creature burrows in to defend her from the heat. The wind was so bleak, that the sun had little or no effect until towards noon, when the weather turned very sultry. We journeyed the whole day in this valley, which in some places extends itself near a mile in breadth. In the afternoon we were alarmed with the fresh tracks of a camel's feet, which make a strong impression in a soft soil. The Arabs do not take them to be more than a day old, and pronounce a party of freebooters to be at hand. No travellers left Ghinnah later than a week before us; and what business can bring any but freebooters into this waste, is incomprehensible to us. Danger seemed to be near us, and scouts were sent forward to advertise us of it.
The

---

* By the testimonies of Captain Norden and Dr. Pococke, these falls are really insignificant; but neither of them penetrated to the second or third cataract.

The robbers were employed in this office, and by the facility with which they traced the suspicious feet, it appeared how difficult it would be to avoid such an expert pack. No hound could run truer upon a scent; nor do I suppose, any hound would be stauncher to the chace. We travelled on, however, without any interruption, and at six o'clock halted to dine. We were in need of refreshment, as the last stage was seven hours, or seventeen miles and an half. But our meat is quite expended, and we were obliged to put up with flour, which also begins to run short, for want, we fear, of œconomy being observed among our servants. By Hadgee Uttalah's first account, we were to have reached Cairo last night; and now he talks of two or three days more! This mistake must have arisen, not more from the delays we have met with, than from his ignorance of the country. It behoves us, however, to be careful of the little provision which remains.

At eight o'clock we resumed our march by the light of the moon, and still found ourselves in the valley. At half past ten we halted to take our repose. The last stage was two hours and an half, or six miles, and by our reckoning we are 246 miles from Ghinnah. Our course to-day has been directed by the windings of the valley, generally to the eastward of N.

TUESDAY, 16th SEPTEMBER.

We decamped at six o'clock this morning, and presently quitting the valley, which is above thirty miles long, we entered upon a plain, over which we travelled for some time. At nine o'clock we came suddenly upon a well, which is situated among some broken ground. The sight of a spring of water was inexpressibly agreeable to our eyes, which had so long been strangers to so refreshing an object. We halted behind the shade of some bushes at a little diftance from it, while we breakfafted, and replenifhed our fkins with that precious article. The laft ftage was three hours, or feven miles and an half.

The morning was very cool and pleafant, and we beheld an hazy fky, for the firft time, I believe, fince we have been in Egypt. The heavens are ufually clear and ferene in this upper province, where I cannot learn the plague has ever extended, during the periods of its greateft rage in Lower Egypt; to which land we are now approaching. Hadgee Uttalah tells us, that he will certainly put us into a boat on Thurfday morning. We cannot be any confiderable diftance from the latitude of Cairo, and have therefore the greater dependence on this promife. While we were at breakfaft we received a vifit from the captain of the robbers, who expreffed a defire to fee a double-barrelled piece, which he heard was in my poffeffion. After the honorable treatment which we had received from him, I could not do lefs than produce it. I went further, to pleafe him, and difcharged it, to fhew him the nature of its conftruction. He was much taken with the novelty of the invention; and after furveying it with particular marks of fatisfaction and aftonifhment, he returned it to my hands. I mention this circumftance, to evince the exceffive forbearance of this man; whofe profeffion is thieving, and to whom a fire-arm of this kind muft have been a very defirable acquifition. He had not left us many minutes, when one of his followers brought us a prefent of a bag of flour, with his mafter's compliments. He had learnt from our conductor, that we were in want of it; and though we did not chufe to be under an obligation to him of this nature, we could not prevail on him to accept of any pecuniary confideration for it. All we could do, was to divide fome rice we had left, and fend the half to the captain; which we had the pleafure to underftand proved a new and acceptable food to him. This is furprizing, confidering the neighborhood of the Delta, which produces fuch

quantities.

quantities of rice. But we muſt remember, that this robber has detached himſelf from the ſociety of cities; and is not likely to meet with any but the common grain, in his progreſs through the waſte.

We loſt the greateſt part of the day at this ſpring. Though our ſkins were preſently filled, the camels were yet to drink, and we had not bargained for the time which this neceſſary buſineſs would take up. As the camels could not go to the well, an hole was ſunk in the earth below the ſurface of the ſpring, over which a ſkin was ſpread, to retain the water which flowed into it. At this but two camels could drink at a time; and it was ſix hours before our camels, which amounted to forty-eight in all, were watered. Each camel, therefore, by this calculation, takes a quarter of an hour to quench his enormous thirſt; and to water a common caravan of 400 camels at ſuch a place as this, would require two days and two nights. A moſt unforeſeen and inconceivable delay to an uninformed traveller!

At three o'clock we reſumed our journey, and ſoon entered a dale, the moſt fertile we had yet beheld. Here graſs, and a kind of wild grain, were intermixed with the fragrant ſhrubs, and afforded a very agreeable change to our cattle, who devoured the freſh blade with unuſual greedineſs. The banks on each ſide of us, were green and ſloping, and the ſoil black and ſoft. From theſe circumſtances, and the courſe of the dale, which winds N. W. towards the Nile, I take it to have been formerly a branch of that river, but which has been long choaked up, except in uncommon inundations. As we went along, we ſtarted ſeveral hares, and ſprang a brace or two of quail; but we are not provided with ſhot to bring them down. At three quarters paſt seven we halted under the bank of the dale, to take our repoſe. The laſt ſtage was four hours and three quarters, or twelve miles; so that by our reckoning we are 266 miles from Ghinnah. Our course to-day was N. by W. and N. W.

WEDNESDAY, 17th SEPTEMBER.

We were mounted before five o'clock this morning, and missing one of our camels, which had strayed, we were obliged to divide his burden among the rest, and to leave a man behind us to look for him. We soon quitted the dale, and ascended the high ground by the side of a mountain, that overlooks it in this part. The path was narrow and perpendicular, and much resembled a ladder. To make it worse, we preceded the robbers; and an ignorant guide among our own people led us astray. Here we found ourselves in a pretty situation! We had kept the lower road on the side of the hill, instead of that towards the summit, until we could proceed no further. We were now obliged to gain the heights, in order to recover the road; in performing which, we drove our poor camels up such steeps, as we had the greatest difficulty to climb after them. We were under the necessity of leaving them to themselves; as the danger of leading them through places, where the least false step would have precipitated both man and beast to the unfathomable abyss below, was too critical to hazard. We hit at length upon the proper path, and were glad to find ourselves in the rear of our unerring guides, the robbers, after having won every foot of the ground with real peril and fatigue. In the valley beneath us, we passed by a fountain of fine water. It gushed from a rock, and threw itself with some violence into a bason, which it had hollowed for itself below. We had no occasion for a fresh supply; but could not help lingering a few minutes to admire a sight, so pretty in itself, and so bewitching to our eyes, which

had

had of late been strangers to bubbling founts and limpid streams. At seven o'clock we reached the summit of the mountain, and travelled until half past ten, over a continued region of hills and dales. This astonishing jumble! this continued ascent! recalls to the traveller's mind the fabled battle of the giants, who, in warring with the gods, heaped hills on hills to scale the canopy of heaven. They are rude, craggy, and barren, and the tracks over them hardly passable. In the bottoms the soil is generally clay, and so moist, as to denote our vicinity to the Nile, which at this season floods the country around. At some openings to our left we once more beheld this noble river—beheld him after a long absence, sweeping his majestic course between the towering mountains. We plainly discerned the tops of those to the westward of his stream; and it seemed as if he had here scooped a channel for his rapid waters out of the solid rock. We gradually regained the low lands, and at eleven o'clock halted among some shrubs, to refresh ourselves and cattle. Here our Arab overtook us with the missing camel. The circumstance of his wandering is very uncommon. The camel is the most staid of all creatures, and remains by the baggage during the night without being picketed. The last stage was six hours, or fifteen miles.

At half past eleven we resumed our march, and soon came to the foot of a prodigious hill, which we unexpectedly found we were to ascend. It was perpendicular, like the one which we had passed some hours before; but what rendered the access more difficult, the path which we were to tread, was nearly right up and down. The captain of the robbers, seeing the obstacles we had to overcome, wisely sent all his camels round the mountain, where he knew there was a defile, and only accompanied us with the beast he rode. We luckily met with no accident in climbing this height, which our people tell us, is the last we shall encounter.

counter. We journeyed over the top until one o'clock, when we defcended into a valley by a paffage eafy enough. Here we were furprifed with the fight of a man and a camel, who were half-concealed by a fpreading bufh. Our fervants were firft, and gave the alarm; upon which the captain of the robbers pufhed on his camel at its utmoft fpeed, regardlefs of danger, and meditating, perhaps, the feizure of fome booty. Our Arabs followed him, and prefently furrounded the man. My companions and myfelf hafted after. Our fituation was difficult on fuch an occafion; but we had already determined on the part we were to take, fhould the diftrefs of a fellow-creature claim our protection. We were bound by the ties of honor, to obferve a ftrict neutrality towards the robbers, except when they infringed the rights of human nature in our prefence. Happily for us all, the man in queftion was no fubject for their depredations. We foon came up to him, and found he was a courier, who left Cairo but yefterday, and is proceeding with letters to fome town on the river. He is known to the robber, or it feems that he would not have ventured through the defart. He tells us that all is quiet again at Cairo. This news, and the certain vicinity of the city, have put us all into good fpirits. The arduous enterprife is nearly accomplifhed, and the palm of fuccefs is at hand!

We left the principal Arabs to entertain the ftranger with coffee, and toiled through the valley until half paft five o'clock, when we halted to dine. We were now joined by thofe Arabs, and prefently after by the reft of the robbers, who had made an aftonifhing march to overtake us. This ftage was fix hours, or fifteen miles. After a light refrefhment of bread, we moved on at feven with the moon, which was now at full, and afforded us a clear light to march over an hilly region until twelve o'clock, when we fpread our beds under a bank, to fnatch a fhort repofe. The Arabs tell us we muft be ftirring before day-break, which,

added

added to our march to-day, pronounces them to be anxious to finish our toilsome journey. This place is but a short distance from the river. The last stage was five hours, or twelve miles, and by our reckoning, we are now 308 miles from Ghinnah. Our course to-day has been N. W. and W.

THURSDAY, 18th SEPTEMBER.

We were roused before four o'clock this morning, that we might get early to the town where we are to take boat. Without our usual allowance of coffee, we marched off directly for the river, to water our camels. The camel is as ready to drink often as any other animal, notwithstanding the large quantity of liquid which his stomach can contain. He is the only animal, who ruminates—if I may so term it—his drink as he journeys along; and is no more oppressed by it, than is the ox with his cud, which he chews at his leisure. We did not lose much time at the river, which we were overjoyed to review. Hence we directed our march to the northward, along the banks of the most delightful river in the world. By the late floods it is, in some parts, double its original breadth, and rushes with a noisy rapidity to the main. The desart here stretches itself to the very banks, which appear infinitely more verdant by the comparison. In our way we passed by a village to our left, called Vel Hadie, and at seven o'clock halted at the town of Ifcour, where we expected to find a boat. But our expectations were vain; although Hadgee Uttalah went himself to the house of the principal officer, to obtain an order for one. While we remained here, I ascended an eminence without the town, and was presented with the most romantic prospect that imagination can portray. The Nile had now surrounded a long slip of land, which appeared to be in the midst of his stream, and displayed a bed of diversified green.

green. A large wood towered its head on this island, and altogether formed a striking contrast to the russet mountains, which overlook his western shores. About a mile from this charming retreat, buried in the desart from common observation, the robbers have their residence. They attended us thus far, and then returned to their tents, which they had pointed out to us on the road, as the dwellings of their families. Their departure was secret, or as we call it, was a French leave. Hadgee Uttalah insinuates, that their captain took this step, in order to shew his disinterestedness, and to save us the pain of being obliged to dismiss him, without a present. If this insinuation be just—and we have no reason to doubt it—there was a modesty in this procedure, which would have done credit to a man of the most liberal education. Indeed, the whole behavior of these robbers has been so extraordinary, and the adventure itself is of so novel a cast, that the reader would scarcely excuse me for parting with them, without making some observations on the subject.

Of all the different tribes of Arabians which we have met with, these tenants of the desart alone, have afforded us unquestionable proofs of generosity and honor. We had sought for these virtues in the courts of princes, and found them in the uncultivated waste. Here no prejudices are harbored, no vain distinctions of religion give rise to despicable persecutions. If the sword be drawn, it is never wanton in its execution, and still respects the laws of friendship and faith. Like the savage inmates of the wild, these robbers rove through habit, and are only rapacious when urged by strong necessity. Man is their foe, more than they are the foe of man. But to these robbers alone this reflection will, perhaps, hold. Banished without cause from society, by the remissness of the laws, and influenced by education to think lightly of their trespasses, why should we marvel to hear of people in this profession, whose morals and manners

manners would not difgrace a city? This pofition is at leaft evident.—By the ftrict connection between them, and the frequent trial to which their fidelity is put, they have formed a character among themfelves, which is unknown to the reft of their countrymen. A character, which has excited this involuntary tribute of praife from a ftranger; and which is, indeed, worthy of a better fate!

The laft ftage was three hours, or feven miles. At ten o'clock we left Ifcour, and profecuted our journey along the banks of the Nile. We met with no villages for fome miles. At one o'clock we faw the pyramids very diftinctly, lying to the weftward of the river. Thefe we had obferved from Ifcour, though forty miles diftant from them; but from their magnitude, conceived them to have been hills of ftone. We now were afcertained of our approach to Cairo; and on my afking our conductor the ufe of thofe ftructures, he told us fo many fables of their origin and riches, as afforded us ample entertainment on the road. Not that the dreams of fuperftition withdrew our attention, from the reality of the vifion which delighted our eyes. We were ftruck with awe, in contemplating thefe amazing monuments of antiquity. Every thing confpired to touch the traveller's mind with the fublimeft ideas. The rude grandeur of the ftupendous mountains behind the pyramids; the aftonifhing height of the pyramids themfelves, which appear to rival the works of nature; the breadth and rapidity of the river which runs beneath them, fo renowned in fong, and fo fertile of uncommon productions, united to raife a picture worthy of a Brooke's* pencil to defcribe. Nor did I confider an herd of camels, that were browfing on our fide of the river, as a fmall addition to the magnificence of the profpect, which was compofed of the moft gigantic objects in nature! In this march

* An eminent painter of Ireland, whofe talents in his profeffion promife to illumine the rifing glory of his country.

two

two of our camels were so far jaded, as to reduce us to distribute what little burdens remained to them among the rest, and to leave them at a village on the road. It was now, that we acknowledged the prudence of bringing the additional camels. We no longer ascribed the measure to any selfish views; and wholly acquitted the Arabs of a design to deceive us; as the difficulties in this mountainous journey were sufficient to break the heart of a camel itself. At five in the evening, we arrived at Tinnah, a town almost opposite the pyramids, where we presently procured a boat to carry us to Cairo, which is but twelve miles distant. The last stage was seven hours, or eighteen miles; so that our journey over the desart, from Ghinnah to this place, has been, by our reckoning, 333 miles.

Tinnah is a small but pleasant town, and stands upon the reputed site of antient Babylon. There are no vestiges, however, of that splendid city; nor any ruins here save those of modern edifices. The houses are prettily shaded with trees, and the environs laid out in fields of grain. It is easy to account for the extinction of antient ruins in a peopled place; but how are we to explain this extinction in a desart, except we recur to the hurricanes of sand in which they may be buried, or rather doubt their existence at once? We met with many spots in the desart, fit enough for cultivation; but not a ruin of any kind, to denote the habitations of men. It is probable, therefore, that the geographers of old wrote without adequate information on the subject; and have given cities and tribes to a waste, which has been desolate since the creation of the world*.

While we supped upon our remaining rice, we were surrounded with crouds of people, who beheld us with curiosity, and learnt our adventures from the Arabs with surprize. At nine

---

* They have even exceeded those whom Swift ridicules—
" Who o'er unhabitable downs,
Place elephants for want of towns."

nine o'clock we joyfully embarked for Cairo. Besides ourselves and our domestics, Hadgee Uttalah and the camel-owners accompanied us in the boat. By them we promised to gratify the drivers, who were forry enough to leave us. The moon was juſt riſen, and without ſail or oar, we fell down briſkly with the current. Every thing wore a placid aſpect, and ſeemed ominous of the ſtate of the capital. We paſſed by many villages, which appeared very picturesque by the pale light of the moon, and at midnight anchored on the weſtern bank oppoſite Cairo, to take a ſhort repoſe.

FRIDAY, 19th SEPTEMBER.

About two this morning we weighed, and ſtood into the khalis or channel, which runs from the river into the city. This channel is of a conſiderable breadth, and was lined on each ſide with trading veſſels and pleaſure-boats; which diſplayed convincing tokens of the commerce and wealth of the capital of Egypt. The ſtrength of the current is here encreaſed, and the boatmen exerted no little ſkill in ſteering through the grove of maſts, which roſe like a wood around us. The ſhores on either hand of us, were adorned with gardens and ſummer-houſes; the dews which fell thickly upon our heads, were impregnated with the fragrance of the paſſing gale, which "whiſpered whence it ſtole the balmy ſpoil." Our minds were now diveſted of the perturbation which had ſo long poſſeſſed them, and were fitted to admit the charming ſcene. It ſeemed to be the effect of ſuch enchantment, as Armida is ſaid to have exhibited to regain the affections of her lover. Erewhile we wandered, like Rinaldo, through gloomy vales and dreary waſtes: And now, are ſuddenly tranſported to the elyſium he found—to ſtately palaces and vernal lands. We went under the ſtern of a Turkiſh frigate, which was galley-built and carried about twenty braſs brafs guns. She was probably stationed here, to protect the channel during the late troubles; but from the bad look-out which the Turkish sailors keep, it would be no difficult matter for an enemy to have surprized her in the night.

At three o'clock we arrived at Old Cairo, and after dressing ourselves in our best Turkish cloaths, we landed our baggage on the wharf, and discharged our boat. We were to remain here until day-break, and my companions and I diverted ourselves in examining the place. In straying about, I came to a garden surrounded by a lofty wall. On one side of it there was a latticed window, which appeared to give light to a bower, as the lattices were entwined with a spreading vine, whose grapes hung in clusters without. As I was admiring the fruit by the doubtful light of the moon, the sound of a guittar suddenly struck my ears. It issued from the window, and was at times accompanied by a female voice. I was too far removed from the performer, to reap the excellence of her skill; but the novelty of the adventure, and the plaintiveness of the tune, kept me fixed, as it were, to the spot. The window was infinitely too high to be scaled without a ladder, or my curiosity to behold a damsel, whom my imagination had pictured out in all the graces of beauty and youth, might have led me into a scrape. I was now called away by the Arabs to depart. They pressed us much to send for asses, a stand of which was in the neighborhood, as we should find ourselves much tired by the walk to the English factory. Our pride was startled at this proposition; and we persisted in our resolution to go on foot, to the great astonishment of the Arabs, who made no allowance for our ignorance of the customs here. We set out accordingly at dawn of day, and left all our servants but Ibrahim, to stay by the baggage, until we sent camels for it. We found the road none of the best, and after going for near a mile, along a dead wall that skirts the channel we had come up, we entered the new city at a

little

little paſt ſix o'clock. The ſtreets began now to be filled with people, and the ſhops diſplayed their various commodities for ſale. The favor of the hot bread had ſuch an effect upon our noſtrils, that ſhame alone deterred us from ſtopping in the ſtreet, to break our faſts with ſuch a new and delicious morſel. In ſpite of our diſguiſe, we were immediately known to be foreigners; and the croud repeatedly expreſſed tokens of ſurprize, which our Arabs told us, aroſe from ſeeing us on foot. To obviate this impertinence, we enquired if we could not proceed by water. A canal was near us, and the Arabs called to the rowers of a gay-looking barge, which took us on board. We were now ſheltered from the ſun, which was waxing warm, and were ſhoved along at an eaſy rate, between the rows of lofty buildings that face the canal. Behind the lattices on either ſide we diſcovered women, in the Greek and Turkiſh habits; and one in particular, of uncommon beauty, who came to the window to taſte of the morning air. Before ſeven o'clock we landed in a line with a quarter, called the *Fils Mooſky*, where the ſeveral European factories are ſituated, and in a few minutes reached Mr. Baldwin's houſe, of whom ſuch frequent mention has been made in this work. Though a perfect ſtranger to our perſons, we were received with great cordiality by this gentleman. Notwithſtanding the many letters which we had addreſſed to him, our ſtory was only communicated to him yeſterday, and that by the Indian Fakeer, who delivered our letter ſafely, after a thouſand difficulties. He was forty-five days on his paſſage; had been taken priſoner repeatedly, by each of the contending parties; and eſcaped detention, on account of his poverty and vocation. We were glad to find this faithful fellow had received his promiſed reward, and wiſhed to repeat our thanks to him.

Mr. Baldwin now congratulated us on our arrival, which he utterly deſpaired of, as ſoon as he learnt our condition. He was ſo conſiderate as to apply laſt night to the bey of Cairo, for a letter to

the

the Shaik Ul Arab for our releafe; and to order one of his fervants to get ready to carry the letter. He had taken thefe preliminary fteps; but owned that he was doubtful of their fuccefs, when he confidered our remote fituation, and the troubles which agitated the country. He was equally charmed with ourfelves, with the behavior of Ifman Abu Ally; and propofes to acknowledge it, in the name of the king and the people of Great Britain. This he fignified to Hadgee Uttalah and his companions in the Arabian language, which he fpeaks very fluently; and defired them to call for our letters and prefents, when they had finifhed their bufinefs in this city.

Now we bade adieu to all anxiety and care. Our troubles appeared to be at an end, and we were only ftudious to confole ourfelves for the lofs of fociety, which we had fo long endured. Peace was reftored to Cairo; and the operations of war removed to the parts we had come from; whither Ibrahim Beg and the fugitive Beys were fled. To recover ourfelves from the fatigues of our journey, to infpect the curiofities of this city, and to prepare for our progrefs to Alexandria, are the points to which our attention is turned. We obtained from the public papers, the moft fatisfactory accounts of our concerns in England; and nothing occurred to damp the happinefs of this day, which I may venture to fay, was the fincereft we had ever experienced. We difpatched camels for our baggage, and in the evening accompanied Mr. Baldwin to a French merchant's houfe; where we found a great deal of company affembled to play at cards. Among them was a very agreeable girl, of Greek extraction by the mother's fide. Her father is a Frenchman, and now at Marfeilles; which has enabled the young lady to obtain a perfect knowledge of the French tongue, and to render herfelf very entertaining to travellers who pafs this way. Though her drefs is confonant to the Turkifh mode, it by no means dif-

figures

figures her person; but has rather something pleasing in its novelty, to the eyes of an European. One of my companions appears to be but too sensible of the charms of the fair Cecilia; and I am told, that this is not the first conquest she has made over the affections of English passengers. The Europeans who reside here, all conform to the Turkish habit; but this is not expected from sojourners like us. As our Eastern cloaths therefore are much the worse for wear, we intend to-morrow to resume our own dress, except at such times as we visit places where it may give offence. The English nation alone, take this liberty with impunity. And I was let into an anecdote of a friend and countryman of mine, who went to the house of the bey here in a shaul turban. This is strictly prohibited to Christians of all denominations; but was nevertheless overlooked in him, because he was an Englishman.

SATURDAY, 20th SEPTEMBER.

We staid within doors to-day, to amuse ourselves with the new publications from England, and to settle our voyage to France. There is a French ship at Alexandria, which is to sail the beginning of next month for Marseilles; and Mr. Baldwin has applied to her agent here for a passage for us. He intends sending dispatches for the *Company* in this vessel, and will be better ascertained of the precise time of her departure.

Misir Ul Kaira, or the City of Anguish, so called from the frequent visits which it has received from the plague, but commonly termed Grand Cairo by us, is situated in the latitude of 30° 3′ N. on an artificial branch of the Nile. Old Cairo nearly faces the river; but the New city is removed above a mile from it, and approaches to the range of mountains which runs through Upper Egypt, and abruptly breaks off here. It is undoubtedly one of

the

the fineſt cities in the Eaſt; which, from the preſent ſtile of architecture that reigns among the Orientals, is but a faint commendation. The houſes are in general built of ſtone, and, being elevated to ſeveral ſtories, would make a grand appearance, notwithſtanding the inelegance of their ſtructure, were not the effect deſtroyed by the exceſſive narrowneſs of the ſtreets. This is one of the cauſes to which the ingenious Dr. Mead aſcribes the birth of the plague in this capital; but experience evinces, that it ariſes from foreign and adventitious cauſes. There has not been a plague here for theſe ſeven years; which is rendered more remarkable, by the commencement of the Ruſſian war at the date of its ceſſation. No one can account for this; though a year ſeldom paſſed by before, without a viſit from it. I do not recollect if any writer has taken notice of a circumſtance, that diveſts this fell deſtroyer of a conſiderable portion of his terrors in this quarter of the world, and opens an ample field for philoſophical ſpeculation. The melancholy conſequences of the plague are well known to us. The laws have been alarmed at its very name; and our ports have been ſo regulated, as wholly to exclude it. The gay metropolis of London was formerly depopulated by it; and, in our own age, we have ſeen the flouriſhing city of Marſeilles rendered a deſart by its ravages. From ſcenes within the ſphere of his knowledge, an elegant and ſentimental poet of our nation thus feelingly deſcribes its baleful influence:

> " The ſullen door,
> Yet uninfected, on its cautious hinge
> Fearing to turn, abhors ſociety:
> Dependants, friends, relations, Love himſelf,
> Savaged by Woe, forget the tender tie,
> The ſweet engagement of the feeling heart."

This picture is juft, fo far as it relates to this malady in Europe. But in Turkey the cafe is altered; and we look in vain for thefe ftrokes of the pathetic. The Mahometans are confirmed Predeftinarians; and are not to be deterred by the fear of contagion, from attending their brethren in diftrefs. The miftakes of the head here expand the heart with the tide of humanity. The dying have their exit fmoothed by the tender offices of friendfhip; and thoufands are fnatched from an untimely grave, by the force of an happy prejudice. It is true, that many are plunged into this diftemper, who might otherwife have avoided it; but the evil is far outweighed by the good which refults from it. For the diftemper is by no means fatal. With care and attention, the greater part of the infected generally recover. I have myfelf feen a man here, who has had the plague no lefs than five times; each of which is diftinguifhed by blotches upon different parts of his body, which he will carry with him to his tomb.

One of the moft noted things here, is an aqueduct which conveys water from the Nile to the caftle, that ftands on an hill in the eaft quarter of the city. This aqueduct runs a very confiderable length. We faw it as we came from Old Cairo, and were told that its courfe is two miles. It is built of ftone, and lined on each fide with lofty gothic arches, which give it a very noble appearance. It is however a modern work; and cannot be claffed among the antiquities of Egypt. Thefe we are to begin upon, as foon as our bodies are reftored to their former vigor. But the pyramids and the catacombs are too diftant for our minute infpection; and we can only regret, that our time admits of our taking but a paffing view of them. Travellers like us, who fall by accident into a country replete with the monuments of paft ages, and whofe time is not at their own difpofal, to gratify the defire of inveftigating the remains of decayed art, can only fkim

X x the

the furface of the ftream they would willingly dive into; and have but the merit of an inclination to extend information.

The late changes which happened here, are confidered of little or no moment among the inhabitants. The depofing of a bey is attended with no tumult or bloodfhed within the walls; where not only the natives but the European factors, are protected from violence by remaining within doors. Though no greater revolution could have taken place in any government, the whole conteft fubfifted without the gates: and during an obftinate battle at Bulac for the fovereignty, nothing but order and tranquillity reigned in Cairo. This idea is carried further here than in any other empire. And fo facred do the Turks hold the privilege of a man's houfe, that fcarce an inftance can be produced among them, of private property being plundered in any revolution in the ftate. A proof of this was recently difplayed. The fugitive beys were, for feveral days, in poffeffion of the caftle which commands the city. When they found it expedient to quit their poft, they retired with their troops through the ftreets, and enforced a difcipline, that preferved the city from the leaft outrage. Nor difappointed ambition, nor grievous neceffity, could influence them to injure a people, who were devoted to a fuccefsful rival, or replenifh their finances, by a mode fo repugnant to their cuftoms. Be it known to the Chriftian leaders of war, that thefe infidels were banifhed their capital—yet voluntarily left it in the enjoyment of that profperity, to which they were loft!

In the evening we went to the hummum, to refrefh ourfelves after our journey. We found it an handfome ftone fabric, crowned with a large dome, through which the light is admitted to a fquare apartment below. In this apartment the company affemble, to undrefs themfelves for the bath; and here they return, to fmoak and drink coffee after the operation; for which purpofe the hall is furrounded with alcoves. There are fmall receffes on every fide of the hall, which contain cocks or fountains of hot and cold water, to temperate the bath, agreeably to the inclinations of every one. The floor is paved with a diverfity of colored marbles, and adds much to the elegance of thefe receptacles of luxury. The ceremony is pretty nearly the fame as in other parts of Turkey; and having been often defcribed, there is no need of a repetition here. I will juft add, that the cuftom is not only cleanly, but healthy to the laft degree; and it is merely the immoderate ufe of it that prevails here, which can occafion its being condemned by the practitioners of phyfic.

SUNDAY, 21ft September.

We were introduced to an * Englifh gentleman this morning, who is in the fervice of the bey. He commands the artillery, and was on the expedition to Syria, in the year 1774, when Mahomet Beg took the cities of Acra and Joppa. During the late difputes he was ftationed in Cairo, and retired with the depofed beys into the caftle. But this was only to fave appearances with the beys, in whofe power he was. His heart inclined to Ifmaul Beg; whom he joined on the retreat of his adverfaries. From this officer, as well as Mr. Baldwin, I gained the particulars of the late revolution. It was quickly conceived, and as quickly executed; and appears to have been the refult of no great intrigues or difficulties. Simple and uninterefting as the event may be held by the fubjects of more ftable governments, the relation of it may give rife to reflections not unufeful, to comparifons not unfavorable to the reader.

At the death of Mahomet Beg the reins of power devolved to

---

* This is more than fufpected to be an unfortunate character, who was obliged to quit his native country fome years ago, on the imputation of a crime of a dark hue.

the hands of four principal beys. Ibrahim Beg, Morad Beg, Muftapha Beg, and Ifmaul Beg, were copartners in the empire of Egypt. The bafhaw, who is fent here by the Porte, has no real influence in the councils. He has not even a voice in affairs of ftate; which he is content to leave to the management of the beys, on condition of being paid the tribute which the Porte exacts. Nay, the beys have fometimes carried matters to fo high a pitch, that there is an inftance of Mahomet Beg's refufing to fubmit to this tax, and denying the fuperiority of the Porte. The fluctuating ftate of the Turkifh government, and the war in which it was then involved, prevented its refenting the infult. But weak as its arms may be, there is no doubt of the ftrength of its politics in this quarter. This revolution was certainly countenanced by the bafhaw; and to him Ifmaul Beg is partly indebted for his fuccefs, in expelling his brethren from an adminiftration, in which they had practifed every fpecies of fraud and oppreffion.

The conteft fuddenly commenced about the end of laft July. Ifmaul Beg marched a body of troops which he had fecretly collected, without the gates of Cairo; and fent a formal challenge to his brother beys, to go out, and decide their differences in a pitched battle. There was fomething fo gallant and open in this proceeding of Ifmaul Beg, and his character was fo far preferable to that of his competitors, that he foon found himfelf at the head of a greater number of partizans, than the allied beys could bring into the field. They met him, however, with apparent refolution, at the appointed place; and the two armies approached near enough together, for the commanders to revile each other for their conduct, in the moft opprobrious terms. Ifmaul Beg firft gave the order for the charge, which was executed fword in hand, though there were boats full of artillery, belonging to each party, at hand, and the troops themfelves were furnifhed

nifhed with fire-arms. But a thirft of revenge, and an eagernefs for blood, which mark the afpect of a civil war, hurried them beyond reflection; and tempted the combatants to truft, as they did of old, to the ftrength of their limbs. The conflict was fharp and bloody; but was determined in about a quarter of an hour, in favor of Ifmaul Beg, who drove his opponents back into the city. Muftapha Beg fled immediately to Upper Egypt; but Ibrahim Beg, and Morad Beg, took refuge in the caftle, which they declared they would defend to the laft extremity.

Their fituation was ftrong, and matters for fome days had a promifing appearance. They maintained a correfpondence in the city, and flattered themfelves with fpeedy relief from Muftapha Beg. But this dawn of hope was quickly overcaft. Their mifconduct compleated what their misfortune began. Jealoufies arofe between the chiefs, and entailed a fudden defection among their adherents. In fhort, they found their numbers fo decreafed, that they judged themfelves unfafe in their poft, and contrived the means of efcape. They retreated at midnight to the Nile, where they embarked unmolefted for Jirje, on boats that had been prepared for them.

This efcape was accomplifhed, as fome think, by the connivance of Ifmaul Beg himfelf, who was glad, at any rate, to be rid of the prefence of his rivals. But he had foon reafon to repent of this ftep. In the courfe of a week, he found the fugitive beys were at the head of a confiderable body of men, which they had raifed upon the river. This force was ftrengthened by a fleet of gallies, under the command of Muftapha Beg. To crufh this danger in its infancy, Ifmaul Beg fent up a large armament to engage them; and had the mortification to fee it return, vanquifhed and difperfed. The tide was now turned, and fuccefs feemed to defert the banners of the victor. Flufhed with this critical advantage, Ibrahim Beg hotly purfued the troops of his adverfary; and

thought

thought of nothing, but re-entering the capital in triumph. Terror preceded his steps, and Egypt prepared herself to submit again to his yoke. In this eventful moment, Ismaul Beg marched without the walls of the city, and, with the concurrence of the bashaw, who has the charge of it, set up the standard of the Prophet; which is only displayed in times of extreme danger, and invites all true Mussulmen to draw their swords in its defence. This manœuvre exceeded his most sanguine expectations. He recruited his army, and revived the spirits of the soldiers to such a degree, that, advancing to meet Ibrahim about the middle of August, he totally defeated him, after an obstinate encounter. Ibrahim Beg is said to have fought very gallantly on this day; and not to have quitted the field, until he had two horses killed under him. He fled with precipitation up the Nile, while the remains of his troops submitted to the conqueror, and has now joined Morad Beg and Mustapha Beg, as I have before mentioned, during our residence at Ghinnah. He was lately followed by considerable detachments from hence, which it is expected will compel the unfortunate chiefs to seek for refuge in another country.

On his return to Cairo, Ismaul Beg was universally acknowledged as the reigning bey, and his title recognized by the Porte. This is a circumstance very agreeable to Mr. Baldwin, and the European merchants settled here, who were much oppressed by Ibrahim Beg, and find a sensible difference in the deportment and disposition of his successor. He is an encourager of commerce, and displays a partiality for the English, whose recent attempts to restore the navigation of the Red-sea have excited his admiration and esteem. The few executions which have taken place since his accession to power, denote his humanity, and exhibit a conduct which wholly deviates from the general line of Mahometan politics.

In the evening we accompanied Mr. Baldwin to the houfe of a Greek lady, who is married to a Frenchman. She is a native of Scio, and, though the mother of feveral children, ftill does credit to the accounts of the beauties of that ifland. She has a daughter about feventeen, in whom are renewed the charms of the parent. Indeed there is no doubt but the Turks poffefs the fineft women in the world, whom their vicinity to Greece gives them an opportunity of procuring. The brother of this damfel is likely to go in the fame fhip with us to Marfeilles, where they have a fifter married: in which cafe, the fair Victoria has given him an unfailing recommendation to our notice.

MONDAY, 22d SEPTEMBER.

We fallied forth this morning in company with the commandant of the artillery, who is kind enough to be our guide in vifiting the curiofities of Cairo. As no Chriftian, without the fanction of the bey, is allowed to ride an horfe here, we were content to mount that humble animal, the afs, in order to be conveyed to the places which we propofed to examine. To obtain that fanction, the fon of a nobleman of the firft rank and family in England, is fuppofed to have made confiderable prefents to the bey, when he paffed through this city fome years ago. But the confequence was, to protect him from the infults of the populace, there was a guard obliged to be placed about his horfe, when he ftirred abroad. The diftinction, therefore, was dearly purchafed, on every account. Every thing grows familiar by habit; and Europeans think no more of beftriding an afs here, than they would of popping into an hackney-coach in Paris or London. It is the common mode of conveyance, and affes are to be found in every ftreet, for the accommodation of gentlemen who are afhamed to be feen on foot. We were not in this fecret

on

on the morning of our arrival here, or we would not have shunned a seeming indignity to incur a professed one.

We pushed on our beasts through a number of extensive streets, in our way to the castle, which stands upon a solid rock nearly in the center of the city. The streets are universally narrow, and so crouded with people, that we experienced no little difficulty in getting along. But this difficulty was balanced by the coolness which reigns in them. The narrow passage draws a constant supply of air; and the height of the houses affords a shade at noon to the passengers below. We were immediately sensible of our approach to the castle. The ground rises pretty gradually, until we got towards the top of the hill. Here it breaks off into an abrupt steep, and we dismounted and left our asses with their owners, before we entered one of the posterns of the castle. The fortifications of this place are in a dismantled state, though the elevation of the hill is a sufficient strength to people determined to defend themselves. We passed through many streets, which are inhabited by the domestics and dependants of the bashaw, who usually takes up his quarters in this fortress. We directed our steps to a building, which is reputed to be the hall where Joseph gave audience to his brethren, when they came to purchase corn in Egypt. This hall is the only remaining part of a large and magnificent edifice; the ruins of which bespeak the wealth and grandeur of its founder. The hall is a square of about sixty feet, the roof of which was a dome, that was supported by a double row of granite pillars. The dome is fallen in; but the pillars pronounce its former loftiness and magnitude. They are each of a single stone, thirty feet high, and about twenty-six inches diameter. There is a cornice of stone above them, which is inscribed with letters of gold, in so obsolete a language, that we are told no one is able to read them.

We

We went from hence to the council-chamber, where the bashaw and the beys meet, to deliberate on public affairs. The apartment is of a vast length, and ornamented with relics of mosaic work, and pillars of porphyry. At the upper end there is a secluded seat for the bashaw, surrounded with green lattices. Here he takes his post in all the vanity of state, and has the mortification of being privy to councils, in which he not only has no share, but which frequently operate against his interest. There is a rope still depending from a beam in this apartment, on which, it is said, a bey was once hung, during some tumultuous disputes at the council-board. There is nothing improbable in this story. But it is not so easy to account, for their permitting this disgraceful instrument of violence to remain in so conspicuous a place. In an adjacent building they shewed us some arms of great antiquity. Among those most worthy of note, are some Roman battle-axes, and a bow of such thickness and length, as would require the strength of a Patagonian to draw.

We were now conducted to Joseph's well. This is another work which bears the name of that Patriarch, and is, indeed, an astonishing monument of labor. It is so deep, that a number of oxen are constantly employed, in raising water for the accommodation of the garrison. There is a team above to raise the water from a chamber below, sixty feet from the surface of the earth. To this chamber you descend, by a flight of steps cut out of the solid rock; and here you find a second team of oxen to draw the water to that level. The authenticity, however, of these works, which boast of so early an origin, has been much doubted by late travellers. It would be presumption in us to give a decision from a cursory view, on a matter which would require a dispassionate investigation. Before we quitted the castle, we ascended a mount of earth, from whence we had an uninterrupted view of the city. It appears from hence not half so large as London

Y y   does

does from the top of St. Paul's; but the extent of the Nile, which has spread itself into a lake, as far as the eye can reach; the cluster of islands which crown the silver expanse; and the majesty of the mountains which bound the smiling scene, give a noble variety to the prospect, which London, with all its opulence and grandeur, cannot afford. We went out of the castle through the principal gate, which faces the great market-place. As we descended to it, we passed between the houses, where the fugitive beys remained, when they shut themselves up in the castle.

We found our asses at the gate, where thay had been brought by the direction of our conductor. On our return home we made a circuit of the city, and had an opportunity of being apprized of our want of consequence in this place. We met with one of the messengers of death, who delivers the fatal mandate to the subject, who has become obnoxious to the bey. He is an officer of the first rank, and is distinguished by a cap like a sugar-loaf, at the sight of which every Christian is obliged to dismount his ass *. We followed the example of our conductor; and as we alighted near the palace of Morad Beg, he took us in to see it. We entered a spacious court-yard, and found a square building with four handsome faces; but could not get in to see it, on account of the female side being inhabited. The women of the bey still reside here, although he will probably be in exile all his life. But such respect do the Turks pay to the characters of women, that there is no danger of their being molested either in person or property, however active the part their relations, or even husbands, may take in a time of trouble. We had a testimony of this respect as we left the bey's palace. No less than thirty women were returning to it, mounted on mules, and attended by a guard of eunuchs. They were vailed from head

* The chiaux of the Janisaries likewise exact this compliment from Christians.

to foot, and we are told, that no less a punishment than death would be the portion of any one, who would presume to remove that curtain. We arrived at Mr. Baldwin's about noon, very well pleased with our morning's excursion, and not at all dissatisfied with the spirit and paces of our asses.

In the evening we walked with Mr. Baldwin in a garden belonging to some Franciscan friars. It is neatly laid out in walks, and is an evening rendezvous for the Europeans of this city. We were here joined by a French nobleman, who is said to be under a temporary banishment from the court of France. He is a man of polite address, and passes for a proficient in the polite arts. We had a very agreeable specimen of his skill in music, as we adjourned to the French factory, to be present at a concert in which he led the first violin, with uncommon taste and execution. Mr. Baldwin bears a part at these little meetings, which are an admirable relief to a mind engaged in business.

SATURDAY, 23d September.

Our departure is fixed for to-morrow evening, so that our stay in this capital will be but short. We would willingly have dedicated another week to so celebrated a scene; but our business interferes with our pleasures. It is with double regret that we now look back to the time which we lost at Ghinnah, and which might have been so profitably spent in the city and environs of Cairo.

Our Arabs came this day to take leave of us. As soon as we could obtain money for our bills on London, we had discharged our notes of hand to Hadgee Uttalah, and given him the promised dress, besides a gratuity to himself and to all the camel-people according to their rank, for their care and honesty in bringing us safely here. We should not have omitted the captain of the robbers, among the number of those who demanded our acknowledgments, could we have promised ourselves the certainty of any token of ours reaching his hand. But our principal concern was to shew our gratitude to the Shaik Ul Arab, to whose friendship we owed more than we could possibly repay. We could not err in supposing, that a proof of our remembrance would make a greater impression at such a distance, however trivial it might be, than a valuable consideration would have done at Ghinnah. He there had it in his power to reject our offerings; but ere this came to his possession we should have quitted the country. We could only consult the genius of the people, to render a slight present acceptable; though we did our venerable friend the justice to believe, that the intention of the present would be its chief recommendation in his eyes. A Turkey carpet for the use of his seraglio, and a piece of purple broad cloth with sattin facings, for a vest for himself, were what we put up on this occasion. To these Mr. Baldwin added some jars of French fruits and Italian sweetmeats, and other rarities of this kind, which he judged would be agreeable to the ladies of the seraglio. We delivered these things into the charge of Hadgee Uttalah, with a complimentary letter from Mr. Baldwin, and another from ourselves. Mr. Baldwin's letter was conceived in general terms. He spoke of the generosity, with which the shaik had behaved towards some of the subjects of the king of Great Britain, and he extolled the merit of the action. He thanked him, in the king's name, for this instance of his goodwill, and begged leave to cultivate the correspondence which had so accidentally arisen between them. A correspondence, he added, which had commenced in a manner so much to the honour of the shaik, and which could not fail to extend his reputation to the remotest corners of the British dominions. Our letter, perhaps, was less courtly, though not less sincere. We recapitulated

the

the favors which we had received from the fhaik. We hinted at the defperate fituation in which his vigilance had difcovered us, and compared it with our prefent happy circumftances. The change we afcribed entirely to his humanity. We lamented our inability to tranfmit him a more liberal token of our gratitude, and entreated him to confider the tender which we had prefumed to make, with his wonted candor and benevolence. Finally, we acknowledged the fidelity of the camel-drivers, who had enabled us to comply with his laft injunctions, and to call the world to witnefs, that our high fenfe of his favors would only ceafe to exift with our lives.

Thefe letters were rendered into Arabic by Mr. Baldwin's interpreter. Sufficient praife cannot be given to that gentleman for the intereft which he took in this affair. Our tribute, fuch as it was, has already been paid him. It remains only for his employers to do juftice to the fpirit with which he fupported their credit, and that of the Englifh nation. At parting he prefented Hadgee Uttalah with a pipe of fome value; and we had the pleafure to fee him and his companions depart, not lefs fatisfied with our bounty towards themfelves, than furprized at our remembrance of their abfent mafter.

It may not, perhaps, be thought impertinent to remark, that the report of thefe Arabs will be of no differvice to the *Company*, fhould they adopt the idea of having their packets forwarded from India, by the way of Cofire and Ghinnah. The port of Cofire is open at all feafons of the year, while that of Suez is fhut up by the northerly winds no lefs than eight months out of twelve. A fact which I have endeavoured to eftablifh in a former part of this work.

Amid thefe agreeable tranfactions, we encountered one of a different nature. After the repeated inftances which Abdul Ruffar had afforded us of his honefty, it appeared that there were moments in which he was not proof to temptation. Ibrahim, ever indolent

indolent and simple, had from time to time lent this fellow money, and since our arrival at Cairo the sum was considerably increased. It was but yesterday noon that we paid up Abdul Russar's wages, at his own request; and at night he decamped in Ibrahim's debt. This intelligence was just now communicated to us, and, from some circumstances, it is probable that he is returned to his native country. To dissipate Ibrahim's chagrin, in some measure, we took this opportunity to discharge our obligations to him. We had advanced some money to the captain on his account, on our leaving the Adventure, and we now presented him with such a gratuity as our finances would admit of. His services were beyond the common class, and were not to be rewarded by any limited wages. Our good-will was only to be bounded by our ability; and he obtained from us a purse containing an hundred venetians. We could have wished, indeed, the sum had been doubled for his sake. But when it is considered, that he will work his passage to India on the ships of next season, and that Mr. Baldwin has generously offered him his table while he remains here, the sum may be carried to his family free of all deductions, and will be no trivial addition to the fortune of an Indian. Notwithstanding this discharge, Ibrahim means to accompany us to Alexandria, and to see us embark for Europe.

Among our other recreations here, we make a daily practice of offering incense to a fair idol, who lives opposite our house. She is a mixture of the Greek and French, as well in her origin as her composition, being as remarkable for vivacity and good-humour in her temper, as for symmetry and elegance in her person. This young damsel quickly found out our arrival, and, like other singing-birds shut up in a cage, began to display her attractions the moment she had caught our observation. She appears at her window every morning and evening, and either awakes our attention with her guitar, or condescends to reply to our

our addresses, which are breathed to her across a narrow street. She has an old mother, who seems to encourage the innocent damsel in her coquetry; and I fear would prove but a treacherous portress to the castle, were some lover, like Jupiter, daring enough to descend to this Danae in a shower of gold. There are numbers of captive nymphs in this city, who sigh for liberty, and would throw themselves into the arms of any European who made honourable addresses to them. Bred up in the circle of French society, and denied the freedom which they hear the females enjoy in France, they repine at their destiny, and would chearfully leave the manners, customs, and country of Turkey behind them.

As we returned from the gardens of the convent this evening, we met a gentleman near the French factory, who is to be our fellow-passenger to Marseilles. It seems, that he is a man of erudition and taste; was formerly secretary to the embassy at Rome; and is now on his return to France from a tour of Greece and Egypt. He was introduced to us by the name of Meillon, and promises to turn out no inconsiderable acquisition to our society during the voyage, and the term of our quarantine at Marseilles.

WEDNESDAY, 24th SEPTEMBER.

We have been preparing ourselves this morning to take leave of this great city. Our stay has not been equal to our curiosity, but perfectly suitable to our designs, which are to get to England with all possible expedition. The packets with which we are charged have doubtless reached London before us by duplicates; but we have private as well as public concerns; and it is time for us to undeceive our friends, and to remove their apprehensions for our safety.

Until the arrival of Mr. Baldwin, about two years ago, the English carried on no commerce in this city. He is still the

only

only merchant of our nation here, and is agent to the company for forwarding their packets to and from India. And, considered in itself, this is a point of no little importance to that political body. The advantage of quick intelligence is no secret to a wise government. The passage home is, indeed, as yet precarious, by the difficult navigation of the gulph of Suez; but the passage out is sure and expeditious. There is an instance, not two months ago, of a Mr. Whitehill coming from London to Cairo in a month. He was charged with the restoration of Lord Pigot to the government of Fort St. George; and it is supposed will get to that place in the same period. A voyage, which seldom is effected by the Cape of Good Hope in double the time!

The decay of the English trade in any quarter, is naturally supposed to give vigor to the exertions of the French. They are avowed rivals in wealth as well as power, and mutually rise on the ruins of each other. But this rule will not hold in respect to the commerce of Egypt. However flourishing the French traffic may be in other parts of the Levant, it is apparently here in a consumptive state. No other symptom of this is necessary to be produced, than the reduction of their establishments. The consulship of Cairo has been struck off as a fruitless expence, by a recent order from France; and it is observed, that a spirit of dissipation and gaming has crept in among the merchants, which was unknown in busy times, and is wholly incompatible with their situation. A decline of this nature will give scope to the industry of the Venetians and other states of Italy, who have factories here, and cut no inconsiderable figures in the commercial scale.

At noon we sent down our baggage to the boat, which we had agreed for to take us as far as Rosetto. We paid but sixteen dollars for the hire of this boat, and, with the assistance of Mr. Baldwin's servants, laid up some cold provision for the passage. The

markets

markets of Cairo are plentifully fupplied with a variety of articles, at reafonable rates. Flefh, fowl, and fifh, are daily expofed for fale; and are ferved up in great perfection at Mr. Baldwin's table, which amply fupports the character of Englifh hofpitality.

At five o'clock we were joined by Monfieur Meillon, and having once more arrayed ourfelves in our Turkifh habits, we mounted our affes and proceeded to Bulac. Bulac is the port of Cairo, where every one is obliged to embark, in order to have his goods paffed at the cuftom-houfe. Mr. Baldwin was fo obliging as to accompany us thither, to fee us on board the boat. We had two miles to go, and in the way, obtained the fight of a part of the city which was new to us; and which every where difplays a face of magnificence, we little expected to find in Egypt. We went through a fquare that is one of the fineft I ever beheld, both in refpect to its extent, and the loftinefs of the buildings which furround it. I fpeak within bounds when I pronounce it to be nearly two miles in circumference; and at this time the area exhibits a beautiful fheet of water, covered with gay boats of all denominations. When the Nile retires within his banks again, the beauty of this fquare will not be loft; as the bed of the prefent canal will wear a drefs of the livelieft verdure, during the other months of the year. We reached Bulac about fix o'clock, and getting our baggage paffed without any delay, we went on board the boat, which we found to be very large and convenient. We are now, for the firft time in our progrefs through Egypt, to be fheltered from the fun, and to travel at our eafe, and in full fecurity from danger. From the fpacioufnefs and convenience of our vehicle, and the charms of this celebrated river, we look for nothing but pleafure in this voyage. Mr. Baldwin has been fo obliging as to fecure us a reception at Rofetto and Alexandria, by furnifhing us with letters to his agents there; and in every refpect, has anfwered the expectations which we had formed from his character and ftation.

ſtation*. We parted with him at ſeven o'clock, when our boat weighed and fell down with the tide. We have the cabbins wholly to ourſelves; but ſhe has ſeveral paſſengers on board, beſides us and our ſervants, and a valuable cargo of coffee. The wind is right againſt us, notwithſtanding which we drop down at the rate of three miles an hour. Juſt before ſun-ſet we opened the pyramids, which were in a direct line behind us. The mountainous ſtature of theſe pyramids was increaſed by the ſetting ray, which had fallen behind them, and exhibited a ſpectacle at once ſublime and picutreſque. The night now ſpread her curtains round the world, and diſpoſed us to reſt. At midnight we paſſed the village of Daranie, on the Delta, where the Nile divides himſelf into two branches, which fall into the Mediterranean at Roſetto and Damiat, near 100 miles aſunder, and form the Delta, one of the moſt fertile iſlands in the world. We took the branch that runs to Roſetto, and continued the whole night to drop down with the current. The wind abated towards morning, and our courſe was conſequently quickened. The reader is here preſented with the courſe of the greater branches of the Nile from Cairo to the Mediterranean, as a ſupplement to the chart of its courſe through Upper Egypt.

* I have learnt, with no little concern, that the ſituation of this gentleman has been ſome time paſt very critical. On the plundering of the caravan, in the ſummer of 1779, between Suez and Cairo, the government bound Mr. Baldwin to prevent a retaliation on the part of the Engliſh, and he was no more than a priſoner at large, until very lately that he effected his eſcape. In this manner has the treaty of commerce between the Engliſh and the government of Cairo, been preſerved ! Thus have the fortunes of many gentlemen, who built their hopes on the faith of nations, and remitted their property from India through this channel, fallen a ſacrifice to the inconſtancy and avarice of a faithleſs race ! Indeed, a revolution has happened in Cairo ſince that deſcribed in this work, ſo the wonder would be, that any treaty was reſpected by ſuch a fluctuating government.

THURSDAY,

THURSDAY, 25th SEPTEMBER.

I rose at day-break, to take a view of the country around us. There was now a fine leading wind, and we went with great rapidity through the water. The navigation of this river is certainly the most delightful, that fancy can picture to itself. To the right of us is the beautiful island of Delta, covered with grain, intersected with canals, and thickly set with large towns and romantic villages. The scene to the left is of a different hue. The banks, indeed, are adorned with handsome cities and extensive groves, and a tract of country as verdant as the opposite; but then the desart appears behind this garden, and gives a noble variety to the prospect. At seven o'clock we passed very near the town of Demischili, on the western bank, and ran by several islands of various forms, which waved with crops of grain. In standing from one side of the river to the other, we ran ashore at nine o'clock, opposite a place called Abuel Hau, where we were detained above half an hour. We find that boats frequently meet with these accidents on the Nile; but the bottom being every where a rich clay, they are productive of nothing worse than the loss of time. There is no danger to be now apprehended from the natives in the day, nor will they even venture to attack any but small boats in the night, in such a situation. The security of this navigation is much amended of late; though our boat is too strong to have shrunk from danger in the worst of times.

By the activity of our people we got afloat again, and pursued our voyage until noon, without any further obstacle. We now found ourselves at the town of Esseiale, on the Delta. We met with but few towns in this last run. What we have hitherto seen are mostly in a ruinous condition; but being all embellished

with

with lofty mofques and the ruins of magnificent ftructures, they cut a very elegant appearance from the water. We were provided with fome roafted fowls, an excellent pie, and fome bottles of wine, to which we paid our refpects with great appetite. It is with difficulty that we can tear ourfelves from the deck on any occafion, as the objects around us are of a fafcinating nature. The towns now began to thicken on us again. We ran by the villages of Nedfgili, Berim, and Feriftah, befides a number of others which we paffed in mid-ftream, and which are to be found in a map that Mr. Neiburh has given of the great branches of the Nile. At five in the evening we went under the town of Schabur, on the weftern bank, and opened a point of the river with a fine breeze. Innumerable are the fmall and large craft which we have met in our run from Cairo, and which convey to the traveller fome idea of the extenfive commerce of Egypt. The exports, however, are chiefly confined to the articles of life, and her corn is diftributed to the different ports of the Mediterranean and the Red-fea. This is the coin in which fhe pays for the coffee of Arabia, and the cotton and filk of Perfia: and, inftead of laying illegal impofts on the merchant, had fhe but wifdom enough to trade upon her own bottoms, without fuffering foreign nations to engrofs the freight of her commodities, there is no doubt that her gains would exceed thofe of every other country.

The wind died away towards fun-fet, which induced our crew to man a pinnace, which has been hitherto a-ftern, to tow us down the ftream. This is of great affiftance to us, and we hope will enfure our arrival at Rofetto in the morning. We have put fome paffengers afhore at feveral places which we have paffed, but fhall carry the principal part of them to Rofetto. Thefe paffengers are lodged under an awning, which extends from the cabbin to the mainmaft, and is capable of containing twenty people.

people. Among them is a poor boy, who loſt his father in the late troubles at Cairo. He has a good appearance, and told his tragic ſtory ſo pathetically, that we were moved to compaſſion, and made a collection among us, to enable him to return to his family, who are at Conſtantinople.

The night is ſerene and unclouded, but we have no light ſave what the ſtars afford. It is a lucky circumſtance, perhaps, for our bodies, that our minds are diſengaged from the proſpects around, and that there is no moon to tempt us to waſte thoſe hours upon deck, which ſhould be dedicated to ſleep. We continued to fall down ſlowly during the night.

FRIDAY, 26th SEPTEMBER.

We had the pleaſure, at day-break, to find ourſelves near the city of Fue, on the Delta. This city is in the latitude of 31° 10' north, and within thirty miles of Roſetto. It is ſtill of a conſiderable extent, and affords an infinity of lofty minarets to the paſſenger's view, whoſe tops were now gilded with the morning ray. Conſidering the want of wind, our progreſs has not been tardy. The country on each ſide of us is ſtill a garden, and exhibits an agreeable variety of fruit-trees and corn-fields, opulent towns and ſequeſtered villages. Now and then we meet with ſmall iſlands, more verdant than the infant buds of ſpring. At ſeven o'clock we paſſed between the towns of Deirut and Disjedie, in the former of which there is one of the moſt beautiful moſques in Egypt. We have found no increaſe in the breadth of the Nile ſince we left Cairo; nor is this ſo much to be wondered at, if we conſider the great depth of the channel, and the multitude of canals which every where divert his waters. We paſſed in the night the grand canal which ſupplies Alexandria with water, and is ſaid to be the work of Alexander. It begins

gins nearly opposite the town of Mehallet Malik, on the Delta; and while it was open for boats, shortened the distance one third, in the voyage we are engaged in. But it would have been a pity to have robbed us of any of the charms of this river. We were still feasting luxuriously on the prospect before us, when we came within sight of the city of Rosetto, which is known at a distance, by the ruins of an antient tower on an hill to the southward of the place. We ran under a mosque situated on an island; and at one o'clock, anchored before the city. We went ashore immediately, and waited on Monsieur Tessier, a French merchant of this place, to whom Mr. Baldwin was so kind as to furnish us with a letter. We were received very politely by this gentleman, who made us a tender of his house during our short stay. Monsieur Meillon, our fellow-traveller, took up his quarters with the French consul, who is but newly arrived here.

Rosetto, or Raschid, is situated in 31° 23′ north latitude, on the western bank of the Nile, and is reckoned one of the prettiest and compactest cities in Egypt. It is the next to Cairo for commerce, if we except Alexandria, and exceeds them both in the salubrity of its air, and the beauty of its situation. The Nile runs in its front, and the sea lies within ten miles of its rear, from whence it is constantly refreshed with cooling breezes. The country about it is a continued plantation of lemon, citron, and orange-trees. We walked out in the evening to survey the city and its environs. The streets are regular, and the buildings in general neat and lofty. We presently quitted the town, and were, in a manner, buried among fragrant groves, where the sun's burning rays never intrude themselves. The walks were strewed with the blossoms of the trees, whose boughs were at the same time loaded with golden fruit. In this happy clime the seasons are joyously blended together; and the

traveller,

traveller, in these retreats, might think himself transported to the regions of fancy*. Here peace and plenty reign. The noise and hurry of a city are not perceivable in this peninsula, which was not the least disturbed by the late revolution in the state, though at so short a distance from the capital. But this may be partly owing to the nature of the Turkish customs. The changes in the government do not affect the subject; nor the evils of public disputes extend beyond those who choose to take a part in them.

On our return home we passed the French factory, which is a spacious edifice, and displays a very handsome front to the river. There is a wharf before it of near a mile in length, which affords a pleasant walk to the inhabitants. On the north side of this wharf stands the house of the late Mr. Wortley Montague, who was so celebrated for his wit and curiosity, and his extraordinary attachment to Mahometan countries; but, perhaps, not less remarkable for being the son of the ingenious lady Mary of the same name. He resided here more than three years; and his loss is still regretted by Monsieur Tessier, and the gentlemen of Rosetto.

We supped and slept at the French merchant's, whose complaisance extended to the procuring us places in a passage-boat, that sails before day-break for Alexandria. We have been obliged to prefer this mode to the usual route by land, which we are assured has been infested by wild Arabs, ever since the commencement of the late troubles. We shall be no losers by the change, as the country between Rosetto and Alexandria, is little better than a desart; and we shall now have an opportunity of examining one of the mouths of the Nile. This mouth, it seems, is so choaked up with a bar of sand, as to render it impassable to any vessel that draws more than nine feet water. The mouth of the eastern

---

* Well did they deserve to be the favorite residence of the beautiful Cleopatra!

branch

branch is more eafy of accefs. Foreign veffels come up almoft to Damiat; and we underftand the Turkifh frigate paffed that way to Cairo. But fhe was obliged to be lightened for that purpofe; and it is only during the inundation of the Nile, that veffels of fuch a conftruction can enter this river, which is navigable for near a thoufand miles, and, were this defect cured, might exhibit fhips of various nations in the heart of Egypt.

SATURDAY, 27th SEPTEMBER.

We embarked at four o'clock this morning on the boat, to which our baggage and fervants had been fhifted the preceding evening. It was a veffel of a different built and conveniency, to the one we had left. It was not very unlike the bark in which we were fo long toffed about the Red-fea, fave that we were now provided with a good awning to fhelter us from the fun, in confideration of a piece of gold which each of us gave for himfelf and fervants. There were no paffengers befides us; and her cargo was not very confiderable. We weighed anchor, in company with thirty fail of the fame craft, and fell down gently with the tide. About fun-rife we found ourfelves oppofite an old caftle on the peninfula, which appears to have been originally built for the defence of the river. We croffed the ftream here, and anchored at the village of Arbut on the Delta, where we were obliged to wait for a wind, to run us over the bar. Here we found the remains of a battery, which had been raifed to anfwer the caftle on the oppofite fhore; and it feems almoft impracticable for any hoftile veffels that can enter this river, to have paffed between them. We found feveral brafs cannon fcattered up and down the beach, of very antient conftruction; but the bore of them is too narrow to engage with the artillery of the prefent times. Arbut is the laft town on the Nile, and the country about it affords little elfe than

date-

date-trees, under the shade of which we rambled about during our stay here.

At ten o'clock a breeze of wind springing up, we repaired aboard, hoisted our sails, and stood for the bar. The river increased all at once in its breadth; the stream began to be considerably agitated; and we had approached within a mile of the bar, when the wind perversely came ahead, and obliged the whole fleet to run under the shore of Delta. The land here has quite lost its fertile appearance. No more the earth smiles with the plenteous harvest; no more the embowering shades half conceal the rustic hamlet. The ground is thinly covered with brush-wood, while the shore of the peninsula is interrupted with frequent hillocks of sand. While we were kept here, our servants dressed us some pigeons, which we had procured at Arbut; and the eating of our dinner helped us to pass away the vexatious moments of delay.

More vessels now joined us from Rosetto. This was the part in which the difficulty of our voyage wholly lay. If the wind continued as it was, we might remain here for a day; and, for our consolation, we were told of boats that had experienced worse luck. The prospect was not the most flattering, and we were about to wish ourselves on the road over the desart to Alexandria, notwithstanding the perils which awaited it, when the wind luckily veered to the eastward of north, and permitted us to lay up well to our point. We immediately availed ourselves of it, and thirty-five sail of us stood for the *bogage* or bar, which we reached about one o'clock. There is a boat constantly at anchor in mid-channel, to direct others through this hazardous place. The waves ran pretty high, and it was our fortune to strike the bank three or four times successively, in performing this passage. The shocks were very smart; but as our boat was light, and the wind fair, we were threatened with no absolute danger. Though the gale began to freshen, and we were obliged to tack twice to fetch the channel,

channel, we got clear of the *bogage* in about ten minutes. This was no trifling piece of good luck, if it be considered, that veffels are fometimes fix or feven hours beating over this bar, and obliged to unlade their cargoes into the pilot-boat, in order to lighten themfelves. Had we been coming into the river at this time, the accident would, in all probability, have been of a ferious nature. The conteft between the wind and the current, which fet us out fo faft, muft be always very violent, and occafion a fea, which would inevitably ftave any veffel, that is unfortunate enough to ftrike the bottom.

The Mediterranean-fea was now before us. The goal to which our earneft looks had been fo long turned, was now happily attained, and we hoped foon to refpire freely after a courfe, run with peril, and won with labor. Like the fteed who approaches his forfaken paftures, we fnuffed in imagination our native air, and every pulfe beat quicker with the thoughts of home. The Nile throws himfelf with fuch an impetuofity into this fea, that Neptune feems to fhrink before his might at this feafon. For a league and more from the bar, the water retains its chryftal hue and frefh quality, of which we convinced ourfelves by an experiment. We now ftood to the fouth-weft, in company with the whole fleet. The fea was fmooth, and the light barks glibly fkimmed the furface. At two o'clock we began to open a bay to our left, which forms the peninfula where Canopus once ftood, and behind which we faintly difcerned the groves of Rofetto. The waves now were confiderably raifed, and our veffel's motion encreafed. But the wind continued fair, and we ran brifkly by a fandy, but not a defart coaft. Date-trees rear their heads behind the fteepy beach, and many of the eminences are crowned with the auguft ruins of ancient caftles. At five in the evening we found ourfelves oppofite to the town of Vickerie, where there is a large caftle in good repair, and a light-houfe for the direction of mariners.

mariners. Here a garrison is constantly maintained for the defence of the coast, which is sometimes insulted by Greek corsairs, and the gallies of Malta. This is a considerable head-land, and there are several small islands lying off it. We once more got in with the land, and smoothed our water very effectually. We descried several sail to the northward, and made the hull of a large three-masted vessel. We were the best sailor in the fleet, and got so much ahead, that at sun-set, our people could distinguish the point behind which Alexandria stands. The coast here is very low, and offers nothing pleasing to the eye. At eight o'clock we could see the lights in the harbor. The night was dark, and we lost the opportunity of beholding the city from this point of view. At nine we anchored within fifty yards of the shore, and sent Ibrahim ashore with Monsieur Meillon, to find out the gentleman to whom we are recommended by Mr. Baldwin. We were preparing to take up our lodging in the boat for the night, when, just before ten o'clock, Ibrahim returned with Signior Brandi himself, who politely came for us at that late hour. We left our servants on board with our baggage, and accompanied that gentleman to an *hotel*, which has been lately set up for the reception of strangers. Here we supped comfortably, and enjoyed a sound repose after our tedious passage from Rosetto.

SUNDAY, 28th SEPTEMBER.

We rose betimes this morning, and sent for our baggage and servants. The house we are in is roomy and convenient; and was originally the English factory, when we had a consul here. Our host is a master taylor, and seems to be an inoffensive Italian. His wife is a Greek woman from Smyrna, talks French and Italian, and promises to render our situation easy during our stay here. We are to pay two dollars *per diem* each, for our bed and board; a price, indeed, rather extravagant, but settled in the best manner by Mr. Baldwin's agent, for the convenience of English travellers.

We walked out after breakfast, to take a view of the antient port and city of Alexandria. We were attended by a Janizary in the English pay, whom it is necessary to have, both as a guide and a protector from the insults of the vulgar. Agreeably to the customs of this place, we had resumed the European dress, discarded our whiskers, and once more looked and moved with freedom and ease. We went directly to the sea-side, to examine the Turkish haven, which lies to the westward of the pharos, and is perfectly secure for shipping when it blows a gale of wind. But this haven is sacred to the Turks, who are unfeeling enough to forbid Christian vessels taking refuge in it, even when it is impossible for them to remain in safety in the common harbor. The melancholy consequences of this restriction have appeared more than once. Particularly in the year 1767, when forty vessels of different nations foundered, or ran ashore in the common harbor, during a violent storm from the north-east quarter. But in spite of this ordinance, Christian vessels will presume at times to peep into this port; and it is not a fortnight since a Maltese privateer chased a Turkish ship of much superior force under the very battery of the pharos, and gave her a parting broadside as she ran into the road. A Turkish man of war of sixty guns was then at anchor here, and, either through want of alertness or resolution, did not attempt to revenge the insult. This man of war is still here, and there are several frigates on this station for the protection of the trade.

We now went into the dock-yard, to see a very bad specimen of their skill in ship-building. Here we perceived a party of females standing on the beach, ready to be embarked in a boat for Cairo. They proved to be Greek slaves, just brought from the Archipelago, and going as a present to the bey of Cairo. This information

tion we obtained from our Janizary, who, at our requeſt, entered into converſation with their guard. The poor creatures ſeemed inſenſible of their ſituation, which, in ſome meaſure, ſuppreſſed the emotions we underwent at the firſt knowledge of their deſtiny. They turned towards us as we approached them; and in ſpite of their vails we could perceive, by their fine eyes, and their admirable forms, that they were objects unfit to be ſecluded from the ſight of the world. This ſudden motion, and the involuntary ſurprize which they betrayed at the novelty of our habit, awakened the jealouſy of their keepers, who immediately hurried them into the boat that was waiting for them. The price of ſuch girls is from four hundred to a thouſand zechins; and their value is enhanced, as much in proportion to their qualifications, as the beauties they poſſeſs. To what a ſtate of degeneracy is the world fallen, when wit, accompliſhments, and beauty, are put up to ſale among the female tribe, in the ſame manner as ſtrength and mechanic ſkill in the negroes of Africa! The latter branch of commerce is indeed an impeachment on humanity; but the former is a diſgrace to the nature and tendency of the finer paſſions.

Alexandria, or Scanderie as the Turks call it, lies in the latitude of 31° 11′ north, on a riſing ground, which deſcends with an eaſy ſlope towards the ſea, and deſcribes a ſemicircle, with the caſtle on the eaſtern, and the pharos on the weſtern point. In this bay the foreign ſhipping lay, and range themſelves abreaſt of the pier which joins the pharos to the continent, according to their arrival. This ſtation they chuſe on account of its greater ſecurity, as the pier breaks the force of the ſea, which tumbles in from the eaſtward. The ſea waſhes the walls of the houſes, and the refreſhing breezes which come from it, contribute much to the healthineſs of the place. The preſent city ſeems to ſtand in one quarter of the old, and does not take up one eighth part of the ground, which may be aſcertained by the antient walls that ſtill remain.

remain. It is reckoned to contain thirty thousand inhabitants of all nations; and a greater medley were never yet assembled together. Gain is the lure which draws them to this mart; the masters of which are the only people who derive no solid advantage from the connection.

I could dwell with pleasure on the minute antiquities of this well-known spot; were they not already described with such precision and elegance, in a work lately published, as to leave a future traveller little to say that can be new, and less that he can hope will equal the manner of so agreeable an author. This work was originally printed in German, and has since been translated into French, and is the production of Mr. Niebuhr, who made the tour of Lower Egypt and Arabia, by the command of his Danish Majesty. I mean to touch, however, on the most remarkable objects of our research; as to observe a profound silence on so curious a theme, would be an insult on the taste and learning of the reader.

We dined in company with a genteel young Swiss, who is on his way to India. He is to embark on the first boat for Cairo, where he means to take his passage on our shipping. It was with no small satisfaction that we replied to his queries of a journey so new to him, and of a country in which we had spent so many years. He was rather mortified, however, when he understood there were none of our vessels at Suez, nor after their arrival, that would sail for India before the next summer.

MONDAY, 29th SEPTEMBER.

We were introduced to-day by Signior Brandi to the French consul. He appears to be a well-bred sensible man, and is well spoken of by our companion Monsieur Meillon, who takes up his lodgings at the French factory. He is but lately arrived here, and

and has his curiosity to satisfy as much as we. We accompanied him in a walk to some of the adjacent ruins. We passed by the Venetian factory, which stands next to the French. This is a very handsome building, and makes a much greater show than any of the foreign factories. Our road lay over a sandy plain, where several granite pillars of a prodigious length, are scattered up and down. They seem to have been brought here with an intention of being used, which has been afterwards given up. When we had crossed this plain, we went under an arched gateway, which, perhaps, marked one of the divisions of the antient city. To the south of it lies a lofty tower in a ruinous condition. It is surrounded by an high wall, and within, there is a grove of date-trees. Here the antiquities commence.

With what concern must the informed spectator view the remains of so celebrated a place! With what regret must he look back on its former beauty and pride, and draw a comparison with its present poverty and decline! I hope it will not be considered as a piece of affectation in any one to declare, that he cannot behold such sights as these with an even mind. The destruction of renowned cities is a baneful prospect to the eye; and the susceptible breast is filled with the same sensations in contemplating their decay, as touch it at the appearance of a venerable character in distress, whom it is beyond the ability of man to relieve. We soon came to an antient temple, a part of which is still habitable, and has been long appropriated to the service of Mahomet. On this account, we found some difficulty to obtain admittance. But the key was at length procured by our Janizary, and we were shewn into the neglected quarter. This is a square of very large diameter, which is surrounded with triple rows of granite pillars of the Corinthian order. These pillars are lofty, and support a roof which is still in a good state of preservation.

The inside of the walls of this temple is inlaid with tables of
marble

marble of various colors, which, for their richness and novelty, cannot but engage the admiration of a stranger. In the area of the square is a stone cistern of very antique mould. It is inscribed on all sides with hieroglyphics, and from a rail which enclosed it, appears to have served for some religious purpose.

From hence we walked through a field of antiquities to a convent, which maintains four Franciscan friars. The building is simple, and suited to the character of its founders. Here we found about an acre of ground, very neatly disposed of. The soil was naturally sterile, but by the industry of these holy fathers, produces vegetables in great abundance. They have a vineyard in some forwardness; and with no small labor and perseverance, have sunk a reservoir to supply the garden with water, which is conveyed thither from a neighboring aqueduct. These innocent creatures were diverting themselves at nine-pins, and carried a content in their looks, which seemed to set the cares and the vanities of the world equally at defiance. The evening was advanced, and we returned towards the city. In the way we were overtaken by a shower of rain. This was such a novelty to us, who had not seen rain for six months past, that we enjoyed it in the highest degree; and were the only persons in company, who would not have dispensed with getting wet to the skin.

The shower was slight, however, and we arrived at the French factory without any damage. The consul now introduced us to his lady, who is a pretty sprightly woman. We readily complied with an invitation from her to play at cards, and spend the evening in her company. It was many months since we had seen a female, whose dress and manners resembled those of our own countrywomen. She appears not to have any great relish for her situation, which, to one of her vivacity, must be dull enough. Indeed, the disposition of the people she is among,

may

may have occasioned her disgust to this country. The French consul lost his life here from a barbarous principle of revenge, about eighteen months ago; and her husband was appointed to succeed him. This would be a sufficient motive for a woman's fears. The particulars of this tragical story I will relate hereafter.

TUESDAY, 30th SEPTEMBER.

We breakfasted this morning on board the French ship, which Mr. Baldwin had recommended to us for a passage to France. She is called the Cleopatra, and is a new, pretty, and commodious vessel. We have agreed with the Captain, Monsieur Calvi, to give him 133 crowns each for our passage, which is indeed a large sum in these seas. But the gentlemen from India are always considered as monied men, and are taxed accordingly, whether they travel this way for pleasure, or are charged with business of a public nature. We find, however, that we shall be accommodated in the most elegant manner; and we must do Captain Calvi the justice to say, that he stated his intentions of providing us with a plentiful table, and submitted the price to our generosity. On our return from the Cleopatra, we passed under the sterns of several merchantmen of different nations. There were but two English vessels in the number, one of which is freighted by Mr. Baldwin for Constantinople.

In the afternoon a large party of us sallied out to take a view of Pompey's pillar, the theme of the present age, and the admiration of past times! Besides my companions and myself, we were joined by the two English commanders of the ships in the harbour, and by Monsieur Meillon, and some young gentlemen of the French factory. We mounted the first asses that presented themselves for hire, and, attended by our Janizary, took the course

course we pursued yesterday. We left the convent on our right, and presently came among broken arches and long pavements; which are the remains of an aqueduct. Several towers reared up their dismantled heads on each side of us, whose appearance pronounces them to have been posts of great importance and strength. A number of stately pillars next engaged our attention. They are placed in two parallel lines, and seem to have formerly supported some magnificent portico. The pillars are of granite, or Thebaic marble, and about thirty feet high of a single stone; and we counted no less than thirty of them still standing. But however choice these columns might be in any other place, they were but foils to the pillar which now appeared before us. We had been buried amid the ruins and the hills of sand, which the winds have thrown up, when, leaving the city by the gate of Rosetto, we came unexpectedly upon the pillar. It is impossible to tell which is most worthy of admiration, the height, the workmanship, or the condition of this pillar. By the best accounts we can obtain, it is an hundred and ten feet high. The shaft, which is of a single stone of granite, is ninety feet, and the pedestal is twenty more. It is of the Corinthian order, which gives a beautiful dignity to its simplicity, rarely to be met with in modern architecture. It has suffered little or no injury from time. The polish upon the shaft has wonderfully withstood the buffeting of the tempest; and it promises to hand down a patriot name to the late posterity of the ignorant native, who has no other trace of the fame of Pompey! The pedestal has been somewhat damaged by the instruments of travellers, who are curious to possess a relic of this antiquity; and one of the volutes of the column was immaturely brought down about four years ago, by a prank of some English captain, which is too ludicrous to pass over.

These jolly sons of Neptune had been pushing about the can on board one of the ships in the harbor, until a strange freak entered

tered into one of their brains. The eccentricity of the thought occasioned it immediately to be adopted; and its apparent impossibility was but a spur for the putting it into execution. The boat was ordered, and with proper implements for the attempt, these enterprizing heroes pushed ashore, to drink a bowl of punch on the top of Pompey's pillar! At the spot they arrived; and many contrivances were proposed to accomplish the desired point. But their labor was vain; and they began to despair of success, when the genius who struck out the frolic, happily suggested the means of performing it. A man was dispatched to the city for a paper kite. The inhabitants were by this time apprized of what was going forward, and flocked in crouds to be witnesses of the address and boldness of the English. The governor of Alexandria was told that these seamen were about to pull down Pompey's pillar. But whether he gave them credit for their respect to the Roman warrior, or to the Turkish government, he left them to themselves, and politely answered, that the English were too great patriots to injure the remains of Pompey. He knew little, however, of the disposition of the people who were engaged in this undertaking. Had the Turkish empire rose in opposition, it would not, perhaps, at that moment have deterred them. The kite was brought, and flown so directly over the pillar, that when it fell on the other side, the string lodged upon the capital. The chief obstacle was now overcome. A two-inch rope was tied to one end of the string, and drawn over the pillar by the end to which the kite was affixed. By this rope one of the seamen ascended to the top, and in less than an hour, a kind of shroud was constructed, by which the whole company went up, and drank their punch amid the shouts of the astonished multitude. To the eye below, the capital of the pillar does not appear capable of holding more than one man upon it; but our seamen found it could contain no less than eight persons very conveniently. It is astonifhing that no accident befel thefe madcaps, in a fituation fo elevated, that would have turned a landman giddy in his fober fenfes. The only detriment which the pillar received, was the lofs of the volute before-mentioned; which came down with a thundering found, and was carried to England by one of the captains, as a prefent to a lady who commiffioned him for a piece of the pillar. The difcovery which they made, amply compenfated for this mifchief; as without their evidence, the world would not have known at this hour, that there was originally a ftatue on this pillar, one foot and ancle of which are ftill remaining. The ftatue was, probably, of Pompey himfelf; and muft have been of a gigantic fize, to have appeared of a man's proportion at fo great an height.

There are circumftances in this ftory which might give it an air of fiction, were it not demonftrated beyond all doubt. Befides the teftimonies of many eye-witneffes, the adventurers themfelves have left us a token of the fact, by the initials of their names, which are very legible in black paint juft beneath the capital. We fpent fo much time in viewing this elegant column, that the evening was too far advanced for us to go further. After providing ourfelves with a relic of this fhrine, we returned towards the port, which is about a mile and a quarter diftant. In our way we mounted an eminence, which has been thrown up by the Turks in digging for antiques, which are frequently found here. From hence we had a fine view of the new and old city and port of Alexandria.

WEDNESDAY, 1ft OCTOBER.

I had a prefent of an antique this morning from Signior Brandi. It is a blue ftone which bears the head of a Jupiter Capitolinus. The fmall collection which I have made, is not worth prefenting presenting to the reader, though the place from which I chiefly drew them, is a proof of their being originals: as neither the skill nor the remoteness of the country of Upper Egypt, can favor deceit in such matters. But a stranger should be very careful how he makes these purchases in Alexandria. Seals have been tendered me for sale, which had all the appearance of antiquity; but on the inspection of a person conversant in *virtù*, turned out to be copies. They are, however, at times, in great plenty in this neighborhood. The people who follow this trade, hit perchance upon a mine of curiosities, when a virtuosi might furnish a cabinet with originals at a small expence. This we saw exemplified. Signior Brandi lives with the Genoese consul, Signior Agostini. At his house we met with several antiquities, which have been recovered from the ruins of this city. Among the most remarkable is a bust of Alexander, finely executed and but little damaged.

In the afternoon we went to see Cleopatra's Needle, which lies to the eastward of the city. We again mounted our asses, and, without any other company than our Janizary, arrived in about ten minutes at the Needle. It is almost close to the sea, and lifts up its head amid an heap of ruins, which appear to have been a circle of magnificent buildings that surrounded it. It is said, there were originally three obelisks which bore this name; and that one of them has been buried by its own weight, and the rising of the sand about it. It is certain, however, that two of them once stood here at about fifty yards asunder. One of them was torn up by the roots in a violent storm some years ago, and "prone on the *ground* lies *groveling* many a rood." These obelisks are also of granite, which is the marble peculiar to this place. They are of a single stone, sixty feet in length, and covered on all sides with hieroglyphics. The one which is standing, yields only in beauty to Pompey's pillar, among the remains of this august city; and it is a wonder that no attempt has been made to transport the fallen Needle to Europe; a similar enterprize to which was effected, I think, in the removal of Trajan's pillar, the greatest boast of modern Rome. What a beautiful termination would it make to one of the vistos at Chatsworth! What a noble addition would it prove to the collection at Stowe! But the expence would be too heavy for any, but a princely purse to discharge, as the relic would be too valuable for any, but a monarch to possess. For a drawing of this obelisk, as well as of Pompey's * pillar, I must refer the reader to the work of Mr. Niebuhr, and to the drawings of Mr. Dalton. The few plates which I have ventured to give, contain views of such things only as are not, to my knowledge, to be met with in other travels.

We contemplated this obelisk with pleasure, and left it with regret. While we looked at the ruins around us, we could not but fancy ourselves carried back to the times of the Ptolemies. Here Anthony revelled; here Cleopatra reigned! Here beauty shed her rosy smiles; here pleasure danced an eternal round; and here, alas! the hero forewent empire and life for the fascinating charms of love! Some hundreds of yards from the spot we had left, is an angle of the antient walls of the city. These walls are still above the level of the ground, and the ditch is still to be distinguished. This is the eastern face, and at certain equidistances, there were round towers for the better protection of the walls. We entered the tower at the angle, which appeared to be less decayed than the rest. There is a circular room in the middle, which at present goes up to the top of the tower: But by a nar-

---

* The author has given a view of this pillar in the frontispiece to his Eastern Eclogues; but a more competent idea can be gathered of it in a collection of prints, published by the ingenious Mr. Dalton in the year 1752, comprizing, among other antiquities, the elevations and sections of the pyramids of Egypt, which must have been a task not less difficult than curious.

row staircase on one side of it, there is a likelihood of there having been apartments above. We made a tour of this face, and on our return home, visited the church of St. Catherine belonging to the Greeks. Here one of the friars led us into a recess illuminated with a lamp, to see the stone on which St. Catherine was beheaded. This stone is held in uncommon veneration; and the fathers are very anxious to persuade strangers, that drops of her blood are still visible thereon. They were under no danger of having this opinion contradicted, through the abundance of our zeal; but they were, perhaps, more pleased, that we had charity enough to leave some silver among them, towards the propagation of this innocent imposition.

THURSDAY, 2d October.

Intelligence came this morning of the loss of five boats on the *begage*, or bar of the Nile, which were among a fleet that sailed two days ago for Rosetto. The young Swifs whom I have before spoken of, was unluckily on board one of them; and we learn with concern, that he has escaped only with his life. If the reader, however, remembers our description of that place, it may seem a greater mercy to him, that the young man did not perish with his effects. The wind blowing in the teeth of a rapid current, must have occasioned a prodigious swell on the bar, which generally proves as fatal to the mariner as to his bark. The French merchants of this city are said to be considerable sufferers by this accident; as they had very rich bales of goods on the boats which are wrecked. But the misfortune of the young Swifs chiefly engaged our attention. Our minds yet smarted with the remembrance of our own distresses; and we were, perhaps, never in a disposition to have contributed more largely, than we now did, towards the relief of a fellow-creature.

ture. So true it is, that calamity is the best physician to mental infirmities, and disposes the passions to listen more seriously to the calls of humanity.

It is laughable enough, to observe the materials and fashion of the generality of the buildings of this city. Marble ready wrought to the hand, is in such profusion here, that in every street you meet with the noble fragments of palaces and temples, applied to the meanest purposes. I have seen a stable supported by pillars of the finest granite, and a cow-house paved with the most beautiful tablets of marble. This view, indeed, is more likely to provoke a sigh than a smile. It too nearly resembles the prophecy denounced against that splendid city, whose regal edifices were to become the habitations of the beasts of the field. But our ridicule is directed against another object. The court-yards of the foreign factories are encompassed with the choicest pillars that could be procured; but the confusion of orders, in which the Doric, Ionic, and Corinthian jar together, joined to the unequal height and diameter of the shafts, rather render the whole a ludicrous than an agreeable assemblage. But as the builders have had convenience more than elegance in view, the want of taste in the disposition is the more excusable.

We took a ride in the evening to the canal which was brought from the Nile, and still supplies the city with water. Our route lay through a road which leads to the S. E. gate, and divides the antient city into two equal parts. This is the high road to Rosetto, on which travellers are accustomed to go on mules, in preference to the dangerous passage by sea. The journey is performed in seven or eight hours, and it is reported that the obstruction to it is now removed, by the gallantry of a Turk, who was attacked yesterday by the Bedouins, or wild Arabs, that have lately infested the country. The captain of the gang was luckily shot by the Turk; and his adherents have fled to other parts. We arrived

in

in about half an hour at the gate. It has been a very superb work, and there are still two columns, which support the pedestal above it, of the most beautiful symmetry and design. The canal is about a quarter of a mile from hence. It still serves the chief purpose for which it was intended; and, in the floods, conveys a sufficient quantity of water to the city, to fill the cisterns for the use of the ensuing year. This expensive labor was necessary to rectify the defect with which this thirsty soil is curst, and is in every respect worthy of its supposed founder. But the channel a few miles above is so choaked up, as to render it no longer navigable for the smallest boats, except for a week or two in the year. There is a large arch thrown over this canal, which appears firm enough to admit of repair. Neither the bridge nor canal, however, have a chance to be restored to their former condition by the indolent and illiberal Turk; although, comparatively speaking, an inconsiderable expence would be the means of reviving, in their full extent, these elegant and serviceable works of antiquity. On the banks of this canal are raised the vegetables, with which the city is supplied; and beyond them the desart stretches to the Nile.

On our return home we made a tour of the western wall of the antient city, which we had not before seen. There are towers upon it as on the other side, and the wall has more frequent breaches in it.

FRIDAY, 3d October.

I employed myself this morning in transcribing an ode, which I had written in detached parts, during our voyage down the Nile. The reader will find it in the Appendix, where it will appear as a companion to the ode to the desart. He may, perhaps, suspect me of another reason than what I before alledged, for not mingling

3 C   poetry

poetry and profe, for putting it in that place. The contraſt between the ſubjects is ſo ſtriking, as to ſet the deſcriptive paſſages of either piece in the beſt light.

Nothing retards our departure but the veſſel's diſpatches, which are not arrived from Cairo. For fear of my being hereafter prevented, I will here communicate the ſtory of the French conſul's murder, ſome circumſtances of which are of an extraordinary nature, and will ſerve to juſtify the unfavorable idea which is entertained of the Arabians, in different parts of this work.

Three young gentlemen belonging to the French factory had been out in the country ſhooting pigeons. They were met on their return by ſome Arabs, who, with their uſual impudence to Chriſtians whom they ſuppoſe to be in their power, demanded their guns. Theſe the Frenchmen naturally refuſed to deliver up; and a ſtruggle enſuing, in which they were likely to be overcome by numbers, one of them levelled his piece, and ſhot an Arab dead on the ſpot. The unexpectedneſs of this action ſtruck ſuch a terror into the reſt, that they immediately diſperſed, and left the young men to make the beſt of their way off. This they effected, but with different fortunes. The guilty perſon knew there was no ſafety for him in Alexandria, although the life had been taken away in defence of his property, againſt an hoſtile aſſault. He bent his way, therefore, to a village on the ſea-ſide, and, without ſuſpicion, hired a mule for Roſetto. Here he arrived with great expedition, and embarked on a boat which was that moment going for Damiat. Happily for him, when he reached that city, there was a veſſel under way for Conſtantinople, in which he eſcaped from the deſtiny that awaited him. One of his companions concealed himſelf in this city, until he found an opportunity to quit it, which his knowledge of the language enabled him to do in ſafety. The other took refuge in the French factory; the ſuppoſed ſanctity of which, he vainly

imagined

imagined would protect him from the resentment of the Arabs. Though he was only a spectator of the accident which had happened, he was doomed to answer for it in the most inhuman manner. The city was presently in commotion; and a mob, headed by the comrades of the deceased, forced open the gates of the factory, after having been denied admittance by the consul, took out the unfortunate youth who remained, and hung him upon the first tree they met with. Not satisfied with this sacrifice, they afterwards cut him in pieces, and exposed his limbs in different quarters of the city.

Here one might think the vengeance of a barbarian would stop. With such a retaliation, that, confounding as it did the innocent with the guilty, is so agreeable to their notions of justice, the Arabs might be satisfied. But their thirst for blood was not yet quenched: As the murderer had escaped, they turned their rage against the innocent man, who had presumed to afford his accomplice a sanctuary. Aware of the unforgiving dispositions of the Arabs, the consul had confined himself to his house for the space of two months, and upwards. He now thought the matter was forgotten, and ventured out as usual to take the air on an ass, along with the Janizary of his nation. This Janizary is esteemed here a sufficient safeguard. He may be so on common occasions, but his authority failed him on this. They were met by a man near Pompey's Pillar, who, with seeming indifference, enquired the consul's name of the Janizary; and being satisfied it was the person he sought, he stepped suddenly behind him, and discharged a pistol in his back. The ball went through the consul's body, and he immediately expired. Thus losing, like the hero near whose column he fell, his life by the treachery of the Egyptian race! The assassin escaped during the Janizary's confusion, and no notice was taken by the government of such an outrage. The French consulted their own dignity, as well as the interests

interests of other nations, when they sent two frigates this summer to demand satisfaction. But whether the force was inadequate, or they have been tempted, by some secret advantages, to give up, as they have done on many occasions, the honor and even safety of their ministers in Turkey, the frigates have departed, without success in their negotiation.

SATURDAY, 4th OCTOBER.

We were alarmed this morning with the report of a vessel being about to founder in the harbor. This carried us to the quay, where we saw a Greek polacre go down in about half an hour. It seems that she run upon the anchor of another vessel as she came into the road, and the crew were glad to quit her with their lives. It is surprizing that these accidents are not more frequent in a port, where vessels are obliged to be always moored, on account of their insecure station. The water is so shallow when the tide is out, that there would be no steering clear of the anchors, were not strangers apprized where they lie. What is done, therefore, in other places for the convenience of the owners, is here enforced for the good of the public. And every vessel is obliged, by an order at this port, to place buoys over her anchors. A failure in this measure subjects her to the payment of any loss she may occasion. And, it is said, the owners of the Greek polacre will recover damages on this ground.

As we were returning from the quay, we met a porter sinking, to all appearance, under a double bale of cotton. He wore jack-boots, in order to keep his knees straight, and walked doubled, with his hands supported on his knees. Were not the fact well known to thousands who trade to the Levant, one would hesitate to mention the enormous loads which the Turkish porters carry. We went to the scales where the bales were weighing, and saw one of

them

them take a bale of 7 cwt. upon his back, and stagger under it to the quay. The distance, indeed, is not very great, and there appears to be as much art as strength exercised in these surprizing efforts of the bodily powers. I have heard more than once, during my residence in India, of the porters in Persia being famous for carrying a pipe of wine on their backs, which is more than 10 cwt. and, with the assistance of a bamboo, or stick across his shoulders, a Chinese at Canton is said to support an equal burden with more ease to himself. It is only in countries, however, where labourers of this kind are scarce, that such vigour is desirable. In Paris or London, where professions are not hereditary, and where every idler is willing to turn his hand to any thing, the inconvenience of this monopoly would be felt. This useful branch of labor would sink in its value, and crouds would languish for want of employment.

We dined on board one of the English ships to-day, where the departure of the French frigates without redress of their complaint, became the subject of conversation. It seems that the French have been much animadverted upon by foreigners here on this occasion; and comparisons been drawn between them and the English, not to their advantage. Indeed, history furnishes many instances of the opposite behavior of both governments in similar cases. Where one negotiates for a redress of injuries, the other dispatches a fleet to command it. And while one is wasting time in unavailing threats, the other employs more certain arguments of conviction with the Mahometan powers. But there is something very mysterious in this procedure of a people, who, in other respects, are jealous of affronts, and enamored of glory. The particular advantages which they derive from the Turkey trade, seem to influence their operations in that quarter; and they aim at the preservation of those advantages, at the expence of their national honor. All Europe

is

is indebted to France, for the trouble she took in scouring the Archipelago of the pirates which infested it, after the close of the Russian war. They were chiefly Greeks, and abounded in such a degree, that not a merchantman escaped being attacked by them. The French frigates every where pursued them with unremitting vigilance; and to eradicate the evil effectually, ran their barks down in general, without firing a gun. The good consequences of these exertions soon appeared; and it is notorious, that there never was a time, in which the Mediterranean was so free of corsairs of all denominations, as the present.

Captain Calvi introduced us in the evening to a Greek family, which consisted of a lady and her two daughters. The latter were very beautiful, but overloaded with a profusion of zechins upon their heads and breasts, which were strung together like pearl *. The eldest of the daughters is married to a man now in France. She pressed our captain much for a passage. He is full; but with the gallantry of a Frenchman, placed his refusal to a desire of preserving harmony among his passengers, which the influence of her charms could not fail to invade. The frankness and pleasantry of this *Provençal* are very engaging, and afford us a prospect of much entertainment during our voyage.

SUNDAY, 5th October.

We attended the service this morning at the chapel of the Genoese factory, where we afterwards dined, on the invitation of

* Among these I perceived a medal of Alexander the Great, in fine preservation. As the characters were Roman, it was probably struck by one of the Cæsars in honor of that hero. I attempted, in vain, to place it among my small collection.

Signior

Signior Brandi. The conful is a polite chearful old gentleman of feventy and upwards, and has ferved in that office with great credit, for above thirty years. He is, however, too much of an invalid to be able to attend to bufinefs, which is managed for him by Signior Brandi, who is alfo agent to Mr. Baldwin.

We accompanied Signior Brandi in the evening to the Venetian factory, where we drank coffee with an Italian lady who is lodged there. From hence we fallied out to a garden, which is about ten minutes walk from the city. This garden is thickly planted with fruit-trees of various kinds, in which we found a very agreeable relief from the fandy views, which every where meet the eye in the environs of this place. Nothing but the happinefs of its fituation for commerce, could have prompted Alexander to have founded a city on this barren fpot. And the rank it keeps among commercial cities at this hour, in fpite of the revolutions it has feen in its religion, government, and cuftoms, demonftrates the acutenefs of that monarch's difcernment. Tyre, Athens, and Carthage, are only to be refpected in the page of hiftory: while the port of Alexandria is ftill crouded with the veffels of different nations; and ftill difpenfes, though in a lefs degree, her bounty through the world.

As we returned home we paffed the houfe of a fair Jewefs, whofe reputation is fpread about this city. It is her cuftom to fhew herfelf daily at her window, to enfnare thofe who venture to gaze upon her. It is affirmed that her charms made a very fingular impreffion upon an Englifh nobleman, who came here fome years ago. He bid very highly for her perfon, but was difappointed in his views. The amour fomehow got wind, and fhe was honored by a wag with his title, which fhe has preferved to this day.

In a converfation with our Janizary this evening, we difcovered that fear was one caufe of the diftinction, with which the

Englifh

English are treated in this country. It is many years since the English trade has declined in the Levant. Their ships of war no more ride triumphant in these seas, and their thunders have long ceased to strike terror through the coasts of Egypt. But the spell is revived. The English have found their way into the Red-sea, and have it at their option to deal with Egypt on their own terms. The reader may remember the assistance which we received in our greatest distress, from the arrival of the Swallow sloop of war at Judda. This sloop mounted about twenty guns, and had carried dispatches from Madras to Suez. Since the Portuguese were expelled Arabia, no vessel of war belonging to a foreign power, had visited that port. Her arrival was a phenomenon, which alarmed the weakness of this government. The jealousies that exist among the European nations, are the basis of its security on the side of the Mediterranean. But on the shores of the Red-sea, it must submit to the power, whose empire in India has given them the navigation and commerce of the Red-sea, without a competitor. And this power is the English. A track, struck out by private adventurers, may hereafter benefit the public; and, under proper restrictions, add to the influence and power of the *Company*, in a measure which might exceed expectation *. Rumor is well known to magnify danger. The force

---

* The instability of the Egyptian government weakens, in some degree, the force of this reasoning. It has been suggested by the ingenious Dr. Russell, whose long residence in Turkey inclines the author to pay a deference to him on a subject on which he is so much better informed, that the discouragement which the Turks give to the trade by Suez, arises from this very cause. The revolutions in Cairo are often annual, and the Porte, consequently, can depend but little on receiving a share of their profits from men, whose footing in power is so slippery. The communication with India by the caravans of Aleppo, turns out wholly in favor of the Turk. The inference, therefore, which the Doctor draws, is very judicious. The commerce by Aleppo would fall to the ground, were that

by

force of the Swallow sloop was estimated at Cairo at sixty guns. Here, she is a first rate! It is no wonder that this government should be on its good behavior, when it has not even a galley on the Red-sea to protect the trade. For though this trade is almost wholly carried on upon Arabian bottoms, were an embargo to be laid on the importation of coffee into the Egyptian ports, the course would be turned to the caravans, through which channel the coffee is delivered at more than double the price, to what it is by water.

MONDAY, 6th OCTOBER.

We are detained here by the most vexatious of all circumstances—the neglect of the agents of the Cleopatra. Captain Calvi has been ready to sail these four days, and his dispatches are not yet arrived from Cairo. To whet our disappointment, the wind has been easterly the whole time; and we might have performed a fourth part of our passage to Marseilles. Natural delays should be borne with patience; but those which arise from human perverseness, are enough to ruffle a Stoic's temper.

We encountered some objects to-day, who beyond all others should engage our commiseration. They were the captain and officers of a French vessel, which was wrecked four years ago on the coast of Barbary. Along with the crew they were carried into slavery; and have now been released by an accident. The emperor of Morocco has sent an embassy to the court of France, and these Frenchmen were selected, among forty others, as a present worthy for a king to receive. The particulars of these un-

by Suez to be established. And this is the secret objection which the Porte entertains to the latter trade; and was hatched, not by the influence of French intrigues, nor the complaints of the religious of Mecca and Medina.

fortunate

fortunate people's story are very interesting, but very similar to accounts already published of captives in the same situation. There is a youth among them of about fourteen years of age. His lot was different from the rest. On account of his youth, when they were first brought to Morocco, the emperor ordered him to be an attendant in the seraglio. This anecdote we had from the boy's own mouth, although he was sometimes at a loss to express himself in his native tongue. His employment was to make coffee for the emperor's wives, and to gather bouquets for them of the sweetest flowers in the gardens of the palace. It may, perhaps, wound the pride of our countrymen to know, that the Sultana is an Englishwoman, who has been elevated to that dignity more than twenty years. She seems to be about forty, and having borne the emperor two sons, is perhaps, on that account, treated by him with a distinction, which her charms no longer command. And in fact, while he pays her only court in public, his private hours are dedicated to a French concubine, who was made a captive by one of his cruizers, and on account of her exquisite beauty, preferred to the seraglio. These barbarians, it seems, are grown nice in their amours! Depopulated Greece cannot afford them a variety of beauty, but they must appropriate the spoils of France and England to pamper their base lusts! Where sleeps the vengeance of those warlike nations, that they suffer these crying injuries to pass unpunished? The gallies of Barbary groan with their men, and her seraglios teem with their females! When the states of Europe learn to distinguish their true interests; when they establish a firm basis of union among themselves; then, and then only, can they hope to see their arms directed against the common enemies of mankind; to see their commerce uninterrupted, their people uninslaved by the refuse of the earth!

The Mahometan Ramazan is commenced. This institute is an imitation of our Lent, except that there is a difference in the mode

mode of abstinence required. The rigid Catholic contents himself with a change of diet; and takes his usual meals without scruple, so that he forbears flesh and certain forbidden things. The life of a Mussulman undergoes a total innovation during this fast. From the time the sun rises until it sets again, the taste of any substance, even water itself, is prohibited by the law of Mahomet. But then the night brings full reparation with it. Excess follows abstinence, and he indulges himself in a variety of food, to be revenged upon the law. The bad consequences of this priestcraft must be sensibly felt by both parties. Our Janizary has been quite unhinged since the Ramazan began. He is now fitter for sleep than action, during the day; and were we to remain here, we should reap little benefit from his services while the fast continued. The streets are now empty of people in the day-time. Towards the evening they begin to assemble in the coffee-houses, and at the corners of the streets; where they wait for the priest's proclamation of sunset. Their faces betray the height of impatience; and at the appointed signal, they start for their dinners with no very temperate intentions.

TUESDAY, 7th October.

The vessel's dispatches are at length arrived, but the wind is so considerably heightened to-day, that the captain holds it dangerous to attempt moving out of his station with it. We must wait for what the morrow may effect in our behalf.

News is just come from Cairo, that the troubles upon the Nile are recommenced, and that war is about to renew its horrors in this unhappy country. The fugitive beys have found means to possess themselves at length of Jirje, about which city they have long hovered. The situation of this post enables them to stop effectually, the navigation of the river. A large armament is preparing

paring at Cairo, to diflodge the rebels from their strong hold. Boats of all kinds are pressed for this service, and the communication promises to be interrupted between Alexandria and the metropolis. The issue of this commotion may, to all appearance, be foretold. It is the last effort of a desperate party, which cannot avail them against superior numbers and discipline. Ismaul Beg has now set a price upon the heads of his antagonists. This barbarous practice is justified by the example of the most polished nations, against those whom the state confiders as traitors. And in all probability, it will now rid the bey of Egypt of his fears. But the accomplishment of this design is uncertain [*]. We cannot sufficiently congratulate ourselves on our removal from those scenes of contention; and count all our toils as happily endured, since we have escaped thereby, the new delays that awaited us.

Ibrahim has just now taken leave of us, to embark on a boat which is bound for Rosetto. He is furnished with recommendations for the English captains who may come to Suez; and there is no doubt of his finding a good opportunity to get back to the Adventure, to which vessel he still belongs. The behavior of this poor Indian has been uniformly honest and ingenuous. Some slight errors which he has been guilty of, were fully retrieved by the importance of his services; and could we command power or riches at this moment, they would be employed in bestowing a more suitable reward on his merits. Henceforth be not virtue appropriated by any particular sect. Let pride be taught to believe, there is no distinction among mankind, but what results from the practice of good and evil; and imbibe, with us, a charitable opinion of the members of every persuasion.

[*] So uncertain, that it appears the very reverse has since happened, and the depofed beys have recovered their power, though at this hour, perhaps, it has again eluded their grasp!

That

That we might be ready for the captain's summons in the morning, we discharged our debts at this place, and presented our Janizary with some pieces of gold, for the trouble that we have given him. The alacrity with which we shall quit these shores, has been quickened by concurrent circumstances. The very air of this city seems to be impregnated with the breezes of the North. Her streets display the habit which is so familiar to our eyes; and her harbor is crowded with vessels, which are bound to the lands of liberty and science. What bosom then can repress its emotions at such a sight? What foot would linger on the strand, when the sail was set for the ports of Europe? Curiosity has been satisfied. Like the hunters who have encountered toil and danger in the pursuit of their game, we anticipate the sweets of repose; and find, that the ardor of expectation constituted the principal pleasure of the chace.

WEDNESDAY, 8th OCTOBER.

The wind being favorable this morning for our departure, the Captain fired a gun, as a signal for us to go off. At seven o'clock Monsieur Meillon accompanied Major Alexander, Mr. Hammond, and myself to the quay, where we embarked on the Cleopatra; and at eleven, weighed our anchor for Marseilles *.

* It may be satisfactory to the reader to know that our travellers, whom he has so long accompanied, arrived safely in England at the close of the year 1777, after a journey of eleven months. It may be supposed that the end of their mission was defeated by the delays they encountered; but they flatter themselves, that the merit of perseverance will not be denied them, either by the respectable body in whose service it was exerted, or by the generous public.

AND

AND now, Madam, it is time to bid you adieu. To pursue the simile of the hunters, whatever satisfaction I may have found in the recital of our adventures, I doubt whether an indifferent person will listen as complacently to the tale. In the review of this volume, I have as much reason to pray for your indulgence, as to hope for your sympathy. While the tear of pity dims your eye, let it prove a vail to the inaccuracies which are almost inseparable from a work of this nature. Nor let this be deemed an unreasonable or arrogant wish. While the major part of mankind are administering to the caprices of the female-sex, while they are feeding their vanity with the grossest flatteries, and perverting their dispositions by an idle compliance with their humours, his presumption may surely be excused, who, actuated by a spirit of philanthropy, and willing to communicate the result of dear-bought experience, endeavors to make one woman of his party, who has reflection enough to weigh the importance of human misfortunes, and zeal enough to promote their publication for the instruction of the world. That he has not offered a trifling subject to her consideration, is the best compliment which he could pay to her understanding; and that he looks for her sympathy in the hour of distress, is not the worst picture which he could give of her feelings. To be a serious member of a thoughtless tribe, is no less an honor to a woman, than to possess a refined heart in a depraved and dissipated age.

I have the honor to be,

Madam,

Your's, &c.

Alexandria, 8th October, 1777.

POSTSCRIPT.

POSTSCRIPT.

JUST as these sheets were going to the press, a letter came to my hands, which, on every account, I would wish to communicate to the reader. The storm is blown over, and the tale that threatened such tragical circumstances, is brought to an happy conclusion. But if any character in this work has secured the affection of the reader, he will not refuse a sigh to its unworthy destiny. If the work itself has interested his passions, he will greedily peruse a supplement, that promises further food for his curiosity. The letter is from Mr. Hammond, one of the number of the unlucky subjects of these adventures, who has possessed resolution enough to hazard the dangers of an inhospitable shore, and to return to India by the route of Egypt. I mean not to anticipate the relation of a friend, but I should do injustice to my own feelings, were I to be silent on this melancholy occasion.

And here let me advise the susceptible reader to close the volume. The ingratitude of mankind is too frequent, to disturb the Philosopher's peace; but the impression it makes on the unexperienced breast, is too deep to be easily erased. But if he dare the conflict, and prefer to mingle his generous concern with mine, let him reflect on the crown of glory which awaits the virtuous dead! Let him, with me, weigh the unimportance of the track, by which the soul is led to the regions of immortality; and while we embalm the monarch's memory with an unfeigned tear, let us hope that our latter prayers may be as acceptable to the Deity, as our latter moments may be more propitious than those of the great Ifman Abu Ally! Unbroken be the reed which moans thy loss, rich pearl of Araby! Sweet smelling like the gums of Aden's vale, to heaven ascend thy precious spirit!

" Grand Cairo, 20th August, 1779.

" I cannot avoid giving you a letter from a place that was once
" so desirable an object to us, however reversed it has been to me
" a second time. I arrived here the 15th July last, after a very
" pleasant passage from Venice, and was preparing, with my
" fellow-travellers, to set out for Suez on the 28th, when, on
" that morning, Mr. Moore, the owner of our vessel, was made
" a prisoner, and detained till four days ago, in consequence of
" his ship, with another at Suez, having been treacherously
" seized by the orders of this government. The ships have since
" been released, and the people are gone to Suez to take posses-
" sion of them again; which we only want to hear of, to enable
" us to set forward. This extraordinary manœuvre, on the part
" of this government, was owing to an English caravan having
" been plundered in crossing the desart from Suez to Cairo, and
" many unfortunate Europeans having perished in the desart.
" The government, upon this, contrived the means of seizing the
" vessels, and have made us enter into solemn engagements with
" them, that no hostilities shall be committed hereafter by the
" English, in consequence of that accident!

" The politics of this country have been a good deal changed
" since we left it. It seems that soon after our departure from
" Cairo, Ibrahim Beg, and Morad Beg, were brought back into
" Cairo, accompanied by our old friend Ifman Abu Ally, who
" was with Mr. Baldwin, and made many enquiries after us. For
" this essential service, the poor old man had his head taken off
" by

" by Morad Beg, about three weeks ago, who was at Ghinnah
" in pursuit of Huffein Beg, one of Ifmaul Beg's partizans!—
" Monfieur Chevalier, the late governor of Chandernagore, ar-
" rived here a few days ago from Judda, by the route of *Cafire*.
" He met with Morad Beg at Ghinnah, who gave him *his* paff-
" port, for his fafety down the river.

" I hope to leave Cairo in about five days, attended by our old
" fervant Ibrahim, who has been wife enough to marry here, and
" is as completely fettled as he well can be. I have advifed him
" to pufh off to India with us. As if I had not been fufficiently
" punifhed for making a fecond vifit to this country, I have had
" the addition of an epidemical ficknefs, which has raged here
" with great violence, and, I believe, has extended to every Euro-
" pean in the place."

THE APPENDIX.

ODE TO THE DESART.

Written on a Journey through the Desarts of Thebais, September 1777.

THOU waste! from human sight retir'd,
By nought esteem'd, invok'd, desir'd;
Where stony hill and sterile plain,
And ever-sullen silence reign*:

Where nought is seen to cheer the eye,
But russet earth and sunny sky;
Nor tree nor herbage bless the ground,
Nor aught to cherish life is found.

Save, where the deer, whom fears assail,
Shoots suddenly athwart the vale;
If chance the sound of distant feet
Approach his lonesome, dark retreat.

O! while thy secrets I explore,
And traverse all thy regions o'er,
The patient camel I bestride—
May no ill hap his steps betide!

* " And ever-musing melancholy reigns." POPE's *Eloisa to Abelard*.

As on we press the burning soil,
And through the winding valley toil,
Still lend some hill's projecting height,
To shield me from Sol's piercing sight.

And should our scrips of water fail,
And horrid thirst my lips assail,
Then, then, thy scanty drops impart,
To renovate my fainting heart.

Nor to thy toiling son refuse
The truffle's leaf, or berry's juice;
These stinted products of the waste,
Luxurious! let my camel taste.

At noontide heat, and midnight cold,
Thy vengeful stores of wrath with-hold:
Nor bid the sudden whirlwind rise,
To blend at once, hills, vales, and skies!

Dread cause! too subtile to define,
Where horror! danger! ruin join!——
Stop, stop its pestilential breath,
That 'whelms a caravan in death!

But chief, whence lies our daily track,
O! turn the roving * Arab back;
Who, tyger-like, infests the way,
And makes the traveller his prey.

---

* The reader will have found that this wish was not granted. We fell in with a party of wild Arabs, and, what was more extraordinary, on the very day that this Ode was written. This meeting, so dreaded by us, was, in all probability, the cause of our preservation. These foes to man, by an unexpected turn, became our friends. They were our guides, when our people were at a loss for the road; they led us to the springs, and supplied us with food, when our water or provision failed us. What an incontestible evidence is this of the weakness of human opinions! of the vanity of human wishes!

As erst the sons of Israel fled
From Pharaoh's reign and Nilus' bed,
Here manna fell by God's command,
And water follow'd Moses' wand:

So may old Nilus passing nigh,
A portion of his floods supply;
Invite the neighb'ring peasant's toil,
To cultivate thine alter'd soil.

So be thy hills with verdure spread,
And trees adorn each naked head,
So in the thirsty vales below,
Discover'd springs be taught to flow.

So, teeming with neglected veins,
Thy marble pay the sculptor's pains;
Who, emulous of Grecian taste,
May give an Athens to the waste!

And on thy furthest sandy shore,
Which hears the Red-sea's billows roar,
May Commerce smile, her sails unfold,
And change thine iron age to gold!

ODE TO THE NILE.

Written during a Voyage down that River. Sept. 1777.

IMMORTAL stream! whom Afric leads
Through barren plains and verdant meads;
Now flaming o'er the Nubian sands,
Now laving Egypt's cultur'd lands;

To mark where first thou court'st the gale,
The poet's stretch of thought might fail:
Might heroes shudder to behold
The wonders which thy depths unfold.

O! place me on thy gentle tide,
When first it leaves its fountain wide;
'Till, threat'ning on the Cat'ract's brow,
It rushes to the world below.

Here, as the joyless wild we trace,
Where Nature shrouds her beauteous face,
The Ostrich—child of want and gloom!
Dips in thy wave his silver plume.

Now, lurking on thy sedgy shores,
The Crocodile his prey explores.
Hark! 'tis a virgin's shriek*—thy flood
She sought—to color with her blood!

No arms the monster can appal—
Bounds from his scales th' unerring ball.
Lo! to avenge a mother's tears,
The Hippopotamus appears!

Now Death assumes his grimmest form,
Thy troubled surface owns the storm;
Like warring vessels, on they move
Their mortal rage and force to prove!

O! haste we from this conflict dire,
And to thy fairer scenes retire;
Where, swelling o'er thy native strand,
Thy waters fatten all the land;

Where on the wide expanse are seen
The tufted grove and island green;
The minaret, that tow'rs above,
The haram—prison gay of love!

As Pleasure, Commerce, spread the sail,
A thousand gallies catch the gale:
Their oars a thousand gallies ply,
Whose pomp refulgent strikes the eye.

* This alludes to a circumstance which happened just before the author came to the Nile, and which the reader will find in page 259 of this work. The frequent combats between the River-horse and Crocodile, in which the former is generally victorious, are too well known to need a comment.

Now bear me down thy weftern arm,
Where Delta looks one cultur'd farm;
By ruin'd cities, nodding towers,
And hide me in Rofetto's bowers.

Hail fhades! who give fuch charms to view,
As ne'er Alcinous' gardens knew;
While bloffoms here their fweets unfold,
Bow'd is the tree with fruit of gold.

And thou fam'd ftream! what tho' no more
The world's emporium as of yore;
Tho' grac'd not with the Roman name,
Thy realm contending factions claim:

A Pharaoh's daughter erft was thine,
Whom pity touch'd with cares divine,
As fhe the prophet chanc'd to note
While in his ozier-bark afloat.

Thou knew'ft a Cleopatra's reign,
Who number'd victors in her train;
A Julius, led by glory's ray;
An Anthony—to love a prey!

A Ptolemy of learn'd renown,
And great Sefoftris wore thy crown;
Thine, Memphis! crufh'd by adverfe fates,
And Thebes—that op'd an hundred gates!

And still shalt thou our homage keep,
While sea-girt Pharos awes the deep;
While left for ages to admire,
Thy pyramids to heav'n aspire!

While Plenty on thy banks is found,
To feed the famish'd nations round;
While Poets strive to sing in vain
The wonders of thy vernal reign!

F I N I S.

www.ingramcontent.com/pod-product-compliance
Lightning Source LLC
Chambersburg PA
CBHW020544300426
44111CB00008B/791